THE OXFORD ENGLISH
LITERARY HISTORY

Volume 13. 1948–2000

THE OXFORD ENGLISH LITERARY HISTORY

General Editor: Jonathan Bate

* already published

This series was conceived and commissioned by Kim Walwyn (1956–2002), to whose memory it is dedicated.

THE OXFORD ENGLISH
LITERARY HISTORY

Volume 13. 1948–2000

The Internationalization of English Literature

BRUCE KING

OXFORD
UNIVERSITY PRESS

*This book has been printed digitally and produced in a standard specification
in order to ensure its continuing availability*

OXFORD
UNIVERSITY PRESS

Great Clarendon Street, Oxford OX2 6DP
United Kingdom
Oxford University Press is a department of the University of Oxford.
It furthers the University's objective of excellence in research, scholarship,
and education by publishing worldwide. Oxford is a registered trade mark of
Oxford University Press in the UK and in certain other countries

© Bruce King 2004

The moral rights of the author have been asserted

First published 2004
First published in paperback 2005
Reprinted 2013

British Library Cataloguing in Publication Data
Data available

Library of Congress Cataloging in Publication Data
Data available

ISBN 978-0-19-928836-6

To Adele and in memory of Nicole

Acknowledgements

I thank the following without whom it is unlikely that there would have been a book on this subject by me:

The National Endowment for the Humanities (which is not responsible for my views) for a Fellowship for Independent Scholars during 2001; the Ball State University Library; the British Council Library (Paris); the Theatre Museum (London); the Ball State University Honors College and its Dean allowed the following students to help at various times with bibliographical and biographical materials—John Harris, Christopher James, Erin McMullen, Ted Fehskens, and Nicole Steward.

Material, interviews, and other information and help was provided by Melanie Abrahams (Renaissance One), Diran Adebayo, Dotun Adebayo (Xpress), Rukhsana Ahmad, Moniza Alvi, Ranjana Sidhanta Ash, Rajeev Balasubramanyam, Bidisha, Paula Burnett, Tirthankar Chanda, Rhonda Cobham, Tim Cribb, James Currey, David Dabydeen, Fred D'Aguair, Leena Dhingra, Farrukh Dhondy, Ian Dieffenthaller, Bernardine Evaristo, Heidy Furlanis, Katija George, Brian Michael Glavey, Harry Goulbourne, Romesh Gunesekera, Marilyn Hacker, Richard Hill (Books for Keeps), Rosemarie Hudson (BlackAmber Books), Aamer Hussein, Catherine Johnson (*Calabash* and Centreprise), A. N. Jeffares, Adil Jussawalla, Mimi Khalvati, Naseem Khan (Arts Council of England), John La Rose (New Beacon), Harald Leusmann, Bénédicte Ledent, Gail Low, Nick McDowell (London Arts Board), Gary McKeone (Arts Council of England), E. A. Markham, Emma Matthewson (Bloomsbury), Arvind Krishna Mehrota, Anne Mobbs, Dom Moraes, Shymala Narayan, Susheila Nasta, H. O. Nazareth, Courttia Newland, Alastair Niven, Jenny Owen, Lauren Onkey, Claire Pamment, Mike Phillips, Steve Pope (Xpress), Alexanda Pringle (Bloomsbury), Jahan Ramazani, Lauri Ramey, Ravi Randhawa, Leone Ross, Cecile Sandten, Chikiu Sarkar (Bloomsbury), Christiane Schlote, Kamila Shamsie, Muneeza Shamsie, Jon Stallworthy, Victoria Tadjo, Jeet

Thayil, John Thieme, Jatinder Verma (Tara Arts), Sarah White (New Beacon), Janet Wilson, and Adam Zameenzad.

William Riggan and Marla Johnson of *World Literature Today*, Paolo Marchonni of *Wasafiri*, Abiola Irele of *Research in African Literature*, Jeet Thayil of *Gentleman* (Mumbai), Erica Waters of *The Caribbean Writer*, and Finn Fordham of *World Literature Written in English* have sent me books to review. Many of my comments are based on reviews I wrote for their journals as well as articles and chapters I have published in *Sewanee Review*, the *Review of Contemporary Fiction, Contemporary Novelists, Contemporary Poets, The Routledge Encyclopaedia of Postcolonial Literature*, James Acheson's *The British & Irish Novel since 1960* (1991), Alamgir Hashmi's *The Worlds of Muslim Imagination* (1986), and my *New English Literatures* (1980), *V. S. Naipaul* (1993), and *Modern Indian Poetry in English* (1987). I am indebted to Anne Walmsley's invaluable *The Caribbean Artists Movement 1966–1972* (1992), Alison Donnell (ed.), *Companion to Contemporary British Culture* (2002), and Prabhu Guptara's *Black British Literature: An Annotated Bibliography* (1986) where I learned of many authors, books, and facts. Jonathan Bate and Lauren Onkey read my manuscript and made useful suggestions.

B.K.

General Editor's Preface

The Oxford English Literary History is the twenty-first-century successor to the Oxford History of English Literature, which appeared in fifteen volumes between 1945 and 1997. As in the previous series, each volume offers an individual scholar's vision of a discrete period of literary history.[1] Each has a distinctive emphasis and structure, determined by its author's considered view of the principal contours of the period. But all the volumes are written in the belief that literary history is a discipline necessary for the revelation of the power of imaginative writing to serve as a means of human understanding, past, present, and future.

Our primary aim is to explore the diverse purposes of literary activity and the varied mental worlds of writers and readers in the past. Particular attention is given to the institutions in which literary acts take place (educated communities, publishing networks and so forth), the forms in which literary works are presented (traditions, genres, structural conventions), and the relationship between literature and broader historical continuities and transformations. Literary history is distinct from political history, but a historical understanding of literature cannot be divorced from cultural and intellectual revolutions or the effects of social change and the upheaval of war.

We do not seek to offer a comprehensive survey of the works of all 'major', let alone 'minor', writers of the last thousand years. All literary histories are inevitably incomplete—as was seen from the rediscovery in the late twentieth century of many long-forgotten women writers of earlier eras. Every literary history has to select; in so doing, it reconfigures the 'canon'. We cast our nets very widely and make claims for many works not previously regarded as canonical, but we are fully conscious of our partiality. Detailed case studies are preferred to summary listings.

---

[1] Since Volume 1, *to 1350*, covers many centuries, it is co-written by two scholars.

A further aim is to undertake a critical investigation of the very notion of a national literary heritage. The word 'literature' is often taken to refer to poems, plays, and novels, but historically a much wider range of writing may properly be considered as 'literary' or as belonging within the realm of what used to be called 'letters'. The boundaries of the literary in general and of *English* literary history in particular have changed through the centuries. Each volume maps those boundaries in the terms of its own period.

For the sake of consistency and feasibility, however, two broad definitions of 'English Literary History' have been applied. First, save in the polyglot culture of the earliest era, we have confined ourselves to the English language—a body of important work written in Latin between the fourteenth and the seventeenth centuries has been excluded. And secondly, we have concentrated on works that come from, or bear upon, England. Most of the writing of other English-speaking countries, notably the United States of America, is excluded. We are not offering a world history of writing in the English language. Those Americans who lived and worked in England are, however, included.

So too with Scottish, Irish, Welsh writers, and those from countries that were once part of the British Empire: where their work was produced or significantly disseminated in England, they are included. Indeed, such figures are of special importance in many volumes, exactly because their non-English origins often placed them in an ambivalent relationship with England. Throughout the series, particular attention is paid to encounters between English and other traditions. But we have also recognized that Scottish, Welsh, Irish, African, Asian, Australasian, Canadian, and Caribbean literatures all have their own histories, which we have not sought to colonize.

It would be possible to argue endlessly about periodization. The arrangement of the Oxford English Literary History is both traditional and innovative. For instance, the period around the beginning of the nineteenth century has long been thought of as the 'Romantic' one; however we may wish to modify the nomenclature, people will go on reading and studying the Lake Poets and the 'Shelley circle' in relation to each other, so it would have been factitious to introduce a volume division at, say, 1810. On the other hand, it is still too soon for there to be broad agreement on the literary-historical shape of the twentieth century: to propose a single break at, say, 1945 would be to fall in with the false assumption that literature moves strictly in tandem with events. Each volume argues the case for its own period as a period, but at the same time beginning and ending dates are treated flexibly, and in many cases—especially with respect to the twentieth century—there is deliberate and considerable overlap between the temporal boundaries of adjacent volumes.

The voices of the last millennium are so various and vital that English literary history is always in the process of being rewritten. We seek both to chart and to contribute to that rewriting, for the benefit not just of students and scholars but of all serious readers.

Jonathan Bate

Contents

Abbreviations

ACLALS	Association for Commonwealth Literature and Language Studies
ATCAL	Association for the Teaching of Caribbean, African, and Asian Literatures
AWWC	Asian Women Writers' Collective
AWWW	Asian Women Writers' Workshop (later AWWC)
BBWG	Brixton Black Women's Group
BTC	Black Theatre Co-operative
BTF	Black Theatre Forum
CAM	Caribbean Artists Movement
CECWA	Caribbean Education and Community Workers Association
CWWA	Caribbean Women Writers' Alliances
DLB	*Dictionary of Literary Biography*
GLC	Greater London Council
IRR	Institute of Race Relations
OWAAD	Organization of Women of Africa and African Descent (later Organization of Women of African and Asian Descent)
SOAS	School of Oriental and African Studies
TBW	Theatre of Black Women
TT	*Third Text*
TWT	The Write Thing
VSO	Voluntary Service Overseas

A Note on References

Brief biographical information on selected authors will be found at the end of the volume, together with bibliographies covering their major works and some recent criticism concerning them. In addition, there are suggestions for more general reading relevant to the literary history of the period. The bibliographies are intended as starting points for further study, not comprehensive listings.

Quotations from prose works written in the period are usually followed by a reference in parentheses to the page number of the edition asterisked in the relevant Author Bibliography. Titles of plays, when first mentioned, are usually followed by a note of the theatre which originally produced them and the date of this production. The date following the title of a film is the date when it was first released. Quotations from poetry give the title of the individual poem, and the collections from which they are taken are asterisked in the relevant Author Bibliography. Publication details for quotations by authors who do not appear in the Author Bibliographies are given in the text.

Introduction

During the second half of the twentieth century the literature of England went through a major change, a change in subject matter and sensitivities as historically significant as earlier shifts in sensibility given such names as Romanticism, Victorianism, and Modernism. This one was often termed Postcolonialism, although, as England has not been a colony for a long time, Post-imperial might be better, and I think Internationalization best.

Unlike previous period changes this one had its basis in a large influx of peoples from elsewhere, especially those of non-European origins, which resulted in the literature of England taking different perspectives from those in the past, having new concerns, and often being focused on the immigrants, their children, and their place in society. Although the amount of immigration was small it seemed large and resulted in new fashions in music, dance, clothing, and speech along with new social conflicts, challenges, and hierarchies, as well as new histories of England. It produced a literature that felt immediate and vital and earned its authors international attention during a time when interest in traditional British literature and culture was being replaced by other English-speaking literatures and cultures. If the nation seemed to be withdrawing into a little England of post-imperial dreariness and irritation, having a diminished relationship to Europe and the United States, or fragmenting into micro-nationalisms, the new immigrants made English literature international in other ways than it had been during the Empire. England was once more at the centre of significant developments, and as England became multiracial and multicultural the claim that they do things better in France no longer applied. England was much better at incorporating people than most of Europe.

The new English literature was a result of larger political and cultural changes. While empires are culturally and racially changed by those they have conquered, England only had small communities of people of colour before 1948 and their contribution to its literature was sporadic. Since the end of the Second World War, however, much of the world had undergone an immense movement of peoples brought about by racial, political, and economic liberalization and the lowering of protective barriers. Europe needed workers to help in rebuilding and many came from the former colonies seeking adventure, better jobs, the securities of the new European welfare systems, and better futures for their children. Others fled the inter-ethnic tensions, civil wars, and tyrannies that the withdrawal of empire had brought or allowed to continue once more. If some came to England in search of work or refuge, many of the new immigrants began as students and stayed on, part of the worldwide expansion of education after the war and offerings of scholarships abroad as a way of gaining influence. Still others were products of the globalization of the economy, who came to the West for any of the reasons why people leave home and move elsewhere if given the chance. In the past such moves might have been more difficult, but with the increasing ease and low cost of international transportation, and the slackening of regulations used to keep out foreigners, England like other western nations had become a place where it was comparatively easy to enter and stay. London was no longer the centre of an empire, but became an international city of racial and cultural mixtures.

England rapidly changed. The immigrants had children who were born and bred English, although often of different skin colours and even religions than most previous English. Mixed marriages and other relationships stopped being exotic, while the counter-culture of the young made fashionable Jamaican speech, 'World music', and much else. There were still racists, riots, and prejudiced police, but England was becoming multicultural and multiracial, a process similar to that underway in other countries including the United States, Canada, New Zealand, and Australia.

The changing racial composition of England as a result of immigration helps explain the new nature of England's literature, but that is only part of the story. There were the continuing ties to the Empire, now the Commonwealth, the attractions of life in London, the ease of being published in England compared with many other nations, interracial marriage. Each writer had a unique reason for being in England and not all were English authors in the sense of having or wanting British citizenship. Some were part of the international community that resided full- or part-time in London. Others had British passports, but culturally never felt at ease in England although there was no other land in which they could be said to be at home. Modern transportation and communications made international lives possible, and some writers divided their time between England and visiting family, gathering materials to write about, or working, abroad. The end of empire resulted in new nations, new areas of interest, and made fashionable reading about decolonization and the culture of Others. There was a market for literature about this new world.

While one focus of this history is on how writing by immigrants and their children viewed England over the decades, another focus is the international dimension in the subject matter, themes, concerns, perspective, history, of the exiles, expatriates, refugees, and other writers living in England. Those born outside England often call upon a different imaginative world from those born in England.

If in the first half of the twentieth century the British writer was likely to be a white, male, upper-middle-class product of a public school, in the last third of the century the writers came from varied backgrounds. The novelist Andrea Levy was born and brought up in London, a child of the so-called Empire Windrush generation, those West Indians who came to England after the Second World War in search of a better future. The novelist Ben Okri, born in Nigeria, was brought to England as a child when his father studied law, returned to Nigeria with his family, but came to London seeking a publisher for his manuscripts. The novelist Salman Rushdie is English as a result of the Partition of India. He was born in Bombay to wealthy, liberal Muslim parents who sent him to Rugby School. A year later his family came to England and became citizens, but afterwards moved to Pakistan. The novelist Kazuo Ishiguro was born in Nagasaki to Japanese parents. The family moved to England when his father, an oceanographer, was employed in developing the North Sea oil fields. The examples could go on with writers or their parents from Egypt, Lebanon, Zanzibar, Sudan, Ethiopia, Ghana, South Africa, Sri Lanka, Grenada, St Kitts, Guyana, Trinidad, Monserrat,

Haiti, and the Dominican Republic. Sometimes the country in which they were born no longer existed in the form they knew it, or the English language in which they wrote was no longer an acceptable national language.

Some writers are products of mixed marriages. The novelist Timothy Mo was born in Hong Kong to an English mother and a Chinese father; he came to England for his education. The dramatist and actor Ayub Khan-Din was born in Salford to an English mother and a Pakistani father. The father came to England during the 1930s, worked as a bus conductor, and married an Englishwoman. The novelist and dramatist Hanif Kureishi was born in Bromley to an English mother and a Pakistani father who was a clerk and political journalist. Considering the varied origins of the new English literature it is not surprising that 'identity' and the assertion of the unique self are often themes, and that some of the writing is auto-biographical, examines personal, family, or racial history, and concerns reasons for leaving places of origins.

This is a history of the literature created between 1948 and 2000 by the new immigrants, their children, and other peoples of colour in England, including refugees, the self-exiled, long-term residents, those who came to England to have careers as writers, and some influential birds of passage. It is not a book about injustice, race, or politics, although such matters often figure prominently in the literature. It is a book about creative writing and some of the contexts in which it was produced. It is not a history about white writers from Australia, Canada, New Zealand, or elsewhere, although many white Commonwealth writers in England also have a sense of difference; limitations of space do not allow discussion of the complexities of the issues and the many white Commonwealth writers. There have long been Australians, Americans, and European writers living in England, but the few Africans, West Indians, and Indians seemed exotic until after 1948. Differences of race, colour, culture, religion may or may not be an issue for a writer, but when there are a large number of writers who are unlike those of the past they change literary history.

While it could be argued that having a discrete history of writing by people of colour is a form of separatism, without such a book the writers are likely to become indistinguishable anchovies squeezed together in a chapter of Postcolonial Resistance stuck somewhere between Irish, Scottish, Welsh, feminist, and gay twentieth-century literary movements. Such a seemingly integrated history ignores a story that needs to be told, and devalues the contribution of the writers in the reimagining of life in England and what it means to be English.

For postcolonialists the internationalization of British literature is 'blowback' in which the former colonials of the Third World take over the imperial centre. Such a Maoist revolutionary model risks continued romantic 1960s sloganizing into a later era. During the colonial period and immediately afterwards, the colonized needed to assert an authentic culture as part of resistance to domination. The assemblage of a 'usable past' was a stage in the process of modernization, part of the process of creating a nation from various groups and joining the international economic and political system. For much of the world those times are past and the assertion of origins has become reactionary, often the basis of post-imperial local tyrannies masquerading as and using the rhetoric of revolutionary movements.

After the counter-culture of the 1960s, society became more liberal and sympathetic towards difference, and postcolonialism became fashionable in the academy as part of the cultural wars that followed the battle over Vietnam. The term postcolonial also changed its significance from a historical period to resistance against what was perceived as dominant western culture. However, by taking over a paradigm of colonial resistance against imperialism, postcolonialism lost touch with the basis of the great migration of the world's people. Rather than the peasants revolting against globalism, people came to England in search of publication, education, better jobs, more secure lives, or adventure. They are part of the globalization of the economy, communications, transportation, education, and culture, not rebels against it.

The Indian writer Pankaj Mishra has explained the situation well:

Modernity, an accomplished fact in the West, remains a fraught, repeatedly frustrated aspiration in other parts of the world. One consequence of this has been the arrival in the revitalized cities of Europe and North America of hundreds of thousands of immigrants; the once-picturesque natives of Africa, Asia and South America, who have had to flee the chaos and diminishing possibilities of their half-modern societies.

... these 'displaced persons' ... contribute, with increasing confidence, to the cosmopolitan life and culture of cities like London and New York. In England itself, there is an ever-growing literature that describes their varied lives; the experiences of colonial subjects who have had to remake themselves out of a bewilderingly diverse material for a new life in the old imperial centre.[1]

The early focus of immigrant writing is nostalgia, memories of a now idealized past, assertions of the self and culture, followed by attempts to build a new life based on new affiliations (such as Caribbean, black, Asian), and an eventual assertion of being part of and having a history in England.

This does not mean there is no literature of resistance in England. Those after the war who came from places where independence and decolonization were still issues continued to write about such matters. South Africans in exile during apartheid wrote a literature of resistance. And the rhetoric of resistance and revolution was taken over by Linton Kwesi Johnson as a Marxist and used by other performance poets. But most of the literature is not of this kind and when posturing is taken into account, even those who claimed to be revolutionaries were writers protesting against the prejudices and discrimination people of colour faced while expecting to be accepted and treated as part of the nation.

Many immigrants undergo a period of transition, an often disagreeable time when it is common to reassert one's now idealized past against the disappointments of the present. This can become institutionalized in the children of immigrants as a way of asserting difference as it can in any group. Add racial discrimination against those who are visibly different and difficulties in employment and housing to the tendency of people to stick to their own for support and there is the basis for a form of resistance and separatism which can resemble the resistance against imperialism prized by postcolonialists. Thus the coming together of various island dialects into the predominantly Jamaican black English used in England, the dialect poetry, the black publications for black readers, the use of

---

[1] Pankaj Mishra, 'Introduction', in V. S. Naipaul, *The Writer and the World* (Knopf, 2002), pp. vii–viii.

Punjabi words, even the attractions of Islamic fundamentalism to some. But such micro-nationalism, with its alternative Englishes, double consciousness, and cultural claims, is not, except for the fundamentalists, serious resistance. Cosmetic re-ethnification is an assertion of identity and uniqueness, and part of the process of demanding a revision of nationality to include former outsiders. Many writers have used the energies and cultural forms produced by ghettos and small revolts as part of their work to show sympathy, affiliation, or because they are new and interesting to use. If they did not they would not be reporting on reality.

Can internationalization contribute to the redefinition of a national literature, especially during a time when nationalism is under attack? One way of answering the question is that those of good intentions hoping to shift England away from nationalism may be undermining decades of British minorities working for acceptance and for a multiracial England. It is morally wrong to say that the idea of English literature, culture, and history no longer matters at precisely the time when it needs redefinition to include Others.

When a literature starts alluding to and building upon its predecessors there is a tradition. By the end of the twentieth century there were plays replying to Errol John's *Moon on a Rainbow Shawl*, novels offering updates of Sam Selvon's *The Lonely Londoners*, fiction modelled upon V. S. Naipaul's early books and his *The Mimic Men*, West Indian and African novelists influenced by Wilson Harris, fiction inspired by the controversy about Salman Rushdie's *The Satanic Verses*. Many novels continued Hanif Kureishi's story of someone from a minority background exploring and conquering fashionable London. The long tradition of notating contemporary black British speech, the increased mapping of areas of London where Indians and blacks live, the focus on specific events which helped form a black or Asian consciousness, the creation of a 'usable past' in the rediscovery of British black and Asian history and the writing of contemporary history are ways in which the culture, racial composition, and literature of England were revisioned and renewed. Whereas many earlier immigrants wrote nostalgically of the places they left and wondered about the choice of coming to an inhospitable England, later books consciously reply by featuring travel to Jamaica, Africa, or Pakistan which results in an affirmation of being British. If born and brought up in, or brought early to, England, what else could a writer be? By the time there were several generations in England issues of nationality should have been moot. Some immigrant writers eventually returned home; others moved on to the USA or Canada. But then authors often travel and the opportunities for a writer in North America are greater than in England.

Whereas other books in this series aim to be definitive, this volume is a beginning. I make opening and concluding claims about the context of the internationalization of the literature of England and its role in a changing England, but my main concern is to survey, map, and make an inventory of creative literature. My decision to arrange this book by decades and literary genres is contrary to the fashion for historicizing discourses, but there is no previous history which needs deconstructing. A chronological approach shows how the writing evolves from stories of immigration to the later assertion of black Britishness and such stages on the way as the black rebel, black consciousness, and gender issues. A background of events and an indication where possible of their effect on literature also seemed useful. While divisions by decade are arbitrary, they are a way to observe historical trends while organizing material.

Most of the early writers were also central to the new literatures being produced in former colonies and their writings did concern problems of decolonization, and cultural and political independence. Alongside such writing a different literature about immigration to England was beginning to appear. Samuel Selvon's novels of black England develop from the situations known by immigrants between 1948 and 1970. V. S. Naipaul's work is based on decisions that others of the time did not make. Linton Kwesi Johnson's young black rebel evolves from the black consciousness and black revolutionary movements of the later 1960s and 1970s. The major performance poets developed during the 1980s as did a body of black feminist and lesbian literature in poetry and for the stage. There are similarities of kind and significance among the many fictionalized stories of family history during the 1990s whether they appear in prose, poetry, or drama. The historical outline then is from immigrant lives and memories, to claims of being British and protest against discrimination, to nuanced stories telling of black and Asian lives which show that areas of England have a rich and diverse history, society, and culture made by immigrants and their children. As much of the English-speaking world became better educated, better qualified, and more financially comfortable, the stories told by immigrants and their children changed from representative hardships to writing about the personal, domestic, and imaginative. The literature I discuss has helped England to reimagine itself; it has contributed to the making of a new England.

If this seems like the return of grand narratives with their notion of progress, I must admit to liking such history. Readers committed to postmodernist anti-narratives, however, will be satisfied by the many writers and groups who seem oddballs in their decade or who do not fit well into any periodization.

I often use the phrase people of colour as an inclusive term for those of African, Caribbean, Asian, and other non-European ethnicities. I have sometimes used 'black' to mean everyone who is not white including those of mixed race. As nothing will ever be totally satisfactory, I have done the best I can shifting between terms as they seem appropriate in the contexts they are used. Some of the authors, especially those who write in popular literary forms, have no racial interests and reject being so classified, but they still need to be included in any history of who and what has been published.

I usually treat an author's writing in one place rather than dividing it between periods and genres, although with a few authors, such as Caryl Phillips and especially Hanif Kureishi, I have discussed theatre and other scripts under Drama as well as Prose. In cases, such as John La Rose, where there are significant authors but not a large body of work in one genre, I discuss the creative writing in a background section. While there are now some recognizable kinds within genres, such as travel literature, or autobiography, usually, as is the case with detective and thriller novels or books of essays, the body of such work is not yet large enough to consider on its own. I have not examined the literature of sociology, history, politics, music criticism, religion, newspaper columns, or sports. My interest is in creative writing and its immediate social and cultural contexts including publishing and sponsorship. This includes theatre and theatre companies. While I have not separately discussed literature written for children, I have indicated its presence and significance.

In the future there will be histories of the literature of England which will integrate black and white without difficulty, but for the present that is a dream. First the histories (as there is more than one story) of how British literature internationalized, became something other than white British-born, need to be written. A good start has been made by C. L. Innes in *A History of Black and Asian Writing in Britain* (2002), but her excellent book only devotes an 'epilogue' to the half-century I discuss.

England's multiracial literature often began from the same seeds that gave birth to the new national literatures of the Commonwealth as many of the authors lived in England directly after the war and their books were published in London. Just as the new national literatures at first often derived from and then modified contemporary British styles and concerns, so England's multiracial writers began with period styles and themes similar to those of white British writers to which they added cultural markers and racial and immigrant concerns. Writing by people of colour and whites often shares characteristics during each decade. Yet something usually changes in the writing of immigrants and people of colour. V. S. Naipaul and Martin Amis are both British, but everything about their background, experience, vision, and writing is radically different. As usual in recent centuries, it is especially in the novel that changing social history is recorded. As theatre is an expensive and difficult art to produce, and requires more than one side of a story, it was slower to accommodate itself to problems of immigrants and their children, but the few early published plays are of high quality and interestingly focus on individuals. That in the last decades of the century the theatre offered exciting nuanced portraits of the conflicts within the black and Asian communities is itself significant of the organizing energies of those involved, of their willingness to air their controversies, and of a supportive multiracial audience.

While there are many exceptions, the history of England's multiracial literature 1948–2000 might be summarized as follows. In poetry a late colonial romanticism, Georgianism, and aestheticism was challenged by a modernist poetry often written in dialect as West Indians replaced Indians; then modernist poetry was both challenged by and incorporated within performance poetry. The central concern of performance poetry with the black and West Indian experience was in turn undermined from within by black feminist and lesbian groups who broadened the ethnic basis of their membership along with gender themes. That many writers also were involved with theatre paradoxically led away from the conventions of performance poetry to a more complex page-based narrative verse concerned with the self and stories in multiple voices. The several decades of West Indian dominance in poetry were replaced by British-born poets of mixed race, often of Nigerian origins, and by writers from new ethnic groups. As a result the Jamaican dialect used as a black 'national' language in most performance poetry gave way to standard English or a racially neutral streetwise diction.

In the theatre the movement was from social realism and Brecht's influence to concern with black British and personal history. While most theatre was by those of West Indian origins, the situation began to change in the 1980s with British-born writers including Hanif Kureishi, the first of several part-Pakistani dramatists. Nigerian dramatists became important.

Immigrant novels of home, social comedy, and cultural conflict were followed during the 1970s by the first books about the lives of the children of the immigrants, the first fiction written for specific markets, the start of writing in England by an African woman, and other firsts as immigrants began to become part of the British rather than their own national literary scene. The 1980s was characterized by Salman Rushdie's novels, the *fatwa* against him, various forms of fabulation, the first publications of many writers from the Islamic world, an increasing number of books by women, and the first books written by the children of immigrants. By the 1990s there was a vital black British literary scene, many authors of mixed race, interest in popular fiction, Indian British novelists, and novelists from many parts of the world settled in England. While subject matter and manner ranged from urban naturalism to surreal fantasies, many of the novels by blacks and those of mixed race looked at what brought the immigrants to England, and the social differences between the various immigrants, while detailing various locales of London as part of a new map of England. Nigerians had replaced West Indians as the most productive literary community and there were many young writers of Indian descent. Those of mixed race were writing of the white side of their family as well as the black, while many black writers were noting similarities between the lives of outsiders regardless of race. Such literature not only reflects social and culture changes, it is one of the ways in which people imagine themselves and in the process change society.

1

The End of Imperial England and the Seeds of the New: 1948–1969

I. New Immigrants

Three ships arrived in 1948 carrying between them about 700 immigrants from the West Indies. Many of the new immigrants were from rural areas of the islands, were fleeing unemployment, had only a primary school education, and were not qualified for jobs in England. England, however, needed workers, and the West Indians were young, active, and soon employed. Thousands followed as a change in American immigration policies, the McCarran Walter Act of 1952, resulted in others coming to England; by 1958 there were perhaps 125,000 West Indian immigrants.

England was still undergoing shortages, rationing, and other effects of the war including a highly disciplined, bureaucratically administered society. The West Indians were thought to create many problems because of their background, colour, and not being hired for specific jobs, but under the 1948 Nationality Act they and others from the colonies and dominions were British and had a right to come and stay. They were the start of what would become a multiracial England with a black working class culturally unlike the existing working class. Although England would in many ways, such as racism, housing, climate, and food, prove disappointing, there were attractions including free National Health, dole for the unemployed, and state-funded education and possible future university education for the children of the immigrants.

Such immigrants added to the middle-class West Indian colonials who came to England to study for university qualifications and professional training unavailable at home. Still others came because with the end of the war it was possible once more to travel and seek adventure. They joined those Indians, Africans, and West Indians who were already living in England or who had helped during the war. England over the centuries had people of colour and at times they had contributed to its literature, but the size of this new movement of immigration would have a lasting effect on British culture, remaking England into a multiracial society and giving its literature a new internationalism when, with the collapse of its empire, it risked narrowing its perspective to Little Englandism. The vibrant, active minorities usually wanted to be English at a time when others were claiming their separateness as Irish, Welsh, Scots, feminist, gay, lesbian, even Northerners. Instead of England ending in fragmentation and the pull of Europe, it was being renewed in a way that made it part of the new internationalism developing during the second half of the twentieth century.

Those immigrants arriving by ship soon became aware that porters and other labourers at the dock were white. There was the grime, crowdedness, and physical unattractiveness of the cities in comparison with the famous monuments of culture the immigrants had heard about. The English seemed to know nothing about geography and had little knowledge of the culture of their colonies. All West Indians were assumed to be Jamaicans. Even the well-intended were likely to ask whether Monserrat was off the coast of Africa and to assume that all Africans spoke one language. Then there was the racism faced in housing, in employment, at the pubs, and when dealing with bureaucracies.

It was not just the West Indians who were surprised by England. In *The Buddha of Suburbia* Hanif Kureishi reconstructs the world Karim's father met in 1950 when arriving from India to study:

London, the Old Kent Road, was a freezing shock to both of them. It was wet and foggy; people called you 'Sunny Jim'; there was never enough to eat, and Dad never took to dripping on toast. 'Nose drippings more like,' he'd say, pushing away the staple diet of the working class. 'I thought it would be roast beef and Yorkshire pudding all the way.' But rationing was still on, and the area was derelict after being bombed to rubble during the war. Dad was amazed and heartened by the sight of the British in England, though. He'd never seen the English in poverty, as roadsweepers, dustmen, shopkeepers and barmen. He'd never seen an Englishman stuffing bread into his mouth with his fingers, and no one told him the English didn't wash regularly because the water was so cold—if they had water at all. And when Dad tried to discuss Byron in local pubs no one warned him that not every Englishman could read or that they didn't necessarily want tutoring by an Indian on the poetry of a pervert and a madman.

Fortunately, Anwar and Dad had somewhere to stay. (pp. 24–5)

Housing in England was expensive, difficult to find, in poor condition, and without expected amenities. Those of colour were likely to face open discrimination and pay exorbitant rent to share what they could obtain. Gangsters soon found this a developing market. Putting together money for a down payment on a house and obtaining a bank loan was even more difficult. Each of Sam Selvon's four London novels is in some way concerned with housing, whether as a necessity of survival or for settling in England. To become a landlord letting rooms and living from the rent of others was to have made it. Selvon's anti-hero Moses leads other West Indians to the promised land of basement bedsitters and eventually himself purchases a dilapidated house awaiting demolition in which he becomes a parody rentier who exploits servants to do his work while he tries to write his memoirs. Decades later V. S. Naipaul would use housing in *The Enigma of Arrival* as symbolic of belonging and contrast the narrator, who needs to build his own house, with the Lord from whom he rented his cottage.

Many who arrived were first housed in hostels before other accommodation or employment was found: there were also student hostels. On the ships the immigrants had met those from other islands and started the process of becoming West Indian: in the hostels they met Indians and Africans. As Sam Selvon's *The Lonely Londoners* showed, they would continue to meet at weekends in bedsitters and a black community would begin to form. There were also clubs where black music—jazz, Caribbean, and African—was played and musical styles and musicians were starting to mix and create a new culture. Music and dance are usually the areas in which new cultural forms are first created, but some forms such as Trinidadian calypso and Indian allegory would reappear in the new British literature.

In general the new writing was realistic. For decades literature by immigrants would mention housing problems; even writers from the white colonies would complain at British landlords, their snooping, small snobberies, and rules against using the bathtub more than once a week. The immigrants complained of British low standards of hygiene and of locking out those who returned late. Having a companion stay over was usually forbidden. The bathtub, shower, and possession of the latchkey were symbols of cultural wars between natives and immigrants. Immigrants, exiles, expatriates, and their children would continue to think of themselves as homeless, because they or their friends had been unaccommodated both physically and socially.

Not all West Indians arrived seeking employment, free health benefits, or found themselves roofless. E. A. Markham recalled his arrival in 1956 and their house in Ladbroke Grove:

The living standard of our family declined in England: we didn't run a car, my mother no longer had a chauffeur, we didn't live in a house of twelve rooms with four others to our name, we didn't have servants . . . People didn't correspond to our notion of 'The English'. The family who rented our downstairs front room were rag-and-bone people (with children our age who eventually had to be ejected because we feared for our own hygiene).[1]

The arrival of the Markhams was balanced by their English boarders' departure to Australia on assisted passage. The Markhams lived next door to Oswald Mosley's right-hand man and listened to Mosley saying that West Indians should be sent back.

Other writers arrived as students on scholarships to the elite universities of the period. By the standards of the immigrants seeking work and housing the students were well off, but they faced snobberies and other wounds including an awareness that they were not regarded as British no matter how well they had mastered the language, literature, and culture. What then was home? Africa? India?

[1] E. A. Markham, 'Taking the Drawing Room through Customs', in F. Dennis and Naseem Khan (eds.), *Voices of the Crossing* (Serpent's Tail, 2000), 14.

The literature is filled with returns, such as that recorded in Naipaul's *An Area of Darkness* (1964), to lands of family origins, followed by awareness that there was no going back, no way of undoing diasporas. Whereas Randolph Stow (b. 1935), an Australian, could in *The Girl as Green as Elderflower* (1980) celebrate returning to the land and culture of his ancestors, migrant people of colour were literally homeless. India made clear that the Indians of Trinidad, British Guinea, and East Africa were British responsibilities, not even employable by the Indian High Commission in London. To be Indian one needed to be born in India. To be African you needed to be born into a tribe. For those born abroad who were raised with awareness of their ethnicity and who assumed that they would return 'home' the failures were a shock.

By the mid-1950s England was in a paradoxical situation; while not wanting people of colour it had become dependent upon them in many areas where whites would not accept employment or where there were shortages of those with professional qualifications. Both industry and public services required the new immigrants who were resented by many, especially by a working class which already felt disenfranchised and now felt in competition with those of a different colour. The new immigrants brought their culture and some brightness to the British scene whether in the calypsos of Lord Kitchener or the late-night clubs offering jazz and other music for dancing. Within decades curries would be thought as British as fish and chips. British officials and politicians kept saying immigration must stop, but England already had a black population which was settling and bound to increase. Immigrants would go to areas where they already had friends, family, or where there were others of similar origins; areas of cities were soon regarded as black or Asian. Racial tensions resulted in riots in Notting Hill and in Nottingham during 1958.

One result of the rapid attempt to produce an educated colonial professional middle class before granting national independence was the creation of a body of writers from the colonies, some of whom came to England as immigrants while others came as students. A few, such as E. R. Braithwaite, arrived during the war to fight for England. West Indian writers in England included John Figueroa who came in 1946 after taking his first degree in the United States; in London he would do further degrees in education while working as a teacher. Edgar Mittelholzer arrived in 1948, left in 1952, and returned in 1956. C. L. R. James (1901–89), an older writer and intellectual, was in and out of England from the 1930s onward, returned in 1953 and left for Trinidad in 1958. He would be back and eventually publish *Beyond a Boundary* (1963), a classic study of the relationship between colonialism, politics, psychology, and race in West Indian cricket. George Lamming, from Barbados, and Samuel Selvon, from Trinidad, arrived together on a small ship in 1950. Both were in their twenties, and came to England to have careers as writers and for life outside the colonial middle class.

There were new small publishing houses interested in the colonies and within three years both Selvon and Lamming were published novelists beginning with the former's *A Brighter Sun* (1952) and Lamming's *In the Castle of My Skin* (1953)—part of the new West Indian literature and forerunners of a black British literature. While their first novels were about race and colonialism in the West Indies, a few years later they would write the first books by West Indian immigrants about life in England, Lamming's *The Emigrants* (1954) and Selvon's *The Lonely Londoners* (1956). During 1950 V. S. Naipaul came to England to study at Oxford on a Trinidad government scholarship; Edward Kamau Brathwaite arrived to study at Cambridge on a scholarship from Barbados. Andrew Salkey arrived in 1952. After working for the BBC and as a teacher he began his career as a novelist with *A Quality of Violence* (1959) and as editor with *West Indian Stories* (1960). Wilson Harris came to England in 1959 and in 1960 began publishing with Faber. Such writers formed a network of sometimes disagreeing acquaintances, friends, broadcasters, reviewers, journalists, and advisers to publishers. Salkey knew Diana Athill of André Deutsch to whom he recommended V. S. Naipaul. Salkey's contacts at Faber led to his being asked to read the manuscript of Wilson Harris's *Palace of the Peacock*, which he recommended for publication, after the first six readers found themselves unable to judge it.

Besides writers, those coming to England included intellectuals who played significant roles in the creation of first a new West Indian literature and then the new black British literature. Stuart Hall arrived in 1951 to read English at Oxford University, became active in politics, and was one of the founders of *Universities and Left*

Review in 1956 which four years later became the *New Left Review*. Hall was part of the transformation of British Marxism into the New Left and influential at the Cultural Studies Centre in Birmingham in reshaping the study of the sociology of culture into cultural studies. His writings over the decades would reflect his identification with the West Indian immigrants and their problems and progress in England. He understood that for the African-Caribbean the concept of diaspora was a matter of social and cultural identity formed in the imagination rather than part of a return to a homeland. He would write studies of the representation of minority youth in the media, and note how a new black British culture was being formed as the young and minorities moved from being on the defensive to a creative position in society. Eric and Jessica Huntley, who would found Bogle L'Ouverture publications, arrived, respectively, in 1956 and 1957 from British Guiana. John La Rose, who would start New Beacon Books, arrived in 1961.

Such writers and intellectuals were also part of the emerging cultural scene in the Caribbean stimulated by the coming of independence. There was a continual movement back and forth as those who published in West Indian journals came to England and as those who had published in England returned to the West Indies. Some West Indians also spent time teaching in Africa. The creation of a modern West Indian literature occurred alongside and often within the start of a black British literature. An early influence on West Indian literature and the establishment of a West Indian literary community in England was Una Marson's *Calling the West Indies*, which was broadcast by the BBC overseas service. Starting in 1943 it began to include literary work by West Indians. In 1945 it became *Caribbean Voices*, a half-hour programme broadcast from London to the West Indies; the next year Henry Swanzy became editor. *Caribbean Voices* became a West Indian literary review on the air with poetry, short stories, short plays, and literary criticism. This helped pull together the scattered English-speaking Caribbean into one literary community and provided a base in London for West Indian writers and intellectuals. For the next decade *Caribbean Voices*, along with similar programmes addressed to India and Africa, brought writers from the colonies into contact with the English literary establishment. In the process a core intellectual and artistic community was formed of immigrant writers. As post-war students came to British universities the writers gravitated towards the BBC, often, like V. S. Naipaul, helping edit *Caribbean Voices* and working part-time or as a freelancer. *Caribbean Voices* paid a guinea a minute for readings and texts which allowed those, such as George Lamming, who were employed as a reader, to avoid seeking other employment and dedicate themselves to their writing.

England already was a centre for Indian, African, and West Indian intellectuals seeking national independence and the end of colonialism. There was the famous 1945 Fifth Pan-African Congress in Manchester whose participants included C. L. R. James, George Padmore, Jomo Kenyatta, and Kwame Nkrumah. This resulted in several organizations. James Berry, later an influential poet and editor, was the secretary of the African and Caribbean Social and Cultural Centre. By the time the BBC *Caribbean Voices* ended, there was a West Indian cultural and political movement with contacts between various groups within the community. The year of the Notting Hill riots, 1958, was the start of the monthly *West Indian Gazette*, which although political became another centre for the writers, while in Bayswater there was the first West Indian carnival. The Institute of Race Relations was also founded in 1958. Over the years its monthly newsletter *Race Today* would be a source of news and analysis about racial discrimination and violence in England.

Most of the Indian writers who came and would come to England were from wealthy or upper-middle-class families; some settled in England as a consequence of the Partition of India. Attia Hosain arrived in 1947 when her husband was posted to the Indian High Commission in London. Although she belonged to the Muslim elite of north India who created Pakistan, she never accepted Partition. Like others from the Empire she was still a British citizen and she divided her time between London and Bombay. The subject matter of her finely grained writing remained the world she had known. She has been claimed as part of Indian and as part of Pakistani literary history. Now she is seen as a British writer. Selvon, V. S. Naipaul, Zulfikhar Ghose, Rushdie, and others would also be claimed by more than one national literature. Many Indians arrived with already existing links to the London literary establishment. Hosain, and earlier Mulk Raj Anand, knew the Bloomsbury group; Dom Moraes had already met Stephen Spender in Bombay. Having come to England at the age of 16 to prepare for university, Moraes was introduced by Spender to Cyril Connolly, E. M. Forster, and Walter de la Mare. Before long he was part of a Soho bohemia that included the painter Francis Bacon and the poet George Barker. He knew few literary Indians in England until he became friendly with Ved Mehta at Oxford.

The West Indian and Indian writers in England during this period seldom had any contact and were uncomfortable when they were brought together by such sponsoring whites as the novelist Colin MacInnes or the publisher André Deutsch. The West Indians were welcoming to Africans, but Indians usually felt superior and were treated better by the British in terms of housing and employment. The stereotypes the British had of them were different. Whereas the black was considered happy-go-lucky, lazy, or criminal, the Indian was thought spiritual, mystical, perhaps part of a princely family. Again Selvon is a guide to the period. In *The Lonely Londoners* Moses tells Indian West Indians to pretend that they are Indians from India to avoid housing problems. This was based on actual situations Selvon knew where West Indians passed themselves off as Indians to British landlords. The temporary alliance between West Indians and Asians as 'black' was a product of a later period after African-Americans proposed a shared blackness with other people of colour and 'black' became a catch-all term for those claiming victimhood. By that time, as immigration of Asians increased, Indians and others from the subcontinent were lumped together under the derogatory label 'Pakis' and had become victims as well.

From 1958 onwards there were increased racial tensions. There were race riots during 1958–9 led by the National Front, and as a consequence the government passed the 1962 Commonwealth Immigrants Act to prevent free immigration by British citizens. Only 30,000 Commonwealth citizens could enter England each year and there was no right to appeal against immigration officers who could bar whom they wished. After 1962 only students and schoolchildren could enter England without problems. This led to a rush to bring family and changed the West Indian population in England from primarily young adult males to families with mothers, sisters, and children. Linton Kwesi Johnson was 9 when he came to join his family.

The Labour Party argued against the 1962 Immigration Act but found that race was a significant issue with voters. A Conservative MP, Peter Griffiths, took Smethwick from Labour in the 1964 general election using the slogan 'If you want a Nigger Neighbour, vote Labour'. Labour won the election, left the Immigration Act virtually unchanged, but passed a Race Relations Bill (1965). The Bill, supposed to outlaw racial discrimination in public places, was powerless to do more than admonish and seek conciliation.

Throughout the 1960s England was affected by international and especially American politics. Many of the same groups that protested against racial discrimination also protested against American foreign policies. Perhaps the greatest influence on attitudes was the independence of former colonies. Within a decade many were granted or fought for independence. Starting with India in 1947, Ghana in 1957, and Nigeria in 1960 the world seemed to be changing. While the West Indian Federation only lasted four years, most of the English-speaking islands were independent nations by 1962. The independence of former colonies and the accompanying cultural assertion, especially the start of a modern African literature, created a feeling that the defeat of colonialism abroad should be a model elsewhere for people of colour.

As nationalism is often based on language, religion, race, and finding a usable past, themes of political and cultural recuperation as well as cultural conflict became part of the literature, themes which a generation later would be imitated in black British literature. Chinua Achebe's *Things Fall Apart* (1958) rapidly became a classic with its use of an Igboized English and Igbo proverbs, the detailed portrait of an interesting, complete, and changing African society with its beliefs, myths, rituals, and the contrast between the perspective of black Africa and the white man with the arrival of imperialism.

The new universities of the new nations, especially in Africa, and perhaps more important, their secondary school systems, added the new literature to their syllabus, thus creating a large new literary market, a market which was enlarged by the interest of the former white dominions, such as Canada and New Zealand, in the literature and culture of the new black nations. At the start of the decade Rex

Collings at Oxford University Press began the Three Crowns paperback books intended for creative writing from the newly independent countries. Wole Soyinka's plays were among its publications. When Collings left, the series was taken over by James Currey who soon moved to Heinemann Educational Books which became famous for its African Writers Series, started in 1962. Heinemann's Caribbean Writers Series followed in 1969. Longman Drumbeat books started in the later 1970s.

The parallel in the United States to decolonization was the civil rights movement which demanded votes and equal treatment in the American South where there were laws requiring racial segregation. Racial protest and models of political resistance in the United States were brought to England by visiting Americans including Martin Luther King (1964) and Malcolm X (1965) who debated with Enoch Powell at the Oxford Union and spoke in London and Smethwick. Each visitor seemed to represent an intensification of the American civil rights struggle. King advocated Gandhian non-violent passive resistance. Malcolm X said the present was an era of revolution and claimed that the struggle by African-Americans was part of the worldwide fight against oppression and colonialism. Stokeley Carmichael arrived in England in July 1967 preaching Black Power and implying that violence was necessary for liberation. Carmichael, originally from Trinidad, was influenced by the role Frantz Fanon gave violence in creating a community and freeing the oppressed from feelings of inferiority. Carmichael spoke to such groups as the Campaign Against Racial Discrimination and the Caribbean Artists Movement. Whereas previous discussions of, say, patois and standard English were concerned with class, culture, and race, Carmichael set them within a larger context of the oppressed and oppressor beginning with slavery. Revolutionaries, especially Fidel Castro and Che Guevara, became the new heroes. During 1968 Rapp Brown, another fiery black American orator, came to England.

Such influences led writers to Black Power and then to the Marxism of the Race Today collective. Soon England would have its own Black Power groups that included Linton Kwesi Johnson and Farrukh Dhondy. In the revolutionary fervour and rhetoric of the late 1960s there seemed no clear distinction among Marxist, Third Worldist, or Black Power. Many of the organizations joined together to form the Black People's Alliance, a self-proclaimed militant front for black consciousness. Some of the writers belonged to a British version of the Black Panthers. Johnson would write poems addressing mythic revolutionary black youths rebelling against the white power structure. Some of the older writers raised in traditions of gradualism, accommodation, and scepticism felt uneasy in a climate of revolutionary rhetoric and fervour.

The end of the Empire continued to bring eruptions when several black African governments confiscated the properties of Asians who were forced to flee. The exodus of Indians from Kenya in 1967 led to a fierce dispute between England, which did not want to admit more people of colour, and India, which said it could not afford to accept the many Indians abroad who held British passports and who were legally as well as morally a British responsibility. In 1968 the government passed the Commonwealth Immigrants Act preventing entry to England by those with British passports unless they were 'patrials'—had British family origins and thus white colonials unlike black West Indians or bronze Indians. By the early 1970s there was the problem of resettling about 50,000 Asians expelled from Uganda. Many, including Muslims, were westernized and entrepreneurial unlike the rural Pakistanis being employed in the north of England for dirty jobs the white British working class no longer wanted. The Nigerian civil war, 1967–70, increased what until then had been a slow stream of Nigerians settling in England. As conditions in Africa deteriorated, a community of Africans in England took root.

During 1968 Enoch Powell delivered his notorious 'Rivers of Blood' speech warning of a race war if immigration of blacks continued; he proposed paying blacks to be repatriated, a topic parodied at the start of Samuel Selvon's *Moses Migrating* where Moses, dissatisfied with his life, writes to Powell saying that he agrees blacks are unhappy in England and he would appreciate money to return to Trinidad. Selvon's novel alludes to people, events, and speeches of the period. When Moses is especially kind to an elderly white woman (who turns out to be an awful racist) it is because Powell claimed that elderly white women were being terrorized by blacks.

Although Enoch Powell was removed from the Conservative Party shadow cabinet, he had his supporters especially among a working class that felt threatened in housing, employment, and social services by immigrants; in London the dockers and meat handlers marched on the House of Commons. This period, one of the low ebbs of racial relations in England, is caught in Kamala Markandaya's *The Nowhere Man*:

As now he saw, walking frail through the streets, such was the oppressive presence of rejection. Heard he whispers that he had allowed to brush him by grown into strident voices that preached a new gospel, a gospel he had not heard since those echoes from Germany before the war. He recalled them now, almost phrase by phrase, presenting hate as a permissible emotion for decent German people. Not only permissible but laudable . . . (p. 176)

Despite such racism England would become a multicultural, multiracial society. The Commonwealth required it. The Africa Centre in Covent Garden opened unofficially in 1962 and was used for productions of plays. The excitement of decolonization and national independence in Africa and the Caribbean carried to such former white dominions as Canada, Australia, and New Zealand. The Empire was replaced by the British Commonwealth and then the Commonwealth.

The mid-1960s began the notion of Commonwealth literature as a way of grouping together writing from former colonies. There were many anthologies of Commonwealth literature such as Heinemann's *Young Commonwealth Poets '65*, a large Commonwealth Arts Festival held throughout England in 1965 with a Commonwealth Poetry Conference in Cardiff, while *London Magazine* in September 1965 produced a large Commonwealth literature issue. Among the many Commonwealth writers then living in England who would stay and settle or go back and forth were Randolph Stow (Australia), Peter Porter (Australia), Fleur Adcock (New Zealand), Mordecai Richler (Canada), Doris Lessing (Rhodesia, now Zimbabwe), and many South Africans (still regarded as Commonwealth writers) as well as West Indians, Indians, and black Africans.

The teaching of Commonwealth literature began in the School of English at Leeds University, when A. Norman Jeffares moved from a chair in Australia, and was part of a new expansion of English studies. The teaching of American literature also started at Leeds at the same time. William Walsh, who was a professor of education at Leeds, published *A Manifold Voice: Studies in Commonwealth Literature* (1970) and edited *Commonwealth Literature* (1973), influential early books in the area. Walsh was made the first professor of Commonwealth literature and courses were soon being taught at Hull, Sheffield, and other northern universities. Leeds University, with Jeffares not far in the background, started *ARIEL* (*A Review of International English Literature*) and the *Journal of Commonwealth Literature* (1965). As new universities, such as Kent at Canterbury or Sussex, started, often with staff hired from the new universities of the Commonwealth or from the red-bricks of the north, they also began offering courses in Commonwealth literature or such areas as African, Indian, or Canadian and Australian literature. The University of Kent at Canterbury soon became a rival and successor of Leeds, especially after Jeffares moved to the University of Stirling, which in turn became another centre for Commonwealth studies.

Commonwealth literature officially began at British universities with a 1964 conference at Leeds University; the papers were published in *Commonwealth Literature: Unity and Diversity* (1965), edited by John Press. This was followed in 1965, also at Leeds University, with the formation of the Association for Commonwealth Literature and Language Studies. Sponsors included the Foreign Office, the British Council, the BBC, and the Commonwealth Relations Office. Soon there were regional branches throughout the Commonwealth and Europe, with the first triennial ACLALS International Conference at the University of Brisbane in 1968. The eighth, at the University of Kent at Canterbury, 1989, was influential in introducing such new black British writers as Ben Okri, Fred D'Aguiar, Caryl Phillips, and David Dabydeen to the international Commonwealth literature community and making many at the conference aware that England now had a new national literature of its own in contrast to Naipaul and Rushdie, who were still regarded as part of West Indian and Indian literature.

Over the decades literary prizes had a role in publicizing the ways the literature of England had changed and become multiracial. The award of the Hawthornden Prize to Dom Moraes (1957) for *A*

Beginning and to V. S. Naipaul (1963) for *Mr Stone and the Knights Companion* showed that Indian and West Indian writers were becoming part of the British literary scene. The Booker Prize, established in 1969, often made Commonwealth and the new British literature fashionable. Winners included V. S. Naipaul's *In a Free State* (1971), Rushdie's *Midnight's Children* (1981), Ishiguro's *The Remains of the Day* (1989), and Okri's *The Famished Road* (1991), along with books by Nadine Gordimer, Ruth Prawer Jhabvala, Thomas Keneally, J. M. Coetzee, Peter Carey, Margaret Atwood, and Michael Ondaatje. Short-listed Booker Prize finalists included novels by Timothy Mo (1982, 1986, 1991), Caryl Phillips (1993), Romesh Gunesekera (1994), Abdulrazak Gurnah (1994), and Ahdaf Soueif (1999).

During 1966 both the Caribbean Artists Movement and New Beacon Bookshop Press began. CAM was started by John La Rose, Andrew Salkey, and E. Kamau Brathwaite to discuss the aesthetics of and give publicity to Caribbean art. They hoped to strengthen links with publishers and put Caribbean art within a global context. Many of the West Indian artists, students, and intellectuals in England at the time participated. At CAM's first public meeting at the Jeannetta Cochrane Theatre in Holborn, Brathwaite read his *Rights of Passage*, part of his ambitious *Arrivants* trilogy published by Oxford University Press. A central work of West Indian literature, *Arrivants* and Brathwaite were to have an influence on black British poetry. Besides making use of a continuum of speech and voices from patois to standard English, and a striking variety of stanzaic forms, the rhythms were more Caribbean than those of Britain.

Although CAM included a variety of views and some participants were to become influenced by Black Power, its founding members and interests at first included the largely new, difficult, modernist, experimental art of such writers as Wilson Harris, John La Rose, and Orlando Patterson, and such painters as Aubrey Williams. Kamau Brathwaite was unique in that he combined epic ambitions and radical experimentation with easy access and clear identification to black cultural nationalism. In general CAM was concerned with the Caribbean and its artists along with Africa and African-America, but some of its sessions would now be regarded as black British. The Caribbean poets reading in October 1971 included James Berry,

T-Bone Wilson, Mustapha Matura, and E. A. Markham. CAM ended during 1972, having run its course. Brathwaite had returned to Jamaica and Salkey in 1974 began teaching in the USA, while La Rose's time went into New Beacon Press and community activities. Whereas Brathwaite and Salkey were oriented towards the Caribbean, La Rose was committed to the community of West Indians in England for whom England was now their actual home.

New Beacon, the first black bookshop and publisher, was the child of La Rose and his wife Sarah White. La Rose would for decades be a leading activist in racial matters especially as they pertained to West Indian immigrants. The bookshop carried publications from and about the Caribbean, about blacks and decolonization. After publishing La Rose's book of poems, *Foundations*, New Beacon Press became a leading small press for Caribbean, black British, and Third World writers. Its third title was Wilson Harris's critical essays *Tradition, the Writer and Society* (1967). It also published books for minority children.

La Rose had an important role in forming consciousness of being black British. At a time when many thought of themselves as exiled from the Caribbean or Africa he said that the youth must recognize that they were in England to stay; the aim of their politics should be to demand a place in society with full rights and obligations. There was a racial problem which would become worse until those in power were forced to examine what needed to be done to make the immigrants and their children part of England. La Rose was the first chair of the Caribbean Education and Community Workers Association (CECWA), which published Bernard Coard's influential pamphlet *How the West Indian Child is made Educationally Subnormal in the British School System* (1971), a founder of the Black Parents Movement (1975), a leading member of the New Cross Massacre Action Committee, and an organizer of the International Book Fair of Radical, Black and Third World Books. On the occasion of the 10th International Book Fair, a committee published *Foundations of a Movement* (1991), a tribute to him. Although the movement represented those who were victims of housing, employment, and legal discrimination, its members were often well-educated professionals with connections to the British establishment. Eric Walter White, secretary of the Poetry Society and director of literature at the Arts Council was the father of Sarah White, John La Rose's wife.

While La Rose's poems included passages of dialect they tended to be abstract and, in the modernist manner, implied a multiplicity of meanings. The compression can become unintelligible. His poetry is in a line of Caribbean poets that includes Wilson Harris, Edward Kamau Brathwaite, and E. A. Markham, each of whom tried to find ways of adapting modernist poetry, especially the surrealist-influenced poetry of Aimé Césaire, to the English-speaking Caribbean. For La Rose poetry should be about the failure to communicate in a culture where there was a gap between sensibility and expression. Many of the poems in *Foundations* (1966) are about the inability to speak, the difficulty of expressing, 'islets of truth | Within me . . . Shouting for diction | truncated | In pained secretion' ('Word Creatures'). In the sequence of poems 'Song to an Imperishable Sunlight' history is used to recall former liberators who need to be known as part of the creation of a necessary black revolutionary consciousness.

La Rose's fragmented multivoiced drama of finding a usable past to construct a sense of the self was taken further by Brathwaite in his more direct and more filled-in evocation of black history and use of dialect, while L. K. Johnson would find in La Rose and Brathwaite ideas from which to create his own poetry of contemporary black youth rebelling. Behind each of the three poets is the Césaire of *Cahier d'un retour au pays natal* (1956). Once the anglophone poets had discovered Martiniquean Césaire's revolutionary mixture of surrealism, modernism, politics, black history, protest, use of patois, and search for black consciousness and speech, there was the problem of how to make use of this breakthrough in English. Césaire established the concept of negritude as a form of resistance to the dominant white culture. In his writing negritude signifies a collective racial consciousness of the black diaspora in contrast to L. S. Senghor's version of negritude which assumes a romantic essential Africanness of passion and closeness to nature in contrast to European rationality.

Brathwaite showed the poets how to use the notion of a black community and how black writing had its own voice, its own sound and rhythms which could best be appreciated as oral poetry rather than on the page. Brathwaite opened the possibility of an oral poetry with a black English voice and diction which was part of a literary tradition with roots in Africa and which shared in the oral poetry of the New World blacks, especially black folk and popular culture. While this might be regarded as a negritude for the anglo-phone blacks, with all the dangers and absurdities of such essential-ism, it was liberating at a time when poets were concerned with use of the voice and when black poets were especially seeking an alter-native to writing within the British tradition. Brathwaite was the theorist of black British oral poetry. James Berry, Faustin Charles, Marc Matthews, T-Bone Wilson, and Linton Kwesi Johnson were nurtured or part-nurtured by CAM. The Radical, Black and Third World Book Fair, which was held annually, was in part a CAM off-shoot, started by La Rose.

The late 1960s and part of the 1970s continued the importation of American black culture and Black Power. A major influence on the new black British writers of the next two decades was African-American writing, an influence from which they would liberate themselves as the contexts were unlike those in England. Ferdinand Dennis recalls reading such books as Stokeley Carmichael's *Black Power*, Frantz Fanon's *Black Skin, White Mask*, Eldridge Cleaver's *Soul on Ice*, and Bobby Seale's *Seize the Time*. When studying for his A levels at a college of further education, he listened to lectures by John La Rose and Darcus Howe and heard Linton Kwesi Johnson in performance with a band. Dennis himself adapted the manner of a black revolutionary. He spoke with black American idioms, and wore a black beret, a black leather jacket, and black trousers. Although born in Jamaica and brought up in England he had, along with others, become a mimic black American. While this gave him historical knowledge and a conceptual vocabulary that as a black British youth he lacked, it applied to a land where there had been slavery and where racial discrimination had brought the United States close to a race war. England was filled with imitation Malcolm Xs, some of whom were idealized by white progressives. The best known was Michael X. This infatuation is the subject of a long critical essay by V. S. Naipaul. Michael X progressed from con man to murderer. Dennis was later to write in *Voices of the Crossing* (2000), 'I have often thought just as the world is increasingly dominated by American culture, so the small population of people of African descent in Britain have become victims of African-American cultural imperialism, mimicking styles and taking on concerns which sit uneasily in the British context' (p. 44).

The counter-culture of the 1960s, its relationship to the rapid development of pop music and drug culture, the protests against the war in Vietnam, the hero worship of revolutionaries, and other cultural and liberation movements of the sixties resulted in a continuing relationship between black culture and the culture of young whites. There was a black world of clubs, prostitutes, and drug dealing stretching from the traditional vice dens of Soho to the then black areas of Notting Hill. This increased during the 1960s with the idealizing of drugs and sexual freedom as part of self-liberation and the revolutionary rhetoric of rock 'n' roll. Rock stars and starlets were proud to be seen in black clubs known as places to purchase drugs and sex, while the police increased their raids and searches in the hope of catching dealers. The story as well as its effect on how West Indians would be seen in future has been well documented by Mike Phillips and Trevor Phillips in *Windrush: The Irresistible Rise of Multi-Racial Britain* (1998). The image of the West Indian had changed from the supposedly clueless immigrants of the late 1940s to (replacing the 1950s image of Cypriots) a criminal class. What began as a means of survival by some during a time when white society was undergoing a cultural revolution led to a continuing antagonism between police and blacks which was to erupt in the riots of the early 1980s.

Several books of the period, such as *Disappointed Guests: Essays by African, Asian, and West Indian Students* (1965), edited by Henri Tajfel and John Dawson, speak of disillusionment by immigrants and black students. Donald Hinds, who at the age of 14 came to England from Jamaica in 1955, was a bus conductor for London Transport in Brixton. While earning qualifications through night classes, he was a journalist for the *West Indian Gazette*, 1958–65, then published with Heinemann *Journey to an Illusion: The West Indian in Britain* (1966), a book of interviews with earlier immigrants, concerning the myths they brought with them, problems of West Indians in England, and how they organized against exclusion and bigotry.

II. Prose: Culture Conflict and Lonely Londoners

After the war there was a small body of Indian writers in England including those who would either return home or move to the USA. Their relationship to traditions of Indian spirituality and legends could be confusing and few wrote about life in England. Balachandra Rajan (b. 1920) wrote his doctorate and lectured at Cambridge University before returning to India, which he represented at the United Nations, then became a professor of English and distinguished literary critic in Canada. He privately printed a small book of modernist poetry and later *The Dark Dancer* (1959) and *Too Long in the West* (1961), two novels that contrast the attractions of traditional culture with modernity. This would be a major concern of the period, and would take such forms as conflict between East and West, spiritualism versus rationalism, or a choice between individualism and the community. Many of the better writers seek a form of hybridity or some expression of both positions. The transformation will be in manner and form as well in vision. The only novel to have an influence on later British fiction was G. V. Desani's *All about Mr Hatterr: A Gesture* (1948). Desani came to England from Kenya in 1926. His parody 'autobiography' tells of a pilgrimage through India during which the amusing anti-hero Hatterr asks seven wise men questions about the purpose of life and which concludes with his understanding that this world is a progress through good and evil. Desani created for his character of mixed Asian and Western origins an Indian English that exuberantly mangles cultures, a mixture which is also found in the structure of the novel. The language reflects the absurdity of existence in which Hatterr will need to live between two cultures and two worlds. Although the novel shares modernist experiments with language and form, it, like later 'hybrids', is also an expression of diaspora cultural conflict. The book transforms Indian spiritual allegory into an Indian-style *Candide* with digressions, stories within stories, and is one of the forerunners acknowledged by Salman Rushdie. Two years later Desani published *Hali* (1950), one of those now forgotten poetic allegorical dramas about Good and Evil that existed alongside modernist literature and which derived from Indian-influenced spiritualist movements. It preaches selflessness, the opposite of the selfishness of *All about Mr Hatterr*. The two works were conceived together.

A Bengali, Sudhin N. Ghose (1899–1965) studied and then worked in continental Europe (1921–40), sometimes at the League of Nations, then lived seventeen years in England as an extramural studies lecturer about India. He belongs to a period when Indian authors such as Desani, influenced by the cultural assertions of nationalism, were, following Raja Rao's *Kanthapura* (1938), experimenting in Indianizing the novel. He published four linked novels about India, *And Gazelles Leaping* (1949), *Cradle of the Clouds* (1951), *The Vermilion Boat* (1953), and *The Flame of the Forest* (1955), which consciously make use of such Indian literary techniques as digressions (especially to explain legends or history), the telling of stories within stories within stories, mixing prose and verse, having heroic characters and characters who are more qualities than individuals, and using as source material the Puranas and Indian folk tales. Although the main character's name changes, the four books make use of an allegorical journey, tracing the hero's life from an orphaned childhood in Calcutta to an affirmation of spirituality. Each of the novels is divided in three parts which correspond to a progression from Hell to Heaven. The narrator of the books seems partly based on Ghose's own biography. After an unsatisfactory year in India as a professor of English, Ghose returned to England in 1958 and published several volumes of Indian *Folk Tales and Fairy Stories* (1961, 1966).

Besides a literary market which brought prestige and money, England allowed freedom to write critically of India. Nirad C. Chaudhuri's (1897–1999) successful *The Autobiography of an Unknown Indian* (1951) led to his visiting England and France in 1955 and *A Passage to England* (1959) praising the English. Later there was his critical study of India, *The Continent of Circe: Being an Essay on the Peoples of India* (1965). Brilliant, a stylist, a scholar as well as an intellectual, highly opinionated and controversial, Chaudhuri was thought by many the best of the Indian writers and a fierce critic of Hinduism and the Nehru-led government. *The Continent of Circe* argued that the Hindus are really degenerate Europeans who were corrupted by the heat and geography of India.

Instead of the India of the nationalists, it offered a history of dissimilar communities ceaselessly in conflict. Chaudhuri moved to England and Oxford in 1970 where he remained throughout his long life, a self-willed exile. His books claim that England had energized India and brought about a renaissance, but as the Empire withdrew in the face of nationalism he saw decay. It is a view sometimes found in the writings of V. S. Naipaul and Rushdie.

Attia Hosain, born and educated in Lucknow, India, came into conflict with her wealthy, feudal Muslim family over her involvement with the nationalist movement and the Left. After Partition she and her children moved to London. The tragedy of Partition and afflictions that accompanied it are the subject of the title story of *Phoenix Fled and Other Stories* (1953); other stories concern feudal society, cultural conflict, how the poor are treated by the rich. *Sunlight on a Broken Column* (1961) is an autobiographical novel, fictionalized memories of the Muslim elite in Lucknow and Oudh during the 1930s and 1940s, as recalled a decade later by a woman who struggled for personal independence against the restricting traditions of Islam and her family. The novel records the confusions, resentments, aggressive words, and love which are part of biculturalism, social change, nationalism, revolution, feminism, maturation, and becoming independent. The story also concerns the loss of power by a social class and the conflicts that resulted in two nations. A portrait of the sexual hypocrisy of the Muslim ruling class, of the superficiality of the colonial elite, and of the treatment of women in Muslim society, this is also a love story: love of what must be hated and rejected if the heroine is to be free, and love of a young man chosen by her emotions rather than by family duty.

Hosain was from a class of Muslim large landowners given special privileges by the British for loyalty; they carried on a feudal way of life well into the twentieth century, until reforms legislated by the Indian nationalists turned them into supporters of Partition. In *Sunlight on a Broken Column* quarrels within the family are a mirror of the larger issues facing society; the fragmentation of the family by modernization, colonialism, language, religion, education, land reform, and Partition parallels the end of a class, its culture, and Muslim India. That Hindu refugees from Pakistan live in the house in which Laila was brought up is symbolic of an inheritance lost with Indian independence.

Laila, who has been given a western education, is conscious of the slavish role of women in Muslim society; she evades an arranged marriage and sympathizes with female servants who are seduced and ruined. While the right to marry for love parallels the struggle for national independence, both personal and national freedom are more complex than the ideal. The nationalist intellectual whom Laila marries is socially and financially below her family, who effectively disown her; to earn money he joins the army, leaving her lonely and isolated. He dies during the Second World War.

Sunlight on a Broken Column is a subtle record of a transitional generation. Like other Indian writers of her generation, Hosain was influenced by the modernist economy of manner and in London participated in BBC programmes broadcast to India. She is a forerunner of those Indians such as Rushdie and Ghose who feel that independence and Partition ended the nation they knew, left them homeless. Their home now only exists in memory. She is also a forerunner of those Indian and Pakistani women who will write about the difficulties of having independent modern lives. Like most of the Indian writers who lived in England her subject matter remained India. Implicit, however, was the meeting of East and West as then understood in which East meant tradition, the past, feudalism, or spirituality.

Kamala Markandaya for several decades wrote commercially successful novels about the East–West encounter. Although she moved to London in 1948 and was married to an Englishman, she continued to think of herself as an Indian and her fiction, except for parts of *The Nowhere Man* and *Possession*, is set in India. As in many 'Commonwealth' novels of the period, her stories can be read figuratively of the nation, and the central themes are social and cultural change brought about by colonialism and later by national independence. While recognizing that as life consists of change India will change, her novels explain India to non-Indians and associate India with inner peace and passivity rather than western restlessness and conquest of nature. Markandaya sensitively portrays relationships between people and their relationship to their environment. Such studies in sensitivity, in which little is said directly, belong to an older era and went out of fashion around the time of Rushdie's *Midnight's Children* as postmodernist energy, fabulation, and verbal play came into fashion, although Amit Chaudhuri continues the tradition.

Markandaya had a run of transatlantic successes beginning with the tear-jerking *Nectar in a Sieve* (1954) with its portrayal of a southern Indian village undergoing a crisis when modern industry, in the form of a tannery, undermines traditions of the past. Although the tannery brings jobs to a village where poverty was the norm it pollutes the environment and causes new discontents. Relationships between the British and Indians are another recurring theme. *Some Inner Fury* (1955) shows the independence movement forcing apart a westernized Indian and her British lover. Often tensions within a family are representative of cultural conflicts as when, in *A Silence of Desire* (1960), the wife of a secularized, British-trained bank clerk trusts a traditional healer rather than have an operation in a hospital. In the tradition of E. M. Forster's *A Passage to India*, sexual relations are metaphoric of the meeting and problems between the two cultures, a topic examined in terms of education, technology, family, and social relations in *The Coffer Dams* (1969) and *Pleasure City* (1982). Markandaya saw that cultural conflict resulted from the market place and modernization. In both novels foreign firms are hired to construct modern projects that Indians cannot build themselves. While colonization brought India a language and knowledge with which to join the modern world, it also brought alienation, decay of communal and cultural traditions, and, as in *The Nowhere Man* (1972), troubled, destructive expatriation. Markandaya was one of the few Indian writers to realize that migration created a need for change from both the immigrant and the host society. The Nowhere Man is a Brahmin, compromised by nationalists, who flees from India to England where, after having survived the war, in which he was a warden and his son died, he is faced in old age by racial violence during the 1960s. *Two Virgins* (1973) concerns two sisters and examines the choices they face between traditional and modern culture as they become aware of their sexuality.

Markandaya uses many conventions associated with the East–West encounter. Often her Indians after seeming to have become westernized take refuge in tradition, while her English characters remain outsiders to India. In *Possession* (1963) a rich upper-class English woman visiting Madras discovers a teenage shepherd with an unusual ability to make art from coloured sand. She buys him from his parents and takes him to England where he becomes a success as well as impregnating a Jewish survivor of the German concentration camps who has become his muse. He then becomes a lover of his sponsor, a woman twice his age. This might have been a story about an older rich woman who discovers and becomes the lover of a moody younger artist, but the novel begins a few years after Indian independence and the relationships in the novel are figurative of those between England and India, the former always capable of getting its way with the latter but unable to understand it. Even the taking up and appreciating of the artist is part of a British taste for things Indian. *Possession* ends in an Indian hillside cave to which the young man has withdrawn with his swami where he is painting calmly with his art devoted to God. The conclusion remains uncertain as his patron claims that now that he has tasted the temptations she offers he will someday return to her. What will eventually possess the young man and by extension the Indian soul: western excitement and material goods or eastern spirituality?

Aubrey Menen would have treated such topics with humour and irony. Author of over twenty books, he was an international figure whose work was known on both sides of the Atlantic. Although he could be argumentative in defence of Indian culture, his usual literary style and tone was the deft, understated, amusing manner of Firbank and Waugh. Born in London of Indian and Irish parentage, he was Roman Catholic, English, and a Nayar, an Indian elite which looked down on British snobbery. The Nayars, who include Menen's cousin the Indian writer Kamala Das, are matrilineal and famed for women divorcing their men by telling them to take their mattress and go. Menen, a homosexual, wrote amusingly of domineering women while protesting their mistreatment in India. Perhaps because he experienced and embodied many incongruities he was a wry satirist in a mannered, elegant prose. From his autobiographies, the *Dead Man in the Silver Market: An Autobiographical Essay on National Pride* (1954) and *Space within the Heart* (1970), it is clear that he rejected nationalism, was lonely, felt alienated, and became worldly.

He treated the spiritual with amusement, especially when it involved a clash of social or cultural perspective. *Rama Retold* (1954) was banned in India for making fun of Indian myths and customs. His Sita is far from a chaste model for womanhood. Its message is that only God, human folly, and laughter are real. His fiction has an unusual range of locations, periods, and subjects. In *The Prevalence of Witches* (1947) a young educational officer of the Indian civil service and a political agent are expected to administer and find they need to become judges of the Limbodians—remote Dangi tribesmen, who blame murder on witchcraft. Many of his novels are based on amusing incongruities. *The Abode of Love* (1956) retells a scandal about a Victorian vicar who established a harem in a country house. In *The Fig Tree* (1957) even the Vatican approves of a scientist's attempt to turn a fig tree into an oral contraceptive to control population, but the fruit turns out to be an aphrodisiac. Menen's irreverence can be seen in his iconoclastic treatment of myths and history. The conqueror Alexander in *A Conspiracy of Women* (1966) is bullied by a woman and in love with his horse. From 1948 Menen lived in Italy for over three decades which provided him with material in *Rome Revealed* (1960) and the essays of *Speaking the Language like a Native* (1962), which debunk tourist Italy.

Whereas the Indian prose writers, many of whom were birds of passage, were mostly concerned with differences between the cultures of Asia and Europe, the West Indians, who came to settle in England, faced problems of what was to be their identity and home along with racial discrimination. Un-British behaviour was thought savage or exotic, but to behave British was to be one of the *Mimic Men* (the title of V. S. Naipaul's novel about the deracinated, British-educated, colonial middle class who inherited power in the new nations). Much of the literature for decades will be concerned with making a transition and with the need for England to be remade.

The most popular West Indian author of the period was E. R. Braithwaite. An RAF fighter pilot during the war, he took a further degree at Cambridge after demobilization, then spent eighteen months unsuccessfully seeking appropriate employment before teaching at a school in the East End of London, the first year of which provided material for *To Sir, With Love* (1959). Anyone questioning whether the educated black West Indian faced discrimination in England only need read *To Sir, With Love*, one of several auto-biographies in which West Indians describe being teachers in England. The portrayal of Braithwaite's first interview for a position as a manager in the electronics industry, a field in which he was well qualified, revealed he was unlikely ever to use his qualifications in England. The refusal by white working-class landlords to rent him a room fills in the other end of the social spectrum. England then was often a place of colour prejudice. A particularly telling example occurs late in the book with the death of the father of the one black student in his class, actually someone of mixed blood. The class pitches in to purchase flowers which no one is willing to take to the boy as they do not want to be seen going to the house of a 'darkie'.

To Sir, With Love is about overcoming prejudice, class and educational as well as racial. Braithwaite, one of the first black teachers in the British school system, was the missionary bringing civilization to the native savages. His students are from a notoriously impoverished and tough part of London, often themselves the children of European immigrants and the unemployed; their families have little money and the places in which they live are overcrowded, damp, without mod cons. They speak and dress poorly, seldom wash, have few academic skills, and have been sent to this particular school because of discipline problems. Braithwaite at first looks down on his students as do many other new teachers. As the students discover he is human and not just a 'darkie', he learns that they are intelligent, in many ways mature, and will be interested in topics if treated with respect. Thus the parallel between Braithwaite and his students.

The effectiveness of *To Sir, With Love* results from understatement and economy. Braithwaite writes in a confident, clear, concise, explanatory manner. There is, however, a tense ambivalence in the prose, reflecting self-control as if the reader were not being told all that is felt. Braithwaite seems too insistent on proclaiming his abilities, attractiveness, intelligence, judgement, and unassertiveness.

Paid Servant (1962) recounts a frustrating period after teaching when Braithwaite, in another first, became a child-welfare officer expected to locate homes for black children, while *A Kind of Home-coming* (1962) describes travels in four West African nations. This was followed by a novel, *A Choice of Straws* (1967), about white working-class racial violence in London told from the perspective of a white hooligan who after killing a 'spade' falls in love with one. Braithwaite portrays the white sympathetically and with understanding. *Honorary White* (1975) tells of six weeks in South Africa when as a distinguished visitor he was temporarily unblackballed. Braithwaite was one of the many West Indians who either returned to the Caribbean or eventually settled in the United States or Canada. Like Sam Selvon's work, their writings can be seen as transitional; they were late colonials who were legally British and regarded themselves as such until racial discrimination made them self-consciously Other.

Edgar Mittelholzer (1909–65) was the first of the post-war West Indian writers who came to England seeking publishers and opportunities for a literary life. After Mittelholzer arrived in England in 1948 he worked for the British Council before trying to live as a full-time writer. He published over twenty novels, and two autobiographies, *With a Carib Eye* (1955) and *A Swarthy Boy* (1963), before his death by suicide. The dark son of a near white father who hated blacks, Mittelholzer's warring self-hatred took the form of asserting his Germanic origins and cultural interests while claiming that the Caribbean must come to terms with slavery, its varied ethnicity, and its black majority. His work is marked by the inner divisions that are often the background of black cultural and racial assertions. An uneven writer, Mittelholzer can offer powerful portraits of obsessions and psychic disintegration, especially of those troubled by the temptations of the flesh, along with characters driven by the will to power and success. Sexual desire is associated with racial interbreeding in contrast to the spiritual. One of his themes is the necessity for the Creole West Indian to accept the black blood of its history, a theme later found in novels of the Trinidadian Laurence Scott, who lives and works in England.

Like many of the writers from Guyana who would follow him to England, Mittelholzer is concerned with the country's past—its plantations, slavery, the Dutch heritage, the Amerindians and their myths—which haunts the present and which often reappears in mysterious, hallucinatory ways. He wrote of the Asian Indians and Amerindians as well as the Creoles of the coast. If the earlier novels gain from their contesting voices, perspectives, and an interest in the history and the mythologies of others, the later novels are those of a white racist. *Uncle Paul* (1963), *The Aloneness of Mrs Chatham* (1965), and *The Jikington Drama* (1965) are narrated by strident monologists who hold that England has gone to rot as a result of its liberalism. That British publishers did not want such novels added to Mittelholzer's despair and alienation.

After Mittelholzer's *A Morning at the Office* (1950) appeared, Sam Selvon, George Lamming, Andrew Salkey, and V. S. Naipaul published novels within the decade and the West Indians were regarded as a literary movement, despite differences of opinion among them. Selvon and Naipaul were to make lasting contributions to British literature, Lamming now seems disappointing, while Salkey's contribution, despite his prolific output as a writer and editor, was as a man of letters who understood there was a difference between those of the Caribbean diaspora and the young blacks born in England. The literature of this generation often expresses the unease of adult immigrants unlikely to feel at home in a new country, nostalgic about the past and the islands they left. The West Indian characters in early novels about England are male adventurers who worry about money, housing, and jobs, while obsessed with inter-racial sex. They live among other blacks and gravitate towards bars and clubs populated by hookers, dealers, and American GIs. There is as yet no sign of a settled black middle class; the women they bed are white working class and sluttish. The narrators are conscious of there being an African-American literature which reflects experiences unlike their own. It would take a while before there were women novelists.

Samuel Selvon began as a journalist, literary editor of the *Trinidad Guardian*, and a poet, but after arriving in England in 1950 he was soon known for his novels *A Brighter Sun* (1952) and *An Island is a World* (1955), concerning the relationship of the rural Asian Indians to the urban black community in Trinidad. Writers from the West Indies would mostly write about 'home' as that is usually the only social and cultural world the immigrant knows in depth. Selvon, however, discovered the possibilities of making literature from the aspirations, problems, adventures, and speech of the black immigrants who came to England after the war.

Moses Aloetta is the central character of a sequence of novels reflecting distinct periods of black British experience. *The Lonely Londoners* (1956) was continued two decades later in *Moses Ascending* (1975) and concluded with *Moses Migrating* (1983). *The Lonely Londoners*, set in the mid-1950s, was based on the adventures told to Selvon by a Trinidadian who had earlier come to England. It is less a reflection of Selvon's circle, with its literary connections and early success, than of someone who arrived too soon, became part of the black working class, failed in his hopes of becoming a writer, and returned home. As can be seen in 'Come Back to Grenada' (1955), included in *Foreday Morning: Selected Prose 1946–1986* (1989), Selvon did not know how to handle this material until he realized that it required Trinidadian English for the narrator rather than, as was usual to West Indian literature, narration in Standard English with conversations in dialect. In blending Trinidadian English with other forms of black English, including phrases current in London and black American English, Selvon created the first novel of black British English almost two decades before Linton Kwesi Johnson achieved a breakthrough in poetry. Selvon's success might be seen as parallel to the writings of Achebe, Rao, and others in the former colonies who were asserting cultural independence through the creation of a literary English that reflected local languages and non-British forms of English. In making novels from loosely connected amusing stories, Selvon had in mind the satiric comic narratives of the Trinidadian calypso singers as well as the British novel of social comedy which he, Salkey, Naipaul, and others inherited and mined in new ways.

The Lonely Londoners begins with a one-sentence opening paragraph. It is the foggy London of the late nineteenth century and modernist writers, with its promises, illusions, and discontents, as now known by the West Indian immigrants. London is cold, threatening, alienating, yet has the fascination of another planet, a version of Augustine's Heavenly City. The phasing is already guiding the reader towards West Indian speech—'when it had a kind of', 'fellar', while the specific locations and bus line are of those immigrant London at this period, as is the situation of meeting new immigrants at Waterloo Station to take them where to stay while they learn about this new place. The disillusioned Moses is a guide, a confessor, and priest for a younger generation of immigrants, 'the boys'. The novel largely consists of stories the narrator tells about Moses' circle, mostly Trinidadians along with an African. While they suffer from racial discrimination, bad jobs, and terrible housing, they are also hustlers, picaros, con men, who learn to survive and enjoy the adventures of life in the metropolis including the availability of white women. 'The boys' have fun despite their world being limited to hustling skirt and getting along on little money. Moses says 'Things does have a way of fixing themselves, whether you worry or not. If you hustle, it will happen, if you don't hustle, it will still happen. Everyone living to dead, not matter what they doing while they living, in the end everybody death' (p. 67). Selvon's strengths are in linguistic invention, the creation of characters, comedy, storytelling, and social observation. The comedy of chasing skirt, even conning money and places to stay, moves the novel in a more creative direction than social realism, the rhetoric of protest, or idealizing of origins. Selvon had found a different way over such ground.

Aloetta's name points towards the level of decorum; Selvon will be like a calypsonian telling about a 'lark', a failed but humorous search for the promised land, an England which the immigrants imagined to be paved with secure, well-paying jobs. Moses, who got there earlier, is the leader of the new questers, such as Galahad. While this is a novel about immigrants, it is also a novel about provincials coming to the big city who participate in a glamorous world otherwise beyond them. There is a ten-page celebration of Hyde Park in the spring written as one paragraph to communicate the feeling of joyful energy and movement 'the boys' have known. While amused at the adventures of an older generation of young male black immigrants, the narrator is aware that their lives passed without accomplishments beyond sexual conquests. For all its celebration of living for the moment and being part of a great city, there is an underlying sadness, especially towards its conclusion, when Moses thinks of the decade he has wasted, unlike those who earned less and yet saved money to have a house and family.

Between the first and second books of the trilogy there was another London novel, *The Housing Lark* (1965), which reflected the problems of immigrants finding decent accommodation and acquiring the financial means to buy property in which to house themselves. As houses and land are common literary symbols for belonging and inheritance, the many times the literature of this period alludes to the difficulties of finding accommodation reflects the insecurity of blacks in England. This is a less serious novel, filled with comic stereotypes of black immigrants; it consists mainly of amusing tales such as about a Trinidadian trying to pass himself off as an Asian Indian to obtain a room and being ejected by a Jamaican who earlier convinced the landlady that he is a genuine Asian Indian.

The second novel of the Moses trilogy, *Moses Ascending*, was described by Selvon/Moses in the preface to *Moses Migrating* as depicting

the changes during that time—a new generation of Black Britons, and an influx of Indians and Pakistanis to add *more* colour to the scene. Moses has ascended to being a landlord, and his language has escalated from the basement to the penthouse, a kind of hybrid mixture of ye-olde and what-happening. (p. xi)

When offered a three-year lease on a house which is due for demolition, Moses rapidly agrees as he wants to be a landlord. He is part of an older generation, however, and does not know the 'new generation of black people'. Soon the basement room has become the headquarters for a Black Power movement which results in Moses being arrested by the police; he barely avoids being left in prison by his friend Galahad who wants to turn him into an example of the mistreatment of blacks in England. Another room is rented by two Muslims who turn out to be one person smuggling immigrants into England. Moses is threatened with death unless he agrees to become part of the scheme. By the end of the novel, Moses the landlord, has lost his top floor 'penthouse' to his white servant Bob and Bob's basement room to Brenda, a Black Panther activist who threatens to reveal his role in the smuggling of immigrants. *Moses Ascending* might be thought an ironic revisioning of *Robinson Crusoe* and *The Tempest* with Moses as Prospero-Crusoe and his white houseboy Bob the Caliban-Friday.

Early in their careers V. S. Naipaul and Selvon, both Trinidadians of Indian descent, revealed, in reviews, an antipathy to the ideas of the other. Where Naipaul began his career with satiric novels about the mixture of cultures in Trinidad and the lack of sophistication of the politics at a time the island was preparing for independence, Selvon's novels promoted racial integration and the Creolization of Indians as part of nation building. Both authors share that Trinidadian sense of mockery and irony found in calypso lyrics and both early developed ways in which to write Trinidadian speech. It is difficult to read the Moses novels without seeing them as similar to Naipaul's early comic novels. It is also difficult to read *Moses Ascending* in which Moses as author has 'retired' to write his auto-biography and not think of the novel as Selvon's version of Naipaul's *The Mimic Men* in which an exiled Trinidad politician retires to a British hotel to write of his past.

After the person Moses was based on decided to return to Trinidad, Selvon started to think of a book which would examine the qualms black immigrants might have returning home. *Moses Migrating* concerns a trip to Trinidad at Carnival time. Moses has tried to become British, a mimic man who travels to the Caribbean to relieve the depression of an English winter. He returns to England, only to find at the end of the novel that because of new immigration laws he might not be allowed entry. Meanwhile it is possible that Galahad and Brenda have sold his London property for very little money to their Black Power group for a new headquarters. The novel is set against the masquerading, heavy drinking, and sexual slackness of Carnival which provides a symbolic parallel to the plot. Moses masquerades as an English penny with the Queen's portrait, repre-sentative of his absurd pretence throughout the novel to be more English than the English. Selvon's model is Swiftian satire with its unstable characterization, changing masks, variety of tones, mixture of comedy and irony, and wide-ranging satire. Such fluidity is also that of the calypsonian whose perspective and values change from song to song. Even charges of mimicry, which are alluded to within the novel, are not as weighty as is sometimes assumed. Carnival itself is mimicry and those who celebrate it are mimics.

The Lonely Londoners began the canon of black British novels. During the 1990s it was a model for two Nigerians writing about London, Biyi Bandele-Thomas's *The Street* and Gbenga Agbenugba's *Another Lonely Londoner*. *Moses Migrating* marked the end of an era when West Indian males came to England as much for excitement and adventure as financial and educational opportunities. Since then black England had changed with an equal number of men and women, families, blacks owning houses and entering the professions, and the various American-style black consciousness movements which Selvon considered a new form of hustling. The power of black feminists was shown when one publicly slapped Selvon while he was reading from one of his novels a passage about sex with a white woman. The incident is mentioned in the 'Special Preface' to the American edition of *Moses Migrating*.

George Lamming (b. 1927) came to England on the same ship as Selvon, both of them sharing the same typewriter. A Barbadian who had moved to Trinidad, Lamming was another poet who found his market as a novelist. He made his reputation with *In the Castle of My Skin* (1953), a novel about growing up during a transitional period of colonialism, which was followed by novels that examined problems in the evolution of the Caribbean from colonies to independence. The semi-autobiographical *In the Castle of My Skin*, set in colonial Barbados, tells of a youth's progressive alienation from the traditional culture of his village through education into the ways of the colonizer as part of the process of preparing for a place in the modern world. The boy's story is set against the transformation of the island from a feudal society in which the white estate owner felt responsibility towards the villagers to the beginnings of a modern black bourgeoisie who have no concern for the effects of their actions on the lives of others. They will replace the colonizers. The novel ends with the main character becoming aware of black America and leaving his island.

The subsequent novels—*The Emigrants* (1954), *Season of Adventure* (1960), *Of Age and Innocence* (1958), *Water with Berries* (1971), and *Natives of My Person* (1972)—might be thought a history of the West Indies and the lasting effects of colonialism. They are poetic, densely written, rather static, allegorical, and examine the nature of freedom and how colonialism has deformed the West Indian psyche. *The Emigrants* tells of a group of people from the Caribbean in a ship to England where they discover that despite local differences they have become West Indians and share similar ambitions that were unfulfillable in their homelands. After their arrival in England there are the usual problems mentioned in novels of the period, such as the cold, the smoke and fog, lack of places to stay, damp, dingy housing, rationing, the distance between places, being mistaken for Africans, their ignorance of the society, even the difficulty for the women in having hair straightened. Comfort or survival often means breaking the law, and soon the police begin to appear enemies rather than protectors. The West Indians meet Africans and learn to see them as brothers and sisters. By the third part of the novel the group is dissolving as each person needs to cope with individual problems in a strange land. While not offering the easy opportunities the Emigrants imagined, England does, however, provide a wider world, a place to make new contacts, explore new roles, although much of their time is spent in basements and cellar clubs. There is a ponderousness, a solemnity, about Lamming's novels which also finds expression in plots structured as diagrammatic arguments to illustrate his belief in the communal and the political.

The autobiographical essays in *The Pleasures of Exile* (1960) circulate around notions of freedom and use the notion of Prospero and Caliban as representing the white colonizer and the black colonized, a theme which will also be found in Lamming's novel *Water with Berries*, a reworking of *The Tempest* in which three West Indians in London represent aspects of Caliban on Prospero's island, and in which there is a symbolic rape of Miranda. Lamming was faced by a problem that obsessed intellectuals from the newly independent nations—if the colonial was taught by the colonizer in the colonizer's language using the colonizer's representations, how was it possible to become mentally and spiritually free? How could you be free of Prospero's views while using his language? Like many others Lamming sought an answer in the peasant as a source of authenticity. Later theorists would argue that only those who have mastered the language and culture of the oppressor can resist and lead decolonization. The search for authenticity leads to origins and roots; the opposite approach leads to hybridity and modernization.

Andrew Salkey (1928–95) came to England in 1952 to be a student at London University and rapidly became part of the group of West Indian writers associated with the BBC; he was especially helpful in promoting the new literature. In *Finding the Centre* Naipaul mentions Salkey advising him with his first stories and helping him towards publication. When Salkey and Selvon left England during the mid-1970s for teaching positions in North America it seemed the end of an era, although Salkey would continue to publish in England, especially with Bogle L'Ouverture, during the 1980s. *A Quality of Violence* (1959), Salkey's first novel, was about the loss of faith which turns peasants towards the Pocomania cult and ritual murder in rural Jamaica during a severe drought. It is similar to Lamming's fiction in its heavily foregrounded symbolism and like many of the West Indian novels of this period it ends with characters going into exile. *Escape to an Autumn Payment* (1960) is the story of such exile as a Salkey-like character finds himself a bewildered colonial in London, his loss of confidence expressed in a confused sexuality. Although the black slang is improbable, the main character is interesting in his unwillingness to face his apparent homosexuality and in the way his indecision is expressed in terms of the freedom London offers in contrast to the staid middle-class moralism of his mother in Jamaica. Salkey's later novels will often treat of those who, in fleeing from the injustices of Jamaica, lose their self-assurance and place in the world. Freedom, losing assurance, and trying to notate black British speech will over the decades remain concerns of West Indian writers in England.

In *The Adventures of Catullus Kelly* (1969) Salkey rewrites *The Lonely Londoners* as a black *Candide*, mocking innocence. The improbably named Catullus Kelly is a cartoonish version of a middle-class Jamaican immigrant in London. Kelly beds white women, lives off money sent by his mother, is unable to understand why he cannot attend racist meetings, foolishly seeks a racist author about whose hyphenated name he is obsessed, loses jobs through such idiotic behaviour as taking the schoolchildren he is teaching to erotic art films, before returning home to end in a mental institution. The novel parodies such aspects of black literary London as working for radio stations and living among intellectuals in Swiss Cottage. At times the parody is explicit—Kelly tells the schoolchildren not to address him as 'Sir' for he is not E. R. Braithwaite. Unlike Selvon and Naipaul, Salkey lacks that Trinidadian amusing touch with satire and irony. *Come Home, Malcolm Heartland* (1976) is a tour through fringe black radicalism and revolutionaries of the late 1960s. Although the novel satirizes unthinking West Indian immigrants who come to England expecting to settle in the middle class and among whites, the new black radicalism is portrayed as habitually fantasizing because of lack of a secure identity, a problem Salkey associates with diasporas.

Salkey began writing fiction for children with *Hurricane* (1964), *Earthquake* (1965), and *Drought* (1966) set in Jamaica, then after Farrukh Dhondy began writing about the black inner city Salkey published *Danny Jones* (1980), a novel for senior school children about being black in England. Danny's father, a Jamaican who came to England during the 1950s, lectures his son about hard work and education as a way to success although he himself has had little success in England. His white wife knows that people in England are limited in opportunities by class and brought up not to have high expectations. Through television, reading, and street talk Danny and his friends have been influenced by black America and Third Worldism. They see their future as unemployment, threats from the police and the National Front, and unending questions from well-paid social workers.

Salkey also edited some of the first anthologies of West Indian literature: *West Indian Stories* (1960), *Stories from the Caribbean* (1965), *Caribbean Prose* (1967), and *Breaklight: An Anthology of Caribbean Poetry* (1971). His continuing influence on black British literature has been the two books he wrote based on the African-Caribbean folk character, Anancy the trickster spider: *Anancy's Score* (1973) and *Anancy, Traveller* (1992). Cunning Anancy is the survivor who comes out on top. Written in varying mixtures of standard and Jamaican English, the stories range from creation myths to the political. Salkey's Anancy is a diaspora African, a traveller, and a writer who retells Caribbean history. In updating a folk character known to children as well as adults Salkey created a model for other writers, such as John Agard, to develop further an African and Caribbean tradition in England.

Many academically qualified West Indians, such as the poet John Figueroa, spent time in Africa. Oscar Ronald Dathorne's (b. 1934) family came from Guyana to England to settle in 1953. Having studied at the University of Sheffield and London University during the 1950s and 1960s Dathorne wrote the light but amusing *Dumplings in the Soup* (1963), a portrait of life in a boarding house for 'coloureds' in a university town. After joining the quest for roots by teaching at universities in Africa, where he set his satiric *The Scholar-Man* (1964), and editing anthologies of Caribbean and African literature, Dathorne joined the exodus to the United States where universities were seeking professors of black and African literature.

Many West Indians who became part of the British literary scene were from Guyana. The racial composition and colonial history of Guyana are especially complex—usually said to be Indian, English, Portuguese, Chinese, African, and Amerindian (and even the Amerindians belong to a number of distinctive language groups ranging from Arawak and Atori to Mapidian and Wapishana). There is also a contrast between the Creolized coastal elite and the vast, still unexplored hinterlands with its still surviving Amerindians, runaway former slaves, myths, rituals, promises of riches and the exotic. Guyana has needed a complex art to express a complex identity and in literature the realistic often covers unexpected forces which suddenly erupt; many stories concern those who leave the coast to seek wealth in the interiors.

One of the most influential writers and theorists came to England in 1959. Wilson Harris's fiction is a surreal magic realism which examines the divisions of Guyana by trying to reimagine history not as one continuous story but as a continual revisioning of characters and events. In his later work this can take the form of reimagining his earlier novels to tell a different tale. Such shape-shifting and revisioning, although arising from the particularities of Guyanese social and literary history, became widely recognized as a natural theory and object for Commonwealth literature where the problem was how to modernize without betraying the 'past' which was supposedly the basis of community. Ben Okri, David Dabydeen, and Fred D'Aguiar are among the many authors who were to be influenced by Harris, who for all his obscurity has come closest to explaining how to use the past creatively and to showing, as Homi Bhabha's well-known essay (included in *The Location of Culture* (1994)) puts it, 'How Newness Enters the World'.

Harris aims at transforming reality through how he envisions it in his writing. Although his writing is often regarded as a precursor of magic realism, it is different from the method developed by Günter

Grass and later by Rushdie in which narrative is an amusing fanciful allegory, a story which while existing on its own is often a parody of real political events. By contrast Harris's stories are seldom amusing, satiric, parodies, or linked to specific historical parallels. They are, rather, imaginative reconfigurations of history and reality in which fixities become unfixed. They are inconsistent, transforming their characters and events in the course of a story, while lacking clear boundaries between living and dead, between races, between victims and the oppressed, between times, between people and their characteristics. Their precursors are the Haitian novels of such writers as Philippe Thoby and Pierre Marcelin with their mixture of surrealism and indigenous legends and magic. There were also Cuban novels exploring similar territory. Harris took such notions further. Because his characters may die and then reappear with different personalities and beliefs, Harris's novels can be puzzling and sometimes impenetrable, but the early ones, especially the *Guyanese Quartet*, are worth the effort. The novels are less a problem than Harris's critical and theoretical writings which may demand trust in Jungian psychology, hermeticism, and other non-empiricist systems of thought.

His many volumes of essays and lectures can be sampled in the *Selected Essays of Wilson Harris* (1999), edited and introduced by the black British poet Andrew Bundy. Bundy regards the fiction as a dreamscape with unfixed boundaries in which people and events are symbols which keep being transformed. He further claims that the curious collection of European influences that has produced Harris's very New World vision argues against enlisting Harris in the cause of postcolonialism. Bundy demonstrates that the essays are related to Harris's fiction in the various periods. The essays on New World writers, such as Jean Rhys, Jean Toomer, Ralph Ellison, Melville, Poe, and William Faulkner, show how opposite archetypes form a different third culture which cannibalistically assimilates adversaries. In other essays the marginalized or occult are the source of imagination and change. Harris is a romantic who finds science with its fixed truths an enemy of the imagination and cultural change. At the core of Harris's vision is a world continually in the process of transformation.

Harris is interested in the subtle links between people which make possible a new person and a new history. To transfigure reality requires a mixture of realism with the magical. The result should open inner spaces to allow a new being to develop both within the text and, Harris hopes, on the part of the reader or observer (a category often found in his novels). The aim is a new community beyond present differences. For all its mysticism it is an attractive vision and in his fiction and lectures an engaging way of envisioning hybridity, cross-culturization, cross-pollenization, and other ways of regarding the emergence of the new, if only because it assumes that people while materially different share universality at the psychic level and that the history we know has many other potential stories that go beyond winner and loser. The eruption of the irrational into the political frees the mind from its polarities, disrupts continuity, rewrites history, and liberates the imagination.

Although Harris began as a poet in British Guinea, he published his first novel with Faber soon after arriving in England. *Palace of the Peacock* (1960) uses a journey upstream through the rivers of Guyana in search of El Dorado, the 'Palace of the Peacock', to show how Europeans disrupted the Indian community and brought it into contact with other races and cultures. Central is Donne (whose name suggests the way Sir Walter Raleigh was both a poet and a deluded conqueror in search of El Dorado), leader of the quest. The final vision of the *Palace* is like that of Dante's *Paradise*. Donne's crew in *Palace* includes those of African, Arawak, British, Portuguese, German, and other stock. The Dreamer is asked to replace Donne, the dead exploring conqueror, as the journey moves upriver and inland towards the original culture of Guyana. Now the Dreamer sees an Arawak woman who becomes part of him and, as they move further into the interior, the heart of memory, there is self-knowledge and fulfilment. The novel is itself a reversal of the seven days of creation, an uncreating of the past, and a re-creation in which Donne, the Dreamer, and his crew become One.

The Far Journey of Oudin (1961) tells of the break-up of a Muslim Indian family as it departs from traditional ways and comes into contact with capitalism. The dead father has had a child outside marriage who is cheated and denied by the survivors. The child seems to be, as identities are not certain, Oudin (Houdini) who is both the exploited worker and Anancy the African-Caribbean trickster spider. Oudin tricks his employer, one of the dead father's sons, and flees into the forest with Beti, their cousin's daughter. This voyage takes on various symbolisms such as Raman seeking Sita, and Europa and the Bull, but shows the lack of sexual and psychic energies in the disintegrating Indian Muslim family in contrast to the bastard child Oudin with his transforming changes of identities. Oudin dies but Beti is pregnant with his child.

After novels about European colonizers and Asian Indian farmers in Guyana, Harris's third novel, *The Whole Armour* (1962), is set among the largely African settlements of the interior. The symbolism is biblical and the main characters are Cristo the hero, Magda the whore, along with Matthias, Peet, Abram, and Sharon. Cristo strips himself of civilization, becomes like a tiger with its skin and claws, and takes on the guilt of history as he is accepted by the Caribs of the jungle. This makes possible a new politics. After Cristo is arrested by the police his redemptive role, the tiger skin, is passed on to Sharon.

The final novel of the quartet, *The Secret Ladder* (1963), like the *Palace of the Peacock*, tells of an expedition which takes seven days through 'the ladder of ascending purgatorial' rivers and a meeting with ancestors. There is a conflict. If the creek is mapped the head-waters will be dammed, which will eventually benefit the coastal rice planters while flooding the inland farmers. Fenwick, in organizing the expedition and mapping the river, offers a model for independent Guyana's politics and represents Harris, who actually worked as such a surveyor, as author. Fenwick is challenged by Poseidon, descendant of an escaped slave, and heir of history. Poseidon is the African past which must be understood and not dispossessed by progress. There is no concluding vision here, unlike *Palace of the Peacock*, but rather a necessary recognition of history by those in power, and the interaction between people.

Harris has written over twenty novels and other books. Most concern Guyana and have similar techniques and assumptions. *The Waiting Room* (1967) and *Black Marsden* (1972) take place in Scotland. *The Angel at the Gate* (1982), *Da Silva da Silva's Cultivated Wilderness* (1977), and *The Tree of the Sun* (1978) are set in London, while *Carnival* (1985) partly takes place in London. It is surprising how little the location has to do with the events or significance. Usually the same characters or characters with similar names appear in novels which refer to each other and their ancestors in Guyana. If there is a character named Marsden there will be a Black Marsden. The racial legacy often works itself through twins or two related people whose merging and changing of identities is reflective of Harris's Jungian and hermetic interests while exemplifying how categories can be transformed over time. Harris revises the plots of novels in later work to show that what appeared fixed can be reimagined. What began as the reimagining of history without the usual dimensions of time and space became a continual exploration of the mystical. While Harris uses the latest fashions in irrationality to re-express himself, he manages to get beyond the burden of history, with its polarities and racial categories, that often oppresses writing and thought by the formerly colonized.

Among the West Indians who arrived in England during the 1950s V. S. Naipaul became one of the best writers of the century. He shared in the creation of a modern West Indian literature, was part of the disillusionment with the fruits of national independence, and contributed to the reinvention of the late twentieth-century international novel and international literary career, bringing an ex-colonial's perspective to a literary kind that earlier writers like Graham Greene had treated with sentimentality as exotic scenery for European adultery and crisis of faith. Naipaul seemed to know instinctively that a major problem of his time was the inability or unwillingness of many areas of the world to make the transition to modernity either because they lacked the resources or would not accept the relationship between the products of modernity and a secular liberal society. He was a constant traveller to and reporter about the post-imperial world; in the process he rejuvenated and made into serious literature many literary kinds such as the travel book and journalist's report. There was an intellectual quality about his work expressing his reading in the world's literature, an engagement with the literature of the places he visited and wrote about, and a knowledge of history and what historians have written. His writing has complexity, an incorporation of opposites, an understanding of the attractions of what he dislikes, even an understanding of and compassion towards those of his fictional characters whose views and behaviour he might be expected to despise.

He learned from his journalist father about reporting and the need to make characters and situations interesting. From the movies he learned of economy, significant visual details, the quick jump from image to image, and rapid change in perspective. A realist concerned with facts who claims to hate 'style', he learned from the modernists the use of literary echoes and allusions to enrich and deepen his fiction. In the linked short stories of *Miguel Street* (1959), and the partly autobiographical novels *A House for Mr Biswas* (1961) and *The Mimic Men* (1967), he made the relationship of memory to the past, especially the difference between memory, reality, and writing of the past, a central theme. Having claimed that Trinidad had no usable history, he researched and wrote *The Loss of El Dorado* (1969; rev. 1973). Believing the novel is a form of social enquiry, he said it died with the societies that made it, but as autobiography, journalism, literary imitation, and history began to find its way into his fiction, he became one of those who were enlarging the boundaries of the modern novel by blurring the line between fact and fiction. Although opposed to avant-garde experiments, he not only mixed kinds of writing as in *The Enigma of Arrival* (1987) and *A Way in the World: A Sequence* (1994), but used foregrounded motifs musically to organize the shifts of time and space in his books. Although his work is unified by recurring interests, obsessions, and themes, each novel is different.

His earliest books consisted of amusing stories of a fragmented colonial society undergoing change. Colonialism in Trinidad had brought together alien peoples whose cultures were incongruous and which were often in conflict with reality as well as each other. His subject matter would become the 'half-formed' societies of the world. Much of what he wrote and what he would write was a composite of real people and events. The amusing *The Mystic Masseur* (1957) was based on a well-known Trinidadian Indian masseur who progressed to mysticism and local political fame. A modern picaroon who seized the day in a culturally and racially unstable society, he was like many of the characters in *The Suffrage of Elvira* (1958) who regard the first national elections by universal suffrage as an opportunity to sell and gain what they can from this unexpected gift of British liberality. Although his appropriation of Dickens's comic caricature was to be followed by others such as Rushdie and Zadie Smith, many who struggled for political independence did not feel flattered and thus began the antagonism between Naipaul and many on the decolonizing Left, an antagonism which would sharpen over the decades. C. L. R. James, however, realized that Naipaul's comedy contains a criticism of the effects of colonialism. James would influence Naipaul's analysis of colonial culture, and of how many newly independent nations were clients of more powerful nations.

Having used up his memories of Trinidad, Naipaul needed to find new material, which also meant devising new forms. In *Mr Stone and the Knights Companion* (1963) he wrote a version of what might be thought the archetypical British subject: the ageing, commuting London office worker. Naipaul could not write such a typical British novel about the grey lower-middle class in a damp British climate without filling it with echoes of modernist poetry and Indian mythology. Not being born in England, he found it difficult to write through the eyes of the white British at home. This was more a matter of society than colour, as he would write convincingly of the British abroad in *The Mimic Men* and *In a Free State* (1971). The prejudices, resentments, and failures of English life were not to be his subject as a writer; instead he applied to the post-imperial world the skills he had formed in analysing his dislike of Trinidad and its problems.

Like such writers as Chinua Achebe and Wole Soyinka, he observed the violence and corruption that the politics of independence brought and worried how people from dissimilar cultures could govern one nation. *The Mimic Men, In a Free State*, and *A Bend in the River* (1979) are novels set against the problems resulting from decolonization in lands that lack social and political stability and where minorities or the weak are trampled upon. Such writings reflect the problem of feeling insecure and homeless, without the protection of a community. The simpler versions of cultural-conflict themes were not appropriate to how he saw himself. He was a utilitarian who knew from his own life and family both the pains of freedom and the humiliations of being without protection, a consciousness intensified by the persecution of Asian Indians in many black-ruled nations of the Caribbean and Africa. Usually the political unrest in his novels involves a civil war during which some white or Indian characters are so enamoured with their own problems and progressive ideas that they are unable to understand the dangers around them.

Behind the comedy of his early fiction about Trinidad was his view that Indian Hindu culture in the Caribbean was incongruous and becoming ossified. In *The Mimic Men* London was little better; the great city he imagined where he would be among the cultured and powerful was belied by the impoverished life he and others led. Imagining India as his home, his land of origins, he travelled there only to recognize in *An Area of Darkness* (1964) that he was a product of the West, especially of the New World, with no patience for Indian poverty, inefficiency, and taking refuge in traditionalism and fatalism. He would write two further books, *India: A Wounded Civilization* (1977) and *India: A Million Mutinies Now* (1990), discussing modernizing tendencies which contested fatalism and caste privilege.

His fiction extends through a series of major novels including *A House for Mr Biswas* commemorating his father's struggle to find a place in the new world, *Mimic Men*'s insight into the causes of the instability of newly independent nations, the linked stories of *In a Free State* about the actual and existential dangers of freedom to individuals and nations, and *A Bend in the River*, which shows the dangerous chaos of African politics since independence. *Guerrillas* (1975) offers memorable portraits of the sexual excitement found in playing with revolution and its tragic consequences. It was based on Naipaul's 'The Killings in Trinidad', a long report on how British fantasies of black sexuality had turned a Trinidadian con man into a fake Black Power leader and his eventual murder of two of his followers.

In seeking subject matter from the supposedly half-made societies of the world, Naipaul became the great international writer of the second half of the twentieth century. Writing about England, however, remained a problem. There is a marvellous story, 'Tell Me Who to Kill' in *In a Free State*, which tells of an illiterate West Indian who, humiliated by his lack of education, sends and then follows his brother to England, where all his hopes evaporate, but except for a few short stories in *A Flag on the Island* (1968) and the early *Mr Stone and the Knights Companion* Naipaul did not write fiction about England again until the autobiographical *The Enigma of*

Arrival (1987), which tells of his reasons for leaving Trinidad, his difficulty being at ease elsewhere, and his career. Although presented as a novel it describes his life, publications, and views; the story is told in two different voices and styles, as fiction and fact, until the two merge into Naipaul's own voice at the conclusion. *The Enigma of Arrival* is set in the countryside of English pastoral poetry and legend to which Naipaul at first feels an outsider. The novel demonstrates him settling, taking root, building a house, eventually becoming part of England. *Enigma* is a celebration of the Indian diaspora. 'Every generation now was to take us further away from those sanctities. But we remade the world for ourselves.' He sees 'life and man as the mystery, the true religion of men, the grief and the glory' (p. 318).

Naipaul's time in Wiltshire on the estate has another dimension. Like many expatriate artists, Naipaul's home is his art and there is a parallel between building his literary and his physical home in England. His landlord has let the estate, symbolic of imperial England, become an untended burden, and is being displaced by an energetic, new, post-war lower- and middle-class order that includes foreigners and former colonials. For Naipaul to have contrasted his career as a writer and his conversion of local houses with the decay and disorder of the manor and the failure of his landlord as a writer is to declare oneself the inheritor, someone who has not only earned his place but who is part of the new order, the new literary tradition of the migration of the world's people. *The Enigma of Arrival* indicated that Mr Biswas's children, after much hard work and learning to adapt, had a house in the very heart of the English literary tradition, which has been reconverted and redesigned to tell and celebrate their story.

If Naipaul has been the great cautionary, prudential, writer of the post-imperial, he was also the voice of change, preaching of the need to adapt, seize the day, and make a mark on the world while there is still time. His novels, such *A Bend in the River*, show his reading of the existentialists Jean-Paul Sartre and Albert Camus. Although desiring security, he knew man makes himself and writing was his means to leave a historical monument to himself. Many of his novels concern those who fail to make something of themselves. *Half a Life* (2001) is the story of Naipaul's opposite, an Indian raised in comfort, with a secure future in front of him, but who does not know what he wants and who wastes his opportunities. He drifts, never takes root, never builds a house, or becomes financially independent. Willie Chandran is one of the wave of students who came to England from the colonies after the war, but Willie is without purpose in England and follows a woman to a Portuguese East African colony from which he will flee when the guerrillas take control.

For Naipaul imperialism is another example that life always consists of people desiring more and trying to satisfy and advance themselves by conquering or tricking others. There is always an unfair social hierarchy which is in the process of changing as people and peoples compete for space, comfort, sex, security. There is always domination, power, and the need for protection; those who lack the means, will, and energy to advance and protect themselves become victims of others or they continue the long human process of flight and migration in search of survival and a better life.

Naipaul sees himself as part of the Indian diaspora and not as black. If he does not have Selvon's interest in creating a black London, he showed others, such as Farrukh Dhondy and Amit Chaudhuri, how to write significant fiction about the former colonies, people of colour, and hybridity without resorting to the clichés of European writing, and that it was possible to see the interest and problems of local life without nationalist stereotypes. Along with such writers as Soyinka and Achebe he examined the problems of decolonization and why national independence led to various forms of tribalism and tyranny. Rushdie, Gurnah, and others follow from their example. There, however, has always been a side of Naipaul's work that shares in what was current writing about England at the time, such as the Little Englandism of *Mr Stone and Knights Companion*, the variant on a West Indian dialect protest story in 'Tell Me Who to Kill', writing about the self in *The Enigma of Arrival*, or the social mapping of Notting Hill and the immigrant literary scene in *Half a Life*. While examining the problems of decolonization and modernization abroad, Naipaul always had an eye on England, especially London.

The Middle Passage: Impressions of Five Societies (1962) initiated a body of post-imperial travel books concerning how those from former colonies view the newly independent nations and other unsettled areas of the contemporary world. Over the decades Naipaul wrote about Argentina, India, Africa, Indonesia, Malaysia, Iran, Pakistan, the Caribbean, even the USA. Others who followed include Shiva Naipaul, Salman Rushdie, and Caryl Phillips. Such national allegories as Rushdie's *Midnight's Children* and *Shame* have taken over Naipaul's application of journalistic reportage and analysis to fiction. A variation is found in the many black British works that seek roots in the West Indies or Africa only to conclude that the author or main character is indeed British. A central theme of Naipaul's writing is how nationalists depend on the technology and products of modernization while rejecting its civilization. *Among the Believers: An Islamic Journey* (1981) and *Beyond Belief: Islamic Excursions among the Converted People* (1998) noted that oil money was being used to export a fundamentalist Islam that regarded the West as its enemy. Naipaul argued that no imperialism is as thorough as Islam which demands of others the denial of their past and culture to become Arabs. Fundamentalism had become an international movement intent on challenging the personal liberty, modernity, and 'Universal Civilization' most of the world now wanted.

He understood the central issues of literature and culture during the second half of the last century, the continuing effects of colonialism, the problems of national independence, the effects of modernization on large areas of the world, the mass migration of peoples, and the internationalization of expectations which conflicted with attempts to restore indigenous ways. He wrote of the pains and desirability of freedom and liberalism while himself being nostalgic for an imagined secure past. Perhaps most important, he showed others that the lives of the colonized, of people of colour, of immigrants, were as significant, interesting, and human, as those of the colonizers and Europeans without needing ideological and racial inflation. Just as Wilson Harris would have an unexpected influence on later writers, so many of the best writers would learn from Naipaul—whether or not they agreed with his views.

The tremendous outburst of Caribbean writing towards the end of colonialism had been brought to England where Selvon showed how it was possible to write about the black immigrant experience through dialect and humour. Naipaul, whose life had made him aware of the dangers of independence without economic means, found it difficult to write about England and turned his attention to the problems of the decolonizing world, especially as it attempted to find political stability and respond to the challenges of modernity when the claim for independence was cultural or racial authenticity. Harris brought to England the problem of hybridizing Guyana's many peoples and cultures into story. He would become a model for those who want to let the imagination roam while writing figuratively of the complexities of history. There will be other strong influences of Caribbean literature on the literature of England, especially during the 1970s and 1980s in poetry.

III. Poetry: Swansongs, Birds of Passage

The most prominent Indian writer in England during the Second World War was J. M. Tambimuttu, a Tamil Indian (he would say Jaffanese) from a Roman Catholic Ceylonese family. Tambimuttu (1915–83) arrived in England just before the war and was soon well known in the literary world, especially in Soho pubs. With no obvious means of support, as a poet, publisher, and editor he helped keep British culture alive during the next decade. Charming and exotic, he knew everyone and between 1939 and 1951 published the better poets and artists in his *Poetry London* and Editions Poetry London. He edited and co-edited various tributes and celebrations including *T. S. Eliot: A Symposium* (1948). He drifted to the USA where he edited *Poetry London/New York*, and was later a guru to Timothy Leary and to the Beatles. His international life was typical of many Indian writers of the time who held British passports, were products of a late colonial blending of cultures, and participated in the fashions of the day.

Indian poetry in England has had no distinguishing features such as the Jamaican English and Caribbean musical forms adopted by West Indian poets. It has not, like West Indian poetry, been in attitude and diction a reflection of an ethnic group or immigrant community. Before the 1990s it seldom dealt in racial or cultural conflict, nor does the poetry offer examples of the empire writing back. A Manchester-born Parsee, Beram Saklatvala (1911–76) was vice-principal of the Working Men's College, London. His father, Shapurji Saklatvala, the famous Communist wartime MP and subject of Mark Wadsworth's biography *Comrade Sak* (1998), was the third Indian to be elected a Member of Parliament since 1880. Beram's poetry included *Stubborn Heart* (1945) published by Tulip Press, and four volumes published by Fortune Press: *Devouring Zodiac* (1945), *The Choice* (1947), *Phoenix and Unicorn* (1954), and *Air Journey: A Sonnet Sequence*. Among his other publications were translations of the *Complete Poems of François Villon* (1968) for Dent's Everyman's Library. He also wrote several books on slavery and the history of the British, Romans, and Christians, some under the name Henry Marsh, the family name of his mother, a white working-class English woman. While his poetry shared in the Georgianism that lingered in some poetry circles until the 1950s, it also made use of the notion of life as a spiritual journey.

As minor Indian poets writing in an older style had no literary market, they often turned to Fortune Press, which was famous for the quality of its paper and design. Fredoon Kabraji (1894–1986) published with Fortune Press during the 1940s and 1950s. His *The Cold Flame: Poems (1922–1924; 1935–1938; 1946–1953)* (1956) includes some of his earlier *A Minor Georgian's Swan Song*. He was a friend of and encouraged by Walter de la Mare. While Kabraji's early poems were set in both India and England, he remained in London during the war and volunteered after Dunkirk. He wrote about love and nature except for a few poems about the war. Such poets were not the alienated students who arrived from the former colonies.

Just as part of modern West Indian literature began in London, so the beginnings of modern Indian poetry in English after the war overlap with the small body of poetry written by Indians in England. The end of the war brought many colonials to England in search of education, culture, or adventure. Most still had British passports. Fortune Press published Nissim Ezekiel's (b. 1924) *A Time to Change* (1952), usually thought the start of modern Indian poetry in English as it had more in common with Auden and the Movement poets than the Georgians. *A Time to Change* reflects the years, 1948–52, Ezekiel spent in England educating himself at public libraries and public lectures, supporting himself at odd jobs, and barely surviving in a shared basement room. The London years would remain part of his personal mythology and reappear later in such poems as 'London' as a place and time of cold bare discipline.

The near invisibility of Indian poetry in England changed after Dom Moraes (b. 1938) arrived in 1955. During the later 1950s until the mid-1960s he was a celebrity as well as a highly regarded heir to the English poetic tradition. The earliest poems were easy to read and romantic in contrast to the prevailing Movement and Angry Young Men. *A Beginning* (Parton, 1957) was filled with dreamy Spenserian and Keatsian echoes: 'I long to die' ('Figures in the Landscape'), 'I am in love, and long to be unhappy' ('Sailing to England'), 'all love became a lie' ('Afternoon Tea'). He seemed 'A happy traveller on a sea of ink' ('Sailing to England'), or, to use the title of a poem, 'A Man Dreaming'; even his confessions asked for sympathy: 'And then he knew his dream for what it was. | At once a sexual panic swamped all his pain' ('A Man Dreaming'). He had a voice, manner, and a feel for language. There were allusions to a childhood and youth travelling with his journalist father (who edited *Times of India*) throughout Asia, loss of sexual innocence, and a religiously fanatic Catholic mother, which partly explained the making of the poet.

He was a Goan Catholic, had a British passport, and was brought up as part of an elite for whom English language and culture were as natural as their acquaintance with leaders of the independence movement with whom they conversed in English and shared mutual respect for British ways. His first book, *Green is the Grass* (1951), published in Bombay when he was 13, is about cricket. After Oxford he edited magazines in London, was publicly linked to a famous actress, and kept Soho lively along with such surviving romantic surrealists as Derek Wright. The self-pity masked a vision of a bleak world in which all is pretence leading to death and final nothingness. He adopted airs of superiority. In his prose *Gone Away: An Indian Journal* (1960) he seems pleased to outrage Indians as if his visit home was to a strange uncivilized land. V. S. and Shiva Naipaul would later bring a more analytical perspective to such travel literature.

Uprootedness appeared in the excellent *John Nobody* (1965), a volume influenced by Auden, in which the first and concluding poems are set in bars. Few of his English poems are set in houses or suggest being settled. Moraes renounced his Indian passport when Goa was 'liberated', and he became one of those who regardless of the place remain homeless, alienated, and in exile. He left for New York, travelled as a UN investigator of human rights abuses, and returned to India as the prodigal son, where he remained a British citizen, part of a reverse diaspora of those who return home to find themselves as alienated as when they left. *In Cinnamon Shade: New and Selected Poems* (2001) was the first major publication of his poetry in England for more than three decades. His life shows the cosmopolitanism that empires can produce, while his poetry illustrates the complexities of artists, difference, alienation, class, and the self-exiled.

Adil Jussawalla (b. 1940) after coming to London to study Architecture studied English at Oxford. He eventually returned home depressed at not taking root in England, after thirteen years, 1957–70. *Land's End* (1962) shows a young poet indebted to such still fashionable models as the seventeenth-century English poets and T. S. Eliot. Although Jussawalla's background was Parsee, some poems echo Eliot's Anglo-Catholicism. The lovely title poem contrasts the geographical place and its tourists with a sacramental view and makes use of such themes as God's creation and the early church founded by Peter. The problem he and others faced was not so much the cultural conflicts made famous by nationalist, Commonwealth, and postcolonial criticism, but rather remaining a talented stranger of another colour in a land where connections, the past, and family still counted for much. For Jussawalla as for Ezekiel life in England eventually seemed a dead end. Jussawalla was one of those who contributed to *Disappointed Guests*.

Two of Jussawalla's Indian friends stayed on. H. O. Nazareth (b. 1944), a film maker, studied politics and philosophy at the University of Kent, Canterbury, joined radical politics, and for a time contributed poems to little magazines. He brought a political awareness along with an interesting persona to poetry. His poems were later collected and published by Jussawalla under the title of *Lobo* (1984) and reflect Nazareth's feeling of Indians being regarded in England as unwanted blacks. Similar to West Indians they are displaced, unassimilated, and face discrimination. Nazareth's poetic models are Byron and the wise-cracking American confessional poet John Berryman. *Lobo* begins with a political perspective on Nazareth's innocent childhood in still colonial Goa. After arriving in England he is suddenly 'You black bastard'. There are the usual references to life in bedsitters, the sterile but crowded suburbs, wondering what the British do behind their drawn curtains, a futile round of affairs, drinking, and late-night talk with political friends. *Lobo* then travels abroad to Spain, the Caribbean, and the United States before returning to London and settling for mediocrity and nostalgia, at 32 an already tamed adventurer and helpless revolutionary. He is a poseur, the uprooted product of colonialism, a bourgeois romantic individualist, a pseudo-Don Juan with political consciousness but without the power and will to shape destiny. Although Nazareth continued to live in London he stopped writing poetry. Jussawalla's other friend, Farrukh Dhondy, found his salvation through involvement in politics of the 1970s and discovered his subject matter in the youth of the new multicultural England.

Zulfikar Ghose was born into a Muslim family in an area of India which became part of Pakistan. That Ghose was made an exile by the Partition of India gave a personal basis to his writings about the relationship of reality to images and words. *Confessions of a Native Alien* (1965) distinguishes between those who are forced or willing exiles and those like himself who no longer have a home to which they can return but who must become natives in an alien nation. The autobiography is useful towards understanding poems in *The Loss of India* (1964), *Jets from Orange* (1967), and *Selected Poems* (1991), which refer to people and events explained in *Confessions*. *The Loss of India*, influenced by Robert Lowell's *Life Studies*, is about belonging to a complex past which cannot be recovered through simple notions of identity, a complexity which for Ghose contrasts with the horrors of Partition. Throughout the volume permanence is contrasted with the need for motion, an opposition which the later poems, and his books of literary criticism, see as a problem in perception created by language and the images in which he thinks. As the past was always unstable and its reality always decays in memory, any permanence is a mistake of language. We never belong in the sense imagined by traditionalists and nationalists.

The two views he discusses, the permanence of a tradition, and its delusiveness, are common to those who are exiles or have been displaced. Both think of the peasant as being at 'home'; the question then becomes whether to try to return to such a home or accept the wider world. But as Ghose admits, the person close to the land is not even aware of the problem, which only arises among those far enough away from such a life to turn it into an image. The solution cannot be a return to a fiction, a fiction enshrined in literary fictions, but in understanding how and why the mind misrepresents. The question whether those who actually live close to the land are conscious of rootedness is examined in relation to Indian Partition in Ghose's novel *The Murder of Aziz Khan* (1967). Aziz Khan, a peasant farmer, has his land and family taken from him by Muslims from India who have created the new Pakistan of laws, contracts, taxes, supposed traditions, and legal violence in contrast to the unthinking feudal world in which Khan lived. Those who create modern nations impose themselves and a false past on those who actually follow the ways of the past.

The formalism of Ghose's poetry and his concern with linguistics have similarities to the Movement poets. He has, however, his own seriousness as a writer which partly is a displacement of the concern with being an alien and partly because he turned from realism towards avant-garde experimentalism. 'This Landscape, These People' (*The Loss of India*, 1964) notes the difference between feeling at home in the natural world in England (he makes no complaints about daffodils being unlike the flowers of India) and being aware that he does not look British and does not feel attached to the people he sees. His attachments are still to family in Pakistan. Then he recalls India and the 'fire' of Partition where he was also 'a stranger'. The present is always transitional between being and becoming. Decades later Moniza Alvi will also write poems in which the attractions of Pakistan are contrasted with the violence of the Partition, but for Alvi the Partition belongs to an imagined past whereas for Ghose such events are recent.

Ghose, for whom English was his third language, had early decided his future was to be an English-language poet. In Bombay he attended Catholic schools, lived in an area without Muslims, and when Partition occurred his father, feeling insecure in India and unattracted to Pakistan, took the family to England in 1952. London was a disappointment, dirtier and less impressive than imagined, and while Zulfikar did not suffer from racial discrimination, and was cricket correspondent for the *Observer*, he was always aware that his looks and skin colour were different from those around him. Over the years his writings moved from the personal towards an impersonality and abstraction as the subject matter changed from memories to an awareness that all attempts to articulate thoughts are likely to be different from the actuality, an interest he shares with Samuel Beckett and which is found later in the fiction of Ishiguro and Gunesekera, where there is awareness of how telling influences what is said.

His particular philosophical linguistic position was clear as early as *Confessions*. Thinking about the Indian 'liberation' of Goa he puzzles over the idea of a nation and rejects such usual characteristics as a particular geography, a race, a religion, a language. What could make Indians feel Goa is Indian except belonging to the same land mass? Concepts like belonging are similarly part of a misleading grammar of beginnings and ends, that are unlikely to be true, which will be pursued through further misleading associations and images.

In this distrust of language he was part of a general movement of thought at the time that critically examined realism and empiricism and which contributed to self-conscious self-referential writing. He was a philosopher of language, a kind of British linguistic deconstructionist, a theorist against theory. This made him take refuge in Art as a form of permanence in contrast to the mutability of the world. He was a close friend of, and influenced by, the experimentalist Bryan S. Johnson, with whom he shared a volume of stories, *Statement against Corpses* (1964), as near as British fiction got at that time to Samuel Beckett or the French *nouveau roman* with their questioning of the conventions of realistic fiction. The volume aimed at renewing the short story as a form, the dying corpses of the title, although many of stories are literally or metaphorically about corpses. In Ghose's *The Contradictions* (1966) love is treated as absurd since there is no way people can know what others think and feel. In the novel sexual behaviour is so subject to misunderstanding by both partners that it seems an absurd farce, a comedy of failure. The titles of the chapters are those of a philosophical discourse.

Many pages of social conversation consist of dialogue about philo-sophical positions.

After living in England for seventeen years, in 1969 Ghose moved permanently to Texas where he claims, in the poems of *The Violent West* (1972), the landscape reminds him of the Pakistan he knew as a child. 'The Remove' notes the irony of Punjabis teaching Punjabis English in British schools while in India the Sikhs and Muslims fight over the Punjab. Most of his later fiction was about Brazil, but novels treating of England or Europe include *Crump's Terms* (1975) and *The Triple Mirror of the Self* (1992), the latter of which mixes images of his past in India and England with settings and possible literary sources of his Latin American fictions, all commented upon by an American academic biographer of a Punjabi Muslim traveller, poet, and academic called Roshan. If there is a message it is that there is never an emancipation from loss and nostalgia, a theme that will be found in many other writers, such as Rushdie and Gunesekera, who have been made homeless by the political changes that followed the end of Empire.

West Indian poets in England during the 1950s and 1960s can seem old fashioned in their classicism and aestheticism, but that is because of the later associations of dialect with vigour, cultural assertion, and modernism. John Figueroa (1920–99) settled in England after decades of moving back and forth between the Caribbean, England, Nigeria, and the USA. Like many in the early Commonwealth period he was both nationalist and British, while having an international life which in his case included Africa and the Spanish-speaking Caribbean. A classicist and translator as well as a professor of education (he was one of Derek Walcott's teachers at the University of the West Indies, Jamaica) he had a light touch which found expression in short love and religious lyrics. He also wrote well-crafted lyrics based on Horace, Sappho, and other classical writers. He edited the pioneering two-volume *Caribbean Voices* (Hamish Hamilton, 1966, 1970), which offered a selection of poetry from the BBC *Caribbean Voices* programmes. Although he seldom wrote in dialect, his amusing 'problems of a writer who does not quite . . .' mocks an American literary critic's complaint that Derek Walcott's poetry was too learned and British: 'Bwoy, you no hear wa de lady say? | Watch di pentameter ting, man. | Dat is white people play!' While conscious of his partly Jewish origins, Figueroa was strongly Roman Catholic; he was critical of hedonism and what he felt was Caribbean lack of discipline. His love poems allude to the temptations of the flesh and are mostly religious; sometimes it is unclear whether the love is spiritual or romantic. In 'The Chase' the mutual pursuit and desire of lovers is that of the soul for God. Some poems are about places Figueroa visited, many of which, such as 'Notre Dame De Chartres' are religious.

Poets who were born and educated during the Empire could remain rooted in Jamaica, be active in West Indian nationalist and cultural movements, while feeling British. Figueroa was highly visible on the Commonwealth literature circuit as a West Indian poet, a lecturer on West Indian literature, and in various guises as adviser, consultant, editor, visiting professor of multicultural, Caribbean, and Third World studies. Living on a small pension in England, always in need of money, often ill and irritable, never comfortable in a cold country where people ate under-ripe bananas and where, as he aged, carrying buckets of coal for the fire became a chore, he was one of those who laid the foundations for a multicultural England, but his poems appeared mostly in small Jamaican editions until late in life when Peepal Tree published *The Chase* (1991).

Although *On This Mountain* (1965) was the first book of poetry by a West Indian living in England to be published by a trade publisher, André Deutsch, A. L. Hendriks remained on the fringes of the British literary scene. His later *To Speak Softly* (1988) was published by Hippopotamus Press, which had a line of good minor Commonwealth poets. With a few exceptions, such as Brathwaite and Walcott, black poets were ignored by mainstream British publishers until the mid-1980s. Hendriks (1922–92) attended secondary school in England, and returned to England in 1964 as a Caribbean director of a television company. He remained a Jamaican poet using such subjects as 'Dawn on Jamaican Hills' and 'An Old Jamaican Woman Thinks about the Hereafter'. Some poems are tightly argued, intellectual, and use a diction that perhaps could have come from Auden or Empson, although other conventions, such as the evocative 'O', are old-fashioned as if Hendrik had not completely accepted the understatement and emotional discipline of modern poetry. The title poem, 'On This Mountain' is almost Victorian in worrying at scepticism and in diction.

In *Madonna of the Unknown Nation* (London Workshop Press, 1974) the Caribbean is a woman, a madonna. Most of the poems in the first half of the *Madonna* have Caribbean subject matter and are open, flowing, colourful, offering an impression of freedom and hope. Then beginning with 'The Migrant' the subject matter, mood, and manner change to the formal and traditional while the titles become sarcastic as Hendriks disapproves of the way England is changing—'Adamson's Mother founding Women's Lib', 'Lullaby in the Abortion Clinic', 'On the Drug Addiction of an Actress'. Instead of the beaches and open streets of the Caribbean there is the ironic 'Neighbour', whose footsteps he hears from an 'adjacent cell', whose flushed toilet makes his own cistern gurgle, and who avoids him by nodding 'civilly' in elevators. The hell of an urban skyscraper is contrasted to Hendriks wanting to love his neighbour and realizing 'that imperceptible wall . . . must always divide us'. The wall is implicitly colour, nationality, and culture as well the notion of the self as enclosed by borders, the theme of 'Boundary'. For someone of his class and finances the problems of the immigrants mostly would have been distant, but in 'Their Mouths But Not Their Hearts' he contrasts the liberal sentiments and politeness of his teachers and neighbours with their limiting conversation to such topics as calypsos and cricket.

'John Crow', from *The Naked Ghost and Other Poems* (1984) published by Outposts, is his excellent, humorous, version of Charles Baudelaire's 'L'Albatros' in which the combination of linguistic nationalism and aestheticism is surprising:

> Poet, man, is like dis Busha of Sky
> Who ride hurricane, an' laugh after shot-gun;
> Upon Earth dey scorn him, so easy fe'tie—
> Him mighty wing' prevent him from run.

Hendriks more than Figueroa uses dialect and touches on matters of race and identity in England, but many of his poems seem muffled by the inheritance of centuries of British poetry. 'Questions to a Bougainvillaea in Eastbourne' makes the obvious comparison between the plant and author as exiles in England. It is noticeable that Figueroa and Hendriks are most striking when using dialect; this is not just a matter of language, it is also the kind of voice and personality found in the poems. It seems that the lack of engagement with questions of identity, race, language, and politics was a limitation that prevented poets of the 1950s and 1960s from developing strong individual voices. That would soon change.

IV. Drama: West Indian Social Realists

The start of West Indian drama in England is intertwined with the beginnings of the new West Indian theatre in the Caribbean. One of the first black West Indian plays (there were earlier ones by white West Indians) to gain wide notice in England was Errol John's *Moon on a Rainbow Shawl* (Royal Court Theatre, 1958). After it received its first stage performance, it became an international hit and continues to be performed in the West Indies. *Moon on a Rainbow Shawl* is a West Indian version of the social-realist-influenced kitchen sink drama of the period. John offers a cross-section of one of the 'yards' in which the Trinidadian poor lived without hope of escape. A central story involves a man facing a conflict between staying to support a woman who is having his child and leaving for opportunities abroad. Winsome Pinnock in *A Hero's Welcome* (Royal Court, 1989; pub. 1993) will look critically at 'yard' drama and John's play. Pinnock's hero returns home and lies about his success in England whereas his life there consisted of little beyond struggling against prejudice.

Lloyd Reckord and his brother Barry Reckord (b. 1926) came to England from Jamaica in the early 1950s, Lloyd to study at the Old Vic School in Bristol. Barry's *Adella* was produced in London in 1954; revised as *Flesh to a Tiger*, it was staged in 1958 at the King's Theatre, Southsea, moved to Cardiff for a week, then opened at the Royal Court in Tony Richardson's production with Cleo Laine and Lloyd Reckord. While the Royal Court was welcoming to dramatists from the Caribbean and Africa, performances were usually limited to dramatized readings on Sunday night. Lloyd Reckord tried to establish the first black theatre company in London. His New Day Theatre Company began in 1960 with two short plays by Derek

Walcott, which after a night at the Royal Court moved to the Tower Theatre, Islington, for two weeks. Although reviewers welcomed the idea of Caribbean plays, they found it difficult to understand West Indian speech. Lloyd Reckord hoped to move his company into the West End but was unable to get financing beyond Barry's *You in Your Small Corner* at the Arts Theatre (1962). Edric and Pearl Connor then formed the Negro Theatre Workshop (1963), which rehearsed plays at the West Indian Students Centre and Africa Centre.

Although Barry Reckord had plays on stage until the mid-1980s, his only published play, *Skyvers*, concerns white teenagers in their final year at a comprehensive school. About the working class in the social realism common to much British theatre at the time, it was produced at the Royal Court, 1963, and published in Penguin's *New English Dramatists* 9 (1966) along with a play by Arnold Wesker. It contrasts the foolish idealism of a new teacher with the scepticism of the students who know that while their future is limited to working-class jobs they will earn more than the teacher whom they consider pitiful. The youths are as intolerant of difference as the middle-class teachers who look down on them. The power of the play is in its language which is full, striking, tinged with threat and violence, feels accurate, and cuts through idealistic nonsense; it is perhaps the best display of British working-class speech on the British stage at the time. Reckord, like E. R. Braithwaite, had taught in a working-class comprehensive school.

The difference between what was performed and what is available in print can be misleading. The novelist Sam Selvon wrote over twenty plays for radio broadcast; one, *Switch*, was performed at the Royal Court in 1977, while those published in *Eldorado West One* (1988) are seven linked, short, unperformed one-act plays written in 1969. Selvon co-wrote the script for one of the first black British films, Horace Ové's *Pressure* (1978), about West Indian immigrants. The small number of plays which reached print are of high quality and an indication that the theatre would be a place that would examine the lives of immigrants in England with a complex realism not always found in the novel and poetry.

2

Transformations: 1970–1979

I. Ethnicity and the Myth of Revolution

The 1970s began badly as tensions between the police and blacks increased. The police seemed determined to impose control on what they regarded as a lawbreaking community which in turn resisted the bullying. In an attempt to close supposed meeting places of radicals and criminals there were police raids on the Black House and the Mangrove Restaurant in Notting Hill. A demonstration by 150 against closing the restaurant was attacked by 500 police and turned violent. Those arrested and charged with rioting became the Mangrove 9, who themselves became a cause for further protests against police brutality and racism.

The Immigration Act of 1971 tried to prevent immigration by people of colour through the concept of 'patriality' intended to limit immigration to those with a parent or grandparent born in Britain except for the reunion of families. Those who did not fall into this category needed proof of employment and a work permit which was only valid for twelve months each time and which prevented the person from changing jobs. Even family members would need to wait four years before coming to England. The Act led to many injustices as immigration officials found excuses to deny people of colour entry to England. They especially questioned whether women were indeed wives and intended brides. Some Asian women were examined for virginity. From 1981 citizenship depended on citizenship of parents not on place of birth.

West Indians in England were no longer part of a large influx of continuing immigration; they were now to become British and as they felt settled, had children, and took root they became black British rather than exiles, expatriates, and immigrants. By the mid-1970s half of the black children in England were born in England.

The first book published by someone black born in England may have been Chris Mullard's *Black Britain* (1973), which looks at British laws on immigration and national social policies from the perspective of a black Briton. An autobiography, it tells the story of the author's becoming aware that he was being brought up according to the expectations of white society, how he became conscious of his blackness, how the race relations industry was staffed by whites, and why Black Power had to develop in response. Like much of the Black Power literature of the period, it is filled with rage and threats. Mullard showed that race relations organizations were out of touch with victims of discrimination and police brutality. The Sri Lankan Ambalavaner Sivanandan, a librarian at the Institute of Race Relations, realized that the IRR would need to become directly involved in British racial policies and conduct whereas in the past it saw its task as preparing reports which led to little action and were likely to be shaped by white interests and policies. *Black Britain* concludes with an account by Alexander Kirby of the crisis of the IRR in which the white directors were challenged by the staff and made to resign, thus allowing fresh blood and new policies.

While the Caribbean Artists Movement, which had more or less died during 1970, had a brief rebirth at the Keskidee Centre during 1972, New Beacon kept going and among its publications of the early 1970s were two books of poetry by James Berry and Salkey's *Georgetown Journal* (1972) and *Anancy's Score* (1973). A second radical black West Indian publisher joined New Beacon Books: Bogle L'Ouverture Publications. Jessica and Eric Huntley arrived in England from Guyana in the late 1950s. They were politically active and published Walter Rodney's *The Groundings with My Brothers* (1969). Their early publications included *One Love* (1971), an anthology of Jamaican poetry edited by Salkey. By 1974 the Huntleys were also running a bookshop out of their apartment. To help raise black consciousness Bogle L'Ouverture published posters and greeting cards by African and Caribbean artists. Soon the focus started to broaden from the Caribbean to West Indians in England

and the new black British literature. Publications included Linton Kwesi Johnson's *Dread Beat and Blood* (1975), Accabre Huntley's *At School Today* (1977), and Faustin Charles's *Days and Nights in the Magic Forest* (1986). Two other influential publishers were Race Today, which published Linton Kwesi Johnson's *Voices of the Living and the Dead* (1974) and Collin Prescod's *Rap Poetry* (1980), and Karnak House, which published T-Bone Wilson's *Counterblast* (1980) and Benjamin Zephaniah's *Pen Rhythms* (1980). In 1975 Darcus Howe and Linton Kwesi Johnson formed 'Creation for Liberation' as a cultural wing of the Race Today Collective. It held discussions, poetry readings, and art exhibitions. Farrukh Dhondy, Howe, and Johnson contributed to leadership of *Race Today*.

The first poetry anthologies that appeared indicate how the West Indian community was beginning to change its perspective from being temporarily to permanently in England, a stage towards black British. Besides the better known West Indians in Salkey's *Breaklight: An Anthology of Caribbean Poetry* (1971) published by Hamish Hamilton, others, less well known, who were in early poetry anthologies included Frank John (b. 1941), Evan Jones, Rudolph Kizerman (b. 1934), John La Rose (b. 1927), and Claude Lushington. Salkey did not include the Jamaican Vivian Underwood (1959–80) whose *Vivian Underwood Poems* (1972) was an early Centerprise success, selling several thousand copies. Frank John was a Trinidadian who self-published cyclostyled pamphlets of Black Revolutionary verse, some of which is collected in his *Black Songs* (1969). As he became more black and African he changed his name to Nkemka Asika. Evan Jones (b. 1927) wrote several good, well-anthologized poems—'The Lament of the Banana Man', 'The Song of the Banana Man'—in Jamaican dialect. At the time of Salkey's anthology Jones was already known as film scriptwriter for *The Damned* (1961), *Eve* (1962), *King and Country* (1964), and *Modesty Blaise* (1965). His *Protector of the Indians* (1958) is a biography of Bartolomé de Las Casas and *Stone Haven* (1993) is an excellent novel about several generations of a Jamaican family. Lushington (b. 1925), a Trinidadian in the RAF towards the end of the war, returned to England in 1955. His poems are in *The Mystic Rose* (1969).

Savacou 9/10 (1974), a Jamaican journal of the Caribbean Artists

Movement co-edited by Brathwaite, Salkey, and Kenneth Ramchand, was a special issue devoted to West Indian writers in England. Contributors included James Berry, Faustin Charles, Stuart Hall, Roy Heath, Linton Kwesi Johnson, E. A. Markham, and V. S. Naipaul.

James Berry's *Bluefoot Traveller* (1976) was the first poetry anthology which claimed to be by British West Indians. It used the term Westindians. Geoffrey Adkins complains in the preface, 'Westindians represent a permanent and talented part of the community here; yet Britain has recognized this so far only in the most grudging way.' Of the twelve poets in the anthology, only Hendriks had published with a well-known publisher. Several of the poets were better known for their general engagement with the black arts scene. Cy Grant, a well-known actor and singer from Guyana, was founder of Drum Art Centre. Although *Blue Foot Traveller* proclaimed a British identity for the West Indian, it was transitional and many of the poets belonged to an older generation. Only Berry, Charles, Johnson, and Markham would become better known writers. Actually there were only eleven authors as 'Paul St Vincent' was Markham appearing a second time; St Vincent was one of his several disguises. All the writers had been born in the West Indies.

Books for black children began with Petronella Breinburg's Sean series published by the Bodley Head Press, starting with *My Brother Sean* (1973), and Buchi Emecheta's books for children, such as *Titch the Cat* (1979) and *Nowhere to Play* (1980), published by Allison & Busby. The first books written specifically for minority youth were also among the first novels written with the new generation of immigrant children, in contrast to their parents, as their subject matter. Farrukh Dhondy's *East End at Your Feet* (1976) was commissioned by Aidan Chambers, general editor of Macmillan Topliners, who wanted books intended for what he hoped would become an ethnic youth literary market. By 1985 *A Multicultural Guide to Children's Books* was published which rapidly sold out. New editions appeared in 1994 and 1999. At first books for children were intended for minorities; later they were sought by mainstream publishers for the British and international multicultural market. By the 1994 edition black and Asian authors born in England joined those born elsewhere. While many of the authors, such as James Berry, Jackie Kay, and Benjamin Zephaniah, are primarily writers of adult books, there are authors, such as Malorie Blackman (b. 1962), who have published a large body of work intended solely for children. The poet Catherine Johnson has mostly written books for children. Publishers, such as Magi, Mantra, and Milet, and a book club, Letterbox Library, were specifically aimed at dual language readers.

The 1975 Notting Hill Carnival was another important event in the creation of a black British community. Carnival in the West Indies was mainly Trinidadian: other islands had smaller carnivals which were distant echoes and pale imitations of Trinidad's orgy of drink, dance, costumes, music, road marches, calypso tents, steel bands, masking, balls, and drama. Carnival in Notting Hill was at first Trinidadian although it attracted the black community regardless of origins. The decision to open the 1975 Notting Hill Carnival to Jamaican reggae groups helped make it a display of black British cultures. Control of the Notting Hill Carnival over the years would always have a larger social significance as it became a famous event attracting tourists throughout Europe and as it led to such offshoots as the Birmingham Carnival in which the black community could enjoy and show the public some of its arts and culture. It meant that the nation had within it a viable, attractive alternative culture whose origins were West Indian but which had taken its own direction in England. Its West Indian tendency towards a seemingly disorderly order and the way it tempted small groups of criminals made it unattractive to the police who kept intervening to restore order and instead produced riots.

Official recognition of the ways British culture was changing took time, but change had begun. Naseem Khan's (b. 1939) *The Arts Britain Ignores: The Arts of Ethnic Minorities in Britain* was published for the Arts Council by the Gulbenkian Foundation and the Community Relations Commission (1976). During 1978 the Association for the Teaching of Caribbean, African and Asian Literatures (ATCAL) was started at a conference at the University of Kent by C. L. Innes. It aimed to promote the study of the new literatures at universities and in the schools and wanted to change the canon and national syllabus. Whereas the School of English at the Leeds University promoted Commonwealth literature, the University of Kent offered an African and Caribbean studies degree.

Unlike Commonwealth literature which included a large component of Australian, New Zealand, and Canadian literature and which was devoted to national literatures, ATCAL recognized that the literatures of people of colour had their own affinities and that a new literature was developing among the diasporas in England.

The 1975 Sex Discrimination Act, while not radically affecting the working lives of most women, gave official support to demands for gender equality. The women's and feminist movement of the 1970s was followed by the formation of black women's, black feminists, and black lesbian groups. They were highly politicized and at first there was a problem about differing concerns of black lesbians from those of other black women. Later problems were inclusion of Asian women and the rejection by some blacks of lighter-skinned women. During 1973 the Brixton Black Women's Group (BBWG) was formed; in 1978 the members created Organization of Women of Africa and African Descent (OWAAD). During 1979 OWAAD changed its name to Organization of Women of African and Asian Descent. Because of internal differences OWAAD ended in 1982.

Not everyone liked the way England was changing. During 1971 there were arson attacks on Indian homes in Newham, possibly by the National Front. When, in 1973, the black workers at Mansfield hosiery went on strike they were opposed by white workers led by a member of the National Front who belonged to the Hosiery Workers' Union. During the 1978 Tory conference Margaret Thatcher proclaimed that immigration must end before England was 'swamped' by other cultures. The next year she became prime minister, remaining in this position until 1990. She moved England towards a liberal market economy and became a target for many writers. The first half of the next decade would be marked by a contest between Thatcher's government and Ken Livingstone's Greater London Council which ended in 1986 when the GLC was abolished. Whereas Labour favoured grants to promote the interests of minority groups, whether lesbians or Asians, the Tories pointed towards financially successful individuals from such groups as evidence that England offered opportunities. The two positions, separatist and assimilationist, aided the transformation of England into a multiracial society, the former in promoting group consciousness, the latter in allowing for individual difference and social change.

II. Prose: Some Firsts

One of the first prose writers to pay attention to the England that mass immigration had produced was Farrukh Dhondy. After coming to England from India during the 1960s to study English at Cambridge University he soon was involved in radical politics. Now a schoolteacher, he wrote a weekly tale about the youths at an inner city school for the Black Panthers' *Freedom News*. An editor asked him to put together the stories for a book aimed at black and brown teenagers as there was little they could read about themselves. *East End at Your Feet* (1976) is the first fiction to use Asian and black British working-class youths as its subject. The odd ways in which influences work can be illustrated by Dhondy's seeing in Lawrence Durrell's *Alexandria Quartet* that if Arabs could be written into a story then so could Indians. Dhondy also learned from Naipaul the need to write truthfully from within a social group with attention to details and conflicts rather than sentimentalizing, stereotyping, and making heroes of people: it helps if the characters, their problems and mistakes, are treated with amused understanding.

The six stories in *East End at Your Feet* contrast traditional culture with the society Indian teenagers inhabit in England. They look at the actualities of the lives of the children of the immigrants and the conflicts they faced at school among the British working class with its antagonism towards immigrant values and aspirations. The insecurities and confusions of teenagers are situated within class and generational conflicts which are as significant as cultural conflict. In 'Dear Maju' a teenager's lack of confidence in his masculinity is intensified by his father's death, which makes him traditionally the head of the family, and by his pretty older sister's attractiveness to the older, tougher, boys at school. As the mother cannot speak English the daughter effectively is head of the family. This story and 'Push's Pimples' contrast British sexual freedom with the Indian view that a family is shamed and dishonoured when an unmarried woman is believed to have lost her virginity. It is a topic through which Rushdie will examine Pakistani culture and politics in *Shame*.

Another theme is how sports or other activities such as painting, in 'Good at Art', can seem a separate world from cultural and racial tensions but be embedded within social contexts. The title story 'East End at Your Feet' implicitly contrasts the immigrant and working-class East End, where the main character lives, with the glamorous West End. His hopes of playing professional football are destroyed when his father dies and his mother takes him to Bombay where he is miserable. Although now living in an apartment with a rich uncle in what Indians consider a wealthy area of Bombay near a beach, the boy feels that in comparison the East End was less smelly, cleaner, and had better housing. His idea of paradise is a return to the East End, his place of origins, his home.

The complications of England as home for someone of Asian family origins feature in other stories. The narrator of 'KBW' is an English-born Indian. When a family that fled rioting in Bangladesh becomes their neighbour on a Hackney council estate, the narrator introduces the son to the school and his cricket team. The new boy, Tahir, rapidly becomes their star bowler. An outbreak of typhoid, however, kills a girl on the estate and rumours blame 'Pakis' for bringing the disease. Tahir's family is attacked by racists while the narrator's helpless father avoids facing the hooligans. Although everyone later assures Tahir that they deplore such racism, his family moves away and he never returns to the team. Such a story is not only about how newcomers are blamed for the problems of society, but also about the violence which erupts suddenly against minorities who may feel part of society and how little they can do about it.

The stories gain in their ironies from being told by youths whose mixed cultural values and perspectives result from lack of knowledge, inexperience, and pressures on them from schoolmates. Dhondy economically makes use of broken English or slang to convey the mentality. This is literature of high quality for teenagers and should be better known. 'Good at Art' is more a Joycean short story than for children, and looks forward to the complexity of Dhondy's novel *Bombay Duck*.

Dhondy followed *East End at Your Feet* with *The Siege of Babylon* (1977), *Come to Mecca* (1978), *Poona Company* (1981), and *Trip Trap* (1984) for this new educational market. *The Siege of Babylon*, based on a real event, tells of three black youths in Brixton trying to hold up a café and keeping four people hostage for several days. The stories in *Come to Mecca* range from tales about the National Front, about Asians exploiting Asians in the East End, and about West Indians, including 'Go Play Butterfly', which concludes with police violence at the Notting Hill Carnival. The title story refers to the British dance hall rather than the holy city; a Marxist faction try to exploit a factory strike to enlist Bengalis in their party, but the Bengalis are against Communism and the young man who started the strike wants the white radical for his girlfriend. British racial violence is more evident in these stories than in *East End at Your Feet* as is minority counter-violence and the choosing of sides. *Poona Company*, set in India, follows Naipaul's *Miguel Street* taking the perspective of a youth growing up to offer portraits of a community through its street life. Instead of one narrator there are several schoolboys and students, who attend cafés at which men gossip and tell stories.

Romance, Romance and *The Bride* (1985) were part of a series of Dhondy's plays broadcast on BBC2 television. *The Bride* contrasts the possibilities of western notions of love crossing boundaries with the tragic results of marriages forced by shame among Asians. *Romance, Romance*, set in Birmingham, is a comedy of generational conflict between a wealthy Indian father and his strongly independent educated daughter. Both are witty and their disagreements are expressed through repartee. The father tries to dissuade his leftist daughter from being involved in her amateur drama group, which is rehearsing a script she wrote concerning generational conflicts. He wants her to marry a young Indian entrepreneur who recently became editor of the Anglo-Asian Conservative Association Magazine and won the Chamber of Commerce award for the most enterprising businessman of the year. Unable to persuade her to meet the young man over dinner, the father asks her to put on her play at the Third Annual Gala of Asian Arts and Cultural Association. The programme begins with a traditional Kathak dance, but, this being multiracial England, two of the dancers are white. Instead of the play the father saw in rehearsal, his daughter substitutes a parody of a Bollywood film in which she dances wildly in an almost topless dress. The father, insulted, stalks off, but the young businessman, seeing the possibilities of turning the daughter into a star in his Indian films, offers her a contract, starting her professional career as an actress and a possible romantic relationship between them. In contrast to the traditional India her father remembers, this is the modern India of movies and international business, racially and culturally hybridized.

Dhondy's debut as a novelist for adults was *Bombay Duck* (1990), a complex multilayered story told by several characters with at times confusing shifts in the narration as the speaker is seldom immediately identifiable. The confusion is significant, a confusion that, like the food named in the book's title, results from the meeting of the East and the West. This is a novel where everyone undergoes some change in identity and nomenclature, like 'Bombay Duck'—an Anglicized pronunciation of a word for a fermented spicy fish (the 'dak') sent from Bombay on the colonial rail system under the British to inland India. In this novel of cultural ironies we are reminded that the early Rastas started wearing their hair in dredlocks after seeing Italian colonial propaganda portraying the Ethiopians as savages with wild, matted, mud-encrusted hair. Most 'authentic' culture begins in such confusion and distortion. Here an international tour of the *Ramayana* with its multinational cast, multicultural pretences, and famous avant-garde English director who brings together the company, alludes to those Peter Brook's projects, such as *Orghast*, *Conference of the Birds*, and *Mahabharata*, that electrified the theatre world after Brook moved to Paris. The director's well-meaning and self-aggrandizing liberalism is innocent about the world outside the West. Hindu fanatics outraged by the production kill the leading lady and cut the leading actor's throat. He survives to tell part of the novel and to read the diary of a former English female columnist who, lacking convictions and seeking a good story, was in charge of publicity for the tour; she later became a masked terrorist in India shooting Hindu fanatics, and herself becomes transformed into a mythic figure.

The other main narrator is XX, who, like Dhondy, is an Indian Parsee from Poona, trying to make a living first as a supply teacher, then as a writer in England. He has changed his name (X standing for Xavier) and identity, but keeps being sent back to India as a journalist by the English or to rescue their straying children. *Bombay Duck* is mostly a sceptical, even cynical, parody of British liberal multiculturalism in contrast to the realities of India and the supposed

Third World. Taking advantage of the fragmented narratives of postmodernism and metonymical symbolism of magic realism, it has many strands and subplots. Dhondy was becoming a lost leader of the 1970s cultural and political revolutionaries, mocking changes he had helped institute.

Except for Dhondy, Indian writing in England diminished in bulk and interest as financial restrictions made leaving India difficult and migrants now preferred North America. Timeri Murari (b. 1941) who first came to England from India as a student when he was 18, divided his time between America and London. He worked for a decade for the *Guardian* while writing a novel, *The Marriage* (1973), and a report on *The New Savages: Children of the Liverpool Streets* (1975).

Sasthi Brata (b. 1939), like Nirad Chaudhuri, rather than writing back against the Empire, lived in England and wrote back against India. Most of his books, witty but lightweight, have only been published in India. His autobiographical *My God Died Young* (1967) recounted the conflicts between the Brahmin culture of his parents and the ideas he learned at the Wesleyan English-language school he attended in Calcutta. After an argument about arranged marriage he left India during 1961 and lived in London where he remained an alienated self-exiled writer conflicted by two cultures. He made his reputation as a novelist with *Confessions of an Indian Woman Eater* (1971), about an intellectual who leaves India and indulges in sex, drink, and talk about existentialism while travelling through Europe. His characters remain on the fringe of society, foreign Hampstead bohemians. *She & He* (1973) is set in Hampstead and concerns the conflicted sex life of an Algerian immigrant, Zamir Ishmael, and his love Sally, and another woman with whom he is also involved. *Traitor to India: A Search for Home* (1975) is another autobiographical novel about a rebel who feels he has no country, while *The Sensuous Guru: The Making of a Mystic President* (1980) is an amusing satire on contemporary American mores involving a fake guru, his woman, and a lesbian friend whom he marries. The guru eventually wins the Nobel Peace Prize and becomes the American president. After his death in a car accident, his wife becomes the first lesbian American president.

While fewer Indian writers came to England for several decades, in their place were writers from Pakistan. Tariq Ali was, like Dhondy, one of the radicals of the 1960s and 1970s who from the time he arrived in England was continually engaged in politics. His many publications during and about the period trace the rise and fall of revolutionary hopes. Besides writing books about Trotskyism and about Indian and Pakistani politics, he wrote of his own life and travels. In the 1990s Tariq Ali would turn his attention from writing books about *The Coming British Revolution* (1972) and *Street Fighting Years: An Autobiography of the Sixties* (1987) to old-fashioned novels on important issues and big themes. They, and the plays he co-authored, continued his battles with Stalinism and Islamic fundamentalism. *Redemption* (1990) is a satire on the various factions of a 1990 congress of Trotskyites. More impressive, although as poorly written, was *Fear of Mirrors* (1998). Like many political novels, it attempts a grand story and has a epic feel resulting from the characters' involvement in major historical events. Ali tells of the rise and fall of Communism as experienced by Central European Jews who, rebelling against their enclosed society and against violent persecutions, were early Communists. The novel moves back and forth between places and times as several generations of family, friends, and lovers devote themselves to the revolution, become disillusioned, are betrayed and exterminated, or want to learn about, explain, or justify the past. A constant theme is betrayal, either from fear of others, personal weakness, lies, or for political reasons. Husbands are betrayed by their wives, children by their mothers, and all are betrayed by their dream of a future of social justice. The novel concludes with several reunions and suggests that some form of Marxism is likely to be a force once more as global capitalism is unable to solve the world's economic and social problems. Ali regards Communism as a noble experiment that went off the track because of Stalin.

Shadows of the Pomegranate Tree (1992) was the first of a pro-jected quartet of novels tracing the history of Islam in its relations to the West, a history intended to show the disappearance of an older, tolerant universalist Islam which was replaced by the orthodoxies of reaction. *Shadows of the Pomegranate Tree* begins seven years after the Roman Catholic reconquest of Granada, a key moment in Arab and Jewish history, and concludes two decades later with the

Spaniards poised to plunder Mexico—symbolically the fall of two empires and the growth of another. Although the Christians had promised the Spanish Moors religious, cultural, and linguistic tolerance, the liberation of Spain led to the Inquisition when Islamic culture was systemically destroyed as libraries of books were burnt and people made to convert. *The Book of Saladin* (1998) tells of the rise of Sultan Yusuf Salah al-Din's family and how Salah al-Din united the twelfth-century Islamic world for the liberation of Jerusalem from the Crusaders. The Europeans not only invade a foreign land, but they are also barbarians with filthy habits, defilers of holy places, liars, killers of women and children, and especially of Jews. Ali's introductory 'Explanatory Note' alludes to its application to the present. The implications are that Arab leaders should stop quarrelling among themselves; they must unite behind a single authority. Or one ruler must have the single-mindedness, virtue, cunning, strength, and patience to bring about unification. The novel is also designed to show that the peoples of the region, such as the Jews, Copts, and other 'people of the book', share a common culture and were united behind Saladin's liberation of Jerusalem.

The Stone Woman (2000) is a family saga set at a country home outside Istanbul at the end of the nineteenth century. The family has served the Sultan for centuries but now is critical of the clergy and awaits the end of the Ottoman Empire and the birth a new society that can compete with Europe. The present generation feels cramped, impotent, like characters in a Chekhov play, and desires larger lives. The truth is that despite the appearance of conventionality their lives have been rich, even romantic. It is difficult, however, to take seriously such conversations as: 'Salman is very depressed by the fact that the Empire has been irreparably decadent for three hundred years' (p. 24). This is a novel in which 'Uncle Memed cleared his throat. Salman smiled. Halil played nervously with his moustache' (p. 27). Ali's own politics can be seen in 'What your philosophers call progress, my dear Baron, has created an inner drought in human beings . . . no solidarity between human beings. No belief in common except to survive and get rich' (p. 26). In each novel Ali has characters make pointed references to Islam being the most tolerant religion in the world, especially towards Jews, but the portrait of 'Jo the Ugly', an American Jew with an immense pitted nose, is not an illustration of tolerance: 'He takes after this mother's brothers who are shysters and rogues, growing rich by robbing their own people' (*Stone Woman*, p. 255); 'who knows but the next hundred years might well be the years of people like Jo the Ugly' (p. 258).

Ali's novels show that the distinction between creative and other forms of writing remains true. There is seldom a paragraph without clichés, political jargon, textbook political summaries, unbelievable dialogue, inappropriate diction, heavy-handed explanations. The structure of the novels can be over-elaborate.

Nigerian British writing starts with Buchi Emecheta, who was the first female African author to live from her creative writings, writing for several literary markets. She expressed the conflict between being an African and becoming British and contrasted how women were treated in Africa and England. Emecheta was already a mother when she followed her husband from Nigeria to London in 1962. The marriage broke up; now responsible for five children, she studied sociology while writing for the *New Statesman* about her experiences as a black immigrant single parent on the dole. Her autobiographical first novel, *In the Ditch* (1972), was published the year she took her degree. Fictionalizing herself as 'Adah', Emecheta offers a portrait of a black woman on her own in London, unfamiliar with the society, uncertain of her rights or where to find aid. It is a well-shaped book with each chapter focused on some incident, character, or example. The structure reflects Emecheta having prepared the chapters for magazine publication; from her study of sociology she was aware that her own life reflected contemporary social trends.

The question of how a divorced Nigerian woman with five children came to be in London studying sociology is answered in Emecheta's next 'Adah' novel, *Second-Class Citizen* (1974). There, as in the openly autobiographical *Head above Water* (1986), we read of her life as a near slave to her relatives in Nigeria after her father's death, her struggle to attend schools, her unsatisfactory marriage, and her growing awareness of herself as an individual. Emecheta realizes that she has been a second-class citizen as a black and as a woman. As a woman she has been brutally and tyrannically treated by African males, while as an African she faces discrimination in England.

Always alienated, she seems continually to write her auto-biography, or that of her mother, in imagining other lives. A sharply defined personality, Emecheta is often emotional and assertive while changing her mind on many topics as if no position were right. After her first books Emecheta wrote for what had become the African literature market place pioneered by Heinemann's African Writers Series. Herself an Igbo, she began publishing novels modelled on those of such Igbo writers as Chinua Achebe, Florence Nwapa, and John Munonye, who depict traditional Igbo society in conflict with European civilization. These novelists contrast the secure organic life of the village with the greater opportunity, freedom, harshness, corruption, and danger of the modern city. Emecheta's novels revise such themes to include female heroines and a feminist perspective. The domination of male over female, which Achebe treats as mostly individual behaviour and which is part of the symbolism in *Things Fall Apart*, Emecheta shows to be that of a master to a slave. She brings to such writing her own struggle to free herself from her village's teaching that women are always the property of some man, and her experiences in England including raised consciousness as a feminist.

While Emecheta was the first black African woman writer to produce such a large body of work, she was an English writer, an African English writer, who had to make her own way as there was nothing like her previously and her work is filled with contradictions as she teetered back and forth between loyalty to Africa and the greater freedom of life in England. Africa seemingly offered opportunities for security, such as a university career which was unlikely in England, but Nigeria was corrupt and mistreated women. Her independence of character made life in Nigeria impossible and her novels challenged the patriarchal assumptions of recent nationalist writers. She also went outside normal publishing circles to distribute such books as *Double Yoke* (1982) and *The Rape of Shavi* (1985) in both England and Nigeria. *The Moonlight Bride* (1980), *The Wrestling Match* (1981), and *Naira Power* (1982) were written specially for the African children's and teenage book market.

The Bride Price (1976) tells a romantic tale in the tradition of popular women's writing, a tale of near-rape, love, and a cursed but happy short marriage which concludes with the bride's death while giving birth to her first child. A sharp sense of how women are financially at the mercy of men infuses the presentation of traditional Igbo attitudes. There is a conflict here between two mentalities. The one is western, rational, individualist, self-willed; the other accepts the wisdom of the tribe, is passive, is fatalistic, and warns that disobeying customs leads to death.

The Slave Girl (1977), set in 1910–47, tells of an orphaned girl who is treated by men as a slave; having escaped, she feels cursed until her husband repays the purchase price for which her brother sold her when they were young. *The Slave Girl* re-explores from a woman's perspective territory previously covered by the Nigerian novelist Elechi Amada, what a traditional society looks like from the inside when it is unknowingly in the midst of change from without. *The Joys of Motherhood* (1979) also covers the first half of the century, from a time when British influence in Igboland was minimal, until after the Second World War, when villagers drifted to Lagos in search of better jobs, and began to understand that under British law women were not slaves. The novel moves from the pastoral of the village to the hardboiled realism of urban economics and power. While the men lose dignity by doing women's work, becoming servants, and washing white people's clothes, many women find they cannot support themselves in the city except through prostitution.

As Emecheta moved from the problems of the past to modern Africa, her subject matter broadened to public themes. *Destination Biafra* (1982) concerns a feminist heroine attempting to mediate between the two sides of the Nigerian civil war; she suffers as a result while emerging as the voice of African sisterhood. In *Double Yoke* (1982) the double focus on a young man and his girlfriend provides contrasting insights into modern Nigeria as experienced by the two sexes. *The Rape of Shavi* (1983) blends criticism of European imperialism with feminist criticism of the male desire for conquest and dominance. The culture is violated by ideas of conquest and the importation of advanced technology. As the formerly peaceful village comes into contact with the outside world it becomes dependent upon selling its minerals for food and guns. The fall from paradise to neocolonialism is rapid.

A decade later, by the time of *Kehinde* (1994), Emecheta seemed finished with Africa, a place where women remained dominated by men. Kehinde likes living in England where she can be alone with her husband and she is safe from the claws of his extended family. He, however, wants to be an African male heading a polygamous family and over her wishes takes her to Nigeria where she feels miserable, especially after he marries a second wife. Kehinde rebels and returns to their house in England, which she owns, where she has an affair with a younger tenant while she works for a doctorate in sociology. When her son tries to evict her by claiming that property in Africa belongs to the husband, she reminds him that in England she owns the house as she pays the mortgage. The meaning is clear: England is a better place for an African woman and it is time to get over sentimentalizing Africa. Such writing was in keeping with the younger generation of Africans living in England and those born in England in which the problem was now the formation of a black British identity rather than African cultural and racial assertion.

Emecheta underwent the usual conflicts of many immigrants in not being at home anywhere, but in time she became black British. The message of her novel *The New Tribe* (2000) is: 'We don't belong in Africa, we're British. Black British maybe, but this is our home now . . . all that roots stuff is so dated. Look how black people have changed the face of British culture. Don't you want to be part of that?' (p. 113).

There were few women among the founders of West Indian writing in England as it was only in the 1960s that there were many West Indian women in England. Some continued to write about growing up in the Caribbean and the conflict between Creole and white colonial ways; while nostalgic, such fiction displaces the tension of being an immigrant in England, a tension treated more fully and directly in later novels. The process can be seen in Merle Hodge's (b. 1944) *Crick Crack, Monkey* (1970), which romanticizes Creole culture as warm, intimate, physical, oral, and passed down through generations of the women of an extended family whereas colonial culture pressures the central figure towards silence, self-centredness, education, leaving home. At the novel's conclusion the heroine is preparing to leave for further education in England. Such books continue a late colonial tradition of semi-autobiographical novels well known from George Lamming's *In the Castle of My Skin*. With Merle Hodge a variant begins in which there is a female self to be discovered as well as an adult perspective. In *For the Life of*

Laetilia (1993) Hodge repeats the cultural conflict formula but the young girl returns to the warmth of Creole culture represented by her grandmother's extended family in contrast to the nuclear family of her drunken father. In such novels aunts and grandmothers stand for Creole culture; their opposites may be a father, teacher, or a striving bourgeois colonial woman.

The story might be said to continue in Beryl Gilroy's *Black Teacher* (1976). Beryl Gilroy (1924–2001), the mother of sociologist Paul Gilroy, came to England from British Guinea in 1951 to study for further qualifications as a teacher but had to accept menial employment before obtaining a position. During the 1960s she wrote autobiographical novels about immigrants, including *In Praise of Love and Children* (1996), which she was unable to publish for several decades. Then she was asked to write *Black Teacher*, which tells of her years as the first black woman teacher and headmistress of a British primary school. Unlike E. R. Braithwaite's *To Sir, With Love* it has no sexual subtext of a handsome, educated, undervalued black war hero winning over his younger, socially inferior white students. At the time it was commissioned, *Black Teacher* was intended to be part of a reform in education as in the 1960s Gilroy was one of those initiating writing intended for the children of multiracial England and there was a demand that something be done about the poor results of West Indian children in British schools. The 1976 Race Relations Act, making indirect racial discrimination a crime, was also part of the context of her autobiography. Hers was the first book to tell of the humiliations faced by black women in England and how they may respond by obsessive concern with their work and self-assertion to prove themselves and those who would follow them to England.

In the 1980s her novels for adults began to be published. In *Frangipani House* (1986) Gilroy tells of Ma King who has brought up several generations of children in Guyana, her own and her children's, especially as the young have emigrated to the United States. As was common in the region, her daughters later took away their children. Her husband has long been dead and now in old age Ma is abandoned and unhappy in an old people's home until she escapes and joins a gang of beggars. After she is found, one of her granddaughters invites her to live with her in America and help bring up her children. *Frangipani House* shows some of the suffering behind the myth of the strong black woman, the isolation of such women, the way emigration leaves them insecure in old age, and the need for them to accept that they too might need to migrate to find a role as the extended family breaks up and can be reformed in new ways.

An immigrant will usually begin by writing about the past as a defence against the experience of migrating and after some years use the new land as possible subject matter. There is, however, the unusual case of Roy Heath who came to England from British Guiana in 1951 when he was 24 and who has written a large, neglected body of work in which he resolutely refuses to write about an England which he dislikes and in which he remains because, he says, of family demands. *Shadows Round the Moon* (1990), his autobiography, concludes, like many books by West Indian exiles, with the author leaving home. Those early years, he claims, are his cultural formation in contrast to which England is irrelevant. For Heath, writing about the Caribbean is a way to keep England at bay. Perhaps that is why he avoids the recent politics of Guyana which with all its horrors might be a rich subject for a writer. Heath also avoids writing directly about the usual topics of identity and nationalism, although, like the politics of Guyana, with its black–Indian racial and ideological divisions, they enter his novels indirectly. Even his narrators are unobtrusive.

Heath writes about Guyana in a realist manner with attention to character, language, class, as if he were a recorder of small, marginal lives uninfluenced by the events of history. It is as if he wanted to preserve his idea of Guyana from reality. The novels, however, undermine their realism. Each goes off course and takes unexpected ways, as can be seen from two novels about murders. In *The Murderer* (1978) Galton Flood has been dominated by his mother, becomes unstable, distances himself from, then kills, his wife. The search for the killer turns out to be pointless when he is discovered to be now a harmless madman. The novel is filled with descriptions of inner and outer disorder. In *One Generation* (1981) the killer has little to do with the story. Heath reveals a country of murderers, incest, transvestites, and other deviants in contrast to the villages of the hinterlands filled with Indians and the descendants of runaway slaves who represent freedom. In these villages there are a variety of myths, rituals, worlds beyond realism.

His early novels detail lives of the Guyanese middle class of the coast and their unexpected relationship to the inland forest and jungle. In *A Man Come Home* (1974) the main character disappears without explanation for long periods and has become strangely wealthy. At the conclusion realism goes out the window when we learn that he has been a lover of a legendary woman in the interior of the country. In the Guyanese imagination the coast is European and the people are of mixed blood, but inland Guyana is exotic, a place of Amerindians, blacks living as Africans, a place for runaway criminals, traditions with strange ceremonies. This other Guyana keeps intruding into Heath's fiction, as it does into that of Wilson Harris and Pauline Melville, as hidden family secrets and as an authenticity with which those on the coast must come to terms.

Heath, Harris, and Melville seem to consider the hinterlands as places to overcome the divisions of history created by colonialism. The wounds of migration, racial discrimination in England, and whatever else has hurt Heath go deep, and made him, like another exile, James Joyce, obsessed with the details of the country he left, a country about which he feels ambivalent. Reality and home for such writers are in the mind, a way to recover the past and remake it.

In contrast to Heath, Shiva Naipaul writes as an Indian alienated from much of the Third World (a term he hated), but unable to settle elsewhere. Shiva, like his older brother V. S., began writing about Hindu life in Trinidad in novels based on their family, and from that perspective turned towards other lands with a critical eye but with less sympathy. His style is dry, distanced, allowing the characters and events to speak for themselves. One of Shiva Naipaul's novels treats of the limited opportunities available in Trinidad, another examines the continuing high costs of the burden of history—especially of isolation and the need to acquire money for investment—and a third treats of the condition of Indians in a black-governed Third World state. Each novel judges the Indian characters as lacking will, ability, and foresight. The early writing is more sympathetic than the later books which seem determined to puncture all the illusions of 1960s and 1970s counter-culture, especially its fake spiritualism and its uncritical admiration for Africa and the Third World.

While his novels show the impossibility of finding 'real life' in the West Indies, they are not set anywhere else. *Fireflies* (1970) and *The Chip-Chip Gatherers* (1973) examine the continuing effects of generations of hardship, traditionalism, money-grubbing, and cultural isolationism on Indians in Trinidad even after many have made the climb from rural poverty to modern urban comforts. *Fireflies* concerns the inner workings and destruction of an extended Indian family which loses its position in the community through bad choices and aiming beyond its abilities. During the course of *Fireflies* the old system breaks down and Indian hierarchy cannot survive modern democracy and the power of the individual vote. Freedom is not necessarily good. The election portrayed is a farce of pretences and vulgarity. In *Fireflies* characters attempt to achieve personal dignity and forge a place for themselves and their children in the world, but at the end there is a disillusioning legacy of failure. This is a quietly angry study of a society without the means of moderniza-tion and personal independence. The fireflies of the title refer to an unlikely rags-to-riches story told by the character Govind, of someone who was so determined to succeed as a doctor that he studied by the light of bottles of fireflies. The story is as improbable as success in such a society where, like the fireflies, bright hopes soon die.

The Chip-Chip Gatherers tells of the harsh life, behaviour, and emotions in a small settlement after the once close-knit Hindu families of Trinidad had fragmented into quarrelling, self-interested, rootless individuals. As a youth, Egbert Ramsaran runs away from the settlement to Port of Spain, but the psychological costs of self-education and amassing money to start a business leave him an emotional cripple, incapable of loving. Returning home where he can bully and humiliate others, he has no use for his riches beyond exercising petty tyranny. Similar failures are common in the novel. Social, family, and sexual relationships form a battleground of pride, vanity, and dominance. Women are especially disadvantaged as there are few jobs for them, they are married off by their parents, and are mistreated and beaten by their husbands, who take mistresses. Just as the peasants endlessly gather the chip-chip, a tiny local shellfish which can hardly provide a satisfying meal, so local lives are unsatisfactory and without purpose.

A Hot Country (1983, published in the USA as *Love and Death in a Hot Country*), Shiva Naipaul's last novel takes place in the context of African-Caribbean nationalism. Influenced by the way the Asian Indians of Guyana (barely disguised as Cuyama in the novel) were tyrannized by the blacks after the latter gained political power, Naipaul reveals the discrepancy between reality and Third World rhetoric. Underdeveloped countries produce underdeveloped souls; colonial rule leads to mob rule. The political situation is, however, presented indirectly as felt by the characters. Naipaul's method here is more economical than in his previous fiction. Early in the novel a father whips his young daughter when she says that she does not believe in God; the father claims that without God his life has no meaning. This can be applied to modern Cuyamanese lives, history, and politics, the fear that there really is no community that can be described as a nation. Independence has brought banditry, cynicism, and lies through destructive politics which ruin rather than build. Everyone speaks of the nation's future as lying in the supposed great wealth of the interior, where no one wants to live. There were similar illusions in the past when Sir Walter Raleigh and others fruitlessly sought El Dorado; now, instead of promises of gold, the black politicians claim that after changing to a one-party dictatorship with an African-style great chief, the effects of colonialism will end and the people will be redeemed.

Shiva shared his brother's wanderlust in search of material and his sceptical view of Africa. *North of South: An African Journey* (1978) is based on six months in East Africa and like his brother's reportage is a mixture of travelogue and essay based on the people he met and observed. The people include hippie drug dealers, whites who pretend to think 'black', and an African who claims to love literature but who does not read. Independence has benefited few. Despite the rhetoric of cultural traditions most Africans want European, especially American, goods. Africans still want to be accepted by whites, but the whites in Africa, especially the settlers, are coarse racists. Africa has always been a place of European fantasies, whether the primitive Africa of the colonials or the Third World socialist Africa of intellectuals. The meeting of whites and blacks has done neither good. Naipaul is especially critical of the Asians who because of their social system allow the African no chance to become part of their society and culture the way Africans can be Europeanized.

Black and White (1980, published in the USA as *Journey to Nowhere*) reports on the Jonestown Massacre, when over nine hundred members of an American cult led by Jim Jones were murdered or committed suicide in Guyana. It shows the often disastrous effects in real life of the illusions of the 1960s and 1970s with its con men, preachers, charismatic leaders, new religions, Third Worldists, fake gurus, African socialists, 'liberation' movements, and communes, a view made clear in 'The Illusions of the Third World' in *An Unfinished Journey* (1986), a volume of autobiography, reportage, and essays. Jones, his followers, and the government of Guyana shared a fantasy of revolutionary salvation. Shiva has his brother's awareness that the usual social and political polarities are unsatisfactory. If one essay in *An Unfinished Journey* discusses white Australian racism, another argues that the promotion of Aboriginal culture in practice confines the Aboriginal in his aboriginality. 'Victim of Ramadan' in *Beyond the Dragon's Mouth: Stories and Pieces* (1984) tells of being mistaken for a Muslim in Morocco and being threatened by fundamentalists for smoking a cigarette and ordering whiskey. In his writing, the search for identity and authenticity is seen as a dangerous obsession, but travel is disillusioning, exasperating. For the migrant nowhere is home.

Some of the first mixed-race authors wrote detective novels. The first 'Asian' British author of detective stories and thrillers was Leslie Charles Bowyer Yin (1907–93), born in Singapore to a Chinese father and English mother. He changed his name in 1926 to Leslie Charteris and became famous for his *The Saint* books. Julian Jay Savarin (b. 1950?) was perhaps the first British author of part-black Caribbean origins to write popular fiction. He is secretive about his life, but he was born in Dominica of African, Mayan, and French origins, and came to England in 1962 for his education. Savarain wrote over twenty novels, most of which have been republished and are usually in print. He began on the progressive rock music scene of the late 1960s, wrote science fiction novels, and then turned to writing detective stories and thrillers. His rock opera, *A Time before*

This, performed in Belfast and London, uses material that became the basis for his four science fiction novels including his *Lemmus* trilogy. His first recording, *Waiters on a Dance* (1969), is an early example of that period's progressive rock. Savarin was a multi-instrumentalist who played a Hammond organ, piano, mellotron, drums, bass, and electric guitar. The album is related to his first published sci-fi novel *Waiters on the Dance* (1976), rapidly followed by *Beyond the Outer Mirr* (1976) and *Archives of Heaven* (1977).

After his science fiction Savarin began writing thrillers in which the hero hunts a master criminal while he himself is being hunted. Although Savarin's plots and dialogue are improbable, his novels are exciting reading. He uses such thriller conventions as the double chase, car chases, the loneliness of the hero, his antagonism towards authority, and his relationship to women who are in danger or killed. His heroes mix Raymond Chandler's detectives in their isolation, alienation, and tough boiled cynicism and Ian Fleming's James Bond in their attraction towards women, cosmopolitanism, knowledge and possession of exclusive luxury products, and relationship to the British secret services. One reason for Savarin's neglect by critics is his refusal to use race as a theme. His part-black characters do not consider race a hindrance; indeed it is often unclear which characters are white and which are black.

Many of his novels have Gordon Gallagher as a central character. Gallagher is part-Jamaican through his mother, part-Irish through his father, an Oxford don. He is ex-RAF, ex-secret service agent, now retired and a professional photographer. The nastier characters refer to Gallagher's colour, but racial issues are not central to the novels which are often linked to each other through recurring characters, both friends like Gordon Gallagher and Pross and enemies like Naja.

In *Wolfrun* (1984) Gallagher is engaged to a beautiful rich white girl who is murdered during an attempt made on his life while they are skiing in France. Gallagher's search for her killers leads him to Africa where in the process of seeking the brains behind the murderers he finds Cubans have rocket nuclear bombs to attack South Africa, a plot he foils although reluctantly aiding the white South African racists, since the resulting war would plunge Africa into chaos. The rockets are being made by a German businessman who was involved in a earlier thriller concerning Gallagher in Australia. In *Naja* (1985) Gallagher works for British intelligence in hunting an unknown killer called Naja and is himself being hunted by Naja. In *Gunship* (1985) the hero is Pross, who was central to *Lynx* (1984) and also appears in *Wolfrun*. Pross, who used to be in the RAF and worked for the secret service, now has a helicopter company, but like Gallagher keeps being dragged back into solving crimes for the government. Despite all the violence, murders, criminals, and deceptions in such books there is a feeling, held by the main characters, that there are civilized standards of behaviour to which people should aspire and adhere, although the evils of life force people into self-protection and revenge.

During the last years of the decade two important novelists of mixed race appeared who remained active into the new century. It is tempting to describe Timothy Mo and Meira Chand as a new start for English literature, but there were earlier mixed-race authors including Aubrey Menen, Beram Saklatvala, as well as Leslie Charteris. It may be significant that until 1990 some of the authors, including Jamal Mahjoub, lived and often wrote about abroad. Both Mo and Chand are realists who present their material objectively, but often seem ironic and critical.

Timothy Mo, who has an English mother, often has Asians and Asia as his subject matter. At the centre of his stories is someone who does not fit within the boundaries of Asian cultures and whose attempt to create his or her own identity is a moral liberation in contrast to the corruptions and hypocrisy of tradition and groups. The early novels combine straight-faced irony and intercultural social comedy with keen observation of how men and women behave in organizing themselves socially and politically. Mo writes of characters trapped by circumstances that tend to determine their behaviour. He has a sharp eye for human weakness while celebrating the way people fight against the odds and act decently even when idealism can be self-defeating. *The Monkey King* (1978) suggests that most people are dependants living off others, and that cruelty and cunning are prime human characteristics: it also portrays an attempt to seek dignity by the financially impoverished half-Portuguese in Macao and Hong Kong. The King Monkey is Mr Poon, a rich Chinese businessman who, wanting more grandchildren to worship him after his death, marries the daughter of his second concubine to Wallace, an educated but impoverished part-Portuguese from Macao. Wallace, like Ng in *The Redundancy of Courage* and Re in *Renegade*, is an outsider and modernizer who survives. Used by Mr Poon to take the blame for a scandal, Wallace leaves Hong Kong for the New Territories, where he comes into his own as a leader, businessman, and husband. Returning to Hong Kong, he replaces Mr Poon as King Monkey, head of the family and Poon's business empire. In this funny but cruel novel few people are likeable. Mr Poon attempts to entertain an English colonial officer by having a monkey tormented; when the Englishman becomes angry at the cruelty, the Chinese think that it must be because they are beating a monkey. Having confused Darwinism with ancestor worship, they decide that the Englishman is angry because they might be tormenting his great-grandfather. Chinese incomprehension of western culture is paralleled by European innocence.

Similar cunning and cruelty can be found in *Sour Sweet* (1982), a novel about the lives of Chinese immigrants and gangsters in England. To their new environment the Chinese bring a past of obligations, criminal gangs, and other ways which will change while adapting to the new land and which have little to do with morality or justice. The novel's title refers to the adaptation of Chinese food to western tastes; the immigrants similarly adapt, and their lives are a mixture of the bitter and the sweet. Whereas Lily is set in her learned behaviour as a traditional Chinese wife, Mui learns British ways from watching television, physically attracts the English she serves as a waitress, and eventually has an Anglo-Chinese daughter who will presumably be part of a new multiracial England. Considering the long history of Chinese immigration to England it is amazing that Mo was the first novelist to treat it seriously. *Sour Sweet* is filled with information about what brings the immigrants to England, the enclosed community of Chinese restaurants and gangs, differences of customs among the immigrants, as well as showing that when the Chinese and English meet they both bring prejudices with them. Much of the information is based rather on research than first-hand experience.

An Insular Possession (1986) is a historical reconstruction of 1833–41 when the British demanded that the mainland be opened to free trade, while the Chinese wished to retain their isolation and prevent the spread of the use of opium. The British wanted to sell opium to pay for Asian tea and for the costs of running an empire; by the end of the eight years they had taken over Hong Kong. Mo examines the events, the people, and the ideas of the period through the voices both of the traders and of those Europeans and Americans who disagreed with them. While we see the Chinese only through foreign eyes, some of the opponents of the opium trade understand local languages and customs, and thus mediate the Chinese consciousness. A theme of the novel is the near impossibility of translating the notions of two such dissimilar cultures into the language and concepts of the other. Every document or speech that needs to be translated is so modified to suit the thought structures of the other society as to be a mistranslation.

The long, impressive opening description of the river serves as a metaphor for the strong currents and continual flow of history, a flow in which such disparate material as garbage and human bodies is to be found. The novel is partly pastiche, a characteristic also found in novels by Ishiguro. The virtuoso imitation of nineteenth-century speech and writing, the long discussions of styles of painting, and the attention given to the invention of early forms of photography bring into focus the relationship of art to reality. In its concern with the nature of illusion, *An Insular Possession* transcends naturalism and shares in the reconstructions of the past that were a feature of British fiction during the 1980s.

Mo's novels explore what results from the meeting of the West and East. While, like Naipaul and Caryl Phillips, he shows that outsiders should be wary as societies are run by those concerned with their own or family profit, his novels usually end on an example of happiness or individual success. Mo is especially interested in what he calls the Renegade, those who through choice, rejection, or birth do not belong. They are hybrids, a sign of the new, the future, and are at the moral centre in an otherwise often divisive, tribal, and violent world. In *The Redundancy of Courage* (1991) the outsider who eventually participates in the community is Adolph Ng, a homosexual of Chinese origins on the fictional island of Danu who is initially educated at a local colonial Roman Catholic school. His classmates will gain their further education in the colonizer's country—many of them serving in its army in Africa—and return home to become the leaders of Danu's political factions. After independence Danu is invaded, conquered, and colonized again, this time by its much larger, also recently liberated neighbours, the Malai; the Danu political elite now lead a bloody guerrilla campaign in which they are outnumbered and outgunned and for which they will die. The invasion and occupation of Danu by the Malai is based on the Indonesian conquest of East Timor and the attempt to turn the former Portuguese colony into an Indonesian province.

Much of the novel consists of Ng's narration of the lives of the guerrillas. It seems an awful life, not worth living, only made bearable by a mixture of extreme idealism and knowledge that capture or surrender means torture and death. Eventually Ng is captured but survives because of an acquaintance, another renegade, who is now working for the Malai. When recaptured by the guerrillas, Ng realizes that he would no longer be able to live such a life: 'I'd rather be a slave in comfort than endure those conditions of freedom. Until now I'd never consciously posed that choice to myself' (p. 371). He saves a Malai officer's son by shooting one of his friends among the guerrillas and buys his freedom.

The Redundancy of Courage examines the complexities of freedom. There is the irony that independence from European imperialism results in a more brutal conquest and colonization by another of the recently liberated nations and that independence leaders soon find themselves fighting to survive in the jungle rather than talking abstruse notions of liberation in colonial comfort. Mo does not reduce his Danuese rebels to caricatures or inflate them to simple heroes. This is a society in all its complexity, whether in the search for food, differing views of engagements and tactics, the improvising of medicines, the treatment of peasants, rivalries, friendships, bravery, betrayals, fear, and incompetence. Ng bears the hardships of the guerrillas and becomes part of the leadership but he is still called a homosexual Chinaman and not trusted. This is a Naipaulian study of the complexities and dangers of freedom and becoming aware of oneself as capable of choice. The novel ends on an upbeat note of claiming the struggle will continue, and Ng can be said to have earned his place in Danu society and history by his unwilling, forced, role in the struggle. What was a way to survive has, ironically, become itself one of the legends of the struggle, thus, one might argue, fulfilling claims that belonging is not racial or being 'native' but having lived fully within a society. But is Ng like one of Ishiguro's narrators telling history in such a way as to justify himself?

There is the ironic title of the novel, a redundancy being an unnecessary excess, a possible view of the liberation struggle, especially in the way it keeps bringing pain and death to the Danuese. Maybe Ng's feline ways of survival are better than the courage to feel pain and willingness to die for a cause? We are often reminded in the novel that the survival of the Danuese as a nation depends less on themselves than on the outside world. The pains the guerrillas suffer and inflict are little more than a way of attempting to influence world opinion.

After *Redundancy* Mo disagreed with Chatto and Windus over the advance for *Brownout on Breadfruit Boulevard* (1995), a novel set in the Philippines, and he self-published it through his own Paddleless Press. Like Emecheta he challenged established trade publishing and found that he could earn as much publishing and distributing his books himself. In *Renegade or Halo²* (1999), also published by Paddleless, the Renegade is Re, born of a black American father and a tribal Malaysian mother who works as a prostitute in the Philippines. Because of size and colour he is nick-named Sugar-Ray, thus Ray, or Re. Those he is raised around speak a pidgin English in which intensity is indicated by doubling the word. As halo is a common Asian iced sweet, a sort of sundae, a hybrid of jellies, candies, beans, and fruits of many colours, he is also nicknamed Halo-Halo, the Halo-squared of the title. Re's life is an allegory of the postcolonial world. His creation is a result of American involvement in Vietnam and the Philippine sex industry; he is educated by Jesuits who train him to think clearly and un-emotionally. He studies law and is soon part of a political gang whose way to power is to do the bidding of those holding power. It is, however, a brotherhood of the elite and he, an outsider, is framed for a murder others commit. This leads to his flight followed by travels to many of the newsworthy places of recent history.

A modern Gulliver who undergoes a late twentieth-century voyage around the world, Re also recalls those picaresque heroes of the early novel who change identities while moving through exotic but dangerous lands where survival is difficult. There are glimpses of Vietnam boat people being raped and killed, of Philippine workers being treated as slaves in the Muslim world, of drug orgies in Thailand, of life in socialist Cuba, even the illegal immigrant Philippine community in London. Re tries to live by a moral code and a British stiff upper lip, but he kills to survive and to revenge his friends. At the story's conclusion he has returned to the Philippines where, ironically, in his native village he learns about the Internet and sees on television the young who have themselves become globalized hybrids, halo-halos of a future.

A British expatriate writing about life in other countries, Meira Chand (b. 1942), was born in England of an Indian father and Swiss mother. After being brought up and educated in England she married an Indian businessman with whom she moved to Japan in 1962. They spent five years in India during the 1970s before returning to Japan. In 1997 she settled in Singapore. Not surprisingly her early fiction, published by John Murray, has as its theme the fragility of identity. Five of her novels are set in Japan. *The Gossamer Fly* (1979) tells of a child who is half English, half Japanese, and who was left with her father when her mother, suffering a nervous breakdown, returns to England. As her father withdraws into himself, a new maid replaces the mother. The novel shows the violent emotions Japanese behaviour suppresses. It is filled with the sights and sounds of Japan. In *Last Quadrant* (1981) an Englishwoman heads an orphanage which brings up the abandoned daughter of a prostitute; there is a crisis two decades later when the mother claims her daughter whom she wants to support her. *The Bonsai Tree* (1983) uses the problems of an English girl who has married a wealthy Japanese businessman to contrast, and show the impossibility of fusing, the two cultures. Chand believes there is no place for a foreigner in Japanese culture. Her later novels are less domestic and more historical. *A Choice of Evil* (1996) takes place during the Japanese occupation of China, from the 1930s until the Tokyo War Crimes' Tribunal after the Second World War, and has an international cast of characters, an epic sweep, and concerns the atrocities the Japanese committed and have tried to ignore. The five years Chand spent in India are reflected in *House of the Sun* (1989) and *A Far Horizon* (2001). The latter is set during the eighteenth century and tells of the events leading to the infamous Black Hole of Calcutta when 146 Europeans were forced into a tiny cell where most died: this led to the British conquest and cultural colonization of India.

Perhaps most striking about the fiction of those who first appeared during the 1970s is the variety of kinds, subject matter, and the origins of the writers. A decade earlier Selvon, Harris, and V. S. Naipaul were still West Indian writers in England. By the late 1970s it is difficult to generalize about, say, Dhondy, Emecheta, Chand, Mo, and Savarin beyond their being English writers who are radically different from each other. Constant themes, however, are the complexities of identity and the instability of life in contrast to rigidities of societies.

III. Poetry: Black Modernists

After Moraes and Ghose, the international side of the British poetry scene for decades would be dominated by West Indians until the black British found their voice. Instead of the Georgianism, aestheticism, and rootless cosmopolitanism of the early post-war years, the poets of the 1970s were mostly West Indians who blended the techniques of modernism with West Indian speech. The results were surprisingly different for each poet. Poems often had two existences, as individual lyrics about practical problems and as part of a volume with an overriding vision and mythology, a practice continued later by John Agard, Grace Nichols, and Amryl Johnson. James Berry made his generation's immigrant's life a subject for poetry, setting it within the larger visionary and mythic structures that E. K. Brathwaite had learned from Aimé Césaire and T. S. Eliot. L. K. Johnson created a diction close to black British speech as used by the young as well as making a mythology of black youth as revolutionary heroes, a black British equivalent of Che, the Black Panthers, and Malcolm X. While diction and racial themes were the usual way in which West Indian literature would become black British, E. A. Markham found dialect was limiting and unnatural for himself. He wrote technically advanced modernist poetry and prose fiction based on the tonalities and range of his Caribbean voice and its counterpoint to rhythms and pitches of standard English.

James Berry was part of the first wave of West Indian migration to England after the Second World War. Where his generation of West Indians migrated expecting to integrate and assimilate into a colour-blind England, Berry argues for group identity and separatism in the form of cultural and political consciousness without a simplistic back-to-Africa pan-blackness. He shares with the younger generation of British West Indians the questioning of Africa's role in their diaspora, Africa's lack of interest in its children abroad, and puzzlement at Africa's inability to better itself. British West Indians understand that their Africa is more desire than fact.

The title of Berry's *Bluefoot Traveller* (Limestone Press, 1976), an anthology from England's Caribbean community, came from a group of poets whom Berry brought together for readings and which was an offshoot of the Caribbean Artists Movement. In the first edition there were twelve poets of whom eleven came to England as adults. The exception was Linton Kwesi Johnson who was 12 when he arrived. Although in the expanded 1981 Harrap edition there were now nineteen poets, some of whom were born in England, the anthology continues an older West Indian political and literary nationalist culture in which authenticity is represented by dialect, the peasant, and the village. James Berry's 'Banana Talk' combines political protest and West Indian speech with Caribbean subject matter. He wanted to bring pride in using Creole English into poetry. The title poem, Berry's 'Bluefoot Traveller', is Jamaican in subject matter and diction: 'Why you stop here? Get news | 'Mericans open up dollar place | in we districk?' This is poetry for immigrants concerned with their identity in a foreign land. Their home remains the Caribbean.

Berry's *Fractured Circles* (1979), published by New Beacon Books, is a selection from two decades of writing, including poems written during the 1950s about being an immigrant, seeking a room in London, and meeting whites. As with Selvon, there is an awareness of time passing without realizing one's hopes. And as with Naipaul there is a concern with achievement, a concern natural to those who came to England seeking a better life, opportunities, and careers. The first poem, 'I spoke to myself', begins 'You can't settle on the ground | like an earth loving rock' and concludes 'I arrested time: | I moved, unaware of kept movements | to devour me'. In the next poem, 'Migrant in London', the speaker feels proud of having arrived in London, but 'Then sudden like, quite loud, I say, | "Then whey you goin'sleep tonight?"'. While representing problems encountered by the Windrush generation, *Fractured Circles* treats the immigrant experience as a spiritual wasteland of angers and memories that needs to be transcended through poetry. The poet is both part of a community and an individual seeking renewal. *Fractured Circles* has an implied narrative combining a history of the immigrant ('Migrant in London', and 'Roomseeker in London') with a metaphysic of life as movement in time. 'Travelling as we are' interrupts the interiorized philosophizing when, on a London underground train feeling 'British among Britons', the poet encounters two white southern American children and their mother: ' "But this is Europe, Memmy. How come | niggers live here too?" '

Like many immigrants, one of Berry's main concerns is with memory, but his memories become stories about rural Jamaica or longings for an Africa of origins. In 'Deprivation' the repetitions, like those of T. S. Eliot and E. Kamau Brathwaite, express a mythology of spiritual drought and desired renewal:

> It is the full time
> in the dazzling time,
> the deathly sacrificial time
> for water unreachable,
> for water wasted
> for water not stored
> for water not given
> for water not recycled
> for water unreceived.

In the final poem, 'Clockhands of Feet', memory reshapes identity: 'I collect pieces of memory now | I rephrase and rephrase words.'

In *Lucy's Letters and Loving* (1982), also published by New Beacon Books, the amusing versified *Lucy Letters* written by Lucy, an immigrant, explains life in London to Leela, her friend in rural Jamaica. The letters contrast the financial and material advantages of life in England with the natural advantages, such as the close friendships and warm weather, of what has been left behind. 'We get money for holidays | but there's no sun-hot | to enjoy cool breeze' ('Lucy's Letter'). The women get jobs and money, stop being dominated by their men, and are influenced by feminism, but they miss their former relationships with men and they miss dressing in their West Indian clothes. After Lucy returns to England from a holiday in the West Indies she worries about losing her past. She is now a British West Indian, someone whose identity is being shaped and changed by her life in England. She decides to save money to buy land at home to which to retire.

'From Lucy: Carnival' illustrates some complexities of life in England for a West Indian. Notting Hill Carnival is based on the extravagant Trinidad Carnival unlike the small celebration in Jamaica. 'A whole London district in | street jumpup . . . A dozen costume ban's, floats galore | like stars. Should see kaftans an' gowns'. Then it turns violent as young blacks and police fight. Soon a black man is on television talking once more about the problems faced by blacks in England, but Lucy has enjoyed herself drinking rum punch and eating rotis with Sue, her friend from Trinidad. The poem represents a black British identity being celebrated with its mixture of peoples and cultures from various parts of the West Indies and its new history of events, such as Carnival and the Notting Hill riots and the conflicts between black youths and the police. Even the phrase 'Black youths' is significant as many of the children of the immigrants have become part of an underclass within England in contrast to the well-off middle-class black intellectuals and professionals symbolized by the black face on TV talking about 'problems all the time'. Berry's consciousness of differences based on origins and class within black England is signalled by shifts in how English is used in each poem. These poems would influence younger writers, such as Fred D'Aguiar, who would use the format of personal letters exchanged across the Atlantic to contrast two cultures and offer insights into social changes.

In his introduction to *News for Babylon: The Chatto Book of Westindian-British Poetry* (1984) Berry declares his purpose as taking 'another step towards the establishment of Westindian-British writing . . . in its own right' (p. xii). Berry's anthology might be contrasted to Paula Burnett's *Penguin Book of Caribbean Verse in English* (1986), which, while offering a useful historical perspective in its selections, is not specifically about 'Westindian British writing'. Much of what Berry says is typical of ethnic manifestos. There are assertions of 'a collective psyche laden with anguish and rage'. More significant is the claim that 'Westindians have had to sort out their sources of identity' (p. xii). *News for Babylon*, as seen by its Rastafarian title, reveals a Jamaican cultural perspective being imported to England as a unifying source of British West Indianness. Berry discusses 'nation language', reggae music, dub poetry, and Linton Kwesi Johnson as part of a counter-culture. While showing how the performance poetry of the 1960s counter-culture, aided by the popularity of Bob Marley's recordings, became Jamaicanized and representative of black England, especially for the young, Berry knows that this cultural style has little to do with many of his poets, such as Markham, but he has no simple way to explain the complexities of black British identities that his poem about Carnival observes.

Berry's early poems assumed a West Indian, especially Jamaican, readership. Some of the poems were first printed in Caribbean publications, such as *Bim* in Barbados and the Jamaican *Sunday Gleaner*. By the time *Chain of Days* (1985) was published by Oxford University Press, Berry had lived in England for over three decades and was now an English writer appearing in *Poetry Review*, *Oxford Poetry*, and *New Departures*. As he made more use of statement, the compact intensity of his earlier poetry was lost. Poems, such as 'In God's Greatest Country, 1945' and 'On an Afternoon Train from Purley to Victoria, 1955' strikingly tell of racial discrimination or well-meant but patronizing ignorance, but those, like 'New World Colonial Child' and 'I am Racism', not based on specific events, can rant. The best of the consciously black poems is 'Two Black Laborers on a London Building Site', based on an event, a London underground train crash which killed thirty people, which has an irony and universality that any minority, or marginalized or persecuted group will recognize:

> Who the driver?
> Not a black man.
>   Not a black man?
> I check that firs'.
>   Thank Almighty God.
> 'Bout thirty people dead
>
>   .   .   .   .
>
>   An' black man didn' drive?

Hot Earth Cold Earth (1995), which republished much of *Chain of Days*, was Berry's first volume of poetry for over a decade, during which he had been mostly active as a writer of books for children. Many poems use an older tradition of protest literature based on class and racial stereotypes, the ballad, folk song, spirituals, and blues. The influence of Guyanese Martin Carter's famous 'University of Hunger' can be seen in the 'I want university' refrain of 'My Letter to You Mother Africa'. 'Countryman O' is an amusing Jamaican dialect reworking of 'Pussycat Pussycat where have you been'. Berry was now writing simplistic poems about blacks as 'my people' in which others are 'robots' and 'captors' and the police are 'the blue clothes gang'. This is from 'I am on Trial after being Juror on a Black Man', another poem built on Martin Carter's poetic conventions and at times his phrasing.

There is no clear distinction between Berry's poems for adults and for children. The introduction to *When I Dance* (1988) mentions that these poems derive from a period of teaching writing to young people. They are 'celebrations' registering 'black people's presence in Britain' and a way of helping create a Caribbean community. Berry sees himself in a nationalist or racial role, affirming the Caribbean culture, origins, and speech of black children in England who he says should study material from black culture. Berry wants to address racial hurts and wants black material on the school syllabus as a way to bring about understanding between the races.

While Berry was a Jamaican making the transition to West Indian British, Linton Kwesi Johnson was the founder of black British oral poetry; he was its intellectual and myth-maker. While taking what was in the air, he was always politically conscious, and represents a continuity between the older West Indian and the new American influences. In 1970, he had joined the Black Panther Youth League and became aware of the Caribbean Artists Movement. He showed his early poems to John La Rose and Andrew Salkey and read Fanon, Césaire, and black American writing. He went through his own early period of writing as a Negritude surrealist and then starting in 1974 was part of the Race Today coalition between Asians and blacks.

Johnson had a similar role in creating a diction and language for black British poetry to that Selvon had in the novel. He heard and built on what might be described as Brixton Creole, the mixture of black Englishes and speech styles brought to and developed within the black Brixton community. Johnson also brought to a larger audience and developed La Rose's view that the West Indian was not a bird of passage in England but now belonged and was British by history and right. It was time to stop looking backward to lost paradises: young British blacks would probably never know the tropics except as tourists. Both blacks and whites had to see clearly that the black Briton was in England to stay. Johnson understood that a change of attitude by and towards blacks did not depend on arguments, it would come about through struggle. If rebellion was to bring respect as well as self-respect, it had to be aimed at those in power who were holding down the black community. Too much energy was going into self-destructive fighting among blacks, the theme of 'Five Nights of Bleeding' in which young black gangs fight each other instead of their real enemy. It was one of the first poems in which Johnson's early experiments came together, and is a classic of contemporary British literature.

'Five Nights of Bleeding' is addressed to black West Indians born or raised in England who, socially and economically disenfranchised, were filled with resentment. It is the first poem of its kind to identify them and speak of their anger in a style that both reflects their violence and their culture, basically the reggae music popular in the clubs. The poem itself re-enacts the situation of black youth in England; it is tense, violent, feels constricted as if it were going to explode. The aim, however, is not just to imitate in verse the social situation; while violence may be cathartic, the real cure is to fight society. 'Five Nights of Bleeding' showed someone who had thought about black society and how to write good poetry for it in terms it understood.

'Five Nights of Bleeding' originally appeared in the magazine *Race Today*, of which Johnson was one of the editorial collective, and soon after in his first pamphlet, *Voices of the Living and the Dead* (1974) published by Towards Racial Justice. The pamphlet includes one other poem, 'Youths of Hope', which is dedicated to Darcus Howe of the collective, and which offers a vision of black youth as an unstoppable resistance against oppression: 'we young lions, youths of hope'. 'Voices' was a verse play which had been performed at the Keskidee Centre the previous year and which celebrates rebels and revolutionaries who died fighting tyranny. Johnson had already developed his myth of himself as part of a generation of young blacks who would fight the police and oppressors in violent battles. He had also created an emotive diction of 'explosive words' to celebrate rioting as a form of liberation and hope. Behind the slogans and chants of the early verse was an existential metaphysic, the young rebel facing death lives in terror.

The temporary influence of Rastafarianism can be seen in *Dread, Beat, and Blood* (1975), published by Bogle L'Ouverture, where Johnson blended street talk with Rastaisms and Jamaican English. He also demonstrated how to write to reggae rhythms, a mastery learned from oral performance with drummers and other musicians. Instead of the imported American jazz rhythms that had previously influenced some black poetry, 'Reggae Sounds' begins with a reggae bass and drumbeat reflecting black British club culture: 'Shock-black bubble-doun-beat bouncing | rock-wisetumble-doun sound music'. Spelling, like grammar, imitates actual West Indian usage in England and contributes to authenticity as well as signalling rebellion. While celebrating black youth, the volume envisions a bloody future as the young rebel against oppression to create eventually a time of peace and love. It is, as the second part of the volume is titled, 'Time to Explode'. Then comes the 'Song of Blood' section with its long prose poem 'John de Crow', which mixes folk tale with a surreal, apocalyptical ritualistic world of murder, death, and spiritual anguish in which the rage of black youth finds release and eventual peace. Part of the text is in capitals: 'SAID THE BLADE TO THE THROAT: MY LOVE FOR YOU IS AS SHARP AS MY TONGUE. and the sound of the death still echoed in their heads.' Various forms of black 'bass culture' (the electric bass having become increasingly important to black popular music as bass and drum nights became a form of dance music on its own) are celebrated next and associated with rebellion, before the volume settles into four poems envisioning One Love. Throughout *Dread, Beat, and Blood* the diction and images are inflected with the biblical by way of Rastafarianism.

For a time Johnson was thought of as a Dub poet, a term he invented to describe a kind of poetry then being written in Jamaica in imitation of DJs dubbing their talk over recordings. After experimenting with using Rastafarian culture as a sign of black Britishness

Johnson decided that the spirituality and nostalgia for Africa was another opium for the people. *Inglan Is a Bitch* (1980), published by Race Today, shows the increasing influence of working with musicians as Johnson's poetry became more song-like with increased frequency of end-rhymes, increased use of chorus, and especially more repetitions of phrases which are used to structure the forward movement of the narrative. The poems are less obscure, no longer surreal, and speak clearly of social and legal injustices. In 'Sonny's Lettah' a young prisoner is serving a life sentence for murdering a policeman who had wrongly attacked his younger brother. Sonny apologizes to his mother for betraying her hopes but he could not watch his brother being beaten by two policemen. The poem is set in a particular time and place, the London of the late 1970s of police enforcement of the 'sus' (suspect) law used to stop and search young blacks. Other poems refer to such recent events as the 1981 riots and the New Cross Massacre in which young blacks died in a fire which many thought was started by the National Front. The volume itself moves from poems of disorganized rage by black youth, anger against the police, 'songs of blood', to poems written to musical beats which are about revolution and a concluding section devoted to 'Peace an Love' and the destruction of Babylon. Phrases such as 'One Love' and 'Peace an Love' bring to mind both Marley's recordings and the earlier flower-power counter-culture.

With Johnson black oral poetry became a form of micro-nationalist cultural assertion in which black England was a suppressed people in revolt. Some characteristics of nationalism and micro-nationalisms found in Johnson's poetry include language (black British English), religion (Rastafarianism), origins (Jamaica, Africa), folk or popular culture (reggae), tradition (orality), and appeals to organizing (resistance), commonality (blackness), generational appeal (youth), and heroism (dying for the cause). Such nationalism is a means of organizing for political and cultural resistance.

When Johnson returned to publishing poetry the Berlin Wall had fallen, the Russian empire had collapsed, and Communism was discredited. *Tings an' Times: Selected Poems* (1991) is partly a selection of older pieces, many revised in style, which provide a history of Johnson's commitments. There are new poems reflecting on the future of Marxism which to him meant people's democracy in contrast to the Stalinist state. The end of Soviet power was as much a triumph for Marxism as for Cold Warriors. 'Mi Revalueshanary Fren', with its punning title, begins:

> mi revalueshanary fren is nat di same agen
> yu know fram when?
> fram di masses shatta silence—
> staat fi grumble
> fram pawty paramoncy tek a tumble
> fram Hungary to Poelan to Romania

The refrain, in street chant style, lists various Eastern European leaders: 'e ad to go . . . jus like apartied I will av to go'. Because the leadership suppressed the masses the whole system exploded like a volcano. Still the speaker is uncomfortable with how the changes in Eastern Europe will affect politics in the West:

> an allow mi av mi rezahvaeshans
> bout di cansiquenses an implicaians
> espehsally fi black libahraeshan.

The title poem, 'Tings an' Times' begins with what becomes a refrain, 'duped I doped I demaralized', and the long poem offers a loose narrative about someone:

> blinded by resplendent lite af love
> dazzled by di firmament af freedam
> im couldn deteck deceit
> all when it kick in im teet
> im nevvah did andahstan
> dat an di road to sowshalism
> yu could buck-up nepotism
> im wife dangerous
> im bredda tretcherous
> an im kozn very vicious

The poem looks back to the days 'wen young rebels did a fite gense oppreshan'. Then in an almost Swiftian or Samuel Johnson list, the speaker thinks of what has happened to the young rebels. This is a black Marxist 'Vanity of Human Wishes'. Some sell out, some rise in the world, some disappear, others become excluded, become middle class, hustle race, live cleanly, become toughs, even 'win di revalueshan in dem hed | all a tun prime minnistah in dem hed'. What has happened to the revolution and revolutionaries when 'wi gat wi council flat', 'wi collah tee vee', 'wi own a lickle place', there are black MPs and blacks on radio and TV? The poem concludes with a celebration of progress and a realization that goals need in future to be redefined by other leaders of 'di dawnin af a diffahrant age'.

By this point in his career Johnson had become a mature craftsman who had mastered an alternative style. The spelling provides phonetic guidance, rhythms are clear on the page, the line breaks and even the lack of punctuation help towards speaking the poem in the mind. Those close consecutive end-rhymes especially in longer lines have a similar manner and clarity, even tone, to such descendants of Boileau as Rochester, Oldham, and Samuel Johnson, except that they also have their origins in black DJs improvising rhymed raps to dancers at clubs. Decades of black British and leftist culture are behind such a poem whether in its allusions to particular songs and slogans, its awareness of how changing circumstances alter political aims, or Johnson's own consciousness that he and others who were leaders of a struggle have changed. The struggle is not over, but it will be different and led by others. *Tings an' Times* ends with 'Di Good Life':

> sowshallism
>   is a wise ole shephad
> im suvvive thru flood
>   tru drout
>   tru blizard

It foresees a time when the flock will return to the shepherd and go forward to greener pastures.

In his later work Johnson has come to see himself primarily as a poet. There are love poems and the Soca-inspired rhythms of 'If I was a top notch poet' in which he amusingly makes a comic bid for recognition with Brathwaite and Walcott by disclaiming such abilities and ambitions. Johnson's influence turns up unexpectedly on others, such as Fred D'Aguiar. That *Mi Revalueshanary Fren: Selected Poems* (2002) was published as a Penguin Modern Classic shows how rapidly what was intended as a part of a revolution became an accepted part of mainstream British culture.

The actor T-Bone Wilson also attended the CAM sessions and learned from Brathwaite and Johnson how to build a volume of poetry around various voices and styles while implying a narrative which goes beyond protest using various aspects of black culture. Poems in Wilson's *Counterblast* (1980), published by Karnak, range from the surrealism common to writers who migrated from Guyana, and lyrics which still use a romantic diction of 'thee', 'thou', and 'thy', to verse in patois. At the heart of the volume is the assumption that the poet speaks for the impoverished and badly housed black immigrant harassed by the police. The speaker is waiting to explode but imaginatively travels to Africa where he is a warrior and hunter. The long title poem mixes the surreal of Césaire and echoes of Brathwaite with specific references to England in lamenting the condition of British blacks.

In James Berry's anthology *Bluefoot Traveller* (1976), G. P. Cresswell Durrante (b. 1937) from St Vincent published a few poems in thick dialect. Linton Kwesi Johnson also had a poem, 'Reggae Sounds', which in its imitation of music was a step towards the new style. By contrast E. A. Markham who is represented under his own name and that of Paul St Vincent was unique. His voice, confidence, the feeling of the verse line, the unexpected changes in subject and argument, and the unusual tone, are personal, different, and treat race, origins, and life in England in a sophisticated, cosmopolitan, amusing manner. In 'Confessions of a Liar':

> I was white in those days and failed
> my exams because of the foreigners next-door
>
> with their all-night dancing and magic.
> What chance did I have in schools
>
> where teachers had de-colonization
> on the brain, and defined Art as Jewish
>
> and made 'Current Affairs' Black? Inevitably,
> I married against my will on the advice
>
> of the Environment; it's all in the Court
> Records. Then I was, as you know, a woman

and didn't care who knew it. No more drudgery
of washing my face and underwear for the brute.

There is much autobiography here mixed in with mocking exaggerations. As he says in 'Anonymous', Markham haunts 'in disguise'.

Markham, who came to England in 1956, began in theatre where he learned to create monologues, characters, and speakable lines. Experimental drama stimulated curiosity for the ways stories could be presented. Markham would increase and multiply his disguises, sometimes perfecting them to the degree that several of his personae would submit poems to and appear in the same issue of a literary magazine without the editor being aware of the deception. It is difficult to decide or distinguish where disguise was a way of handling and distancing matters concerned with race and class, a way to be ironic, a way to be avant-garde, a form of amusement, an eccentricity, or a development of how poets assume masks. Over the decades he would write poetry and prose of varying quality ranging from classic to unreadable. He did not want to be limited by notions of identity and thought of himself as a West Indian European who had worked in Germany and Sweden and lived in France when he was not in England.

Even his plain unmetaphoric verse can be difficult to understand due to its economy, compression, changes in voice and tone, ellipses in scene and narrative, and use of personal allusions. Markham mixes facts and fiction without warning, invents places and persons; even the footnotes he adds to his poetry may be parody. The verse itself presents problems because, although based on iambic feet and usually presented in regularly formed stanzas, there is much metric substitution and other means of creating variety. Each mask he uses has a different way of speaking, a different diction, a different feel to the voice. Several of his personae have taken on lives of their own, appearing in his publications as if they were real people.

Raised in Montserrat (which he likes to explain was the only Irish colony) Markham had little contact with West Indian Creole culture and its African survivals. His literary and social scene in England was not Brixton. The disguises were a way to avoid racial categorization with its accompanying expectations as to subject matter, diction, and attitude. In the 'Notes' prefacing *Living in Disguise* (1986) he says:

The Sally Goodman poems . . . grew out of the author's close contact (and empathy) with groups of women writers and performers operating . . . in New England and in Koln. Part of the interest was trying to create work which, though not alien to the individual consciousness generating it, nevertheless didn't go out of its way to confirm the usual biological prejudices.

We were concerned that the tendencies (both academic and popular) to colonize tracts of contemporary writing, subjecting them to fairly arbitrary rule as 'Jewish', 'Black', 'Women', etc., territories, was causing (bound to cause?) them to develop literary constitutions (and politics) unhealthily dependent on the aid of a gratuitous *adjective*. . . . And besides it was fun. (n.p. but actually p. 6)

In introducing his poetry in his *Hinterland* anthology, he asks why a poet should be limited to a choice between two contrasting voices: black Creole and Standard English. Other voices are possible. Among Markham's personae were Paul St Vincent (a young black intent on surviving the inner city), Lambchops (a naïve black), Philpot (Lambchops some fourteen years later), and Sally Goodman (a white feminist from Wales). These masks and others keep appearing in his books, meet and comment on each other, and on Markham and his writing, and provide an imaginative world that intersects with, participates in, and parodies the autobiographical. St Vincent not only appeared in magazines and anthologies but was the author of several pamphlets in which he often wrote about 'Lambchops'. Much of Markham's writing is autobiographical and a way to speak through a mask although viewed in a fun house of distorting mirrors. Markham's postmodernism comes from his complex personality, experience, and an instinct for complication, experimentation, ingenuity, and unwillingness to be categorized.

A product of modernism, cosmopolitanism, travel, he is also a West Indian immigrant who is aware, although he distances it, of being regarded by others as black, and he continues to have contacts with 'home'. He has been in most anthologies of black British and West Indian poetry, he was part of the black performance poetry scene of the 1970s and 1980s, and, besides writing many poems about Montserrat, he organized and co-edited *Hugo versus*

Montserrat (1989) to raise money for relief after Hurricane Hugo severely damaged the island. He also edited *Hinterland: Caribbean Poetry from the West Indies and Britain* (1989), which offers a canon of major writers.

Before *Living in Disguise*, he had published *Human Rites: Selected Poems 1970–1982* (1984), which includes groups of poems titled 'West Indian Myths' along with love poems and a selection of Lambchops and Philpot. Throughout the volume real life is contrasted to or disguised by mythologies; usually the perspective is ironic. 'West Indian Myth I' has 'Man in a hurry | | hunting new skins in London' and ends with him 'years later, right where he began', which is a more complex racial treatment of the theme of time passing. In another poem the speaker thinks back (as Markham will often do) on the family house in Montserrat and in still another recalls the tourists who came to 'the hot island | to smell native armpits, to screw' ('West Indian Myth 6'). The amusing Lambchops poems mock an innocent black university graduate hoping to avoid stereotypes by immersing himself in white elite culture, while Philpot seems trapped by his relationships to the women he bedded, their children, their other lovers, and their relationships to each other. The West Indies and death are possible escapes. The volume has tight-lipped humour, precision of language and form, and many themes that will recur in other volumes. Like many avant-gardists Markham keeps looking back.

In *Towards the End of a Century* (1989) Markham dropped his disguises. His concern with his family and the past is imagined as a return to a place that has changed and people who have aged or died. Nostalgia for a now-gone Caribbean is enclosed within awareness of his own history and that of the century, all of which will be rewritten to its own purpose by the future: 'My "fact" | can be denied, a casuality of memory | like the trick of editing out a nation's butchery' ('The New Season (ii)'). While there are no masks, there are mazes and other barriers. Many poems, especially those about former loves, are self-mocking and imply the situation may be imaginative.

The first part of *Letter from Ulster and The Hugo Poems* (1993) consists of verse reflections in Northern Ireland. It begins in 'Hinterland' with Markham 'In Portrush, home for two months' thinking of himself as a wanderer who has 'Explored the world, tasted its strangeness', and reached a place like home, surrounded by the sea and with connections to Montserrat. He addresses a lost love, recalls three hundred years of colonization of Montserrat, and in 'Letter for Ulster' imagines himself a younger poet on his imaginary island St Caesare. In the Hugo poems, Kevin represents the original Irish settlers 'Who set foot on your Emerald Isle in the 1630s'. *Misapprehensions* (1995) commemorates the death of Markham's mother and of his friend Andrew Salkey. Written in loose sonnets and with some stories in prose, the volume continues Markham's imaginative return to Montserrat and his past.

Markham is always unexpected. The travel book *A Papua New Guinea Sojourn: More Pleasures of Exile* (1998) recalls 1983–5 when Markham was the first media co-ordinator of the Enga Province in the highlands of New Guinea. First he had to create the media and decide upon its local functions before coordinating it. He was thought African or a Black American or asked if Montserrat were near London. He was doing a high-level job defined by the World Bank while on a VSO salary. After Markham published an article making a hero of a woman beaten to death by her husband who thought her an adulterer, the clan declared war on him by drummers playing non-stop outside his office, a sign that he was to be killed. Markham was made to apologize and forbidden to ride in a car near the clan. *A Papua New Guinea Sojourn: More Pleasures of Exile* is very literary. The subtitle alludes to George Lamming's *Pleasures of Exile*; Markham even submitted his reports in verse to the World Bank, which offered to renew his contract, this time at a high salary, a temptation he resisted. Markham is a do-gooder who often misjudged matters. A failed video projector caused a riot in which the disappointed audience attempted to kill Markham and his staff. The police chief told him that next time he should test the projector before the show.

Markham's preferences for the experimental are clear in *The Penguin Book of Caribbean Short Stories* (1996). Whereas previous anthologies of West Indian stories reveal a taste for naturalism, well-made plots, and nationalist messages, Markham's choice as editor is recent fiction which takes chances, challenges realism, avoids chronology and typecasting. The punning title of his convoluted novel *Marking Time* (1999) alludes to the various layers of a story about a J. Alfred Prufrockian West Indian writer and teacher in England who is marking scripts and planning courses for the next semester. He is marking time in the sense of wasting and also judging it. Pewter is chasing Lee, a married women with whom he has earlier had an affair and whose husband dies about halfway through the book. Pewter desires her but knows it is too soon, so he must wait. *Marking Time* recalls Pewter's past, his relationships to Lee, and his childhood on 'St Caesare' (his invented island—with a pun on Césaire). As the main male characters are aspects of Markham's life and imaginings, the title also puns on 'Markham Time'. The novel moves at the pace of a very slow snail just as Pewter keeps revising lists of things to do, which never get done. The novel raises such questions as is this the life for which the narrator left the West Indies? The book ends with Pewter at an airport leaving for he knows not where. Writing his life has been marking time; after he has marked it he reverts to being a wanderer.

The poets of this period and those who followed in the 1980s often seem like giants in their larger-than-life personalities and personae, the forms they attempted, and in their struggle to bring the resources of Caribbean and modernist literature, and the West Indian or black British voice, into their writing about life of England. Each remains distinctive, yet each was responding to the challenges of being a West Indian in England.

IV. Drama: West Indian Playwrights and Black Lives

Black theatre in England for decades mostly consisted of West Indians in England writing about 'home' or watching plays about the Caribbean and Africa by West Indian and African dramatists. Similarly Asian theatre at first consisted of a re-creation of Indian culture in England through dramatizing works by Tagore or creating theatre around Indian myths and rituals. Plays by British West Indians were thin on the ground and the repertoire of the new companies consisted of plays by black Americans or a few West Indians who travelled between New York, Canada, England, and the Caribbean, such as Edgar White whose ritualistic dramas were performed during the 1970s at the new black theatres.

In 1970 two community-based theatres opened, Keskidee in Islington, and Dark and Light in Brixton, which produced black and Asian plays and allowed directors, actors, and technicians opportunities for training. TEMBA (Zulu for 'hope') was started in 1970 by the South African actor Alton Kualo and mostly took South African and a few black American plays on Arts Council-funded tours: in 1985 leadership, as artistic director, passed to the dynamic Alby James, who immediately began producing plays by Tunde Ikoli, Michael Ellis, Jacqueline Rudet, Trish Cooke, Benjamin Zephaniah, and other black British dramatists. When, however, TEMBA, as the most successful and by then oldest black British theatre company tried to move beyond the limitations of ethnic theatre and included during its season plays by Shakespeare and Ibsen, Arts Council funding was withdrawn and transferred to two newer black groups, the Black Mime Theatre and Double Edge Theatre. The question of the nature of black theatre was not directly faced, but funding was withdrawn because TEMBA was moving from a small to middle-sized company and it was claimed that management would not be up to required standards. After 1991, twenty-one years, and forty-four productions, TEMBA was finished, a victim of those who believed in supporting ethnic separatism rather than have black theatre strive for the standards of the National Theatre. The black theatre community argued over such policies and the controversy continues.

By the mid-seventies the Jamaican Yvonne Brewster (b. 1938) was becoming a leading black director. In 1985 she became one of the founders of the Tawala Theatre Company, based at the Cochrane Theatre, London, the longest lasting major black company. The first plays Tawala produced were by such West Indians as C. L. R. James, Dennis Scott, Trevor Rhone, Edgar White, and Derek Walcott, or by Africans, rather than black British. Brewster selected and edited for Methuen *Black Plays* (1987), the first collection of black British plays; two more volumes followed (1989, 1995). She has been openly critical of policies requiring separatist companies without white actors.

Publication of drama is always difficult as the market is smaller than for novels and as publishers are unwilling to print play scripts before their text has been settled by a major production. The publication of contemporary drama has usually been in the hands of a few publishers willing to risk the market through specialization or because a dramatist has fame in another area. The main English publisher of black plays since Michael Abbensetts's *Sweet Talk* (1973) was Methuen until 1989 when Nick Hern Books appeared. A few plays and screenplays have been published by Faber. Amber Lane Press, which began in 1978, was during the early 1980s the only publisher of younger black dramatists. Amber Lane published Caryl Phillips's *Strange Fruit* (1981), *Where There is Darkness* (1982), and *The Shelter* (1984) and Hanif Kureishi's *Birds of Passage* (1983), as well as Biyi Bandele-Thomas's plays of the 1990s. Oberon Books published the experimental *Plays* (1997) of the actor Sol Rivers and other new writers, while Faber's new StageScripts published texts by Winsome Pinnock, Tanika Gupta, and Parv Bancil.

During the 1970s there were two outstanding West Indian dramatists: Mustapha Matura and Michael Abbensetts. Mustapha Matura's first plays were the short experimental dramas, published together as 'Black Pieces', performed by the Ambiance Lunch-Hour Theatre Club, at the ICA, London, in August 1970. They contrast the attractions of white society with black consciousness and, as is all his work, are intended to provide roles for black actors. Mustapha Matura's *As Time Goes By* (Traverse Theatre Club, Edinburgh, 1971) tells of an Indian Trinidadian who came to England on money from his girlfriend to earn academic qualifications, quickly became distracted, then married, and lives as a fake guru who sells drugs to hippies. He is like one of those Jonsonian con men who tricks and is tricked, around whom the other characters in the play circulate. Time has gone by for the diaspora who think their condition is temporary and for those talking of return. The immigrant cannot return home, but life in England can be a slow slide downwards. Ram is an Anancy trickster, like many characters in the early fiction of V. S. Naipaul, or Selvon's novels, who has learned to adapt while his wife has not, but behind the adaptation is a loss of ideals and dignity. *Welcome Home Jacko* (The Factory, Paddington, 1979) offers a later period of the diaspora in which many young black British West Indians inhabit hostels and prisons, have Black Power posters on their walls, speak patois, admire Africa, listen to reggae, but are trapped and have little chance of bettering themselves.

Matura's plays have amusing West Indian dialogue, with much wit, irony, sarcasm, and wordplay, but behind the comedy is disappointment, hurt, and anger.

Many of his plays are set in and allude to politics in Trinidad. *Play Mas*, produced at the Royal Court in 1974 with costumes by Trinidadian Peter Minshall, contrasts Ramjohn Gookool, a tailor who lives in the self-enclosed Indian Trinidadian world with his assistant Samuel, who rapidly becomes involved in black politics. National independence has been costly to the Indians, brought Trinidad's two major racial groups into conflict, and the nation is ruled by a ruthless, corrupt political party. The first act takes place before national independence in Ramraj's shop in Port of Spain, the second act significantly takes place in a police station in independent Trinidad. There is a national emergency and the play ends during Carnival with an attempted revolution. The background is similar to that of V. S. Naipaul's *Guerrillas*. Using the costumes of Carnival as metaphor for self and nation, *Play Mas* is visually interesting, while like many of Matura's plays its comedy seems to float on an underlying despair.

Rum an' Coca Cola (Royal Court, 1976) portrays Trinidad dominated by the American dollar as seen by two Calypsonians. *Meetings* (Hampstead Theatre, 1982) contrasts Jean's obsession with business, modernization, and meetings to Hugh's desire to take it easy and enjoy old-fashioned Trinidadian food. Such plays show that while governed by a party preaching black nationalism and socialist slogans, Trinidad is losing its identity to American and international business. *Playboy of the West Indies* (Tricycle Theatre, 1984) and *Trinidad Sisters* (Donmar Warehouse, London, 1988) also concern Trinidad before and after national independence. The first sets J. M. Synge's Irish play in a Trinidadian fishing village from which the men leave seeking employment; the second is a revisioning of Chekhov in Trinidad (the sisters want to leave for Cambridge) towards the end of the British Empire. *Independence* (Bush Theatre, London, 1979) is mostly a dialogue between two barkeepers, one nostalgic for the old days of foreign tourists while the younger wants to be an independent farmer. Speaking in the name of the people the leftist government allows no criticism by the people, while making mistake after mistake.

Michael Abbensetts was among the first to portray the lives and characters of British West Indians in their complexity. His characters have been in England for decades. *Sweet Talk* (Royal Court Upstairs, 1973) concerns the tensions within a black family and how people destroy their marriage and themselves. Tony is good at repairing electrical equipment; he rebuilds radio and television sets after he comes home from work to the bedsitter. Instead of saving money to buy a house or start a business he gambles and keeps dreaming of a big break although for years he has been a steady loser. He is bitter with life, sarcastic, unlikeable. The marriage is under strain and he is unfaithful to his wife who brags of her faithfulness. She holds a job, is ill, tired, and, ignoring her husband's advances, saves affection for their son. She risks her life by becoming pregnant again although she knows that she may die giving birth. While Tony blames his obsession with betting upon living in a white country, his wife claims he will not save for the future and wastes his abilities in talk of some day becoming an accountant. He says he cannot live and work without love and respect. The give and take between the husband and wife is witty, wounding, and reveals a bond beneath disappointments.

Abbensetts's *Samba* (Tricycle Theatre, 1980; pub. Eyre Methuen, 1980) also concerns unwillingness to accept reality. Trinidadian Alfred Lewis came to England when he was 21. Passing himself off as Alfredo Lamas, an Argentine, he became an arrogant, wise-cracking, highly successful band leader. His Argentine Gauchos, playing Anglicized Latin American music, were famous during the 1950s, toured the world, and were favourites of royalty, until rock 'n' roll ended his career. The play juxtaposes scenes from the past with the present, twenty years later, when Lewis owns an unsuccessful mini-cab business which he is likely to lose. He is vain, unwise, and tries to hide his origins as West Indian. He opposes his daughter's marriage to an employee because he is black and only a cab driver. Alfred remains socially ambitious and unwilling to accept change. He refused to marry the mother of his child as she was white working class; instead he married a rich upper-class white divorcee who soon divorced him, took his Hampstead house, and kept him indebted though alimony. The play is interesting for the lives going on around Alfred, for its complexity of time scheme, and for the fullness of story. The interior conflict takes place offstage when Alfred's desire to regain his position overcomes his pride. Such plays have a complexity of characterization and awareness of social distinctions and ambitions that only V. S. Naipaul, Timothy Mo, and a few other novelists had so far achieved.

3

Fragmentation and Internationalization: 1980–1989

I. Demanding Rights

The riots of the first half of the 1980s were viewed by many blacks as a revolution against their treatment by society especially by the police. The first riot occurred in Bristol, April 1980; there were disturbances throughout south, central, north, and east London April–July 1981—Croydon, Brixton, Wood Green, Hackney, Newham, Battersea, Notting Hill, and Southall. Brixton rioted again in 1982. During 1985 riots ranged from Brixton in south London, and Broadwater Farm (Tottenham in north London), to Handsworth in Birmingham.

Michael Keith shows in *Race, Riots and Policing: Lore and Disorder in a Multi-Racist Society* (1993) that often the 'riots' were little more than late-night drinking public disorders in which police arrested few blacks but many whites and Asians. Where riots did take place, there was a history of tension between police and sections of the black community. These were not the unemployed youth riots offered as a cause of social explosions and mythologized in the poetry of Linton Kwesi Johnson; they were planned confrontations between the police and older blacks who had experienced years of heavy-handed and discriminatory law enforcement. Those escaping the law would seek refuge in such areas, thus compounding the conflict between the police feeling it needed to keep control and members of the local community wanting a liberated zone.

Much of the tension, as reflected in later novels about police stopping black youth, was the result of 'sus' operations in which police, trying to regain control of black areas and keep pressure on potential criminals, required black youths to identify themselves and justify their presence in the area, a situation which led to heated words, and arrests for disobedience. The police sometimes stopped and planted drugs on those assumed to be dealers. It was a recipe for interracial trouble and the assumptions on both sides continue to plague the black community and police in England. Significant was the New Cross Massacre of January 1981, a fire that killed many, which was blamed by West Indians on National Front racists, and which the police claimed was the result of careless smokers at the party. The police were unwilling seriously to investigate but gaoled protesters.

The riots made those in power conscious that something needed to be done besides trying to re-establish police control. After Thatcher's 1986 abolition of the Greater London Council brought an end to many of the minority organizations it financed, some governmental bodies, such as the Arts Council, consciously directed funding to minority culture. The appointment of David Dabydeen (1982–5) and Alastair Niven to the Literature Advisory Panel of the Arts Council of Great Britain and Niven in 1986 to the Arts Council of Great Britain's Ethnic Minorities Committee showed that even under the Conservatives England would move towards multiculturalism.

Niven, a white, had been actively involved in the teaching of Commonwealth, especially African and Indian, literatures, and was one of those who moved up to senior administrative positions where they promoted black British culture. In 1987 he became director of literature for the Arts Council of Great Britain and led the fight against cuts in funding at a time when there was talk of abolishing support of literature. He was a member of the steering committee of the 1989 Silver Jubilee ACLALS Conference at the University of Kent where black British literature had a prominent place, and Niven would in 1997 move to the British Council as director of literature. The Arts Council in England and the British Council abroad promoted the new minority writers, whether they were British, immigrants, or residents, on readings and tours with the result that contemporary English literature had a multiracial and international appearance. Niven's career, and others could be cited, meant there was continuity among those influencing government policies regardless of which party was in power. A generational change was taking place in time to support a tremendous release of social energy in the study of black and Asian English history and an outburst of creative writing and other arts by people of colour. After the mid-1980s it was impossible to keep to the image of England as a nation of white people and their culture with some exotic immigrants. That England was over.

Increased government attention to people of colour occurred alongside such influential studies as James Walvin's *Black and White: The Negro and English Society* (1973), published by Allen Lane, and Peter Fryer's *Staying Power* (1984), the first major history of black people in England; *Heart of the Race: Black Women's Lives in Britain* (1985) by Beverley Bryan, Stella Dadzie, and Susanne Scafe; and Rozina Visram's *Ayahs, Lascars and Princes: The Story of Indians in Britain 1700–1947* (1986). There were now also black and Asian newspapers in England and radio and TV shows devoted to the two communities. Black Audio/Film Collective began in 1983 and by 1985 a black British film movement had appeared. The politicization of the arts continued and, as can be seen from Hanif Kureishi's films, Thatcher and her attempt to change England from a welfare to a laissez-faire state gave artists something at which they could shoot. Thatcher's rhetoric of traditional British values threatened the new immigrants and their cultures.

Hazel Carby's often-cited polemic 'White Woman Listen! Black Feminism and the Boundaries of Sisterhood' appeared in *The Empire Strikes Back: Race and Racism in 70s Britain* (1982). During the 1981 conference of the Organization of Women of African and Asian Descent there were angry words between those who wanted the conference to be concerned with racism and those who had formed a panel to discuss the problems of black lesbians. The arguments challenged assumptions that racial matters should triumph over matters of sexuality. The first Black Lesbian Group in England was formed in 1982. In 1984 there was the 'We Are Here' conference of Black Feminists as distinct from black women. The next year, 1985, over two hundred attended Zami1, the first national black lesbian conference in London at which black meant both African and Asian. Zami 2 was held in Birmingham in 1989 and included lesbians of Middle Eastern and Latin American descent. The Gay Asian Group was formed (1981) and quickly became the Gay Black Group, then the Lesbian and Gay Black Group (1985). Although the term Black now included Asians, the two would separate as can be seen by the start in 1988 of Shakti for South Asian bisexuals, gays, and lesbians. The first book about black lesbian lives in Britain was Anna Khambatta and Valerie Mason-Jones's *Making Black Waves* (1993), a pamphlet published by Scarlet Press.

As lesbians of colour came out of the closet, black and Asian lesbian publishing started mostly in the form of small presses devoted to the work of black women in general. During 1983 Da Choong, Olivette Cole-Wilson, Bernardine Evaristo, and Gabriela Pearse formed the collective Black Womantalk, the first black woman's press in England. In 1987 they edited *Black Women Talk Poetry*, the first anthology of black women's poetry in England (two earlier anthologies were limited to four writers in each) and in 1991 *Don't Ask Me Why*, an anthology of prose and poetry. The importance of the volumes was that the authors were black British not black women immigrants, and not necessarily lesbian.

The Sheba Collective began the Sheba Feminist Press in 1984. *Dangerous Knowing: Four Black Women Poets* (1984) included Grace Nichols, Jackie Kay, Barbara Burford, and Gabriela Pearse; it was advertised as the first collection of poetry written by British-based black women. Such collections belong to the cultural assertion phase common to nationalist or micro-nationalist movements in which community, origins, language, suffering, and difference are emphasized as a way to mark off the group from the Oppressors. Gabriela Pearse's 'Queiro' wants to 'Get beyond the patriarchy . . . and love the witches.' She warns 'To Whom It May Concern—I'm Proud!' She is of mixed race and complains that at school she was treated as an 'Honorary White' as her 'shade' was 'not stridently offensive'. 'Soft Evening Blues' concludes by celebrating her 'moustache'. Common to such writing are assertions of pride, worth, and bonding. The title of the volume comes from 'Untitled' in which Burford tells other women that their 'mystery' is 'creative fruitfull-ness': 'It is a bloody . . . dangerous knowing'. Such poetry often inverts norms. In 'The Nth Day of Christmas' Burford (b. 1944) turns musical comedy symbols of beauty, romance, and frivolity into a black feminist hell. Although the poem concludes 'Bitter, twisted and frustrated? | Damn right!' Burford has an appealing sense of humour which is less true of 'Introspection Blues' with its discussion of rejection and rejecting, slights and self-loathing.

Sheba Feminist also were the publishers of *Gifts from my Grandmother* (1985), a volume of poetry by Meiling Jin (b. 1956), a Guyanese of Chinese parents who came to England as a child, and Burford's *The Threshing Floor* (1986). Sheba's *Charting the Journey* (1988) was co-edited by Jackie Kay, Gail Lewis, Shabnam Grewal, Liliane Landor, and film-maker Pratibha Parmar (b. 1955). The Urban Fox Press was founded by Maud Sulter (b. 1960) in 1989. *Let It Be Told* (1987), edited by a South African, Lauretta Ngcobo, celebrates the new black feminist rage for expression by reprinting extracts from Marsha Prescod's *Land of Rope and Tory* (1985), Sulter's *As a Black Woman* (1985)—both published by Akira—Amryl Johnson's *Long Road to Nowhere* (1985), Ngcobo's own novel *Cross of Gold* (1981), along with poems by Grace Nichols, Valerie Bloom, and a useful list of further reading. The period's desire to move from bourgeois individualism to communality can be seen in the number of books with several editors, the formation of publishing collectives, and that Beverley Bryan, Stella Dadzie, and Suzanne Scafe wrote as 'The Collective'.

Although Kay, Evaristo, and Nichols were to become part of the new canon of British writers, many of those who were published by the collectives and in such anthologies were part of a movement and would not be heard from again as creative writers. Lauretta Ngcobo was one of the many South African exiles, black and white, in England at the time and she remained active as an essayist and author of a second novel, *And They Didn't Die* (1990). After thirty-one years in England, she returned to South Africa. Similarly Zoë Wicomb (b. 1948) studied and taught for eighteen years in England before returning to South Africa in 1990. Whereas many black South African exiles moved on to North American universities, white South Africans tended to settle in England.

One of the better known feminist writers of the period, Suniti Namjoshi (b. 1941), is an Indian. Namjoshi had published four volumes with a small press in India before she came to England for a year in the late 1970s. Sheba Feminist published her animal *Feminist Fables* (1981). It and the playful story of a bisexual modern goddess in *Conversations with a Cow* (1985) are both unusual prose works unlike most feminist writing of the time. Who else would have lesbian cows discussing the different pleasures given by men and women? Namjoshi settled in England in 1987. *The Blue Donkey Fables* (1988), in prose and verse, range in their satire from feminism to the human condition. It is suggested that a new creation of the world without people would be a happier place. As her work has developed, it is less limited by feminist and lesbian politics. *The Mother of Maya Diip* (1989) is a Swiftian satire in which a feminist utopia is shown to be a tyrannical murderous place of savagery towards men which has its own matriarchal hierarchies and idolatries. Power once more corrupts. Whereas most West Indian and Asian woman came to England to settle, Namjoshi sought the freedom of an exile.

The Asian Women Writers' Workshop, later the Asian Women Writers' Collective, was the first writers' workshop for British-based Asian women. Until its formation (1984), writing by women of Asian origins had been sporadic in England, the earlier writers had been forgotten, seemed distant, and were part of a late colonial elite. Subsequent large-scale Asian immigration produced a different group of women who were feeling the consequences of dislocation, strained marriages, and such cultural changes of the 1970s as the feminist movement and the shift from the self to group politics. The Asian Women Writers' Workshop began as a way to bring women together to end their feelings of isolation and give them an audience which would make their writing feel worthwhile. The combination of having an audience, the excitement of such projects as anthologies, and the feeling of a supportive community meant that the meetings were eagerly attended, especially as several of the group were then going through problems with the men in their lives.

Early discussions included whether it was permissible to read love poetry addressed to men and whether the AWWW should be a feminist collective. If the latter, should the editors of anthologies be identified? What was intended as a way to keep the languages of the authors' origins alive soon proved impossible and English won.

Another problem was that Asian meant South Asian. Attempts to add other Asians were mostly unsuccessful as were attempts to create a national chain of such workshops. The group remained London-based educated South Asian women.

The Asian Women Writers' Workshop began with GLC support and was one of the projects of the 1980s when a supposedly 'loonie Left' was transforming London into a modern multicultural city, or rather recognizing and supporting what London was becoming. In keeping with the times, the Asian Women Writers' Workshop after a year or so changed its name into the Asian Women Writers' Collective, but its essential function was the weekly meeting at which Asian women would read their writings to each other and gain the support of the group. The reading of manuscripts aloud influenced the content, style, and length of works: the preferred manner was short and punchy. The founding members included Ravi Randhawa, Rukhsana Ahmad, Rahila Gupta, and Leena Dhingra. Meera Syal and Tanika Gupta joined later and appeared in their anthologies. Like many other literary movements it did not so much end as fade away when, during the mid-1990s, members pursued their own interests. One crisis was *The Satanic Verses* affair which divided those who believed in free speech from those who felt they should support the Muslim community.

While the AWWW itself only produced two anthologies of short stories for general circulation, several of the authors wrote novels, plays, and film scripts and were included in the many anthologies of the period by women writers or concerning exiles and immigrants. Besides Meera Syal and Tanika Gupta, AWWC members who are playwrights include Joyoti Grech, Maya Chowdhry, and Rukhsana Ahmad. The AWWW anthologies and others of the period were published by feminist presses such the Women's Press and Virago. The first AWWW anthology was *Right of Way* (1988). *Flaming Spirit* (1994) was compiled by Ruksana Ahmad and Rahila Gupta to celebrate the tenth anniversary of the workshop and consisted of twenty short stories on such topics as young women rebelling against their families, women fearing their fathers, rape, betrayal by white friends, British racial prejudice, and the poverty which made families migrate to England.

As Susheila Nasta (2002) has pointed out, the demand which had started during the 1970s in the USA for stories about ethnic and women's lives helped create within a decade a market for stories about black and Asian British women. Farhana Sheikh's novel *The Red Box* (1991) builds on what had become a formula by having two contrasting English schoolgirls of Muslim families interviewed by a woman of similar origins doing research for her teaching. The novel shows class differences brought from Pakistan, an obsession with shame especially in regard to women, and conflict between generations in England. While Virago remained the most visible and successful publisher in England of women's writing, its sometimes stereotyped notions of ethnicity perhaps led to the publication of Rahila Khan's *Down the Road Worlds Away* (1987), which was actually written by the Reverend Toby Forward, a white male.

From the mid-1980s onward the Women's Press was close to the black and Asian scene and published such works as Sharan-Jeet Shan's *In My Own Name* (1985), the two AWWC anthologies, Rukhsana Ahmad's *We Sinful Women: Contemporary Urdu Feminist Poetry* (1991), and Pauline Melville's *Shape-Shifter* (1990). Although a co-operative, leadership came from a white South African who was politically active in protest movements and who was married to an Indian. Financial support came from a wealthy Indian. The Women's Press at first published black American writers and with the profits published many of the first books about black and Asian life in England in contrast to stories of exiles and nostalgia. Its success, and that of the other non-mainstream presses, came from the large number of small black bookshops that started during the 1980s. There was a readership, market, and places of distribution for books about blacks and Asians. While neither the Women's Press nor the earlier founded Allison and Busby exclusively published black literature, they discovered many of the new writers and helped move such writing towards mainstream attention.

That many of the writers came from the Commonwealth meant that there was a continuing relationship between those, especially scholars, who followed Commonwealth literature and the new black and Asian British literature. *Kunapipi* (the journal of the European branch of the Association of Commonwealth Literature and Language Society) published work by, interviews with, and criticism of many Commonwealth writers living in England, while special issues were devoted to such topics as 'Women Writers' and 'Black Britain'. Anna Rutherford, the editor, an Australian who taught in Denmark, also ran Dangeroo Press, which published the two first books of poetry by David Dabydeen and the first versions of some of his scholarly books about black England. The 1989 ACLALS conference at the University of Kent was notable for the presence of many of the younger black British writers, such as Ben Okri, David Dabydeen, and Fred D'Aguiar as well as such established figures as Sam Selvon and John Figueroa.

Wasafiri was founded during 1984, with Susheila Nasta as editor, by ATCAL. When ATCAL collapsed the magazine moved to the University of Kent and eventually to Queen Mary & Westfield College in London and broadened its range to include Asian and Associated Literatures. *Wasafiri* was lively and carried creative writing, artwork, reviews, interviews, and took a strong interest in the new literature being written by those of Asian, African, and Caribbean origins in England. It had many special issues and was a place where critics and artists often argued with each other. *Third Text*, founded in 1987, aimed to be a major international journal to analyse the ways the West claims its authority to judge the world's art and to discuss and evaluate formerly marginalized artists. Largely theoretical and more concerned with art than creative writing, *TT* has devoted issues to the concept of black art and black aesthetics, and the question of freedom of expression raised by Muslim reaction to *The Satanic Verses*.

Recognition that there was now a black British literature (boundaries undefined) began in the 1980s with Prabhu Guptara's bibliography *Black British Literature* (1986), sponsored by the Greater London Council and prepared under the guidance of the Centre for Caribbean Studies at the University of Warwick, and several poetry anthologies, James Berry's *News for Babylon: The Chatto Book of West-Indian British Poetry* (1984), and E. A. Markham's *Hinterland: Afro-Caribbean and Black British Poetry* (1989). *The New British Poetry 1968–1988* (1988) had a substantial section of 'Black British Poetry' selected by Fred D'Aguiar. For the first time black British literature was represented on a large scale in a mainstream anthology.

The title of *News for Babylon* came from the Rastafarian idiom which was popular in the counter-culture especially among young blacks who, in being rejected by white Britain, identified with the Rastafarian idealization of Africa as home, with feeling opposed to white society, and with the creation of an exclusive language for the group as a means of identification. Many of Berry's new poets were British-born, the children of immigrants, and the volume as a whole indicated a movement away from West Indian machoism, racial self-mockery, and similar attitudes that had been characteristics of much West Indian literature. There was a change in sensibility. The black oral poetry scene began to move from the margins towards the centre of British culture as performance poets broadened their audience through association with the alternative comedy scene.

The continuing relationship of black British militancy to the West Indies can be seen from Huntley's Bogle L'Ouverture bookshop being renamed the Walter Rodney Bookshop in 1980. The original title came from compounding the names of Toussaint L'Ouverture, who had led Haiti to its independence against France, with Paul Bogle, who was executed for leading the Morant Bay rebellion in Jamaica. Walter Rodney (1942–80) was a brilliant radical historian from Guyana famous for such books, published by Bogle L'Ouverture, as *The Groundings with my Brothers* (1969) and *How Europe Underdeveloped Africa* (1972). He had been influenced by Rastafarianism, Pan-Africanism, Marxism, and the Cuban revolution. During the previous decade he had visited Marxist Cuba and Grenada and had been banned from re-entering Jamaica where he was a lecturer at the University. In Guyana he was arrested for revolutionary activities and killed by a bomb.

The First International Book Fair of Radical, Black and Third World Books was held in North London in 1982 under the sponsorship of the publishers New Beacon, *Race Today*, and Bogle L'Ouverture. New Beacon had started fifteen years previously. The fair was opened by C. L. R. James. James had first come to England sixty years earlier where he discovered Marxism. James (1901–89) after decades of wandering, and having at various times been expelled from the USA and Trinidad, would spend the final years of his life in Brixton, lionized by those associated with *Race Today*. Darcus Howe was a nephew and Linton K. Johnson was a visitor.

During these years Allison and Busby republished many of the books that made his reputation decades ago, such as *The Black Jacobins: Toussaint L'Ouverture and the San Domingo Revolution* (1938, 1980) and *Mariners, Renegades, and Castaways: The Story of Herman Melville and the World We Live In* (1953, 1985), and his recent Pan-Africanist writings such as *Nkrumah and the Ghana Revolution* (1977, 1982). Howe and Busby edited *C. L. R. James' 80th Birthday Lectures* (1983) for *Race Today*. James had for a time been lodged with Farrukh Dhondy, who was his cook and chauffeur. Dhondy in *C. L. R. James: Cricket, the Caribbean, and World Revolution* (2001) would look back on this period with disillusionment.

The Book Fair of radical and black books brought the increasing number of black publishers to the attention of potential readers and the new black bookshops and brought the new black and Asian writers and interested scholars and critics into contact with each other as the Book Fair was also a cultural convention of lectures and public discussions. England now had a black community conscious of itself and its history, and its culture was starting to gain recognition by those in a position to offer state patronage. The American invasion of Grenada ended the increasingly radical revolution of 1979–83 and caused several Grenadan writers and intellectuals to move to England, adding a further level to Caribbean consciousness in black Britain.

During the last two decades of the century the black British literary scene was enlivened and kept politicized by authors from Grenada. Many were published by the new, often small, presses, such as Peepal Tree, the Women's Press, Karia, and Mango, which were created specifically for West Indian or women writers. Merle Collins (b. 1950), who came to England in 1983, left Grenada after the American invasion ended the Marxist revolution of 1979. Her novel *Angel* (1987) recounts three decades of Grenadan social and political history. It begins with the burning of two plantations as part of the widespread regional unrest during the late thirties, the rise of nationalist leaders in the Caribbean labour unions, independence, and the corrupt authoritarian rule of the leader. Particular to Grenada was the coup that replaced the leader by a popular Marxist, Maurice Bishop, and the bloody massacre of Bishop and his followers by revolutionary purists, which in turn led to the American invasion.

The story follows Angel through childhood, her years in a convent school, her time studying at the University of the West Indies in Jamaica, her return to Grenada as a radical teacher, and her role in the secret ruling Communist Party group. She is wounded manning a machine gun against the Americans who take her to the United States to save her eyesight. The titles of chapters and the dialogue are in patois, which Angel tells her students is as good a language as English when they really only want to prepare for their Cambridge English examinations instead of discussing politics. Although Collins varies the perspective through the contrasting opinions of different characters and by the use of letters from abroad, the novel makes a historical case for the Bishop revolution and suggests that while the coup against him was foolish, the American intervention was wrong and another example of whites telling blacks they know what is best for them.

While *Angel* offers a social and political history much like those 1930s and 1940s novels influenced by social realism, it is more interesting in its use of orality, folk forms, letters, and variety of perspectives. Although there are many different voices, the continuity is provided by women. As in much West Indian fiction written by women, the novel offers a portrait of an extended family through several generations of women. Whereas the men of older generations worked on plantations or sought work in the United States while the women remained at home trying to survive with the children, Angel is part of a new generation with the advantage of education and a choice of professions, and which was influenced by Black Power and other international movements of the 1960s and 1970s.

Collins's two volumes of poetry are *Because the Dawn Breaks* (1985), reflecting the emotions and events resulting from the 1979 revolution until 1983, and *Rotten Pomerack* (1992). She was a member of African Dawn, which performed dramatized poetry to African music. She co-edited with Rhonda Cobham an anthology of writing by black women in England, *Watchers & Seekers* (1987).

Jacob Ross (b. 1956) also came to England because of the American invasion of Grenada where he was director of cultural affairs, 1979–83. After his arrival in England in 1984 he rapidly became part of the black cultural scene. He was a founder in 1984 of the Arts Media Group to respond to media misrepresentation of black and minority arts. He edited *Black Arts in London* as well as *Artrage*. With Kwesi Owusu, Ross wrote *Behind the Masquerade: The Story of Notting Hill Carnival* (1988), which claims that the Notting Hill Carnival is descended from Africa by way of Trinidad and tells of Notting Hill and local Carnival history.

Ross's *Song for Simone & Other Stories* (1986) consists of powerfully realized short stories about childhood, youth, and injustice in Grenada. It was the first book of prose published by Karia Press, which previously only published poetry; it was intended as Karia's entry into the market for young adults and older children. After sharing with Joan Amin-Addo the editorship of *Voice, Memory, Ashes* (1998), Ross published *Away to Catch the Dust and Other Stories* (1999), another collection of intense, well-crafted, often amusing, stories about an unnamed Caribbean island, obviously Grenada. Ross's focus is close up on his characters in their social communities.

Still another Grenadan who continued to write about childhood on the island was Jean Buffong (b. 1943), who came to England in 1962. A lawyer by profession, and author of two novels, *Under the Silk Cotton Tree* (1992) and *Snowflakes in the Sun* (1995), like the other Grenadans she was politically and culturally active in such groups as the Caribbean Women Writers' Alliance. CWWA was started in 1994 by another Grenadan, Joan Amin-Addo (b. 1948), who besides being head of the Caribbean Studies Centre at Goldsmiths College, edited *Mango Season* and Mango publications. Fiction about childhood remained a subject for others from the Caribbean. Janice Shinebourne (b. 1947), of Indian and Chinese descent and married to an Englishman, wrote about growing up in Guyana in her novels *The Timepiece* (1987) and *The Last English Plantation* (1988).

If the 1960s to the mid-1980s was a period of cultural revolution, from the mid-1980s consolidation and cultural conservatism was in the air. There was a feeling that it was time to accept the social changes of recent decades but not allow them to expand further. One major area of cultural conflict was the schools and their role in preparing the young for the future. Within the consolidation the cultural wars continued, although as the young rebels became lecturers, administrators, and recognized artists, rebellion shifted from the streets to committees and academic studies. With responsibilities came the recognition that something new was needed beyond the antagonisms of the past.

The sociologist and cultural theorist Paul Gilroy (b. 1956) first came to public notice with his *'There Ain't no Black in the Union Jack': The Cultural Politics of Race and Nation* (1987), the same year that he published *Problems in Anti-Racist Strategy*. Influential on recent black British thought, putting it in touch with such new theoretical models as the deconstructive version of Marxism which offers analysis of the social creation of reality and its discourses, Gilroy's books have tried to find ways to go beyond the polarities common to discussion of nation and race in which there are fixed markers of Us and Them, positions which he finds as disheartening in blacks and progressives as in whites and conservatives. While his work is part of the new multicultural, multiracial England, he distrusts official government affirmative-action policies which have the unintended effect of reinforcing racial categories and making acceptance of minorities feel imposed rather than natural. Instead he prefers such groups as Rock against Racism, rooted in the youth movement, which had a wide social base and united various struggles in a counter-culture. *'There Ain't no Black in the Union Jack'* finds a model in black popular music for social change that avoids traditional racial and national categories.

Gilroy wants society to recognize that in the meeting of supposed opposites both sides change and indeed that they continually have been changing in the past through their interaction. It is as wrong to speak of a white culture or England uninfluenced by black culture as it is wrong to assume that there is a black culture that has been uninfluenced by contact with Europe and whites. In *The Black Atlantic: Modernity and Double Consciousness* (1993) Gilroy turns his attention to African-American culture to show the ways in which its spokespersons have ignored the continual historical interplay between European and black thought. Besides noting how theorists of black culture often reapplied or inverted the ideas of European philosophers, Gilroy points to the years influential black Americans spent in Europe and how this broadened their view of the world. Studying in detail a few selected writers, Gilroy offers a powerful argument that African-Americans cut themselves off from the insights of someone like Richard Wright after he left the USA for Paris. African-Americans created an isolationist view of the black tradition which not only ignores black European and black British history, but ignores real Africa and its continuing historical relationship with the rest of the world. Black culture, like all culture, is neither pure nor does it become tainted and 'complicit' by recognizing that it shares history with others.

Although Gilroy's ideas have similarities with such other theorists as Homi Bhabha in recognizing that culture is hybrid and syncretic, and that notions of class, race, and nation have historically changed, he assumes a material basis for culture which distinguishes his concepts from the chaotic arbitrariness of postmodernism. His revision of African-American culture has behind it the awareness of how obsession with American racial history can prevent the critical understanding of the slave trade and its relationship to the modern world of capitalism and the Enlightenment. How can society move beyond former ideas of identity? He is, to take the title of another of his books, *Against Race: Imagining Political Culture beyond the Colour Line* (2000). For all his analytical sophistication, Gilroy has similarities to Wilson Harris's way of envisioning change through breaking down categories and reimagining history.

The riots of the late 1970s and 1980s were the beginnings of a new start in how England was regarded by its minorities and majority. For the former it meant a shift from thinking of themselves as a diaspora idealizing a homeland to which they would return; instead they were fighting to be recognized as British with the same rights as the majority. The majority learned that they could not withdraw into a dream of a racially and culturally homogeneous England; England would need to be understood as multicultural and multiracial even if such notions ranged in meaning from a coalition of separate cultures to a melting pot of hybridity. The writers who appeared during the 1990s, if periods can be simplified, recognized that individuals carry within them more than one culture and often belong to more than one ethnicity or class or, in some cases, more than one nation.

Until recently, black British culture had been characterized by

West Indian immigrants. Salman Rushdie's *Midnight's Children* (1981) and *Shame* (1983) showed that there were other ethnic groups to be considered, and the controversy that followed publication of Rushdie's *The Satanic Verses* (1988) revealed that talk of an easy pluriculturalism was naïve, especially when the Ayatollah Khomeini issued a *fatwa* calling on Muslims to kill Rushdie and his publishers, a *fatwa* supported by many Muslim leaders in England who demanded that those born into Muslim families should be judged by Islamic law. By the end of the century England had over a million and half followers of Islam, many of whom thought of their primary identity as Muslim. While London and other large cities continued to absorb the immigrants and the cultural variety they brought, the decaying working-class towns of the old industrial North would sometimes become battlegrounds for young British Asians defending their turf against resentful, unemployed white males and racist groups seeking to create trouble. After the election of the first Muslim MP in 1997, two Muslims were appointed peers in 1998.

II. Prose: From Exotic to British, Almost

Fabulists

During the 1980s the British novel appeared reborn as writers turned their attention beyond England and foregrounded the techniques of fiction. Along with the new subject matter and styles there was an increase in the publication and quality of fiction by writers of foreign backgrounds; this included the first generation of writers who were the children of immigrants or taken to England at an early age and brought up as British. Whereas Salman Rushdie became a voice of diasporas, one of his central themes was the conflict between the authoritarian traditions of the past and the social changes caused by the West. By contrast, Hanif Kureishi, born in England, would write about individual lives and generational change within British society. Some authors were from places that had not previously produced much writing in England.

Salman Rushdie was prominent on the literary scene throughout the 1980s. While there were exceptions, such as Desani and Harris, immigrant fiction had mostly been realistic. Rushdie brought the new international magic realism to the English language novel; *Midnight's Children* would influence creative writing during the decade in many former colonies where national politics and cultural contrasts were the main discourses. In such writing, the world of the folk imagination blends with modernity and was a way through which Rushdie's own multicultural identity found expression. Rushdie brought the intonations of the subcontinent, especially Urdu, into English. While his language exploded in many directions, his novels felt improvised, energetically growing in many directions at once without care about the ways they branched or whether they led anywhere. After *Midnight's Children* it seemed that writing had to be self-reflective and reveal in manner and structure the fragmentation of the postcolonial condition whether in the incongruities of tradition and westernization in former colonies or in diasporan lives. Whereas Zulifkar Ghose's experimental fiction was burdened with theories about philosophy and language, Rushdie comically mixed languages and cultures, fantasy and reality, history and autobiography. Besides G. V. Desani's comic mangling of cultures and languages in *All about Mr Hatterr: A Gesture*, Rushdie's models were novels by Günter Grass and Gabriel García Márquez suggesting a political allegory by using fabulous events which correspond to history.

In *Midnight's Children* (1981) and *Shame* (1983), plot alludes to the histories of modern India and Pakistan but reality is transformed by cartoonish exaggeration, humorous stories, and absurd images and symbols; the fabulous is a way to treat the political without sacrificing art to the literal. It was evident from his first novel *Grimus* (1975) that Rushdie liked science fiction and Hollywood films; yet he also modelled his digressive manner and extraordinary characters and events on the methods of Indian art, the fairy tale, and other ancient and non-western models. A science-fiction version of a pilgrim's progress towards an ultimate reality, a parody update of the Indian spiritual journey, *Grimus* takes place in many dimensions including a film version of a mythical American southwest. It anticipates *Midnight's Children* in such narrative characteristics as the enclosing of stories within stories, the seemingly endless transformations of characters into other avatars, and in the evolution of the story into a cosmic allegory of creation, life, and destruction.

Just as Grimus creates, preserves, and destroys worlds, so in *Midnight's Children* the political allegory continues a battle between aspects of creation and destruction recounted in Hindu mythology. Whereas most earlier Commonwealth experimentalists, such as Wilson Harris of Guyana, kept to the high seriousness of Modernism, *Midnight's Children* has a joyful self-debunking, self-consciousness. Filled with outrageous puns, literary parodies, and clever twists of the plot, it often tricks the reader. Saleem Sinai, the narrator whose life is at times similar to the author's, and who is born at midnight, 15 August 1947, when India gained its independence, views himself as a metaphor for the nation. The allegory can be as absurdly literal as a lost tip of Saleem's finger representing separatist movements, or as fanciful as when Saleem is used in East Pakistan as a tracker dog during the revolt that led to the creation of Bangladesh. Saleem's family's past touches on important moments of Indian history concluding with the Emergency of 1975–7.

Like many books by exiles and immigrants, *Midnight's Children* is about the preservation of memories which Rushdie treats as the equivalent of Indian pickle-making, the chutnification of history, and as the incarnation of an eternal cosmic mythological struggle involving Shiva, 'destroyer of the midnight children', who is also 'Shiva-the-procreator'. In a further twist, Saleem the writer is found to be a changeling, a part-British false heir to Indian identity who thinks he represents recent history, whereas Major Shiva is discovered to be the true heir to the nation. Each of Rushdie's novels contrasts the liberalism of modernity with the repression and authoritarianism of those who claimed to speak for traditionalism. It is especially in the treatment of women that the modern western world differs from non-western cultures. *Midnight's Children* begins with a German-trained medical doctor, representing what was then the apex of western science, who must examine a woman through holes made in a cloth so he does not shame her family by seeing her nude. At the conclusion, tradition returns in the violence of Major Shiva.

At a time when cultural decolonization was a main theme of the new national literatures, Rushdie criticized the governments of newly independent nations and brought attention to Islam's feudal notions of shame and the intolerance of its fundamentalists. Although satiric of the founding and subsequent history of Pakistan, *Shame* does not have *Midnight's Children*'s near fit to actual events. The narrator says that one must write what appears to be fantasy, as in the present world realistic writing is likely to be banned and ineffectual. *Shame* examines a culture for what it has produced in terms of a political state, a way of life, and the treatment of women— as when an immigrant Pakistani father in England slits his daughter's throat for the supposed shame she caused. A culture of shame gives rise to repression, tyranny, and violence. For Rushdie the Partition of India took away his country, divorced the Muslims of the sub-continent from their past among the Hindus, and brought religious fanaticism to the land that is now Pakistan.

The Satanic Verses (1988) continues from the earlier novels in themes of displacement, living in more than one culture, and allegorizing the immigrant experience. The science-fiction world of *Grimus* is recalled in the dropping through space and living in many dimensions—here representing the immigrant's movement through cultures and mentalities. As in *Midnight's Children*, the plot incarnates a struggle between good and evil in which it is unclear which is which. Like the earlier novels, *The Satanic Verses* makes use of traditional oriental and oral literature, including *A Thousand and One Nights*. A virtuoso display of storytelling, *The Satanic Verses* self-consciously alludes to itself, to other texts, to theories of art, and to postmodernist theory. It is a parody Bible, moving from a Fall to an Apocalypse, and continues Rushdie's examination of contemporary Islam, while celebrating the Bombay and India of his origins. Woven into the novel are allusions to Rushdie's relationship to his family. *The Satanic Verses* was Rushdie's first novel in which large sections of the story are set in London and its strongest satire is aimed at England, especially Margaret Thatcher's government. It concludes with what appears to be Rushdie's own imagined reconciliation with his father in Bombay: a reconciliation necessarily imagined as his family had moved to Pakistan.

The Satanic Verses examines kinds of exile, and the fanaticism that drives those who seek to change the world. As can be seen from

The Jaguar Smile: A Nicaraguan Journey (1987), Rushdie had Marxist sympathies; he felt that as an Indian he belonged with the oppressed, and that the regimes he criticized were returning to the ignorance and brutality of feudalism. He was often in trouble. Mrs Gandhi as prime minister of India sued him in court for the suggestion in *Midnight's Children* that to ensure her power she had her son killed, which the novel implied was feudal dynastic practices continued into contemporary India. *Shame* was banned in Pakistan for insulting the state and individuals. Fundamentalist Muslims in India and England claimed Rushdie insulted Islam in *The Satanic Verses*. On 14 February 1989, the Ayatollah Khomeini of Iran declared that Rushdie and those who helped publish his book must be killed. The affair pitted those who believed that free speech is the most important right against those who felt Enlightenment secularism affronted their faith. Those defending ethnic and religious minorities were embarrassed when many Muslims demanded the death of an author, burnt his books, and called for an Islamic England. What had brought a crisis among the multiculturalists was England's first contact with the effects of a new Muslim fundamentalism. While Rushdie followed scholarly sources in retelling older stories about Mohammed's life, his novel became a pawn in the mobilization of Islamic sentiment against the West's liberalism. As a result several publishing houses were bombed and translators killed.

After the *fatwa* Rushdie was forced into hiding, moving from place to place. *Haroun and the Sea of Stories* (1990) is in part an allegory of Rushdie's situation, especially his loss of his wife at the time, and a claim that writers draw upon a pre-existing sea of stories upon which they elaborate, whereas writing to an ideology or command kills inspiration and shuts access to the sea. *The Wizard of Oz* (1992) is an essay about the film which he had seen in Bombay as a child and which had influenced his imagination, an example of the transcultural in modern lives. *Imaginary Homelands: Essays and Criticism* (1991) argues against the approach still used by some Commonwealth and postcolonial literature critics in which the presence of anything deemed native, such as local flora, fauna, places, and characters, and a national form of English, is thought of value. Rushdie's view is that such nationalism is reactionary while the exile is in a privileged position to combine elements of past and present, the local and international, to create a modern literature. Many critics felt that while V. S. Naipaul continued to look back on the wounds of the colonial past, Rushdie had defined a positive post-imperial hybridity which was useful for understanding diasporas.

Throughout Rushdie's writing there is nostalgia for the Bombay of his youth. Bombay, the most cosmopolitan city in India, a place where many tongues are spoken in mangled and marvellous mixtures, with a thriving commercial film industry ('Bollywood'—which often figures in his novels), is the home to which his imagination returns. *East, West* (1994) includes memories of his teenage years in England and refusal to choose between two cultures. Most of the short stories in *East, West* concern such choices and conclude with some affirmation of Indian or Muslim values, affirmations which, coming as a surprise, feel ironic.

Rushdie's later fiction suggests someone coming to terms with exile by accepting that the world has always been a place of migrancy and cross-cultural influences. At the conclusion of *The Moor's Last Sigh* (1995), Moraes Zogoiby flees an apocalyptic Bombay of gang wars, bombings, and communal violence for Spain. There he is imprisoned and forced to write his personal and family history. Moraes is the Moor of the title, although he is Jew, Christian, and Indian. His mother's side of the family is descended from the Portuguese who settled in Goa and his father's side can trace its lineage to the Christian reconquest of Spain when both Moors and Jews were expelled. They have been Indian for centuries despite the attempt of Hindu nationalists to treat them as alien. Rushdie's view of history as a record of change, conquests, flights, migrants, is not unlike the vision behind many of Naipaul's novels, but whereas Naipaul seems unhappy that changes have occurred, Rushdie is preposterously cheerful and optimistic, a difference represented by the former's careful realism and the latter's fanciful magic realism.

The Moor's Last Sigh along with *The Satanic Verses* made 'diaspora' central to modern discourse; it offered an alternative vision of the start of the modern world which instead of beginning with Columbus began with the expulsion of the Moors and Jews from Spain. *The Moor's Last Sigh* is another version of *Midnight's Children* using an improbable, fantastic family history as a way to tell the story of modern India decades later. In *The Moor's Last Sigh* Indian history is told from the perspective of the South, with its many minorities, rather than the Hindu–Islamic North; there are now fanatical nativist thugs who violently destroy whatever they regard as non-Hindu. The wandering Jew has become the wandering Moor, symbolic of India's threatened minorities and the rejection of the westernized elite that founded the nation. Like Scheherazade, the narrator staves off execution by telling, or inventing, his Thousand and One Nights.

Having brought the post-imperial novel of disillusionment into the international mainstream, unfortunately experienced the effects of Islamic fundamentalism, and written a powerful book about diasporas, Rushdie wrote in *The Ground beneath Her Feet* (1999) and *Fury* (2001) about the celebrity produced by globalized popular music, fashion, and mass youth culture. While pop music was a major influence on the new hybridized international culture of the last quarter of the 20th century, the two novels lack the engagement and social texture that usually grounds Rushdie's novels in reality. In *The Ground beneath Her Feet* the myth of Orpheus and Eurydice is retold as two Indian lovers who become international rock stars. It is Rushdie's most accessible novel, understandable without knowing Indian history and culture, as it alludes to or imitates such cultural icons as John and Yoko, Sid and Nancy.

The first half of *The Ground beneath Her Feet* takes place in Bombay. The perspective is that of the Parsees, a small minority of Persian origins who flourished for a century by adopting British ways, becoming the modernizers of India, who since independence have become increasingly threatened and marginalized. Rai, the narrator (Rai the popular Francophonic fusion of North African Arabic with rock music), says that these are his last memories of Bombay. The main characters leave for England and then move on to New York (where Rushdie himself moved when he came out of hiding). Rai proclaims New York the centre of the modern world while claiming that the USA is the world's bully. Rushdie's subject matter is celebrity, the 'buzz' that British journalism brought to influential New York publications. Rushdie and his main characters moving to New York was part of a process which was driven by the emergence of the United States as the world's main power and its entrepreneurial capitalism as the source of global liberalization. Significantly, to establish the fame and international credentials of its main characters, part of Kureishi's *The Buddha of Suburbia* also takes place in New York.

Writers of Pakistani origins in England range from those, such as Attia Hossain and Rushdie, who were left homeless by the Partition of India, to those such as Rukhsana Ahmad and Tariq Ali who came to England as wives or students, and those who, like Aamer Hussein, are residents while remaining Pakistanis or who, like Kamila Shamsie, use London as a place to write. Their work differs from those with one Pakistani parent such as Hanif Kureishi and the dramatist Ayub Khan-Din who were born in England. One reason for a body of writing by Pakistanis in England is that Pakistan has encouraged, at times demanded, the use of Urdu. For English-language users, life can be more comfortable in London than at home, especially as the cultured landed families of Islamic northern India have been replaced by Pakistani military, corrupt businessmen, and religious extremists. For some who left India for Pakistan where they felt or found themselves regarded as alien, England is a further stage of migration, part of what has become an international life.

Adam Zameenzad, who came to England in 1974, is another maker of highly imaginative stories. His novels combine postmodern irony, fragmentation, non-linear plots, and self-reflective playfulness, with a wide body of learning and what might be thought exotic settings, whether the Third World or Third Street in lower Manhattan. They range in location from Pakistan in *The Thirteenth House* (1987) and Africa in *My Friend Matt and Hena the Whore* (1988), to South America in *Love Bones and Water* (1989). *Cyrus, Cyrus* (1990) is international. *Gorgeous White Female: The Comic Adventures of a Demented Nonager* (1995) takes place in Italy, England, and New York. Zameenzad often writes of underdogs, the marginal, the rejected, those without means, the losers. Children are central to his fiction as main characters or as involved observers.

The Thirteenth House (1987), his brilliant first novel, is about Pakistan. Like all of Zameenzad's novels it is told through a complicated technique in which the narrator has an unusual relationship to the story and his own story takes over the focus of the novel. The main tale concerns Zahid, a lower-middle-class Pakistani office worker, a continual failure who gives lessons to children to earn extra money. Zahid rents a small house, the Thirteenth House of the novel's title—an imaginary sign of the zodiac for those who have undergone so much pain that they can no longer feel. Zahid becomes deluded by a holy man and his followers who eventually kill the narrator and take Zahid's money along with his daughter and pregnant wife. After being accused by the police of murder, Zahid is beaten and tortured until insane. In the novel the problems of marriage are metaphors for the problems of Pakistan. Zahid's belief in a holy man has its parallel in Pakistan's turning towards Islamic extremism to solve its problems. Zahid has become so much a believer that he does not understand that his wife is pregnant by the holy man.

My Friend Matt and Hena the Whore (1988) is set in a newly independent African state where the government is under siege by leftist guerrillas. Both sides terrorize, kill, and purchase weapons rather than feed the people. At the novel's conclusion the children climb over heaps of mutilated dead while four political factions quarrel. *Love Bones and Water* (1989) offers a strange tale about a dead, mutilated grey man brought back to life by a boy called Peter who passes him on to villagers who care for him. The village represents an older, more natural, if economically weak, world of peasants and rituals that is being destroyed by modern economics. The novel teases with an allegory in which the grey man is a version of Christ. The villagers have biblical names as do Peter and his uncle Paul. Under all the irony there is a message about the necessity of love.

The later novels are those of an internationalist obsessed with language and fabulation. There are few details of clothing, little interest in the psychology of relationships, or concern with individuals in depth. Language itself is foregrounded in the form of puns, verbal ironies, absurd comparisons, aggressive use of street or sexual turns of phrase, even boring rants. Zameenzad holds postcolonial ideas about the guilt of the West towards the Third World, but he also shows that the Third World consists of a bloodthirsty, raping rabble although the brutality of the poor has social and economic reasons.

The later novels can leave an impression that seriousness is absurd. There seems little reason why the stories take one direction rather than another; motivation or cause and effect are mocked by the characters being caricatures. *Cyrus, Cyrus* (1990) is an example of the joys and boredoms of postmodern fabulation. *Cyrus, Cyrus* is supposedly a confessional autobiography told to Zameenzad by Cyrus Cyrus after the latter has mysteriously disappeared from a British gaol where he was being held for multiple murders, including those of his own children. Like many of Zameenzad's fictions the story concerns one of the marginals of society, here an Indian untouchable latrine cleaner whose family become Christian converts. Cyrus (having no other name he repeats the one he has) is a product of a rape and regards himself unfortunate in every way, being dark-skinned, ugly, and having a birthmark supposedly a sign of the devil. A life of disasters drives him to Pakistan, back to India, to the USA, England, even Hell. At times the novel, like *Midnight's Children* or *Shame*, attaches the narrative to such public events as the secession of East Pakistan, its invasion by Pakistan, and Bangladesh's independence with Indian help, help which Zameedzad treats as political scheming. The story keeps being side-tracked by digressive fantasy in which myths and spiritual notions are literalized; Cyrus is eaten by and lives within a tiger which keeps reappearing to chase him after he has been liberated by another spiritual force.

Gorgeous White Female (1995) takes the reader to Venice, then England, before settling in Manhattan's East Village populated mostly, in this book, by panhandlers, the down and out, blacks, and gays. It is a book about losers and those who feel like them. The main character, Lahyayani Brendan Cenna, a 12-year-old, hates his Indian father, Raj, and is obsessively in love with his white, blue-eyed mother, Marilyn. Lahya thinks himself ugly because he is a 'black' male like 'dadso', and wants to become a white blue-eyed blonde like 'Mumsy'. Lahya, ironically, is transformed into an aged white female unable to walk in her high red heels. That the goddess Kali is supposed to be the narrator and sometimes addresses the reader adds to the purposeful artificiality and self-displaying inventiveness, along with the mockery of those who sacrifice life to such fantasies as western notions of beauty and Hollywoodish white America.

While Rushdie and Zameenzad could claim Indian literary sources, Ben Okri appeared to be working within African traditions, especially those associated with the Nigerian Wole Soyinka who wrote about contemporary politics within a setting of Yoruba mythology and the presence of spirits. Unlike Emecheta, a Nigerian who eventually became a British African writer, Okri lived mostly in England, but, because of a formative decade from the age of 9, he began as a Nigerian writer and for almost two decades continued to write of Africa. His first fiction was in the brutal realism then used to describe life in Lagos, but it soon became an expressionism in which the ugliness of reality results in the artist's imagination forming sickening images. *The Landscapes Within* (1981) shows how reality is conveyed through an expressionistic surrealism, a technique Okri learned from such writers as Amos Tutuola, Wole Soyinka, and Ayi Kwei Armah. His writing alludes to his models as sources of symbolism, to authenticize his perceptions and to make analogies. Okri, like Emecheta, transformed African literary models into new forms. Born of parents from two different tribes, Igbo and Urhobo, he adopted the literary manner and symbolism of a third, Yoruba, which he cross-pollinated with Wilson Harris's shape-shifting and Latin American magic realism. He used the imagery, literary traditions, and mythological world views of various African ethnic groups along with his readings in European and world literature.

Although his sentences are rich in poetic similes and symbols, Okri's tone and rhythm are flat and trance-like. He does not accept that there is one mode of being; there is no clear distinction between the living and the dead, or the imagined and the actual. He is concerned about how the past influences the present. His early novels *Flowers and Shadows* (1980) and *The Landscapes Within*, and the short stories of *Incidents at the Shrine* (1986) and *Stars of the New Curfew* (1988), show the brutality and injustice of contemporary Nigeria, including the horrors of the Nigerian civil war. Stories suggesting that the violence and corruption of modern Africa have their origins in traditional cults may be followed by stories of emotional purgation through initiation into traditions. Usually there is an attempted reconciliation.

In the early fiction the main character is a sensitive young man representative of the country's future who during his relationship with a woman discovers the brutality of his elders. The situation is Oedipal with love for a caring female challenging an older, violent male. The central themes are the lack of love and caring relationships in a society brutalized through the harshness needed to survive. The underlying causes have their origins in secret societies dominating others through fear and violence.

In Okri's poetry, such as the sequence *An African Elegy* (1992), he uses the convention from African oral poetry that 'We' is both personal and collective. Lack of communal morality is expressed in the novels through images of excrement, disease, and poverty, with spiritual disorder finding its physical counterpart in filth, stink, clogged sewage, electricity failures, and rotting bodies. While the predominant images are of an African wasteland of faeces, foul odours, and diseased, deformed, or murdered bodies, there is the hope that understanding will lead to a better future.

The Famished Road (1991) is about the recurring patterns of African mythology, history, and politics. The attempt to escape the pattern becomes symbolic of a history that must be resisted to live fully and improve Africa. Awarded the Booker Prize, *The Famished Road* made Okri an international star, and appeared a seeming successor to *Midnight's Children*, a lengthy 'Commonwealth' magic realist novel, concerned about the fate of former British colonies. Mythic, non-naturalistic, sprawling, moving rapidly between this and the spiritual world, set in an unnamed Africa that resembles Nigeria on the eve of independence, *The Famished Road* seems to comment on the politics of new nations on the verge of being born. There is a vicious Party of the Rich and a distrusted Party of the Poor, much personal and social corruption, and people brutalized in choosing sides. Okri is concerned with how Africa became what it is. The central story tells of Ma, Dad, and Azaro, a nuclear family unlike the extended families of Africa. Azaro the narrator is a spirit-child who in Nigerian belief is born, soon dies, and is later reborn and dies in continuing cycles. Wole Soyinka, from whom Okri inherited many of his images, had already transformed the mythology of born-again children into the equivalent of Hindu cycles of reincarnation. Azaro defies the other spirits to remain in this world and is aware of spirits who live alongside humans and interact with our world.

The Famished Road made use of African customs, had an African story, and while the political dimension was unclear beyond the grisly dishonest politics associated with Nigeria, the novel had the charm of a folk story with an amazing mixture of the real and spiritual worlds. *The Famished Road* also was a proclamation of the right of the artist to be a storyteller whose moods and fancy shaped the tale. While using a Yoruba tradition of fiction, Okri moved beyond the African literary market into the literary mainstream, appealing to the many readers of Rushdie and other magic realists.

While *The Famished Road* synthesizes aspects of African story-telling, the continual reimagining of the same characters and places in new ways is less the influence of Africa than of that consummate shape-shifter Wilson Harris. Harris's *Palace of the Peacock*, with its surreal revisioning of history and characters melting into each other and changing roles and significance, is Okri's main model. Instead of the mixture of realism and expressionism in the earlier novels, Okri now had a way to allow his imagination full play. Azaro is not only a spirit-child, he is also a storyteller, someone who keeps seeing visions that others do not. While a giant step beyond the realism of Okri's early fiction, the method became the endless making up of ghosts and spirits and their doings in *Songs of Enchantment* (1993). *Infinite Riches* (1998), the third part of *The Famished Road* trilogy, continues the story of Azaro's family, his friends, the conflict between the Party of the Rich and the Party of the Poor, the election campaign, and Madam Koto and her bar. The story takes place during the final weeks leading up to the withdrawal of the British and an election that will determine who rules the new nation. There are new elements here including some crude anti-colonial propaganda and caricature, almost thrown in as expected of a postcolonial writer, and the use of the Book of Revelations which will become characteristic of Okri's later writing.

Okri still had not faced the problem of what an author writes after using memories of the society known in youth. Between *Songs of Enchantment* and *Infinite Riches* Okri wrote two novels showing contrasting directions towards which he was attracted. *Astonishing the Gods* (1995) has few concrete events, places, or people and allegorizes how the meeting of cultures in colonialism brings about a fall from innocence and a journey of discovery. Invisible because his contented peasant family was unnoticed, a boy grows up without conflicts until he attends school, learns from others of his invisibility, and discovers he is not part of history. He flees overseas and learns the ways of the world. After seven years he arrives at a strange port (the echoes of V. S. Naipaul's *The Enigma of Arrival* seem intended) where he chooses to be stranded. In this city with its avenue of mirrors he finds transcendence and suffering and feels he is dissolving into light and peace. Many visions follow with such messages as 'Things are what they are. That is their power . . . If they meant something they would be less . . . What you see is what you are, or what you will become' (p. 11). The wayfarer sees majestic sights, crosses strange bridges, and reaches the city of the Invisibles where he hears strange harmonies. A guide leaves him alone before the gates of a city. When he cannot read the language of a scroll, a new guide appears and he enters. New mysteries keeps occurring until at the conclusion the boy 'who had left home in search of the secret of visibility . . . found a higher invisibility, the invisibility of the blessed' (p. 159). This is the least compelling of Okri's versions of life as a journey towards enlightenment.

Dangerous Love (1996) returns to the Nigeria of Okri's earlier writings. While it has visionary passages, it is a novel of Lagos in all its stains, smells, excrement, arguments, and violence. A major strand concerns a young woman unwillingly married by her family to a brutal older man and her love of a young painter who lives in the same compound with his drunken violent father. After a beating the woman runs away from her husband and returning home she is mistakenly killed as part of an intervillage quarrel. In an example of how history becomes lies, she is said to have been a willing martyr in the cause of peace. The only gain is that the young man learns how to make paintings about his dead love without detailing her features. *Dangerous Love* continues Okri's themes of an Africa, particularly Nigeria, which has long suffered from its secret cults, selfish leaders, tribalism, violence, and corrupt, inefficient administrations. At one point a character alludes to Hemingway in speaking of his friends as a doomed generation. A green scumpool is often mentioned as the subject of a painting made by Omovo, the young man who is the main character in the novel. Omovo alludes to the original model for Okri's technique, Armah's Ghanaian novel *The Beautyful Ones Are Not Yet Born*, a title which Omovo thinks might be appropriate for one of his paintings. *Dangerous Love* is concerned with the art of the

African novel, its models, and Okri's own sources. In a note at the end of the book Okri mentions that *Dangerous Love* is a major revision of *The Landscapes Within*, written when he was 21 and Nigeria was still fresh to him, a novel which has remained central to his vision. It could be argued that the success of *A Famished Road* trapped Okri into repeating a formula. *In Arcadia* (2002), in which a British film crew journeys to Paris to explain what they understand by happiness, seems an attempt at renewal. It once more shows how Harris's *Palace of the Peacock* continued to haunt writers as a model for social, cultural, and creative revisioning. Here a TV crew undertakes a mysterious journey from the hell of their individual lives towards an imagined ideal, a world felt to exist within memory.

Another writer influenced by Wilson Harris's work was the Trinidadian Faustin Charles (b. 1938). In 1962 Charles emigrated to England where he joined the literary scene as a poet, editor, storyteller, and lecturer on Caribbean history and culture. He was associated with the Caribbean Artists Movement and wrote several poetry chapbooks before Bogle L'Ouverture published his novel *Signposts of the Jumbie* (1981) and verse *Days and Nights in the Magic Forest* (1986). Charles's politics are in his subject matter and use of language. In *Signposts*, written in heavy dialect, a teenager asks an Obeah-man to help find the parents he never knew. Instead of finding his roots in the ways expected, he sees conflicting images from many times. If it is impossible to retrieve the past, the youth finds he can create his own modern version in Carnival with its symbolic masks. In a final twist we learn that the allegory we read is a tale told to children in a rural village. The titles, like Charles's second novel, *The Black Magic Man of Brixton* (1985) and the anthology he edited, *Under the Storyteller's Spell* (1989), show how Harris's mysticism and refusal to keep to the rules of realism easily become tales for children. Charles is a storyteller fascinated by magic, animals, and rural life. He contributes West Indian dialect and appropriate settings, such as the Caribbean, to the moralized animal tale, and keeps the Caribbean cultural tradition alive in England.

Caryl Phillips, David Dabydeen, and the poet Fred D'Aguiar used fragmented, polyphonic narratives to characterize their identities as British West Indians. They were transitional between the immigrants and the black British in having been born or lived in England most of their lives while re-establishing connections to the West Indies. Their work is concerned with representation, race, and history while showing how a diaspora continues to feel uprooted. Phillips has said that home is where you want to be buried and, alluding to the notions of the Black Atlantic, he wishes to be buried in the Atlantic between England, Africa, and America.

While Caryl Phillips, David Dabydeen, and Fred D'Aguiar felt outsiders because of the humiliations they faced when young, their sense of identity was strengthened by the black consciousness and radicalism of the 1970s. They are graduates of British universities where their study of English included the analysis of power in terms of race, gender, sexuality, and class, to which they brought a strong sense of the relationship between dominance, exploitation, slavery, and prejudice. They are concerned with analysing representations of the past. In *Caribbean Literature in English* (1999) Louis James treats the writers together when discussing 'African (re)possession'. After showing how the eighteenth-century linguistic texture of Phillips's *Cambridge* complicates interpretation, James contrasts Dabydeen's long poem 'Turner' with D'Aguiar's novel *Feeding the Ghosts*. Dabydeen notes how in J. M. W. Turner's picture *Slavers Throwing Overboard the Dead and the Dying* the slaves are subordinate, marginalized, to the central drama of the hurricane and saving the ship. The poet tries to feel as one with a shackled slave, but the perspective of the painting makes this impossible; he has himself become shackled by the painter. D'Aguiar's *Feeding the Ghosts* (1997) replies by telling of a female slave who manages to hang on to the ship after being tossed overboard. The novel imagines her experience (which Dabydeen says he cannot do) caught between life and death, reality and dream, and in itself shows it is possible to redeem black history through reimagining. Such reimagining is Wilson Harris's influence on British West Indian writers.

Dabydeen's poem 'Turner' is an example of the reinterpretation of the past by unpacking its technique as well as its symbols. Turner's romantic scene is read in terms of capitalism's attempt to impose itself on nature through slavery and plantations, the resulting slavery and devaluation of African life, and the precariousness of such an economic and social order. The painter's placing of the figures and their importance has ideological significance. Form is not neutral but continues to influence how the future will read the painting, an influence Dabydeen as poet feels although he attempts to imagine himself as one of the marginalized slaves. In attempting to create a usable black past, writers researched records of the slave trade and wrote novels in which slaves and the situations they inhabit are more complicated than the usual outline of capture in Africa, the Middle Passage, torturous work and death in the Americas. Many novels rewrite this story to give slaves personal histories and make them agents rather than victims.

Caryl Phillips often writes about purity, outsiders, and those like Othello who compromise. Like V. S. Naipaul he feels that those made outsiders by history or choice are often harmed. It is necessary for blacks to be conscious of their blackness and to distrust whites, but being limited to racial identity is impoverishing and false. His first novel *The Final Passage* (1985), about his parents and the Windrush generation, was followed by *State of Independence* (1986), about someone returning twenty years later to a West Indian island, where he is distrusted as alien. *The European Tribe* (1987) tells of Phillips's years as one of the few blacks at Cambridge University, his trip to the United States where he discovered black American writing, and travel across Europe where he found people clannish and unwelcoming. Phillips says blacks are more comfortable among themselves and mentions feelings of affinity with Jews as another victimized minority.

With *Higher Ground* (1989) his writing changed from its former linear plots and single voice to polyphonic writing with several voices and narrative strands, and the kind of fragmentation and self-conscious storytelling associated with postmodernism. As in most of his later writing, the African slave trade is the starting point for what are tales of the diaspora to which there is a white, usually female or Jewish, counterpart. Here the first story is the voice of an African who works for the slave traders, but falling in love with a trader's African woman defies his employers and is himself made a slave. The second narrative concerns another black rebel whose defiance of whites is also self-defeating. A radicalized criminal of the 1960s writes letters which become increasingly shrill and psychotic as his mental condition deteriorates. Both stories show dangers to blacks living among whites. People form clans and either reject outsiders or use them until a time they can be destroyed. The third story is of a Polish Jew in England during the 1950s who also mentally deteriorates in a land where she is uncertain whether she is Irene or Irina. Each story transforms a well-known literary kind, such as the older slave narratives or black radical criminal autobiographies of the 1960s. Phillips, like D'Aguiar and Dabydeen, shares the post-modern taste for rewriting along with a post-imperial revisioning of the literature of the past. While Phillips remaps the African diaspora he avoids the sentimentality of back to Africanism and black essentialism. In a world of tribes any outsider is endangered and should be wary especially of the dangers that come with being in love.

Cambridge (1991) re-examines through its central character the history and identity of those Africans who were among the first black writers in England. Imitating eighteenth-century prose in such works as *The Interesting Narrative of the Life of Olaudah Equiano* (1789), Phillips tells of an African who is enslaved, converted to Christianity, and sent from England to Africa as a missionary in a nearly hopeless situation in which he becomes financially and morally isolated from his sponsors. He is once more enslaved and sent to a West Indian plantation where the brutal overseer, refusing to accept Cambridge's Christianity, sexually takes his common-law wife. After being struck by the overseer, Cambridge kills him during the struggle and is himself hanged. The stiff manner of the eighteenth-century style contributes to the ambiguity about Cambridge's actions: was the killing accidental, does he repent, or are his prayers lamentations for his condition? His many changes of name throughout his life parallel the many different situations in which he finds himself and the many layers of his identity.

Contrasted to Cambridge is Emily Cartwright, an Englishwoman whose father is absentee owner of the plantation. A sense of duty drives her to the West Indies where she is so overcome by the differences and isolated as an English lady that she becomes a virtual prisoner of the overseer who cheats her father. Rather than being able to help the slaves, she is one of several white women in Phillips's novels who become outsiders and victims. She keeps a diary written in a sentimental style of affected language and exaggerated sensibility.

Crossing the River (1993) also begins in the eighteenth century when an African sells his three children to a slave trader. The various voices and stories represent the father's memories and lamentation for his actions two hundred and fifty years later, along with the stories of his children. One is emancipated and returns from England to Africa to proclaim the white man's civilization and religion, but is abandoned by his sponsor, a white homosexual who wished to get rid of the evidence of his guilt. The story of the second son is told by an Englishwoman who during the Second World War was the lover of a black American soldier and had a child by him, whom, under social pressure, she abandons. Like the Africans of the diaspora, she has become an outsider. The 'river' of the title is both the Middle Passage and a decision which changes a person's life.

The Nature of Blood (1997) returns to the similar experience of the Jews and Blacks in the two Venice chapters of *The European Tribe*. The novel begins in Cyprus towards the end of the Second World War, when Jewish refugees were turned away from Palestine by the British. It ends in Israel with a 'hero' who, having left his wife and child in the United States so he can fight for a homeland, is decades later ageing and lonely. This is a book about memories, desire, history, ethnicity, isolation, and imagining 'home'. The literary imitations, interruptions of the fictional frame, and inter-weaving of stories are Brechtian in breaking uncritical involvement with the characters to aid objective analysis and judgement. A story about a Jewish family destroyed by the Nazis is mirrored by a retelling of *Othello* and the history of the Jews of fifteenth-century Portobuffole (who fleeing persecution in Germany were allowed to settle near Venice and once more victimized, a background of *The Merchant of Venice*), a portrait of refugees becoming Hagannah soldiers, and Ethiopians discriminated against in Israel.

Phillips shows history's contradictions: the more successful strangers are in rising in society and becoming assimilated, the more likely there will be resentment and violence. While Jews were needed in Venice to lend money, the people resented and the Church wanted to destroy them. The acculturated German Jews remained a people without a home whom the Nazis wanted to destroy. The Jews in Israel, however, brought with them European racism in their treat-ment of the Ethiopians. While showing how groups treat those felt to be alien, and how social hierarchies use and keep power, *The Nature of Blood* recognizes the force of loneliness, and the need for love and belonging. Such emotions energize life but can be self-destructive. Othello's isolation and loneliness in Venice drive him towards the dangers represented by Desdemona and hope of assimilation. Men rise in society by gaining the love of women towards whom they later behave badly and, like Othello, destroy.

While the slave trade uprooted many from Africa and stranded them abroad, Phillips does not believe it possible to return to Africa nor for the diasporan black to be assimilated in white society. He is interested in individuals and aware that others are in a similar predicament to those of African descent. *The Atlantic Sound* (2000) is a travel book concerned with the remembrance of the slave trade. It retraces the route of the ships from Europe to Africa to the New World. Phillips visits Liverpool to see how the city, once the largest port in England devoted to the slave trade, recalls its past and is struck by the lack of British urban planning and the grim faces of the inhabitants. His guide, a local black radical, blames everything on Jews and says that the Liverpool blacks, with their long history in the city even before the slave trade, resent newer immigrants and recent African refugees. Phillips travels to Ghana where the slave trade is only remembered to attract black Americans and other tourists: he is told that the upkeep of the historical records should be paid by those of the diaspora, 'your' people, not Africans. So much for black unity. Phillips then visits Charleston, once the largest American port for the importation of slaves. His subject is a white judge from one of the old Caroline family who had a role in gaining African-American voting rights. As a result he and his wife were ostracized by local whites and even some African-Americans avoided them. A conclusion tells of African-Americans who live in Israel and who believe that Africans were the original Jews although they are culturally black Americans.

The title of *A New World Order: Selected Essays* (2001) refers to the supposedly contemporary condition of having roots in several places but not being at home in any, a condition exemplified in Phillips's autobiographical introduction with its rapid shifts of scene between Africa, New York, St Kitts, and Leeds. Changes in location change little as modern communications, culture, and economics are transnational. The essays are about black literature and the complications of being 'black'. Some essays look at the ways African-American culture has been harmed by racial obsession. A discussion of the experience of West Indian immigrants sharply skewers George Orwell's famous essay 'England, Your England' with its idealization of the British character. Phillips notes that the riots of the 1970s and early 1980s took place in what were once slaving ports, cities which had an unacknowledged history of racial discontents. While Thatcher's campaign slogan 'Labour says he's black, Tories say he is British' took white middle-class behaviour as the norm, it transformed racial exclusion into social and economic inclusion. Soon there were black members of Parliament, black faces on television and national sports teams, while black music and fashion became part of style. Phillips observes that multiculturalism cannot be different cultures living side by side. 'A truly multicultural society is one which is composed of multicultural individuals; people who are able to synthesize different worlds in one body and to live comfortably with these different worlds' (*New World Order*, p. 279).

David Dabydeen is one of those who, having read postcolonial theory and sociology, saw race, class, and gender as ways to analyse society and rewrite western history and its stereotypes. Another concern is the relationship of the Asian Indian to being 'black', a question raised by the African-Caribbean tyranny that drove many from Guyana, and the tensions between Asians and blacks in England. Have they enough shared history for their stories to intertwine? Although Dabydeen's parentage was primarily Indian, there were also some African connections. In Guyana he was aware of the bloody violence between those of African and Indian stock as politics became racially polarized. Throughout his writing there is a tension between being, socially, a 'Black West Indian' and his interest in his Indian origins. In England, as seen in his first novel, *The Intended* (1991), he became a 'Paki' and 'black' to taunting schoolboys although he was a South Asian West Indian and conscious of his difference from most of the Asians and African-Caribbeans he knew. The novel itself in theme, language, and form is intended to avoid assimilation into the white British canon and simplistic ethnic positions by recalling the Oxford-bound narrator's past in Guyana and at school in England among other immigrant children as well as his fantasy of becoming white. 'The Intended' is an idealized white woman, the white muse, to whom the narrator hopes to elevate himself in contrast to his 'black' past.

The 'black' alliance in England during the 1970s between Indians and West Indians influenced Dabydeen's creative writing and scholarship. His contribution to the recovery of black history includes *Hogarth's Blacks: Images of Blacks in Eighteenth Century English Art* (1985), and the editing of *The Black Presence in English Literature* (1983) and *Early Black Writers in Britain* (1993). Although an Indian in Guyana and a black in England, Dabydeen's work reveals contradictions between such identities and a desire to subvert them. Like many West Indians, Selvon for example, he will complain of racial discrimination while mocking clichéd victimization and liberal correctness. One of Dabydeen's strengths has been the use of amusing irony, and self-conscious literary art along with the topics and conventions of postcolonial literature. *Slave Song* (1984) is black West Indian dialect poetry modelled on medieval English lyrics. The interplay between the two, while fun for the knowing, brings out similarities; the desires, complaints, and fears of both the West Indian and the English peasant are part of a shared humanity and the result of repressive social structures and the power of injustice in both societies. Dabydeen and D'Aguiar were aware of other British writers exploring regional dialects in poetry, especially of Tony Harrison's remaking of tradition by translating the medieval mystery plays into modern Yorkshire dialect.

Dabydeen undermines the social realism of dialect in *Slave Song* by treating the volume as an academic edition with notes and glossary. Many of the poems are intended as replies to or parodies of previous British literature and its conventions as when, in 'Guyana Pastoral', the description of the dead raped girl evokes symbolism from the aubade. Having written from the perspective of a black West Indian in *Slave Song*, Dabydeen writes as an Indian in *Coolie Odyssey* (1988). The two dialects are different. 'Coolie Odyssey' begins in Swiftian pastiche with 'Now that peasantry is in vogue | Poetry bubbles from peat bogs . . . coughed up in grates North or North East' as a reason to 'hymn' his own 'wreck'. The volume tells of the journey of peasants from India to Guyana and of their children to England. The 'slave' and 'coolie' represent the two sides of the

West Indies that came together for a time as 'black' in England. Dabydeen's early work can suffer from manipulating the symbolism that had become commonplace to academic studies of postcolonial literature. He wants to show someone caught between English and two Guyanese cultures, a broken self revealed through broken language and fragmented form.

A reliance on postcolonial theory and previous texts informs *Disappearance* (1993), a novel set in an archetypical English village where a young Guyanese engineer is being employed to stop the ravages of the sea against the land. The symbolism of the outsider reclaiming the English heritage as well as the setting and some names allude to V. S. Naipaul's *The Enigma of Arrival*, another novel about an outsider learning to understand the ways of a village. What at first seems in Dabydeen's novel peaceful and settled proves to have a history of deception, corruption, and deviance, as well as the violence of empire abroad. Besides parallels to Conrad's *Heart of Darkness* there are echoes of Wilson Harris's early novels: parallels are suggested between the village and Guyana, the narrator's battle against the sea having similarities to engineering the rivers and falls in Guyana. As the narrator comes to see England as more complex than stereotypical, so his sense of history is revised and there is the fusion and revisioning of peoples that Harris's novels intend.

The Counting House (1996), like novels by Caryl Phillips and Fred D'Aguiar, imagines from the few historical details that have survived a history of the nameless. A list, a British biscuit tin, and a drawing of Rama remain of the nineteenth-century Asian Indian presence at Plantation Albion, British Guiana. The novel follows Rohini and Vidia from their rebellion against impoverished, unchanging Hindu India to contact between the indentured Indians and freed blacks in Guiana and the tragedies caused by two strong-willed women. Sexual desire and sexual power drive the economic, political, and social system. The story can be read as an allegory of the colonial plantation system, of how international capitalism disrupted societies while bringing the world's people together, of the racial divisions of Guyana, and of the problematics of 'black' in black British.

Although each of his novels concern representation, notions of Otherness, and resistance through rewriting canonical texts,

Dabydeen's sense of humour complicates his fiction. *A Harlot's Progress* (1999) begins in the late 1760s when Mr Pringle of the Committee for the Abolition of Slavery has tracked down 'Mungo', supposedly the oldest Negro in London, who three decades earlier was famous through William Hogarth's *A Harlot's Progress* prints as a whore's servant and accomplice. Now the Abolitionists are remaking the Negro as a victim of slavery saved by Christianity, and need Mungo to provide personal details to a story already outlined, beginning with memories of Africa, the slave ship, labour on a West Indian plantation, being taken to England, servant to a Lord, purchase by a Jew, servant to a prostitute, and 'redemption' by the Abolitionists. Pringle's fiction is intended as Mungo's autobiography.

Mungo resents how representations of his life are part of a cultural war among whites, but he needs the money that Pringle pays. Mungo is a slave of the white man's economics, puritanism, and desire, associated in the novel with perverse sexuality, figuratively and often literally buggering the Negro due to attraction, the wish to dominate, and the excitement of guilt. Mungo attempts to free himself from such demands by imagining other histories of a fantastic kind. They are a parody history of Otherness, comprising desire, the grotesque, the fantastic, irony, and the sardonic. The prose often pastiches conventions of eighteenth-century fiction and art. While contributing to the rescue of black eighteenth-century England from the formerly neglected margins of social and cultural history, Dabydeen is concerned with the poor, the servants, the whore, and the Jew, their relationships and how society treats them. He does not make minorities or the poor more moral or attractive than their stereotypical representations, but he gives them complex characters and lives, and sees them as humiliated and kept dominated through the ways they need to survive.

A Harlot's Progress, like most of Dabydeen's writings, concerns sexuality in its many forms. Whether beaten, sodomized, bought, sold, evangelized, or fantasized, there is always desire, fear, attraction, love, sensuality, passion; that is life. Imagining the erotic is also the life of a writer; Dabydeen as author is another Mungo. The characters Mungo creates want to be treated in an idealized fashion, which, while amusing, expresses the competing demands made on an author. Dabydeen implies, as Derek Walcott has often said, that taken from Africa the African has lost his original name and cultural memories. He becomes a new man, a mixture of picaro and existentialist. Instead of endlessly lamenting, celebrate the paradoxical liberation that resulted from the slave trade in a diaspora of interesting and exciting lives in other lands. While this is a book claiming England's place in the Black Atlantic, Dabydeen is as attuned to the history of Indian indenture as the Middle Passage. Mungo's apparently made-up African language is a version of Hindi; images of Christ are described as a blue god because Dabydeen has Shiva in mind. *A Harlot's Progress* is heir of Wilson Harris's *The Guyanese Quartet* with its role-changing, ever-renewing spirits of the past revisioning history. They, however, have discovered sexuality and that life can be fun.

After *Midnight's Children* British publishers were increasingly likely to accept manuscripts about abroad from novelists with non-British names. Kazuo Ishiguro and Timothy Mo were part of the new generation writing about large international events. Although Mo and Ishiguro were often mentioned together because of their Asian names, they had different backgrounds, Mo being a product of a racially mixed marriage while Ishiguro's parents settled in England because of the father's job. Whereas Mo has used his connection with the Orient as the basis for writing novels about Asians, Ishiguro has denied there is anything specifically Japanese about his work, despite his first two novels being mostly set in Japan and interviews revealing an awareness of Japanese literature and cinema. That such sources have substituted for direct experience may explain his attraction towards pastiche. Whereas other writers, such as Caryl Phillips, Dabydeen, and A. S. Byatt, have imitated older styles, Ishiguro subtly assumes the manners of Japanese films, British interwar popular fiction, and other identifiable artistic kinds, but without calling attention to the parody the way postmodern literature does. His choice of this technique is appropriate to the narrator and role of memory in his fiction. There is another radical difference between Ishiguro and Mo. Starting with *Remains of the Day*, Ishiguro's central character is white British. Selvon and Dhondy wrote about black lives in England, Mo wrote a novel about Chinese immigrants in England, but Ishiguro created a convincing portrait of the British and their society in *Remains of the Day*, and in *The Unconsoled* of a famous English pianist in Europe.

Although Ishiguro has mentioned Chekhov's influence on the way his novels seem plotless and without action, the manner of his characters keeping a calm surface during emotional turmoil seems more Japanese than western as does how his characters speak in roundabout ways, often suppressing the truth to save face. Among Ishiguro's earliest publications were three stories in Faber's anthology *Introduction 7* (1981). Each story uses a monologue to reveal more about the speaker than that person intends. In each, the precise facts of what happened are not clear as the reader can only piece together what has been said by seeing through the narration to a different story. 'A Strange and Sometime Sadness' seems like a trial run for *A Pale View of Hills*. It is told by a Japanese woman who came to England after the Second World War and who is estranged from her daughter Yasuko. Yasuko is named after the mother's friend who died in the atom bomb attack on Nagasaki, an attack from which the narrator escaped without any harm. This claim should make the reader wary of the truth of the narrator, a wariness that should extend to the tale she tells of not being jealous of her friend's boyfriend and of her friend's willingness to give up marriage to take care of her father. We look through trick perspectives on what is likely to be disguised jealousy along with anger by the narrator at her own daughter leaving her alone in old age. Ishiguro often uses this technique of narrators falsifying history and inventing parallel stories to save themselves from shame or as a way of implying criticism. There is also displaced violence in that the narrator's Japanese acquaintances are killed by the bomb while she escapes untouched. It is as if she wanted to hurt her daughter the way the people in her memories die.

Ishiguro's novels refine such narrative techniques. He usually writes about false or misleading memories, indicating how people displace emotions and transform the past for their own benefit. His fiction concerns angry relations between children and their parents, betrayal by close friends. Characters are isolated by personality, migration, culture, or career. A theme of his early novels is the contrast between older Japanese culture and the modern westernized world of individualism and self-centredness. While looking critically at Japanese culture he is interested in its complexities and like the magic realists he associates the personal with the national. His first two novels treat of the effect on individuals of Japan's defeat in the Second World War. As the world changes, his narrators are now in the wrong, even the wrong place. There is also generational conflict as the young regard the old as guilty. There is a self-reflective element as the narrator may be an artist (such as a painter or pianist) or someone seeking the truth about the past, such as the detective in *When We Were Orphans* (2000). Most of the novels have some relationship to the Second World War. Two have to do with Japan, one with those who were pro-Fascist in England. Although the themes remain similar, Ishiguro has experimented with the form and technique by moving from the melancholy understatement of his first novels to the Kafkaesque humour of *The Unconsoled*, which, like fragments of a dream, avoids any finality.

A Pale View of Hills (1982) consists of the memories of Etsuko, a Japanese widow who often recalls Nagasaki during the American occupation after the war, when an older generation of nationalists refused to accept that the young rejected unthinking obedience and patriotism. If the old order is tyrannical and unrepentant, the younger generation is selfish. The choice seems to be between the living death of the past, which provides protection and guidance, and the new American democratic way of opportunities and insecurity. Etsuko is in England and her memories seem self-excuses especially in relation to her estranged daughter.

While *An Artist of the Floating World* (1986) appears Japanese in its economy and selection of detail, the narrator's indirect ways of telling and the effect are similar to the contradictions produced by the unreliable narrators of other modern novels. The title alludes to the Japanese painting genre *ukiyo-e* (floating world). The novel tells of a Japanese master painter, of whom the narrator was a disciple, who captured in his work the fleeting, changing pleasures of life. The narrator, by contrast, rejected such hedonism, and became a follower of the nationalist movement, painting propaganda in a heroic, patriotic style, as a result of which he became prominent and wealthy. He betrayed his friends, and after the war he is unrepentant and shunned. Whereas many of his nationalist acquaintances commit suicide as a form of apology to society, he pretends to be an old fool, but this is a protective mask which allows him first to avoid, then adapt to, the attitudes of post-war society. Eventually he indicates his sorrow for his past behaviour in such a way as to lose nothing.

The novel reflects Japanese culture during half a century, from the supposed decadence of the early 1900s through the nationalism of the thirties to the Americanized society of the post-war years. The theme of change is expressed throughout the novel in descriptions of the growth and decay of various urban areas, changes in painting and building styles, as well as in the career and attitudes of the narrator. The babbling old painter is revealed as a cunning national-ist who adjusts his manner (if not his views) to a new age. He is also an Artist of the Floating World, someone who in his own way has enjoyed the pleasures of his time. At the end of the novel the narrator is waiting for Japan to recover from its humiliating defeat.

Each of Ishiguro's novels evolves from the concerns of his first. There is an exiled or alienated narrator recalling his or her past in a manner which conceals part of the truth and which the reader suspects is a way to make shame or guilt acceptable. While Ishiguro plants clues the story is incomplete, fragmentary, and the ending unresolved, although the telling proves consolation to the narrator. Usually there is loss of face, a coming down in the world, and an attempt to recover from humiliation. It is seldom clear what is loss of memory, self-deception, or lying. As he moves from the melancholy understatement of his first two novels to the Kafkaesque humour of the lengthy *The Unconsoled* (1995), Ishiguro develops an under-stated flat style for his unreliable narrators as well as ways of organizing his fiction by themes rather than through the unfolding action that is usually thought of as plot. He occupies a middle ground between the realism that dominated British fiction in earlier decades and the fanciful inventions of Rushdie or Julian Barnes. His novels are imitations of stereotypes, more pastiche than realism. The first two novels seem realistic but besides the labyrinth created by the characters' telling of the stories, they are also the Japan of movies, of popular mythology, in which deviousness avoids conflict and shame. *Remains of the Day* participates in postmodern fashion for pastiche writing about the past in the manner of the past, perhaps best known from A. S. Byatt's *Possession*.

Stevens, the elderly English butler in Ishiguro's third novel, *The Remains of the Day* (1989), speaks in a tortuous, stiff, formal style while defending his former employer, an English lord who worked to appease the Nazis and after the war was in disgrace. Like Ono, the artist of *An Artist of the Floating World*, who misjudged his loyalties in pre-war Japan, and who finds that history will not forgive him, Stevens tries to rewrite history. The butler and England of *Remains of the Day* are imitations of a mythic past when the nation was run by those who owned great country houses and were served by devoted employees willing to forsake any other life for the privilege of doing their duty. With a few twists it could be a novel by Evelyn Waugh, or even P. G. Wodehouse. Such pastiche is also criticism. The social order it seems to celebrate is shown to depend on repression and exploitation. In doing what he perceives as his duty Stevens is a failure as a human being, as brought out by how he treats his father and a woman who is attracted to him. That the grand house is now owned by an American has a similar significance to the West Indian narrator of *The Enigma of Arrival* building his house in the English countryside by demolishing several cottages. England is being taken over by Others: Americans and immigrant people of colour.

The Unconsoled imitates the manner of dreams and Central European symbolism in which what seems incongruous and surreal implies a hidden story. This is a novel about an artist, a concert pianist, in which hidden memories of a failed and denied past, especially a family past, unwelcomely intrude upon the present. In a further development of the unreliable narrators of the previous novels, it is not clear who is the narrator or dreamer. In these novels what is said about others or even the landscape carries more importance than is at first obvious. The narrators are people with an above-ordinary sense of duty and ambition who retell their lives in such a way as to give themselves dignity. The novels need to be thought about and read again to see what has been hidden and to piece the narrator's stories together into the story behind the tale. That the stories have some connection to the author's own relationship to Japan and his parents seems likely, but like many dreams and memories of the past the connection is unstable, perhaps at times misleading, or uncomfortable.

Hargurchet Singh Bhabra (1955–2000), a Bombay-born Indian raised in Leeds and London and educated at Reigate Grammar School and Trinity College, Oxford, had a successful career in the City, then in 1984 followed his family to Canada, where he wrote international thrillers. His brilliant *Gestures* (1986), published by Michael Joseph, was awarded the Betty Trask First Novel and the new Fulbright–Raymond Chandler prize. It was followed by four thrillers written under the name A. M. Kabal, *The Adversary* (1986), *Bad Money* (1987), *Union Station* (1987), and *The Cull* (1988), and, one written as John Ford, *Zero Yield* (1990). As H. S. Bhabra he also wrote another serious novel, *Peru* (1988). In 1989, he moved to the USA with the hope of becoming a scriptwriter. He was arrested while climbing the Golden Gate Bridge in San Francisco; afterwards he was a television interviewer in Toronto, became increasingly eccentric, and committed suicide.

Gestures contrasts those who hold power with the humane liberals who, from moral scruples, do not act when they could influence society. While Bhabra valorizes the individual, the liberal spirit, the morally informed over the realist, the organization, and the rich, the former fail or are killed while the latter survive, remain in power, and control the world from behind the scenes. The world is essentially corrupt and its amorality cannot be changed. Like Caryl Phillips and Dabydeen, Bhabra has used Jews as representative outsiders. The industrialist in *Gestures* has a Nietzschean will to power, the same will to be master that drove Fascism, while Manet is Jewish in his scruples, his continual reference to a moral and religious tradition in which he does not believe. He represents Europe at its best, as the industrialist represents Europe at its worst.

In writing about Jews and other minorities Bhabra could write for a broad readership without being limited to matters of race. In examining the role of finance in politics, his novels are also, however, about empires and colonialism. The consul in Venice

wrote the standard work on the effects of the crusades on eastern Mediterranean trade . . . instead of their being holy wars, but Howard was the first person to examine their economic basis and effects . . . I suppose at the time people didn't want to be reminded that missionaries and the white man's burden were only aspects of empire. Howard might as well

have called his book *Trade Follows the Flag, or Stealing from the Darkies.*
Right book, wrong time. (p. 61)

Nations and individuals seek their self-interest. Only those with
riches are free and even the rich will be sacrificed by nations in their
own interests unless so powerful as to be necessary.

While such characters as Manet self-destructively follow moral
values, others live cautiously by establishment rules and climb the
ladder of success. They may admire the brave, but they know that
organizations are to be obeyed. In the hierarchy of survival and
power, however, the super-rich, the international financier, outranks
the organization and nation. Ultimately everything depends on the
power of money and who controls the money. Bhabra often refers to
the way the Nazis treated Jews and how those who profited from
Jewish extermination camps escaped punishment after the Second
World War. The confiscation of Jewish property, the enslavement of
Jews in labour camps, their extermination, and the unwillingness of
the victors after the war to punish those responsible are Bhabra's
representation of the economic exploitation and enslavement of
others.

His novels share the obsession of international thrillers that
history is a conspiracy of the rich and powerful. In *The Adversary* the
archaeologist Chas Winterton is a self-exiled desert rat in Egypt,
cataloguing the library of a minor Coptic monastery while seeking
a great discovery that will bring him fame and a triumphant university professorship. After discovering a letter proving that the
Copts, not the Roman Catholics, are St Peter's heirs, Winterton and
the letter are hunted by a psychotic sadist priest from Rome, the CIA,
David Medina, and Medina's beautiful sadistic female bodyguard.
Medina, a fabulously rich American financier, funds Islamic fundamentalists since turmoil gives Medina more control in buying,
murdering, and manipulating others. The priest belongs to a secret
group operating from the Vatican since the Inquisition. Typical of
Bhabra is the isolation of the main character, the exotic scholarship,
the international cast, the complexity of plot, the sudden reversals in
relationships, the assumption that behind every story is another and
another.

The years Bhabra worked in the City as a financial consultant left its mark in his view of human nature. *Bad Money*, based on Sir Thomas Gresham's Law that 'Bad money drives out good', concerns competing and co-operating Russian, American, and Vatican criminal and financial empires. They have the power against which the individual can only offer foolish, romantic, moral resistance. The novel starts with four murders in different parts of the world that are eventually found to be linked to a complex money-laundering scheme. While such popular fiction is disappointing in comparison to *Gestures*, it shares a vision of the international power of money and organizations, a power which although evil and corrupting is a force of life and the basis of social hierarchies.

East Africans and Arabs

The increasing internationalization of England's literature can be seen by its writers from East Africa and the Arab world. During the 1980s Ahdaf Soueif began publishing autobiographical fiction concerning the cultural conflicts of an Egyptian woman educated in English and living in England, while in the late 1980s two writers from Arabized East Africa began publishing novels. Abdulrazak Gurnah found his way to England after the dominant elite was overthrown by non-Arab Africans in Zanzibar. By contrast, Jamal Mahjoub was born in England. Soon there were other writers from the Arab world. Leila Aboulela, born in Cairo (1964) of Egyptian and Sudanese parents, was brought up and educated in the Sudan where she graduated with a degree in economics at the University of Khartoum, then came to England to study statistics. She wrote a novel and a book of short stories while living in Scotland, before following her husband abroad. 'The Museum' was awarded the Caine Prize in 2000 for African short stories. Tony Hanania, author of *Homesick* (1997), *Unreal City* (1999), and *Eros Island* (2000), all published by Bloomsbury, was born (1964) in Lebanon, educated at Winchester and later at the Warburg Institute, and worked for Sotheby's in Madrid and the Tate Gallery. His first novel was based on his years in an English boarding school during the Lebanese civil war.

Whereas Souief is critical of European imperialism, and Aboulela of western culture, Mahjoub seems alienated from both England and the Sudan, while Gurnah is troubled by both East Africa's Arab past and the black nationalism that replaced it. Gurnah has objected to studies of Commonwealth and postcolonial literatures being concerned with the relationship of Europe to the colonized whereas most of the world has had a long complex multilayered history involving many peoples, cultures, languages, and conquests. His writings examine this occulted past and its effects. One of his themes concerns the need to have ambition to define oneself. Ambition caused people to explore their world, journey outwards, and may end in failure, but those who lack ambition become victims of family, friends, those in power, and their own depression. He writes about individuals who are uprooted, alienated, and unwanted and therefore are, or feel, resentful victims, yet their condition offers possibilities unlike those who do not attempt to change their lives. The novels are about outsiders and the narration remains within or near their consciousness. Their tales are set against a history of Zanzibar in which feudalism after national independence was replaced by revolutionary thugs. History consists mostly of the selfish taking from the weak.

Memory of Departure (1987) tells of a young man, Hassam Omar, of a part Arab-African family headed by a brutal drunken father who beat his eldest son to death and who earlier in life sold young men to Arabs for sexual use. There is now a revolutionary black socialist dictatorship in Tanzania when anyone with Arab blood is treated as a public enemy. Hassam cannot afford to go to university which could be his escape from the slums in which his family now lives. His sister accepts the corruption of society and prostitutes herself. As the novel ends, Hassam is a sailor on a ship transporting poor migrants between countries as he tries to reach a part of the world, such as England, where he might make something of himself.

Memory of Departure is one of Gurnah's novels where a disillusioned young person leaves home but finds in freedom the exchange of bondage for insecurity and near poverty. Gurnah examines the Naipaulian problem of being 'unhoused'. Ambitions are frustrated by lack of means and opportunities. Gurnah, like Naipaul, depicts a world in which various individuals and groups compete and in which achievements easily crumble without support. Besides treating of migration and journeys, the novels examine the relationship of memory to identity; the stories are of exiles and immigrants caught between memories of the past and their present life. Gurnah questions Arab and European imperial narratives while showing that independent Africa is troubled by its present governments.

Memory of Departure was the first of several novels which seem part autobiographical. *Pilgrim's Way* (1988) tells of a former student who works as a hospital orderly in Canterbury, faces indignities, and recalls his past. He was part of the local elite in Zanzibar, fled after the black revolution against Arabs, and came to England with insufficient savings. After he fails his examinations he is stranded, encounters racial prejudice, and is threatened by hoodlums. Bitter, he isolates himself from others, and feels humiliated by his work while being unwilling to admit to those at home what his life has become. This is Gurnah's immigrant version of *Dangling Man* or *Notes from Underground*. The thwarting of the African's ambitions makes him resentful and turns him towards living alone in a rotting, filthy house.

Admiring Silence (1996) could be *Pilgrim's Way* two decades later and recounts the dispiriting memories of an unnamed man of part-Arab descent, who, when he was 42 after twenty years of being away, visits Zanzibar. Since he moved to England in the late 1960s he has become a teacher at a boys' school and lives with and is losing interest in an Englishwoman who is the mother of his daughter. Feeling discontent, surrounded by racial prejudice, he invents his past and that of Zanzibar. Trying to keep his worlds apart, he never tells his family about his Englishwoman. When he returns to Zanzibar he sees that his supposed memories were lies meant to comfort him in exile. Zanzibar is an impoverished place of inter-racial quarrels ruled by local thugs who seek revenge on the formerly ruling Arabs. It is disillusioning, a society symbolized by over-flowing, broken, stinking, filthy toilets. The narrator returns to England but Emma has found someone else and he is at home nowhere, another dangling man.

By the Sea (2001) refers to the coast of Tanzania and to a British seaside town where one of the two narrators, another exile, now lives as a political refugee. As the novel opens he is being interrogated by immigration and pretends not to speak English. The organization and sentences of the opening paragraph do not read like normal English prose and in the following pages the narrator will make minor mistakes in usage and think in Swahili or Arab words. By the conclusion he has met, learned that he is distantly related to, and formed a friendship with another exile who regarded him as a family enemy. We learn the complicated family histories of both men, the pettiness, squabbles, treacheries, and hatreds of the formerly dominant part-Arab community, and how the subsequent Black Power revolution in Zanzibar punished those with Arab blood while destroying the economy and imposing a tyrannical single-party state. Recounting the past as exiles allows the men to understand what made them.

The effects of being a resentful outsider and the temptations of withdrawing into separatism are examined in *Dottie* (1990). Dottie is a young black Englishwoman whose mother, a prostitute, died when the girl was in her teens. After her mother's death Dottie tries to keep her brother and sister away from what she feels is a white world that will humiliate them. Such separatism is self-defeating. Dottie's sister is of subnormal intelligence and would be better left in the special school where a social worker placed her. Similarly the brother, who rejects his family past, would be better left with the white middle-class family in which he is happily placed until Dottie manages to bring him home, which results in his rapid deterioration into drugs, drug dealing, crime, murder, and his own death. Dottie eventually earns secretarial qualifications and moves out of factory work to respectability. A powerful portrait of Dottie's impoverished world and dotty feelings, the novel shows that British blacks have complex, pre-Windrush, histories that need to traced and told. A grandfather was a Pathan who ran away from his tyrannical brother and in helping the British during their empire building ended up in Cardiff where he married a Somali woman.

The two volumes of *Essays on African Writing* (1993, 1995) that Gurnah edited, along with his essay on the Zimbabwean Dambudzo Marechera, avoid narrow cultural nationalism or black essentialism. Rather than insisting upon the nationalist's distinction between tradition and outside influences, Gurnah claims that African writers naturalize international influences. His novels show a world of change in which Africans have always been part of a larger world.

Paradise (1994) portrays East African societies on the eve of the First World War. The Arab traders backed by Indian financiers dominate the region and deal in goods and slaves. The latter are Swahili-speaking Africans from many tribes. The Germans now claim the area but they and the British are seldom present. The story is seen through the eyes of Yufu who at the age of 12 becomes a slave to a trader. Besides portraying an area of Africa dominated by Arab expansion which was being challenged by European imperialism, and showing continuing Arab involvement in slave trading long after it was banned elsewhere, *Paradise* concerns alienation and freedom. Yufu and others are uprooted as slaves and must learn to adjust to another society. Home depends on memories and Yufu can no longer remember the past. His parents dead, Yufu can only flee from his Arab master to the feared Germans, from one imperialism to another. Life is a journey; there is no paradise, only dangers, trades, changes in status.

Paradise is related to Conrad's *Heart of Darkness* in the Arab trader's journey to the interior of Africa, and to Achebe's *Things Fall Apart* in offering a view of the last moments of a part of Africa before European colonization. In explaining the origins of the town where he lives the trader claims: 'You'll be thinking: how did so many of these Arabs come to be here in such a short time? . . . buying slaves . . . was like picking fruit off a tree. They didn't even have to capture their victims themselves . . . There were enough people eager to sell their cousins and neighbours for trinkets' (*Paradise*, p. 131). Gurnah's style is in places imitative of Arabic and Swahili, although not to the degree of Achebe's Igboized English in *Things*. Gurnak's fiction is rich in ironies, parallels, historical detail, characters with secrets and unexpected pasts, foreshadowings of horrors, and allusions to other works of literature. The writing is powerful, obsessive, difficult to stop reading. It has intensity, a complex vision, and claims to greatness.

A few years after the publication of Gurnah's first novel, Jamal Mahjoub's *Navigation of a Rainmaker* (1989) appeared in the Heinemann African Writers Series as did his next two novels, *Wings of Dust* (1994) and *In the Hour of Signs* (1996), also set in Sudan. Whereas Gurnah is concerned with the results of Arab dominance on the East African coast, Mahjoub portrays those deracinated as a result of Africa's contact with Europe. Often this is expressed through a journey. *Navigation of a Rainmaker* tells of a product of a mixed English-Sudanese marriage, a son who, tired of racial humiliations in England, attempts to settle in the Sudan where he remains a disillusioned outsider working for a foreign petroleum company. The novel is written in the manner of a thriller with emphasis on action, plot, ideas, and mood, but with little depth of character. The first half takes place in the north of a Sudan which is becoming Islamized and trying to put down a rebellion in the south where there is oil. Although there are allusions to the continuous history of the Arabs enslaving and selling the Africans of the south, Mahjoub makes unnamed outside powers responsible for the rebellion as they want to stir up trouble and gain oil rights. This allows the central character to redeem himself through killing an African-American who is working for those seeking oil. What began as a novel about lack of belonging concludes with the hero dying to save the Sudan from outside interference. Set against this story is another tale, poetically told, of a nomad trying to lead his family through the desert to the south to avoid the drought, and an inset story about a 12-year-old boy killing the killers of his father and regaining his family's camels. These parallels contrast those who were born in and understand the desert with those from outside who do not know how to live with and attempt to exploit it. The earth, the land, is the nation over which others fight and die.

Mahjoub seems uncomfortable with hybridity. *Wings of Dust* tells of the previous generation, those from Sudan who went to Europe just after the Second World War seeking education and who assumed that national independence would be a straightforward good which they would inherit. They are Mahjoub's equivalent to Naipaul's *Mimic Men* who because of their education fail to understand the corruption, instability, violence, class hatred, and intolerance that can follow the withdrawal of imperial order. Colonialism has made them, they cannot rule the former colonies for long, and fleeing to Europe they discover they have no homes. This is another novel which feels fragmented and in which character and probability are neglected to illustrate a world of change, chance, the unexpected, and war—a view of the world made explicit in Mahjoub's next novel. *In the Hour of Signs* tells of two decades of war in the late nineteenth century in which a charismatic Mahid led his followers in rebellion against their Turkish and Egyptian rulers. The result was chaos, reflected in the movements of the novel and the many brutal deaths, which led to the siege of Khartoum leaving the British in control. This is another novel with crude jump shifts, lack of character development, a civil war involving outsiders, a world out of joint, contrasts between the impoverished majority and the elite. Contrasts are made between those who know and those, such as the British, who do not know the ways of the desert. There is once more the destabilizing effect of religious fanaticism. Mahjoub shows that nations consist of different peoples, social classes, and religions, which must live with each other.

Mahjoub's novels are also about the difficulty of knowing and making a truthful narrative about the past. *The Carrier* (1998) looks back to the early seventeenth century when the start of the scientific revolution was beginning to put Europe ahead of the Islamic world. A slave is sent from Algiers to Europe to seek an advanced telescope. This is another journey of exile, isolation, and the dangers of freedom, especially for the intellectual or educated, as the slave originally had to flee from his master in what is now the Sudan, and from that time onwards lived on his wits, chance, and what others make him do. The story is told complexly as it is researched and imagined in the twentieth century after strange scientific instruments are found in Denmark.

Ahdaf Soueif is a feminist anti-colonialist also concerned with the relationship of Europe to the Arab world. Her feminism is complicated by recognition of the need many women have for children, their need for the security of family, and by consciousness that self-liberation may be at the cost of harming others, and that the results can be disappointing. Soueif's progressiveness is also held in check by nationalism. Notions of hybridity and improving the situation of women conflict with ideas of authenticity. She identifies with the women who seek a modern Arab culture without imitating the West. Like many expatriates she asserts an identity based on history, in her case a history of anti-imperialism in the Middle East. Although she seldom directly expresses her views, her writings seem part of a generation of Egyptians who rejected Anwar Sadat's opening to Israel and abandonment of anti-westernism. Her central character is often someone like herself who has mastered English, fallen in love with English literature, lived in England, but becomes critical of imperialism and wants to associate herself with her original culture.

Aisha (1983), a loosely knit novel told through eight stories, concerns Aisha, a young Egyptian woman stranded between Arabic and western culture. In one story an 8-year-old Aisha is told by her 15-year-old nanny Zeina of the latter's forced and humiliating marriage, the test of her virginity, and her submission to a sexually brutal husband. Aisha avoids an arranged marriage but marries someone whom she does not love and who does not share her interests. She fails to have a child and, in the concluding story, joins in a folk ritual hoping to make herself fertile. The stories introduce many of the themes that will be central to the later fiction where West and East clash, where women are unsatisfied by both cultures, where freely chosen marriages are no more successful than arranged ones, and where the desire for children must be fulfilled while curtailing freedom.

Aisha reappears as Asya in *In the Eye of the Sun* (1992), a novel about a feminist's failed marriage to a dry intellectual that has parallels to George Eliot's *Middlemarch*. Moving between various Middle Eastern cities and using passages from Arab newspapers, this long, detailed novel recalls the anti-western politics of Gamal Abdel Nasser, his death, the 1967 war with Israel, and the rise of Anwar Sadat. Asya ignores public events, tries to immerse herself in western culture, but is forced into an arranged marriage with impotent Saif, who works for Syrian intelligence. Unhappy with her marriage she studies in England for a doctorate, sees in England's monuments symbols of imperialism and exploitation of Arabs, blames England for the creation of Israel, and becomes disenchanted with English literature. Bogged down in her research at a provincial university, she starts an affair. Learning of the affair, Saif accuses her of selfishness and ignoring the consequence of her actions on others. Seeing the parallel between her personal life and her neglect, as an intellectual, of Egypt, she returns home where she teaches birth control while wanting a child of her own. Soueif usually ends her books with symbols suggesting triumph through identification with the past. At the conclusion, as Egypt Americanizes under Sadat, Asya sees an ancient statue of a smiling woman with whom she identifies.

The seven stories in *Sandpiper* (1996) concern the problems and break-up of marriages either in the Islamic world or where western women have married Arabs. Inevitably the perceptions of those of the Arab world differ from those of the West. The contrasting cultures are mutually destructive and women seem victims of both the West and Islam. Two of the stories set in England concern a broken marriage between Egyptians, and are reimaginings of Asya. In the second of the stories Asya's mother-in-law arrives with part of Saif's family in the hope of bringing the two together. She is disgusted with a culture in which preparing food and having babies are not the most important desires of a woman or in which respectable women have affairs. By contrast the estranged wife can no longer understand Egyptian cruelty towards animals.

Soueif's pointillist, complex layering of memories of different times, and purposeful vagueness about details, is itself exotic, offering sketches with few events to support the symbolism and themes. For all their delicateness and her knowledge of the Arab world, most of the stories replay stereotypes about cultural clash, the restrictions of the Arab world, and the supposed attractions of its men. When in 'Satan' the mother-in-law is shocked by her son not turning up for a meal she has prepared and which she then forces on the pregnant wife of another of her sons, the scene seems a Woody Allen sketch about a Jewish mother. The most powerful story, 'The Water-Heater', concerns sexual repression. An older brother who is head of the family and a model of Islamic religious observance marries his intelligent younger sister, who hoped to go to university, to someone she dislikes, before she even graduates from school because the brother, who has kept himself chaste, is incestuously attracted towards her.

The Map of Love (1999) uses two love affairs to sketch in more than a century of Egypt's relationship to the West from an Arab perspective. It is like Ruth Prawer Jhabvala's *Heat and Dust*, a novel with a double plot in which, as a writer researches the past, the past and present have similarities. The love and marriage of widowed Lady Anna Winterbourne to the Egyptian nationalist Sharif Pasha al-Barudi at the turn of the century parallels, in the 1990s, an affair between the (symbolically named) American Isabel Parkman and Omar-al-Ghamrawi, an Egyptian-Palestinian musician, political writer, and activist. Omar is modelled upon the critic Edward Said and the later pages of the novel turn into a lecture. Here is the real Middle East which the West can only know by accepting that present problems derive from colonial history. The novel can be read as criticism of western interpretations of the Arab world which are dismissed as prejudiced. There is even a passage defending diaspora intellectuals (like Said and Soueif) from claims that they are unrepresentative cosmopolitans who tell an alienated western intelligentsia what it wants. While providing a historical background for understanding current cultural tensions, Soueif sacrifices narrative probability and character psychology for politics. The British, Americans, and 'Zionists' are stereotyped. The Arabs except those in power are good.

Although politics influence her treatment of characterization, representation, and themes, Soueif's style is deft, light, subtle; *The Map of Love* is impressively complex in form. Soueif is a self-conscious, sophisticated writer, and her book is modelled after, and a critique of, the 'Oriental tale' as well as an Arabization in Sharif Pasha al-Barudi of the Byronic hero and all the romanticism that goes with it.

A different perspective is offered by Leila Aboulela. Using a lyrical, melancholic stream-of-consciousness style, her fiction tells of those from Egypt or Sudan living in the West faced by conflicts between freedom and tradition. Whereas Mahjoub and most writers from the West assume conflict results in continuing alienation and exile, Aboulela's characters miss and return to the securities of faith, home, and Islamic notions of 'justice'. In *The Translator* (1999) a young Sudanese widow is a translator of Arabic at a Scottish university where she falls in love with her divorced, secular boss. After he refuses to convert to Islam to marry her, she returns to the Sudan where she feels comforted by faith and being at home. Aboulela has been termed by Islamic critics the first halal writer in English. Her emphasis on faith contrasts to the politics of Ahdaf Soueif who regards fundamentalism in the Muslim world as a reaction against western cultural imperialism. *The Translator* has been understood as a criticism of the expressions of female sexual desire in Soueif's writings, especially Asya's affair in *In the Eye of the Sun*.

Becoming and Being British

While in *Sour Sweet, Remains of the Day*, and *Dottie*, writers such as Mo, Ishiguro, and Gurnah explored life in England as their subject matter—they were preceded by Selvon and Dhondy—it took time before West Indians began writing fiction about family life in England and generational conflicts as their English-born children developed different values. Dabydeen, Caryl Phillips, and D'Aguiar wrote more about the past than the present. In the early 1980s, however, some smaller presses began publishing the first black British fiction, such as Norman Smith's novel *Bad Friday* (1982) published by Trinity Arts Association. *Railton Blues* (1983) by David Simon was one of the first novels to combine the disappointments of West Indian immigrants in London with the specific tensions that had developed on the front line in Brixton, Railton Road, during the late 1970s and 1980s. While offering a portrait of a community and making use of patois, the novel is stereotypical with Caribbean men violently mistreating and leaving heroically stoic Caribbean women for white women, the unemployed young turning to Rasta and drugs, white hatred, police brutality, and official harassment, concluding with a riot. The attempt to write realistically about those who lived unhappily in England was not successfully treated in prose fiction for another decade when Courttia Newland, Rocky Carr, and Alex Wheatle would write about the 1980s.

The Jamaican Joan Riley, beginning with *The Unbelonging* (1985) and *Waiting in the Twilight* (1987), was among the first to write novels about West Indian women settling in England, the racial and sexual prejudices they faced, and the complicated lives they developed among themselves. While *The Unbelonging* continues traditions of writing about the shock of life in cold England, especially at school, in contrast to the warmth of a Caribbean childhood, it shows that dreams of return to a tropical Eden result from disappointments in England. The young woman returns to the Jamaica from which she was uprooted when she was 10 only to be horrified by the poverty, crime, and ugliness. She is told to return home to the England from which she came, which parallels the white schoolgirls in England telling her to go home. While the novel shows the young girl brutalized by her drunken father, which explains her fear of men, especially black men, she does not listen to advice, or facts, and rejects help; humiliated by her family history, she assumes that everyone is her enemy. As in many books written by West Indian women, the father is a violent sexual predator who beats his daughter and attempts to rape her. His own frustrations with his life in England are passed on as feelings that whites hate blacks. Riley shows why some West Indian women in England have developed self-destructive traits to cover fears and insecurities. The British welfare system aids the girl after she escapes her father and supports her until she goes to university. That when she returns to Jamaica she has a masters degree and can afford to stay at a tourist hotel shows that she has a future which would have been impossible had she remained in Jamaica.

Riley's *Romance* (1988) tells of several generations of West Indians in London and the relationships between them. The focus is especially on two contrasting sisters. The younger, and seemingly weaker, dreams of marrying a blonde white man after she was abused by a black man. Similar to the central character of *The Unbelonging*, she escapes reality by reading romantic popular fiction and imagines herself a thin, blonde, white heroine. To avoid confrontation she takes the easiest way, even confessing to a crime she did not commit. She has a series of white sexual partners and has a child by a violent racist. Her older sister is so anti-white and so drearily responsible that she drives away the younger sister who manages to live on her own and take care of herself. The elder sister is married to a man so often turned down for promotions that he has lost self-confidence and does not understand he is running into prejudice. The novel ends on an upbeat note as the elder sister finds a way to begin working towards a college degree. This is in contrast to the earlier *Waiting in the Twilight* with its story of an older immigrant woman whose life in England consists of failure and who thinks about what her life might have been.

While the texture of Riley's writing is thin, the characterization simple, and the stories lack drive, she offers a contrast to the absurdities of popular white romantic fiction. She has purposefully set out to depict the failures, the wounded, the unglamorous, among black women. She presents a world of dead-end jobs, the unwillingness of people to seek medical aid, the fear and violence of the police, and the many friendships and family relationships within the black community that help people survive. Riley's characters are intended as ordinary, working-class black immigrants, neither villains nor idealized. They are, however, imprisoned by the past, by their family history in Jamaica and by the hurts of the early immigrants to England. *A Kindness to the Children* (1992) begins with a black British woman going to Jamaica from which her parents left. 'Sylvia thought of the years her parents had spent trying to convince her that she was British. If only they had realized what it would mean: to be here where no English voice intruded and most every skin was black' (p. 2). But at the conclusion of the novel she gives away a copy of the *Jamaican Gleaner*: 'There is nothing in it to concern me' (p. 312).

Except for pieces in anthologies, the first noteworthy publication by an Asian Women Writers' Collective author was Ravinder Randhawa's novel *A Wicked Old Woman* (1987). It is the first novel by a woman set within England's Asian community—in this case Indian and Pakistani—and remains controversial because of its unusual structure and style. There appears to be no plot as the main character, Kulwant Singh, recalls the past or listens to the history of others as she visits family and old friends. Without reading attentively and awaiting information, it is often difficult to understand how the characters are related or know each other and where their stories intersect. The manner of narrative is oblique and fogged with distracting wordplay and cleverness. Kuli ('Coolie') Singh is an obvious pun as is Maya's uncertainty of what is real. Mark's name is inverted to Karma. His initials also form MAD. Kuli's teenage love is called Him-Him.

Kuli, scared of the passion of her teenage, white English boyfriend whom she had been seeing behind her parents' back, decides to become a traditional Indian wife. She demands that her parents arrange her marriage; an Indian, sight unseen, is soon imported for her. Having been raised in England with western notions of romantic love, and still dreaming of her schoolboy lover, Kuli is unaffectionate towards her hard-working husband who eventually leaves her and their children for a younger woman. Kuli's children hate her for losing their father. She seems cold, unforgiving, and disguises herself in old clothes as an old woman with a walking stick (symbolic of her past blindness, her feeling wounded and old, and a weapon to hurt others). The novel begins with 'Stick-leg-shuffle-leg-shuffle', a refrain which recurs whenever she visits the next person.

As the past emerges, a portrait of a group of women (family, relatives, friends, enemies, acquaintances) builds along with their troubled relationships with men who leave the women with wounds when they depart for younger women or fame, and take the fruits of what was joint labour. The men are driven by lust which the women avoid. Rani kills a man while defending herself against his violent advances. While the novel reads like feminist complaint against men, that is the perspective of Kuli, who blames unsatisfactory relationships on being culturally neither purely Indian nor purely English. The novel concludes with the women healing each other through collective involvement, especially as they join in supporting other women in an anti-war protest. This is paralleled by the joint effort to provide political and legal support for Rani. Kuli gives away her walking stick and Oxfam clothing and her life is renewed by living in the present. Her search through memory has taught her to forget the wounds of the past. Randhawa asks if people can live without love and finds love through collective responsibility in action. Joint political action with other ethnic groups is implied by the mention of a black woman and the parallel story of white Caroline.

A Wicked Old Woman is a history of the lives of Asian women in England. Kuli's mother knew and learned no English as she wanted to return to India and it was assumed that girls would remain culturally traditional. At school the children are mocked as different, find friends and protectors, attract boys, and begin creating a new life in England. The novel mentions many events of British Asian history such as the attacks by the National Front who poured petrol through letter boxes to kill and frighten Indians. As the women begin to organize, there is an Asian Centre which acts as a refuge, Asian women become journalists, and Asian women become part of British history, joining in various political protests. At times the issues sound similar to those of the black writers of the previous decade: 'And because we're here to stay we have to leave a legacy for the future, for the children to whom India will be just another country . . . They'll be British by birth but never by colour' (p. 144). 'How come we never learnt about the Indian soldiers who fought with the

Brits. Looks like a deliberate suppression of the facts to me. I mean that's what multi-cultural education should be about, not Diwalis and sari parties' (p. 156).

Collectivism and concern with Asian women as a group is common to AWWW authors except for Leena Dhingra (b. 1942) who is attracted to the aesthetic side of literature. Her novel *Amritvela* (1988) is complex, circular in form, with many seeming digressions, stories within stories, and retellings of Indian mythology. The story concerns an Indian who when young is brought to England, marries an Englishman, feels lonely when work separates them, and visits India to relearn her culture before settling again in England. Deracinated after the Partition of India left her family stranded in Europe, Dhingra in her novel and short stories is concerned with individuals who feel isolated and homeless because exiled and who need to create a sense of identity.

The same desire to explain the lives of Asian women in Britain that led to the formation of the AWWW also influenced Sharan-Jeet Shan (b. 1945) to write and Women's Press to publish *In My Own Name* (1985), which began while she and her husband were quarrelling over divorce. Although Sharan-Jeet (the Shan is a pseudonym) is a Sikh, her book is an excellent introduction to the notion of shame that gives Rushdie's novel its title. She shows the pressures an Asian woman feels from her upbringing, family, and community, as well as her isolation in England. Fathers, elder males, and husbands were gods to be obeyed without question; women were nothing. At medical school in India, however, she fell in love with a Muslim. Her father claimed she had shamed the honour of the family, isolated her in a locked room in a village, drugged her, and beat her over many months until she agreed to an arranged marriage. The man her father found for her was a liar who lived in one room with his brother in England and sent the money he earned to his family in India while falling deeply into debt. He treated his wife as a slave, continually beating her, ignored their children, and claimed that because of her reputation she was lucky. After sixteen years of hatred during which her husband's behaviour became increasingly violent, she divorced him, which resulted in her parents and other Sikhs claiming that she had once more dishonoured them and refusing contact with her. She eventually gained qualifications as a teacher, supported her family financially, and learned to use the British legal and welfare system to become independent and the head of a single-parent family. Sharan-Jeet's autobiography is rich in detail conveying how those who suffer grave and brutal injustice feel guilty and seek compromise. She, however, never gave up until one day she left, took a new name, and started a new life with her children. Her story shows that domination of Asian women by men is more thorough than in the West and that few women will have the emotional and economic resources to part from their larger family and community. Unfortunately the Cambridge University Press 1991 edition of the autobiography has an afterword in which Sharan-Jeet tells of having become politically conscious of 'racism, capitalism, neocolonialism, sexism and numerous other "isms" '. While the West Indian and Asian women were in a sense writing allegories about groups of women, the detail of their writing and focus on individuals was a step towards mapping the actuality of England as it changed. Asian women were mixing regardless of differences in backgrounds, becoming active in politics, having careers, and writing of lives that differed radically from the past in India or Pakistan.

At a time when West Indian and Asian women were writing of their new lives in England, Hanif Kureishi was already known as a dramatist and for his film scripts. His first novel was the semi-autobiographical *The Buddha of Suburbia* (1990). Of mixed race and raised in England he was a central figure in the shift from writing about origins, exile, and cultural conflict to the complexities of contemporary England. His plays and film scripts of the 1980s looked at how British life was changing with the presence of large numbers of Asian immigrants, the class distinctions among the immigrants, and how their children were becoming part of English society. His fiction of the 1990s turned away from immigrants and social issues to the intimate, the loss of excitement, dreams, and love as one ages. While he did not deeply explore the significance of being of mixed race (the way Bernardine Evaristo or Ayub Khan-Din would), he was the first black or Asian writer to move beyond the immigrant and racial experience to an intense body of work about the Self and the life it leads in relationship to desire, the body, love, sex, age, and work. While this later fiction can be repetitive, it is a superb achievement.

In 'The Rainbow Sign' (1986) Kureishi discusses prejudices at school in a London suburb, his visit to Pakistan and its attractions, and how he was formed by the ideals of 1960 London with its hedonism, subversions, and liberations. As a youth he had admired the American Black Power advocates, but being half white he could not find comfort in black separatism. The increasing restrictions of Islamic rule had no attractions for him, especially as it did not allow the artist freedom. His love of popular music and its cultural symbolism is seen in *The Faber Book of Pop* (1995), which he edited with Jon Savage. In 'Eight Arms to Hold You' (1991) he tells of his admiration for John Lennon, comparing him with Brecht as a spiritual and artistic model. Instead of being part of a diaspora, Kureishi accepted being British. Linton Kwesi Johnson anticipated him in accepting being British and writing about life in contemporary England, but Johnson's poetry was political and written for blacks about blacks whereas Kureishi was concerned with living fully. This is different subject matter from that of Naipaul and Rushdie; it is partly the difference between being an immigrant and being born in a country. In Kureishi's writing the desire for change and renewal is expressed though sexual relationships; eventually themes of race, social justice, and personal social advancement disappear to be replaced by stories of couples uncoupling and the costs.

The Buddha of Suburbia (1990), his first novel, begins a new era when the children of immigrants write as English:

My name is Karim Amir, and I am an Englishman born and bred, almost. I am often considered to be a funny kind of Englishman, a new breed as it were, having emerged from two old histories. But I don't care—Englishman I am (though not proud of it), from the South London Suburbs and going somewhere. Perhaps it is the odd mixture of continents and blood, or here and there, of belonging and not, that makes me restless and easily bored. Or perhaps it was being brought up in the suburbs that did it. Anyway, why search the inner room when it's enough to say that I was looking for trouble, any kind of movement, action and sexual interest I could find, because things were gloomy, so slow and heavy, in our family, I don't know why. Quite frankly, it was getting me down and I was ready for anything. (p. 3)

Karim is not like his father, who came to England from India in 1950, twenty years previously. Karim, at 17, is a product of the cultural revolution of pop music and of the sixties, with their sexual freedom, drugs, multiracialism, multiculturalism, and instant fame. He is the forerunner of the excitement of making it in London that will figure in the novels of Meera Syal and Atima Srivastava. *The Buddha of Suburbia* is about desire and liberation and their costs, especially the wounding effect of change on family and those with whom one has emotional ties. *Buddha* offers contrasting portraits of those affected such as Karim's abandoned mother.

Haroon, Karim's father, came from a well-off Bombay Muslim family to England as a student, married a white working-class woman, and settled into a dull, secure job at a time when most of the family moved to Pakistan. Now a father of two grown children Haroon is bored, disappointed, and turns to Oriental philosophy with its conquest of desire by wishing nothing. Such platitudinizing makes him a guru to the ageing hippiedom of the suburbs. Soon he is intertwined with erotic, ambitious Eva, and divorces his wife while Karim finds mutual satisfaction with Eva's son. Karim follows Eva and Haroon to their new flat in West Kensington where she and Karim begin their social and cultural advancement and Karim becomes a brown sex object for the liberal establishment.

The Buddha of Suburbia is a version of the Balzacian novel about the provincial who comes to the metropolis and the ways and the costs of making it. Rather than an orphan, Karim is the new breed produced by divorces and a multiracial England. The novel also reworks in the context of the counter-culture revolution, modern literature's celebration of the rebellion of desire against socially and morally imposed limits. Karim is a product of the British class system. The famous rock musicians he admires have emerged from working-class or middle-class suburban families. He has also been affected by racism in British schools. He regards his father's belief in the superiority of England and its ways as a colonial mentality. Racism is seen by Kureishi as white working-class resentment at immigrant competition and achievement, while professional-class liberals are often patronizing.

The Black Album (1995), Kureishi's portrait of post-swinging London is set in 1989, the year after the publication of *The Satanic Verses*. The title comes from an album by the singer Prince. The liberations of the sixties, the ideologies of the seventies, massive immigration, and Thatcherite economics have resulted in acid raves, slavish followers of any anti-western slogan, universities in which no one reads, sex without love, increasing unemployment, angry minorities, angry white men, and the collapse of liberal culture. This is an update of Waugh's *Decline and Fall*. It is also 'The Second Coming', but as warning. Things have fallen apart, the best lack conviction, there is social, emotional, and intellectual anarchy, while fanatics demanding unthinking obedience gain followers among the angry and disillusioned.

Shahid Hasan is 'black British' but trapped between skinheads and Muslims who both consider him Pakistani. His father thought himself finished with Asia and Islam, but a boom-bust economy, working-class resentment, postcolonial theorists, and the expedient multiculturalism of Labour Party politicians have destroyed the national consensus. Shahid attends a college staffed by poorly qualified teachers, mostly disillusioned sixties radicals, for whom their brighter students write about the cultural significance of Prince recordings while others take drugs or burn books. Shahid is seduced by the well-practised attractions of a college lecturer who teaches him many new pleasures, including designer drugs. He is threatened by Riaz, leader of a group of Islamic fundamentalist toughs who claim that free thought or individuality lead to western decadence, inaction, lack of respect for and betrayal of the Third World, especially Islam.

In an analogy to *The Satanic Verses* affair, Shahid rewrites some of Riaz's poems and is forced to flee for his life with his lover who, having tried to discuss Rushdie's book in her class, is hiding from Riaz's gang. Kureishi is too much a fan of popular culture, and knows contemporary British taste too well, to have an unhappy ending. Once he gains the attention of television, Riaz moves from book-burning and violence towards mainstream ethnic politics. The narration reflects Shahid's use of drugs. While the unfixed tone and structure of the novel imitates Ecstasy-influenced, hallucinatory feelings, *The Black Album* is a plea for the superiority of real literature, scepticism, and England, in contrast to those who regard them with scorn as the products of elitism, the Enlightenment, and racist imperialism.

Some of the ten stories in *Love in a Blue Time* (1997) compress desire, indulgence, and subsequent frustrations into a few dream-like, yet highly colloquial pages where everything appears to happen at once, in the present, with no time for reflection. An effective technique is the sudden, unannounced, unprepared shift into the mind of someone on drugs, having sex, or into the midst of a likely disaster. The effect is less the strung-out psychedelia of the 1960s and more a speeded-up version of the amusing but self-destructive drug-taking found in writing of the 1980s, especially in novels of Martin Amis, where Ecstasy and cocaine are part of glittering success. In the title story a now well-off rebel trying to move from advertising into serious film making and from one-night stands to marriage and fatherhood almost throws everything away in a swift return to debauchery once he meets a former admired companion in excess. There is no return to youth; the financial and creative fruits of work are quickly jeopardized. Kureishi offers a contrasting perspective in 'Nightlife', the main source of the film *Intimacy* rather than the novel with that name; it concerns a man to whom a woman he hardly knows comes once a week for sex. Wounded by his marriage, he has withdrawn from a previously successful career and wants to exist without anxiety, demands, or deep feelings. His family, wife, children, job no longer matter to him or give him pleasure. All he has is this strange encounter with this woman which costs him nothing financially or emotionally, but it offers him little beyond bodily pleasure and if she leaves he will have nothing. The stories dealing with race are more complicated. In 'With Your Tongue down My Throat' a hypocritical, dictatorial Pakistan elite is unfavourably contrasted to an impoverished, sluttish, drug-taking England. 'We're Not Jews' is a small classic which offers another perspective on the world of *The Buddha of Suburbia*. Azhar has been bullied at school and, after his mother complains, he and his mother are harassed and threatened by the bully and his father, their neighbours who consider her marriage to a Pakistani as a betrayal. The story is packed with personal histories. Azhar's mother is white British and the bully's father used to date her although she now looks down on him as 'common'. While her husband is cultured and from a good family, he only has a factory job and speaks English in an Indian manner. Son and mother are embarrassed by the way the father's family crowd into their house which smells of curry and speak Urdu and Punjabi.

When the father rants of leaving England for home he has never been to Pakistan. England is the only home they have. Further complexities are suggested by allusions to the Partition massacres, apartheid in South Africa, and the gassing of Jews. The story's title comes from the mother's defensive 'We're not Jews' when taunted.

In his later work Kureishi looks back on his ideals of a liberated, hedonistic, subversive 1960s as his characters grow older and are faced with the responsibilities and boredom of settled lives. Although the narrator of *Intimacy* (1998) complains at being locked into a what has become a loveless relationship, the perspective is ironic. The woman is not what the narrator claims; he turns down her offers of sex, affection, concern. He has been consistently unfaithful, likes comfort and order but refuses to help around the house. Another irony is the lack of attractiveness beyond youth and excitement of his new object of desire. An uneducated suburban runaway with no mind or interests beyond playing in a rock band, she sleeps around, and drifts through life. *Intimacy* is a beautifully written book. The prose is concise, at times approaches the aphoristic and epigrammatical, has short lyrical outbursts, and follows the shifts in mood and focus of the narrator's mind. The registers and tones range from the intellectual and moralistic to the erotic and obscene, but there is always control, precision, economy, rhythm. *Intimacy* records the nuances, politics, and ethics of personal crisis in middle age.

Laments for the passing of unrestricted pleasure were followed by asking how people lived together, how it was possible to restrict desire, how love could last without betraying the soul of the now ageing young rebel, a view present but questioned in *Midnight All Day* (2000). The ten stories mostly concern the difficulties of living with another person, the fear of losing freedom, the disillusionments of intimacy, and the greater fear that if this relationship does not work there will be no others in future and one will be left lonely, a failure. While marriages here are prolonged quarrels, life without continuity and attachment, especially without children to bring up, without someone to care for and love, is thin and bitter. The stories are about choice. In several stories the lover meets the husband of the woman with whom he is having an affair. In one the lover says you have had your chance, now it is mine, and accepts responsibility for the woman and her children. In 'That Was Then' Kureishi examines how the imagination unpredictably transforms bits and pieces of experience into art, especially as the sexual drive is the basis of change and fame as in 'The Penis', an amusing parable about the relationship of sex to art and work. The penis of a handsome porno star becomes detached, is chased through London as it attracts admiring females, until weary of fame it is captured and reattached to its owner, who must work harder to pay for the operation. In *Gabriel's Gift* (2001) Kureishi examines from the child's perspective the breakdown of a relationship, the departure of the father, and the mother's financial problems. Gabriel's father eventually learns that the excitements of youth cannot be regained; helped by Gabriel's art he marries the mother. Such fiction is part of the shift of focus to the self and private lives that becomes a feature of poetry, drama, and the novel during the 1990s as minorities felt more settled in England and attention moved on from group politics.

III. Poetry: Performance and Dialect

Black British poetry after the mid-1970s was often dialect-tinged performance poetry with protest themes. Despite claims of its African origins it was similar to written verse except for its dramatic effect and improvisation in performance. Most poets wrote, as most British West Indians spoke, in both Standard English and dialect. Like much of black literature, performance poetry shares in the trends of white culture, such as the renewal of popular oral poetry by the Beat and Liverpool poets, but has its own history, particularly the development of a Jamaican tradition of dialect verse. The large Jamaican immigrant community, Jamaicanized British West Indians, and black feminists proved a core audience which rapidly expanded across colour lines. While the centre of Dub music was London with its large West Indian population, several poets lived in university towns within commuting distance of the metropolis. Levi Tafari lived and published in Liverpool where because of the port there has been black community over the centuries.

Valerie Bloom's *Touch Mi, Tell Mi* (1983), published by Bogle L'Ouverture, continues an older Jamaican tradition. Bloom (b. 1956) uses rural Jamaican English and subject matter except for protest poems about such topics as police brutality and the government spending money on nuclear power. Her poems are more like the amusing monologues that Louise Bennet had introduced to Jamaican poetry than Linton Kwesi Johnson's rapid, energetic, streetwise, politically focused, modernist-influenced, urban verse. In Bloom's poems Jamaica is 'home'. In 'Language Barrier' she claims 'Jamaica language sweet you know bwoy'. Her use of iambic quatrains with alternating abab rhymes is like the conventional English forms that Bennet and other Jamaican poets inherited from colonialism. Bloom would become an author of books of children's verse.

By contrast, Jean 'Binta' Breeze (b. 1956) was one of those at the Drama School of the University of the West Indies in Jamaica who developed Dub poetry during the 1970s by consciously turning DJ voice-over raps into performance poetry. She soon moved away from the limited rhythms and political themes of Dub to poetry about personal feelings. During the mid-1980s she began living part of the year in England where she became popular on the black and feminist scenes. In *Riddym Ravings & Other Poems* (1988), edited by the Jamaican literary critic and poet Mervyn Morris for the *Race Today* poetry series, some of her dialect poems can be difficult to understand because development is through associations. While this is the method of many post-Bob Dylan popular songs, Breeze's poetic line is sometimes minimalist (one word a line), and associations can pile up through wordplay with no clear logic. She has, however, a good sense of structure and her poems have refrains and end with a return to their opening motifs and phrases.

Riddym Ravings means loose associational poetry to rhythm (usually the bass and drums). A few poems, such as 'eena mi corner', concern Dub music and attempt to imitate the music with its hypnotic beat; 'dubwise' snakes down the page in one or two word lines with various indentations meant to represent a lady writhing to the broken rhythms of the dance beat. 'Arising (for youths of Azania)' is a dialect Dub celebration of youth rebellion in which the schoolteacher is the voice of the system's oppression. While the sentiments are those of many pop songs of the time in which it was claimed that education makes a student just one more brick in a wall, the mythology is like Johnson's black rebel:

> like is concentration camp you wann sen wi
> teacher sey
> tun to you history book
> an let mi tell yuh bout Captain Cook
> so mi step outa de class
> before she tek mi tun ass
> a fi mi people pon de crass
> an bomb a shatta glass
>
> .   .   .   .
>
> mi a mash it in guerilla style
> mi a flash it in guerilla style

Many poems such as 'Her Course' are about women and contrast light-skinned middle-class ideals with the lives of poor black women. A speaker's red-skin middle-class mother 'gets high | on clean children'. This contrasts to a poem telling of a woman with dirty bundles of clothes in a tenement yard whose only source of water is a standpipe.

The title poem is subtitled '(the Mad Woman's Poem)' and the speaker claims to have a radio in her head through which, significant of the origins of such poetry, a DJ plays and raps. She is one of the crazed and impoverished of Kingston with its filth, lack of manners, prostitutes, and guns. In the refrain she wants to return to the countryside; instead she is returned to a hospital for the insane. She is the black version of the feminist mad woman in the attic, while the DJ in her head is a way to signify that this is a woman who can talk tough like the male DJ.

Spring Cleaning (1992), published by Virago, offers a complex personality, a 'Red' (light brown) woman rebelling against both white and black domination while appealing to feminist sisterhood. Most poems are set in the West Indies and are versions of women's consciousness themes; the volume ends by claiming the poet is an expression of her readers and community. Verse and prose alternates in *On the Edge of an Island* (1997), published by Bloodaxe, a book about life in Jamaica which concludes with a mother telling her daughter 'At least in England dem respec de kine of work yuh do.'

The Arrival of Bright Eye and Other Poems (2000), also published by Bloodaxe, uses childhood friends to represent the Caribbean female experience. There is a narrative of a poor rural childhood, schooling, the discovery of sex, shame, migration abroad, break-up of family, homelessness, seeking love, identification with black sisters, and concluding poems affirming Caribbean and African culture for those of the black diaspora. The volume mixes poetry and prose monologues. 'The first dance' metaphorizes the biblical creation of the world, and the potentiality of a woman's body, as like the rhythm of the spheres and life. Creation begins as drumming rhythms without sound. This allows Breeze to reinterpret creation as black, 'black silence breathed | and there was motion . . . giving birth to motion'. In 'Learning', an amusing prose poem, there is a contrast between authority as represented by the teacher and what is sexually learned at school. 'A Cold Coming' is an obvious pun; the prose poem tells of a Jamaican equivalent to a pyjama party between the speaker and her friend Faith. This is followed by 'Shamaa-lady', the one poem republished from *Riddym Ravings*, in which in response to the 'telegraph bush' 'she jus pack er shame | an gawn'. In 'flowering' the speaker is with a woman who 'finally let me in', but 'I never touched her again.'

'The Arrival of Brighteye' tells of a girl left behind with her grandmother in the Caribbean when her mother leaves to better herself in England. Years later Brighteye lives unhappily with her remarried mother in England, the mother's new husband, and the younger children of the new marriage. The monologue is a complaint at migration to England and the instability of the Caribbean family: 'ah don't belong here, but ah don't belong dere eider'. As in many of the poems there is a need for love, especially mother love. In 'Duppy Dance' which concludes the volume there is an assertion of African origins in various incantations and of doing without men. The message is 'we don't care man | is Africa we need'.

Unlike most Dub poets of the 1970s and 1980s, Benjamin Zephaniah was born in England although he spent his youth in Jamaica before returning to England. Whereas Linton Johnson could be aloof, intellectual, and more concerned about his message and art than popularity, Zephaniah saw himself as an entertainer with a political perspective. He will use any means to communicate. He was one of the first to use complicated electronics to score his poetry. Zephaniah's poetry is thin on the page, it only has value when performed. When Johnson withdrew for some years from the oral poetry scene, Zephaniah became a star and possibly the most popular poet in England, the subject of TV programmes.

After self-publishing *Pen Rhythm* (1980), Zephaniah made three recordings, *Dub Ranting* (1982), *Rasta* (1983), and *Big Boy Don't Make Girls Cry* (1984), before his first book was published. *The Dread Affair: Collected Poems* (1985) begins with proclamations of the poet as a rebel, as a Jamaican, a martyr, a Rastafarian, a youth, from the ghetto—the pose of Johnson's rebel, but with less seriousness. He is for 'my people', drumming, and against 'corruption', 'them', the police, Miss World, wars, Rome, Babylon. He cites the Bible, wants blacks to stick together and return to Africa. Zephaniah is a crossover poet, a black writer who speaks from a racial position while assuming that white and black youth are part of the same working class oppressed by capitalism. The perspective is Rastafarian plus counter-culture with praise of John Lennon and rocking while high on ganja. Many poems are short chants, slogans to be repeated outside a police station or on a march; some could have taken their themes from a Bob Marley recording as such words as Mother and Love are continually repeated. Grammatically he uses the Rastafarian 'I' and similar signs of affinity: 'Come little children rock with I | the beat of the drum will never die | drummers beat, drummers beat' ('Beat Drummers'). Zephaniah as performer has a likeable, amusing, self-mocking, personality. His voice is clear, soft Jamaican-British, and his pronunciation is British with Jamaican touches. He reads in many contrasting tones and rhythms: he comes close to polyphony when he uses electronics to imitate records using overlapping voices.

Zephaniah was for a time writer-in-residence at the Africa Arts Collective in Liverpool which resulted in *Inna Liverpool* (1988). Despite his popularity it was not until *City Psalms* (1992) that Zephaniah was taken up by a mainstream poetry publisher, Bloodaxe. By then reggae had been overtaken by 'dance hall' and Zephaniah was up to date: 'Dis poetry is designed fe rantin | Dance hall style, Big mouth chanting.' 'Dis Poetry' might be considered Zephaniah's poetics and a declaration of the poetics of those who attend his readings: 'I've tried Shakespeare, Respect due dere | But dis is de stuff I like.' One problem of male performance poets is mixing a bad boy hoodlum image and counter-culture posing with the softer, fashionable 'new man'. Zephaniah is in favour of all good causes. *City Psalms* begins by criticizing 'Macho Man' who cannot cook or sew, but demands his food and 'Woman' be ready on time. The poet asks Macho Man to help him 'Save de Whale' and give up drunkenness for herbal tea. This contrasts with the continuing vague leftism of 'Black Politics of Today' with insistence on being a rebel and allusions to Nicaragua and Chile. In such poems black oral poetry becomes mainstream entertainment: 'Me vocabulary is changing I don't use coloured or bitch | Because I am Vegan I will no eat de Rich' ('Black Politics of Today'). This Zephaniah was a peaceful Rasta poet addressing Babylon with love.

In *Propa Propaganda* (1996), also published by Bloodaxe, 'The War Process', 'Who Dun It?', 'City River Blues', and 'Belly of de Beast' need to be read polyphonically but it is difficult to know how other poems might be read as they seem scripts for oral performance. By contrast 'Terrible World', Zephaniah's parody of Louis Armstrong's recording of 'What a Beautiful World' ('I've seen streets of blood | Redda dan red') is too easy to recite. Many poems have little interest on the page. 'More Animal Writes' is a joke animal protest chant: 'They have the power | We have not, | Animals must stick together.'

Zephaniah risked becoming a cutesy multiculturalist for soft-hearted weepies. In *School's Out: Poems Not for School* (1997), published by AK Press, Zephaniah repositions himself as the descendant of slaves and as the black youth from a broken family who gets into trouble and fails at school. He tries to keep alive the pose of the black rebel who speaks Black English and who is honest in contrast to middle-class hypocrisy. There is an easy available cluster of assumptions to draw upon—'Me name was problem child', 'rumours make me homeless', 'We are the Human Race', 'Rich wants a war'. Despite talk of representing the people his assumptions are contemptuous of most people. In 'Robots of the Future': 'You see them on trains, they like to hear what papers say . . . They never did think for themselves, | (And they were never able).' Zephaniah has also written several plays for theatre. *Job Rocking* (1987) performed at Riverside Studios and published in Brewster's *Black Plays 2* (1989) is a long verse poem in several voices. While its subject is unemployment, Zephaniah claims it is rap verse for dancing in which rhythm is more important than the meaning of the words.

A number of small presses supported performance poetry in Caribbean English. Nubia Publications included Shakka Gyata Dedi's *Afrikan Hartbeat I* (1982). Desmond Johnson's first volume, *Theresa and My People* (1983), was published by Black Ink Collective. Desmond Johnson, a Jamaican, then founded Akira Press, which published his *Deadly Ending Season* (1984) and became one of the main publishers of West Indian poetry during the mid-1980s. It liked politicized poets like Jacob Ross. Akira published in 1985 Glynn Martin's *De Ratchet A Talk*, Marsha Prescod's satirical *Land of Rope and Tory*, Maud Sulter's (b. 1960) *As a Black Woman*, Anum Iyapo's *Man of the Living, Woman of Life*, Morgan Dalphinis's *For Those Who Will Come After!*, and Merle Collins's volume of poetry about Grenada, *Because the Dawn Breaks!* Other Akira publications ranged from books about black people in Britain and folk tales from Zimbabwe, to Mike Phillips's first book, *Smell of the Coast* (1987), before going bankrupt. Such publications were often supported by grants from the GLC during a time when the Mayor, Ken Livingstone, made London into a multicultural city where the formerly marginalized seemed to hold power. When Thatcher dissolved the GLC the new subsidized presses collapsed whereas the older minority publishers who refused subsidies, such as New Beacon and Bogle L'Ouverture, survived.

Although John Agard was one of the early performance poets, he and Grace Nichols are different from the Jamaican-influenced reggae and Dub poets. While aware of Kamau Brathwaite's use of dialect, mythology, and Africa origins to create a linked volume of poetry, their roots were southern Caribbean culture: coming from Guyana they were predisposed towards the rhythms, sounds, and symbolism of Trinidadian steel band, pan, and Carnival. The rhythms of calypso are more syncopated than reggae and there is a verbal texture of puns, ironies, innuendoes, and satire along with narrative and drama. The steel bands with their pans can have an orchestral range of sounds and harmonies as well as the complex drumming rhythms found in Trinidad where African, Indian, and Latin American beats combine. Carnival offers ritual, myth, visuality, and a structure which has been thought dramatic. Agard's poetry has always been complex and reads well on the page as well as in performance. The volumes he and Nichols have published are unified by themes and story; their cultural affirmations are intended as political.

Shoot Me with Flowers (1973) was self-published in Guyana at the time of flower power, peace and love, the Beatles, Black Power, and the anti-war movement. While Agard developed from the counter-culture and its radical politics, the poems in this volume concern the intimacy of personal relationships. As he comes from the southern Caribbean, Agard's style of performance, models, and use of Creole are close to Trinidadian calypso with its fanciful invention. He brought this tradition to the cross-pollinating black and counter-culture performance poetry scene in 1977 when he moved to England. *Man to Pan* (1982), while political, 'celebrates the evolution of Steelband, a cycle of poems to be performed with drums & steelpans' ('Himself Interviews Himself', *Mangoes and Bullets* (1985)). It begins with 'Pan Recipe', which claims the origins of steel band in the 'rape' of a people for centuries which is expressed in drums along with the mixture of bloods in shanty towns. The interest of the poems is in approximations of the various rhythms and tones of pans in a steel band: 'and to me octave | is a word dat rhyme with slave'.

> Beethoven to kaiso
> shantytownsound turn concerto
>
> is another classic
> Anancy trick.

There are some visually shaped poems meant to represent rhythms and sounds.

In *Limbo Dancer in Dark Glasses* (1983) Agard continues developing protest poetry into something larger, mythic, inclusive. There is flow to the volume as groups of poems develop into other groups and the limbo dance moves through various stages from birth to death with the promise of resurrection. It becomes the dance of life, the survival instinct, the will to protest, sex, another name for the libido, the black slave's survival dance. Agard's acknowledgements are to Wilson Harris and Kamau Brathwaite, the former for seeing the limbo dancer as a kind of god, the latter for bringing into the poetry the origins of the limbo dance as a movement by the Africans on the slave ships. The place of the volume within a West Indian context is furthered by a dedication that includes Grace Nichols (Agard's wife) and the poet James Berry.

The Limbo Dancer, like the Palm Tree King and the Wanted Man, is one of the personae Agard created by combining street characters and carnival masks with Johnson's young rebel. Agard treats the limbo dancer as having many meanings ranging from slave and all those who have suffered persecution, to a force of nature. The volume begins with the 'Limbo Dancer's Wombsong', which sets the tone of the dancer as an amused and amusing cool cat who speaks English with some traits of West Indian dialect. Born of the 'Mother of universe' he stretches from Africa to Brazil. He is six million Jews, he is Stephen Biko, all the oppressed victims of evil. In 'Limbo Dancer at Immigration': 'It was always the same | at every border | at every frontier', he is not wanted. His dance is a revolution. He is part of the masses, the protesters at Greenham Common, those who held a vigil for the dead at New Cross, he is among the children of Soweto and the miners of Gdansk. He is Christ, a black entertainer, someone who will always return.

Because many of his best poems are in volumes published in the Caribbean or self-published in England, Agard has needed to keep his work before readers by republishing early work. His next volume *Mangoes and Bullets* (1985) consisted of selections from *Shoot Me with Flowers* (1973), *Man to Pan* (1982), *Limbo Dancer in Dark Glasses* (1983), *Palm Tree King* (1983), and new poems (under the title of *Wanted Man*). It begins with a mock 'Himself Interviews Himself' and a 'Dedication': 'Remembering Walter Rodney & Maurice Bishop | two of our Caribbean dream-doers'. *Mangoes and Bullets* is partly about politics. 'Immigrant Neighbours' compares the white British when 'your immigrant neighbours | slaughter a sheep | in view of the street', or have a loud all-night party, with whites viewing 'a video nasty':

> Why can't these foreigners
> be more like us
> why can't they act civilized
> and organize a decent fox hunt

Agard has become a voice of immigrant England. Many poems express the relationship of literature to black and left politics. Agard amusingly assumes the persona of a wanted man, wanted because of his crimes with standard English. In 'Listen Mr Oxford Don' 'I didn't graduate | I immigrate',

> I ent have no gun
> I ent have no knife
> but mugging de Queen's English
> is the story of my life
>
> . . . . . .
>
> I ent serving no jail sentence
> I slashing suffix in self-defence
> I bashing future wit present tense
> and if necessary
>
> I making de Queen's English accessory
> to my offence

Lovelines for a Goat-Born Lady (1990) is dedicated to Grace Nichols. Goat-born refers to the sign under which the 'lady' was born and the poems have many usual motifs of love poetry but with a Guyanese difference. She is referred to as 'Mudhead woman'; 'mudhead', a footnote explains, is a Guyanese term of affection for those from the low-lying silted coastland. The poems are charming in their use of West Indian terms, and the many variations Agard finds: 'Starapple of my eye | my firefly in pitchdense of night' ('Lovepoem Slowly Turning into a Lullaby'). He is her 'lizard', in later poems she is pregnant: 'Your belly big with child | is geography made new' ('Moonbelly (A Pregnancy Sequence)'). At times Agard sounds like Donne: 'Lead me to your wanton parts | that I may graze | with holy glee' ('Lead Me'). Many lyrics are of the slight but clever kind associated with e. e. cummings. 'Jumbie Romance' concludes 'we tongue locked | in a syntax of yes'. Some poems play with simple political slogans to identify sex with the good and pleasurable. In 'Epilogue', 'Erogenous zones | are nuclear free zones'. Several poems are simple double entendres. 'Grandma's Advice' is little more than an extended double entendre on 'pussy' ('stroke it every night'). Like other protest poets of the 1980s Agard had become accepted and tamed.

From the Devil's Pulpit (1997) offers a 'Book of Temptation': over 120 short, witty poems providing the Devil's perspective on the Bible, history, and life. This Devil is more a comedian than an advocate of sin. This is tame stuff. Poems include 'Glory Glory Be to Chocolate', 'Light Up Your Pipes', 'Coffee in Heaven', 'Mona Lisa You Teaser', and 'Lucifer Relaxes with a Michael Jackson Video'. The Devil is a conventional moralist complaining at the horrors of nationalism, ethnic hatreds, and civil war in Rwanda, Ireland, and Bosnia. Agard does have a philosophy; life consists of balance, opposites, temptations, curiosity, excitements, pleasures, every god needs a devil, every order needs a disorder, every established hierarchy needs sceptical mockery. Like most of the rebel black performing poets Agard had become mainstream, part of middle-brow culture.

Agard early began writing books of children's verse which include *Laughter is an Egg* and *No Hickory, No Dickory, No Dock. Get Back, Pimple!* (1996) shows that there is no clear division between his children's and adults' poetry as it republishes some poems from *Limbo Dancer in Dark Glasses* and *Mangoes and Bullets*. While most of the verse for children treats of such topics as 'Exams Blues', 'Not-Enough Pocket-Money Blues', 'Blind-Date Blues', others, such as 'Angela Davis and Joan of Arc Rap', are political. This is poetry for teenagers which mixes dating, life in the disco, and the latest styles with progressive politics. Many poems are about poetry and being a poet. The fourth section, 'God in Blue Denims', largely concerns teenage identity and dreams—'Who Are You?', 'In My New Trainers', 'Rebel Heart', and 'Into the Unknown'.

Weblines (2000) contained a new book, *Come Down Nansi*, along with the again republished *Limbo Dancer in Dark Glasses* and *Man to Pan*. There are by now enough allusions in Agard's poems to his masks as spider, trickster, pan man, limbo dancer, to form an African-Caribbean mythology. In *Come Down Nansi* it is Anansi the trickster spider, a folklore character derived from West Africa with a long Caribbean literary history that includes Louise Bennet, James Berry, and Jan Carew. Agard follows the path of Andrew Salkey's *Anancy's Score* and *Anancy, Traveller* in his own Nansi variations. These new poems make less use of dialect than earlier volumes and seem written for British West Indians rather than West Indians.

Many poems are dramatized Caribbean revisions of folk tales. Some poems, such as 'The Coming of Debt', seem influenced by those spiritual lyric allegories of George Herbert, but there are allusions to Africa rather than Christian doctrine. Agard's recurring themes, motifs, and masks offer those of African descent a history and shared culture to have as their own. 'How Anansi Helped Skygod Get One Hundred Slaves from Earth' concludes: 'and because my kith and kin have lost their names | I must build a covenant of broken webs'. 'From grandmother Ma' ends: 'I will spin proverbs | bridging two worlds.' The next poem begins: 'Hide talking drum | in skin of English words.'

Performance poetry by black British women shares in the explosion of writing by black women during the last quarter of the century. Grace Nichols first made her reputation with *I is a long memoried woman* (1983), a sequence of lyric poems linked through a story concerning the spirit of the African women taken to the New World as slaves. In theme and manner it belongs to a time when black feminism was creating its own mythologies and 'respect' had become a demand. A representative black woman is imagined journeying over many centuries from her life in Africa through the Middle Passage to her life in the Caribbean on a plantation. A series of scenes in the form of lyrical monologues intended for performance, *I is a long memoried woman*, Nichols suggested, could be staged with accompanying African drumming. The woman is at various times I/us/we, and represents the many places from which African women were brought to the New World, which becomes a place of rebirth. The importance of memory is affirmed in questing for ancestry, a mythology, a history, a community, a model for black womanhood. A vision with similarities to Brathwaite's trilogy, the poem is also a justification which recalls the origins of the black woman and her history of keeping her dignity and resisting her oppressor. Even when she appeared docile and happy she was angry and planning her escape; what her masters understood as compliance was rape. As is common in black feminist writing, womanhood is identified with being a mother, raising children. There is strong affirmation of sexuality which is regarded as political.

After the dedication to the memory of Nanny the Marroon (a Jamaican who fled slavery and remained free) and to all people fighting for their liberation, and 'To my enlightening sister poets', the sequence of poems begins with images of birth and creation; the Middle Passage bringing the slaves to the New World is a new genesis. After recounting injuries, injustice, resistance, and various cultural survivals, the speaker offers an assertion of women choosing their destiny. Africa, its rituals, its communities, may appear lost in the Middle Passage but is the basis for a new identity, a new mythology, with roots in the past. The poems are about healing in contrast to isolation and dislocation. Recalling the history of black women is the Muse of song. The epilogue claims that having lost her original tongue in crossing the Atlantic, the poet has grown a new one from the old. Poetry is her way of healing old wounds, redeeming by remembering the past as a prelude to moving forward.

The influence of Brathwaite can be felt throughout, especially in such ticks as dramatically repeating phrases and the way the poem is printed on the page is an indication of timing when being read aloud: 'And yet ...... | And yet ...... '. Nichols through Brathwaite is indebted to T. S. Eliot, poets of concise metaphors, striking images, and memorable phrases.

One of Nichols's concerns is the black female body. *I is a long memoried woman* includes poems about sexual pleasure, pubic hair, the menstrual cycle, giving birth. Nichols identifies the sensuous female body with nature, creativity, and poetry. It has been whipped, raped, it has given birth to children, but now its appearance is judged by standards of white culture. *The Fat Black Woman's Poems* (1984) echoes feminist criticism of thinness as a standard of beauty, a criticism especially common among black females. These are a different kind of black consciousness poems, more playful, shorter, more about difficulties of being a black woman in a white culture. It is a commonplace that beauty among mature African women is judged by large hips, buttocks, thighs, breasts, even fat. The first poem of the volume begins 'Beauty | is a fat black woman' and offers two brief portraits of the woman in natural settings. In the next poem the fat black woman is sitting on a monarch's throne in Africa and claiming it as her right while surrounded by chiefs. Such are the proper contexts in which to understand the beauty and cultural history of black females. Next we are offered a different perspective on old representations of the fat black woman as an Aunt Jemina. She felt murderous while acting the part to feed her children. There is a poem about London shops not carrying dress sizes large enough for fat black women, but, as the next poem says, she is 'feeling fine' and there is no need for her to diet or exercise. *The Fat Black Woman's Poems* make up a quarter of the volume which otherwise consists of poems about blacks in London and memories of Guyana. Nichols is nostalgic for a lost tropical garden of exotic-sounding flowers and fish while admitting that poverty and hope for a better future drove women abroad to cold London.

In *Lazy Thoughts of a Lazy Woman* (1989) a witty poet turns white bourgeois values upside down. The first poem praises dust, scum, fungi; the next praises grease which 'reassures me that life | is naturally sticky' ('Grease'). There is a parody of Walt Whitman, 'I sing the body reclining', a schoolgirlish 'With Apologies to Hamlet': 'To pee or not to pee | That is the question.' Another poem asserts 'Wherever I hang me knickers—that's my home.' Instead of being a good housekeeper, this is a black feminist praising her body. There is a 'Spell Against Too Much Male White Power', an 'Ode to My Bleed', and 'My Black Triangle', which 'carries the seal of approval | of my deepest self'. Once more the second half of the volume consists mostly of poems about childhood in Guyana in contrast to racial and other problems in London. Some poems are in patois and several return to the need to recall black female history and origins in Africa.

Whole of a Morning Sky (1986), Nichols's novel for adults, tells of the migration of a family from a rural village in Guyana to the capital just before national independence. There are strikes which hurt the population, shops are set ablaze and looted, the British soldiers try to restore order, but soon the Asians and blacks are killing each other and neighbours are murdered. In contrast to the disruptions of male politics and the father's hardened view of life, the mother holds the family together and the various women in the novel form a female community for warmth and survival. The novel is mostly told through the perspective of the two daughters who were growing up in the early 1960s; there is a contrast between the fore-grounded social and family life and the distanced but threatening political violence which is often the topic of conversation between the adults. The novel portrays Guyana as a paradise destroyed by male politics but made liveable by the ways of women.

Sunris (1996), a sequence of poems offering a myth of women, begins with a short prose introduction in which Nichols recalls that as a child Carnival in Guyana seemed to her a form of rebellion against her father whereas when she saw Carnival in Trinidad it was filled with magnificent visual imagery of deities and famous people. The book ends with a short glossary of the dates and characters mentioned in the poems. They include the Hindu Kali, the Amerindian Kanaima, the Chinese Kuan Yin, such African gods as Legba, Ogun, and Shango, along with the sixteenth-century Aztec Emperor Montezuma and the British Long-man carved on the hills of Southdown. This is a more multiracial Nichols in keeping with the shift from black separatism to multiculturalism during the 1990s both in England and the West Indies. Her remembering is not now limited to African roots. She brings wider interests, especially towards the myths of the past, to England and its ancient monuments.

Many of the glossed figures appear in the title poem 'Sunris' where the speaker describing the carnival procession becomes possessed by the dance rhythms and emotionally participates in the life of the figures. The sequence is a celebration of rebellion which makes use of Caribbean speech, imitates the rhythms and tones of the music (especially the pan drums), and concludes with the speaker herself becoming the incarnation of the Caribbean heritage as the new goddess Sunris who combines Iris and the Sun. The use of Creole and the many figures from various cultures is a way of affirming the multiplicity of the black female personality and of Caribbean society.

Nichols's children's books are set in a mythic and secure tropics of caring family, rural villages, forests, alligators, mangoes, bananas, lizards, parrots and parakeets, and dancing crabs. *Come on into My Tropical Garden* (1988) invites the reader to 'taste my sugar cake and my pine drink . . . you can pick my hibiscus | and kiss my chimpanzees' (p. 3). The people in the illustrations are black West Indians. Nichols and Agard co-edited *No Hickory No Dickory No Dock: A Collection of Caribbean Nursery Rhymes* (1992), mostly imitations and parodies of traditional children's verse. Some are by Nichols and Agard, others remembered from childhood in Guyana. Besides this mouse claiming he did not run up the clock, there is a version of Humpty Dumpty fixed with superglue.

Another regular on the black female performance circuit was Amryl Johnson, a Trinidadian who came to England at the age of 11. She often wrote as a nostalgic West Indian although her auto-biographical prose travelogue, *Sequins for a Ragged Hem* (1988), mixes a tourist's survey of the beauty of the islands with impatience and disillusionment. Many of her poems contrast a warm, visually beautiful, Creole-cadenced Caribbean with a lonely, cold England. While she sometimes wrote about dragging the chains of slavery and other 'I am a black woman' clichés, other poems offer a strong, quirky personality seldom at ease in her relationships, especially the many love affairs to which the poems allude. While using themes of black feminist verse, Johnson has an instinct for lyrical abstraction and song. There is a seriousness about being a poet: her later books are allegories about poetry.

In *Gorgons* (1992) Johnson imagines Medusa returning and being horrified at what she has done; this becomes a metaphor for having looked but not really seen. Medusa has seven daughters, each of whom is the subject of five poems and who represent such characteristics as dependence, fighting for freedom, restlessness, rebellious sensuality, and frustrated bitterness. There is also a mysterious male character with different names who represses the women. Several lyrics suggest that Gorgon's story concerns the process of writing and its inspiration. Amryl Johnson has more a sense of architectural structure than a gift for verse texture. Many poems are either statements or depend upon repetitions for effect. 'Could Would Wood Burn?' opens with a feminist version of Brathwaite: 'She could do it | She could do it all | She could do it all all all'. 'Dual Vision' runs variations on 'You are a Woman of Determination | you have tenacity'. In 1995 the London Arts Board commissioned and published in its autumn *News* her *Rainbow Dragon Trilogy* to celebrate the thirtieth anniversary of the Notting Hill Carnival.

Fred D'Aguiar's use of traditional verse forms and his sophisti-cated essays in literary criticism make him appear outside the simplicities and slogans of black performance poetry, but his early publications show how he developed from such a context. 'Dread-Talk' in *Mama Dot* (1985) reveals the unexpected influence of L. K. Johnson on D'Aguiar, who was at first unclear how to apply London

Creole to his poetry about the years when he was sent from England to live with relatives in Guyana. Practice reading to drumming while attending the Brixton Black Ink workshops resulted in 'Mama Dot': 'Born on a Sunday | in the kingdom of Ashante'. While most of his poems are in standard English, some, such as 'Mama Dot Warns against an Easter Rebellion', use D'Aguiar's version of dialect: 'she not sayin a word, be we hearin her | fo de ress a dat day an evry year since'.

His first volume of poetry was about people in Guyana, especially his Guyanese grandmother, Mama Dot, who is treated as a mother Africa, the voice of black folk experience. Another figure in *Mama Dot* is 'Papa-T', his grandfather: 'When Grandad recited the Tennyson learned at seas, | I saw companies of redcoats tin-soldiering it.' Papa-T also used Guyanese speech: '*If yu all don't pay me mind, | I goin ge yu a good lickin an sen yu to bed*.' Papa-T and Mama Dot comprise two sides of D'Aguiar's cultural and literary inheritance, the black folk and British literary tradition. In 'Letter from Mama Dot' Guyana has changed from the Eden of recalled childhood to 'another South American dictatorship' in which 'Everybody fed-up in truth; since independence | This country hasn't stopped stepping back.' His second volume of poetry also returns to memories of Guyana, *Airy Hall* (1989) where Mama Dot lived: 'The red sand road, houses well back, | Trees there to collect dust.' These are poems about a place rather than people. 'Airy Hall, Mid-Morning' is when 'Someone revs a tractor | Left idle or turning over long.' 'Airy Hall Iconography' with its subtle end rhymes describes such local fruits as the tamarind, mango, coconut, guava, paw-paw (papaya), and sapodilla: 'The Sour-sop's veneer is the wasp | treading air at the vaulted honeycomb.' Both volumes have a tri-part structure, beginning with poems about what is remembered, then digressions, followed by a concluding long poem, such as the auto-biographical Wordsworthian 'Guyanese Days' in *Mama Dot*: 'As a child I worked this land half-naked, | Growing into patched, taken-in clothes.'

The Audenesque *British Subjects* (1993) turns from nostalgia for Guyana to the complexities of being black British and to identification with Africa and its diaspora. 'A Gift of A Rose' recalls a beating by two British policemen under the 'sus' law: 'Now when I see the police ahead, I take the first exit.' 'Home' tells of returning to the warmly familiar red telephone boxes, grey skies, and 'Chokey streets' of England in contrast to 'H. M. Customs' examining D'Aguiar's passport, 'the stamp, British Citizen, not bold enough | for my liking and too much for theirs'. D'Aguiar's concern with the history of England in relation to the slave trade and its earlier black communities can be seen in 'At the Grave of the Unknown African' recalling,

> shipload after shipload that docked,
> unloaded, watered, scrubbed, exercised and restocked

> thousands more souls for sale in Bristol's port

He, a 'black Englishman', is told by the dead African, *'Say what happened to me and countless like me, all anon. | Say it urgently.'*

As D'Aguiar explored black history in his writings he needed longer narrative forms. *A Jamaican Airman Foresees His Death* performed at the Royal Court Theatre Upstairs (1991), published in Brewster's *Black Plays 3* (1995), includes a range of Englishes, in this case from Standard and Scottish to Jamaican, to show the complexities of black British experience. While about the history of blacks in England and white racial prejudice against them, the play also concerns visions and the ironies of history. Taking as its starting point W. B. Yeats's 'An Irish Airman Foresees His Death' with its supposedly aristocratic posture that the superior person dies in pursuit of visions and ideals while knowing that reality and causes will betray, D'Aguiar shows a black Jamaican who abandons the chance of advancing financially and socially at home to defend England and, more important, as he wanted to fly. Alvin is a black colonial Icarus who will fall after having flown too high as an RAF gunner and in winning the love of a white woman. The eighteen scenes are short and change rapidly in manner from the poetic and symbolic to the realistic and in places to harsh caricature and protest. The style ranges from verse to prose with many literary allusions and echoes. Characters sometimes become the chorus commenting on events. Although such disjuncture of modes since *Midnight's Children* is often said to be postcolonial postmodernism, the play is more a mixture of early modernisms, part dreamplay, part Audenesque agitprop, part Brecht.

The Longest Memory (1994) treats black history in prose with the sensitivity of verse. The novel contrasts two slaves: a father, representative of an older generation that has learned to survive by identifying with the power and ways of the white master, and his rebellious son. The story alludes to the differences between black moderates and radicals. The father prevents his son from escaping supposedly to help him survive, but also to hide the father's sins. Many of D'Aguiar's works include a guilty father and a strong woman. Here the young black slave's love of a white woman symbolizes a future that might overcome the divisions created by racial prejudice.

In *Dear Future* (1996) D'Aguiar returns to Guyana and shows how politics and exile destroy a family. The novel's themes include the role of the West Indian woman as family head, the fragmentation of family in the West Indian diaspora, and the creation of the 'black' Briton from a variety of nationalities, religions, and cultures. As in the novels of Wilson Harris, who is the model for D'Aguiar's version of magic realism, history is retold in new forms and fantastic stories to permit renewal and avoid the burden of the past. While the corruption, racial divisions, and violence that characterized Guyanese politics are neutralized by fantasy, humour, and grotesque caricatures, this remains a story of damaged people. In British Guiana different groups of the world's populations were left with each other at independence. The resulting violence was made worse by ideologies and American and British interference. *Dear Future* shows how this history separated children from parents, how some offspring became British while others died in Guyana, and what being a British West Indian or a black Briton means beyond the simplicities of race relationships. The mother's man in London is a Muslim who tricks her Hindu-Indian-Portuguese children into being circumcised by a Jewish rabbi, a trick to which she consents as she hopes to remarry until she learns that the Pakistani wants her as a second wife. *Bethany Bettany* (2003) uses a child brought up in London and Guyana and many narrative voices to treat of a broken family as an allegory of the brutal politics of Guyana since independence.

D'Aguiar returned to verse for *Bill of Rights* (1998), a complex retelling of the Jonestown, Guyana mass suicides and murders, and for *Bloodlines* (2000), a story narrated in some 480 eight-line pentameter stanzas set in the antebellum American south. It tells of a black female slave, the white son of a neighbouring plantation owner, their love, his disinheritance, their attempt to escape, their capture, her death giving birth to his brown son (the narrator), an imagined return to Africa, and such later events as the white man seeking his lost black love. D'Aguiar aims for an old-fashioned pathos in this love story about a couple, which is also intended as an allegory of white–black attraction and hate. Instead of a modernist Eliot-Césaire-Brathwaite fragmented epic vision revealed though lyrics, common to early Berry, Agard, and Nichols, D'Aguiar's strong storylines belong to an older tradition of narrative verse as resurrected by Vikram Seth in *Golden Gate* (1986) and used during the 1990s by Jackie Kay and Bernardine Evaristo. The long association of black poetry with modernist verse poetics had passed.

IV. Drama: Black, Black Feminist, and Asian Brecht

Black British, in contrast to West Indian, theatre started with British-born Hanif Kureishi and Caryl Phillips who were brought up in England and their subject matter was England. There were also many new black theatre groups such as the Black Theatre Co-operative (BTC) 1979, co-founded by Mustapha Matura, which in 1999 was renamed Nitro. The Black Theatre Forum (BTF) started in 1985 to 'stimulate the development of Black Theatre in Britain' and organized an annual Black Theatre Season 1985–90. In 1995 it started a newsletter *Frontseat* edited by Bernardine Evaristo, who also wrote about black theatre for *Artrage*. The 1980s and early 1990s were the time of such black female drama groups as Theatre of Black Women (TBW, co-founded 1982 by Evaristo), the Women's Troop, and Munirah. Many started with grants from the GLC. From the mid-1980s there were black female and lesbian plays including Jackie Kay's *Twice Over*, which has white and black actors, performed by Gay Sweatshop, a British gay and lesbian theatre company founded in 1974, in 1988. Many plays of 1980s reflect arguments over black consciousness, black feminism, and black lesbianism. Most lack depth of characterization or character development, but gain their effect from being abrasive and from a conflict between what is demanded and what is possible. The lack of depth is often purposeful, part of the Brechtianism of the period in which dramatists and producers followed the German Marxist play-wright in avoiding empathy with characters while using 'distancing' effects which help the audience see the play as a situation requiring objective analysis rather than emotional sympathy.

Many plays concern black separatism versus some form of assimi-lation, or the in-betweenness of those of mixed race. Some characters are extremely disagreeable as hurt and rage become self-destructive and their rhetoric of black pride escalates. Of Jamaican parentage, British-born Michael Ellis was one of the new black dramatists and his plays and their places of publication participate in the black con-sciousness of the time. His *Chameleon* was produced by TEMBA in 1985, directed by Alby James, and toured for almost a year. It is included in Brewster's *Black Plays I* (1987), published by Methuen. The chameleon is a black man in the lower ranks of management in a large firm. He claims that there is no racial discrimination in the company or country and tries to behave as a white, but his office is isolated, hidden away in the building, and, although he is head of a section, he has only one secretary. He avoids causing trouble while having an affair with and hoping to marry the daughter of his white boss. The other actor is his recently appointed secretary. She is con-sciously black, demands her rights, and fits such stereotypes as being a single mother, always late for work, argumentative, politically active, and was fired from her last job for hitting her boss for what she considered mistreatment. She claims to be trying to make a man of the chameleon by pointing out how he is deluding himself. After a confrontation in which he threatens to call the police she quits. Although he is a scared windbag, the woman's behaviour is self-destructive. In a play about the survival of the individual versus identification with a community, tension results from contrast between empathy with what the woman says and knowing that her rebellion will end badly.

The novelist Caryl Phillips began by writing powerful, bitter, and confusing plays during the 1980s. *Strange Fruit* (Studio Theatre, Crucible Theatre, Sheffield, 1980) feels as if it were written from the front lines of racial, gender, and generational conflicts. The mood is angry, tense, filled with threat and potential violence, close to insane.

Dialogue appears to consist of nerves snapping; dislike and hatred have replaced love. The strange fruit is not the lynched black American of Billie Holiday's recording, but two children brought to England by their Jamaican mother because she wanted them to have a better life than was possible with her drunken irresponsible husband. As an immigrant she suffered from poverty, racial humiliations, difficulty obtaining employment and housing, but now she is a schoolteacher who has created a decent life and brought up her two sons with a view to bourgeois careers. Instead they want to be black revolutionaries; they have contempt for their mother as an imitation white and they plan to rob a bank and return 'home' to Africa. The older son first visits Jamaica where he learns that he is an unwanted outsider, there is no international black family, and his mother lied in claiming that his father was a dead hero. The younger brother who spends his time smoking pot and talking to other young rebels refuses to listen to the truth, accuses the older brother of wanting to be white, and leaves home with a bag of guns and a pregnant 16-year-old white whose child he fantasizes will be a 'warrior'.

Although this appears a play about frustration and pathology within the British black community there is, as in most of Phillips's work, a parallel white character. The girl is a strange fruit of a racist Roman Catholic family; because of her religion she does not use birth control and refuses to have an abortion. She allows the young black man to humiliate her as she hopes to marry him. In this play about obsessions, return 'home' is not possible; it is necessary to tell the truth and act rationally or else rebellion becomes suicidal. There is respect for the older immigrants and what they endured in contrast to the young who waste their opportunities in fantasies.

Where There is Darkness (Lyric Theatre Hammersmith, 1982) is another emotionally violent play which weaves back and forth in time; it concerns conflicts between West Indian men and women and between parents and children as well as the myth of home. Albert has heartlessly used women and his friends to get to and advance in England. Now, well-off, he is brutal towards his white wife, and is a demanding patriarch towards his son whom he expects to continue ascending the social and economic ladder. Instead of going to university the son wants to marry a black woman he has made pregnant. In the quarrel which follows, the woman says she will not marry someone who is afraid of his father, and the father, who tends towards the delusional, collapses thinking he has lost his son. While showing the costs of taking root in England, the play reveals a Jamaica that everyone hoped to flee and to which return would be foolish.

Phillips's *Playing Away* (1987), a television play directed by Horace Ové, is a comedy of manners in which quarrelsome black cricketers from Brixton play a white village team in rural England. The match is arranged, despite scepticism on both sides, by an ambitious black professional and a white liberal. Although the trip begins with the shambles of stereotypical black behaviour, the Brixtonians win after the village team falls apart when several of them quit following a disputed call. Rather than believing in fair play, many locals expected the umpire to take the side of whites, an expectation that reflects a class division in the village represented by two pubs, one for politically liberal professionals, the other for working-class racists. Although an amusing play, there is barely suppressed violence and the rape of a black woman by three white youths. Phillips offers a view of both black and white anger beyond the platitudes of a multiracial, multicultural England.

Some dramatists avoided the limitations of political theatre and by working against the grain of the times got further into the complexities of black British life. Alfred Fagon (1937–86) came to England from Jamaica in 1955 and held many odd jobs before becoming a television actor and writer in 1969. During the 1970s his plays began being performed by such alternative companies and theatres as the Almost Free Theatre, the Metro Club, and Foco Novo Theatre Company. In the 1980s there were productions at the Tricycle and the Royal Court at which *Lonely Cowboy* (1985) was performed. The play takes place in a newly opened restaurant in Brixton during 1984. Brewster includes it in *Black Plays 1* (Methuen, 1987) for the 'sheer wonderful madness of leaving most characters dead or dying at the end of what might have been seen as a light comedy of Brixton manners'. She finds it 'interesting to hear the viewpoint of a writer nearing fifty years old on the concerns and development of a Black British population' and notes 'the subtly captured rhythms and speech eccentricities of a generation raised by immigrants' (p. 8).

Another play in Brewster's first anthology is Tunde Ikoli's (b. 1955) adaptation of Maxim Gorky's *The Lower Depths* to the East End. Born in London to a Cornish mother and Nigerian father, Ikoli became an assistant director at the Royal Court where his first play, *Short Sleeves in Summer*, was performed in 1974. His association with the Foco Novo Theatre Company as resident dramatist began in 1977. *Lower Depths* (1986), which was first produced by Foco Novo at the Birmingham Rep (which encouraged plays by minority writers) before moving to the Tricycle, is another instance of a black, in this case mixed-race, dramatist transforming a theatre classic as did Matura. While European texts provided a model, they revealed to writers similarities between people and situations they knew and those elsewhere; the works imitated showed ways to write about the Caribbean, Nigeria, or black England. Ikoli also wrote *Scrape off the Black* (Riverside Studios, 1983), published in Brewster's *Black Plays 3* (1995). *Scrape off the Black* is a witty, farcical, yet bitter, portrait of the consequences of a mixed-race relationship once the joys of love and sexual passion have been replaced by a gaoled black husband, an ageing white woman living on welfare, and two criminal sons.

The first of the significant black women dramatists to come to wide attention was Jacqueline Rudet (b. 1962), an East Londoner who lived in Dominica during her youth, and who was part of the new black feminist literary and theatre scene. She formed Imani-Faith in 1983 as a drama group for black women. Rudet likes plays in which there are revelations of secrets and their effect on families who need to come to terms with the supposedly scandalous. *Basin* (Royal Court Theatre Upstairs, 1985) concerns two black female friends who become lovers to the scandal of another friend; in the process the West Indian word 'Zammies', for close female friends, is extended to the common condition shared by black women. Although character development and psychology is sacrificed for the illustration of ideas, the dialogue is concise, sharp, clarifying. In *Money to Live*, performed by the BTC at the Royal Court Upstairs, in 1984, and published in *Plays by Women 5* (Methuen, 1986) edited by Mary Remnant, several women become strippers, a mother confesses that she was a prostitute to support her family, one of her daughters admits to an abortion, and her son impregnates a

17-year-old who may have an abortion. There are suggestions that masturbation is all the sex that a woman needs.

Rudet tries to write about problems of black society without being concerned with issues of identity. *Money to Live* shows what black women do when needing to earn money to support their families or their desires. In the play the men are unable to find employment or unwilling to work for the money needed by a family. The men are irresponsible, only concerned with having sex and moving on although they expect women to bear and keep their children. The play asks whether sex work, here in the form of being a stripper, is degrading and contributes to the dangers of rape, or whether it is a way to turn the table on men for financial gain in a society in which women, especially black women, are otherwise at a disadvantage.

There are powerful speeches in favour of an economic-based feminism. Some of the women do not enjoy stripping, others do, a few become so excited by the crowd that they want to perform sex on stage. While money is needed for independence and to avoid feeling trapped, happiness might require keeping in contact with family and the past. Issues raised in the play include black speech: 'If talking properly is "acting white", then pass me the emulsion. Do I need to restrict my vocabulary in order to retain my black friends? Why must black people be inarticulate to be "black"?' (p. 160). Although lacking subtle characterization and a range of tones, *Money to Live*'s speeches, conflicts, and revelations—along with visual interest in the form of dressing, undressing, and body movement—make for a powerful play.

The poet and novelist Jackie Kay was a dramatist with the Theatre of Black Women where she learned to construct narrative and poems for oral performance. Influenced by the African-American Ntozake Shange in its variety of styles, *Chiaroscuro*, produced by the Theatre for Black Women (Soho Poly, 1986) and published by Methuen in Jill Davis's *Lesbian Plays* (1987), ranges in technique from directly addressing the audience to singing poetry as four women revise themselves and seek others identities in telling their histories. Each of the women comes from a different background, Nigerian, Asian, mixed Caribbean and white, and an orphan with no knowledge of her parents. The sexualities also range from uncloseted to anti-lesbian. The heated conversations discuss issues of race and sexuality and how they are imposed by society. While the mixture of presentation is appropriate to Kay's theme, such experimentation was common to black women's theatre of the period, reflecting its roots in encounter groups, performance art, and the alternative theatre of recent decades.

Publishable plays written by those of Asian descent were late on the scene. The Royal Court actively scouted potential writers and actors and kept them attached in various capacities so that they could learn about theatre and make contacts from the inside, whether watching rehearsals, selling programmes, or at Sunday night readings. Hanif Kureishi's *Borderline*, produced by the Joint Stock Theatre Group (Royal Court, 1981), was the first play with Asian characters on a major stage by an author of part-Asian descent. Kureishi had early become associated with the Royal Court and the Joint Stock Company, which was predominantly white, consciously interracial, and experimental. The play, based on interviews, reveals how several generations of the Asian community at Southall have accommodated to England while under threats of violence by whites. There is a clear relationship between immigration policies and how Asians are treated. Even Pakistanis will exploit Pakistanis using fears of deportation to obtain cheap labour. The play concludes with young Asians preparing to prevent a Fascist meeting in their neighbourhood. Such a play is not only about Asians but also about how whites force others into stereotypical roles. Brechtian in analysis, the play has changes in perspective—a complexity furthered by some white actors having Indian roles.

Kureishi's concern in many of his early plays was with the declining working class in Thatcher's England, the ways this shaped resentment against immigrants (still the topic of novels such as Meera Syal's *Anita and Me*), and the excitement of London in contrast to the suburbs. He avoided making Asians and blacks passive racial victims; he portrayed them fighting for their defence while exploiting their own people. Although he disliked the collapse of the Welfare State, he felt that individuals shape their own fate. *Birds of Passage* (Hampstead Theatre, 1983) examines social fragmentation when a working-class family loses its jobs and needs to move. It sells the house to a tough-minded wealthy Pakistani who boarded with them while supposedly a student, but who was keeping his eyes open for business opportunities. There is racial violence in the neighbourhood, but Asif does not care as he feels above the working class and says he will buy many homes and fill them with Asian immigrants who will fight the racists. Besides revealing how attitudes are influenced by wealth and class (the rich Pakistani holds the same views about the British working class and impoverished immigrants as any upper-class Tory), the play shows that while money divides people into Us against Them it allows people to shape their lives. Tough-minded but rational, Stella escapes from the working-class suburb by becoming a prostitute in London; this allows her to meet people and results in a job in New York. In a related story a working-class couple who had become wealthy and moved into an upper-class neighbourhood is hurt by the recession and sells their house. The racist husband who had become a Tory offers to work for Asif as he needs the money. Social position including attitudes about race and sex is based on who has money.

Kureishi came to wider public attention with his screen scripts which belong to a time when the new Channel 4 was investing in films about unusual aspects of British life. *My Beautiful Laundrette* (1984; pub. 1986), directed by Stephen Frears, is a portrait of Thatcher's London showing the effects of free enterprise where the only value is the individual making money. Society has broken down as is seen in family, marriage, business, sexual and racial relations. Freedom allows people to pursue their own interests, but the cumulative effect is a world of naked power, thuggery, and anarchy. *My Beautiful Laundrette* offers a Brechtian analysis, a homosexual Pakistani British *Mother Courage* in which we empathize with Omar, even if he is crooked and sounds like a thug in his quest to become a self-sufficient businessman. Such a mixture of empathy and criticism is common to Kureishi's writing.

In the opening scene of the film before the credits, a door is removed and tenants, including Johnny, who are behind in their rent, are evicted. The large body of someone who appears dangerous looms up, clothing is thrown out the window. Property rights are seen as force, power, foreshadowing the jobless, alienated, homeless, violent white working-class layabouts implicitly created by Thatcherism—resentful youths who are attracted to neo-fascism and attack immigrants. Taking the metaphor further, one could argue that everyone becomes homeless in a land where money creates power and power creates money and people no longer belong to society but see the world in terms of us against them. This is not a film in which the immigrants and the children of immigrants are portrayed as likeable victims. They are the object of white, especially white working-class, prejudice, but the Pakistanis in the film who have become financially well off through business and crime employ others to do their dirty work. Whites are as dispossessed as the immigrants. Johnny and Omar are lovers, but Johnny is continually made aware that without Omar and the Pakistanis he would be another unemployed, homeless white youth. As one of the young whites says, the Pakistanis were supposed to come to England to work, now they employ whites to work.

This is Kureishi's version of Brecht's *Three Penny Opera* with its representation of liberal capitalism as crime. The story illustrates the need to accumulate capital for investment, the exploitation of the work of others to create an enterprise which if it succeeds will generate further businesses. The laundrette represents capitalist enterprise. Omar rents it from his uncle Nasser and needs money to invest. To get the money Omar steals the drugs that his relative Salim is importing and has Johnny sell the drugs on the street. The original capital for the business thus results from crime and from Omar's exploitation of Johnny, his friend and now employee and lover. Johnny is like an exploited wife. Homosexual relations here are treated as similar to heterosexual relationships; both are based on power and exploitation as well as attraction and attachment.

In *My Beautiful Laundrette* the family is the central symbol of human relationships. The portrait is multifaceted. Family protects, enables Omar to get started, but family is also inhibiting and exploitative. Family was also one of Thatcher's values, part of the neo-Victorianism she claimed to represent although the film implies that in Thatcher's free-enterprise England family relationships have broken down with the fragmentation of society. The young thugs have no family, Johnny has left home and has no place to live until given one by Omar's uncle for his work in evicting others from Nasser's properties. Instead of the various ethnic groups being united against racism they turn against each other in the battle for survival. Johnny and Omar rob from a West Indian family to get money to repay Salim for the drugs they stole from him.

Family relations also break down for the young Pakistani. Tania, the daughter of Nasser, is alienated by talk of Pakistan and its customs. Her father plans on marrying her to Omar but she wants to run away with Johnny; when he refuses she leaves on her own. The close family relationships of the past enabled the Pakistanis to survive and get ahead in England as shown by how Omar is given a start by Nasser, or forgiven for stealing drugs by Salim, but the move to England results in the children of immigrants having different cultural values; within a generation family relationships stop being the basis of lives. Omar has no deep loyalty except to his laundrette. It is part of the complexity of the story that while Omar exploits his white working-class lover, they have known each other since school and are closer to each other than Omar is to his family. Theirs is the only successful relationship between two people in the film.

Sammy and Rosie Get Laid (1987; pub. 1988) looks critically at the progressive culture intended to replace the family. For many in the film's audience it was a sign of disillusionment with the excesses of 1980s 'loonie Left'. What had been liberating was now doctrinaire. The film begins with an allusion to the 1980s riots in Brixton and other black communities. The riots are, in the politically correct language of the time, described as a 'revolt' and seen by those involved and their supporters as an equivalent to the independence struggle of the former colonies. The film ends with Margaret Thatcher's voice as bulldozers raze the buildings erected by a delightful group of squatters. The film is set in London during the early 1980s when Ken Livingstone was mayor and the GLC promoted an alternative culture led by minorities. The main characters are representative. It is not clear what Sammy does for a living, but he takes hard drugs and lives with Rosie, a white radical feminist journalist. While they allow each other sexual freedom, they demand consistency in their unbourgeois behaviour.

Whereas Sammy and Rosie are cynics who have strayed in from *Liaisons dangereuses*, discuss each other's lovers, and are generally unlikeable, Dave and the squatters seem like peaceful 1960s hippies in a bitterly divided England where the cultural revolution of the GLC stops at the suburbs, the latter a foreign territory to most of the characters. Dave wants to fight the way black people are treated, but he cannot see the positive results of the riots. Another sympathetic character is, surprisingly, Sammy's father who, after having had people killed and tortured to impose order and modernization in Pakistan, is now on the run, hunted, and fearful. He has come to England to hide and give his wealth to Sammy whom he wants to start a family. Lost in the violent London of the 1980s, and often physically harmed, he is only befriended by Dave and by Sammy's American girlfriend. Sammy wants his money without helping him, Rosie regards him from a political perspective as evil, and culturally as the patriarchy she hates. A Pakistani lesbian wants him punished and argues that Sammy's willingness temporarily to house him is an example of the excesses of liberalism. Eventually he hangs himself. The film is Brechtian in its denial of empathy for most characters and in the way it makes the audience ask what went wrong with the idealism that first brought together Sammy and Rosie, how it differs from the intolerance of the right, and what might be done. Incidental attractions of *Sammy and Rosie Get Laid* include the presence of two future writers: Meera Syal as the lively self-righteous lesbian warrior and Ayub Khan-Din as the often emotionally dishonest Sammy.

London Kills Me (1991), a film Kureishi wrote and directed, is another updating of *Three Penny Opera*; it examines the attractions and realities of unlimited freedom, especially chemical paradises. Kureishi offers a parallel between Thatcherite laissez-faire capitalism and the drug culture, especially how the 1980s version of the counter-culture was unlikely to benefit those born without means to participate in its economy. The new drug culture of the late eighties is part of and similar to the illusions of the junk bond economy of the period. The power arrangements of society are repeated in the drug world. The customers for the drugs are those who eat in high-tech fashionable restaurants. If Clint were not selling them drugs he would be their waiter.

In the short story 'My Son the Fanatic', in *Love in a Blue Time*, Farid seems little more than a bourgeois youth rebelling against his parents and the story about generational conflict. Parvez's beating his son at the conclusion is the anger of a parent who has worked hard and sacrificed to give his child what he never had himself and finds himself and his life treated with contempt. The film version, *My Son the Fanatic* (UK release 1998), is a fuller story, a love story about Parvez, the father, and Bettina, the English prostitute for whom as a taxi driver he sometimes pimps and with whom he finds the affection denied at home. Whereas the film is hostile to Islamic fundamentalism, portrayed as dangerously violent and intolerant, in the short story version the immigrant father eventually loses his temper with his fundamentalist son in a conflict between generations that questions the father's own liberal tolerance. Kureishi's 'Introduction: The Road Exactly' explains that the story had its origins in a young friend who supported the *fatwa* against Salman Rushdie, and locates the development of British Muslim fundamentalism in racial and economic discrimination and the excesses of liberal freedom as represented by the 1960s. This is too pat, a repeating of sociological clichés. Kureishi has created a better, more complex, story than his explanation. That Minoo, the mother, has been sending Parvez's earnings to her relatives in Pakistan, that she claims only they love her, that she is stuck in the house knowing no one while Parvez drives his taxi and explores the world, that the son is indulged and has picked up the anti-capitalist rhetoric of the intelligentsia, is a richer story than the sociology of the 'Introduction'.

Kureishi returned to writing plays with *Sleep with Me* (Royal National Theatre, 1999). Set during a weekend in the country, it looks at a time of dissatisfaction when a group of friends are breaking up and reforming relationships. Stephan is a famous writer who has won an Oscar, he is rich, and in demand by producers and women. Although he takes drugs, he is disciplined and works every day. Otherwise he seeks the freedom and excitement of youth. The basic material resembles Kureishi's novel *Intimacy*. Stephen is about to leave Julie and their children for a teenager who has none of his intellectual interests and with whom he does not expect to stay for long. Indeed he finds it difficult to remain in any relationship; he is only interested in himself and his work. He is no longer the radical of the early 1970s, and regards all ideologies as expressions of resentment; what people create is the only value. The 'erotic anarchy of the imagination' is the basis of all art and ideas. There is an unresolvable conflict between Stephan's vision of freedom and the many inhibitions and duties that are part of a relationship between two people.

Although he says he loves the children, the play begins and concludes with Julie comforting a baby with soothing words. She is the one who has cared for the children and it has left her tired, irritable, and, for Stephan, no longer desirable. A central theme of the play is 'duty' as represented by children.

In contrast to Kureishi's concern with how England affects its immigrant community, British-born Harwant Bains (b. 1963) focuses on the history and traditions of the Sikhs in *Blood* (Royal Court Upstairs, 1989), a powerful play with the grotesque violence of Jacobean tragedy. It begins at the Partition of India with a dead woman being raped while her husband is forced to watch and their son escapes. Two years later the son and a relative are immigrants in England living in one room. Fed up with factory work, the son seduces an Englishwoman into supporting him through prostitution while the relative saves his wages to bring a wife from India. The son seduces the wife, the relative kills the prostitute, and they supposedly go separate ways, but the son eventually has the child of his union with the wife work for his gang of drug dealers. This son kills him to take over the gang. Throughout the play we are reminded of how the Sikh tradition of being warriors, endless quarrels over land, and the murderous violence of Partition resulted in the first generation of immigrants to England willing to work end-less hours to provide better opportunities for their children, but who are also absolutely amoral in their ruthless drive to succeed. There are flashbacks or other reminders of the violence the child had witnessed and a parallel is implied between those who killed his mother and his behaviour in England. *Blood* is a way to understand community history and how it has influenced the children of the immigrants.

4

England's New English Literature: 1990–2000

I. Celebrating Multiracial England

The arrival of SS *Empire Windrush* fifty years earlier was celebrated in 1998 as symbolic of the start of the country's new ethnic, racial, and cultural diversity. Dabydeen edited for *Kunapipi* 'The Windrush Commemorative Issue: West Indians in Britain 1948–1998' while Nia, an imprint of Xpress, published Vivienne Francis's *With Hope in Their Eyes* (1998), a compilation of interviews with those who arrived on the ship and others from the West Indies who were in England during the 1950s, including soldiers who stayed on after the war. More analytical was *Windrush: The Irresistible Rise of Multi-Racial Britain* by Mike Phillips and Trevor Phillips (1998), which began as interviews for a BBC2 series of TV programmes about the Windrush generation. The series was produced by Trevor's Pepper Productions. The authors note how laws intended to exclude further black immigration resulted in the men bringing over the wives and children they had left behind and the black community settling into respectable families. The women seeking the warmth they expected in churches found they were unwelcome, and this produced the Pentecostal black churches which provided them with a sense of community. Mike Phillips's later part-autobiographical, part-fictional *London Crossings* (2001) retold the history of West Indian immigration, settlement, and transformation into black British through a narrative of Phillips's life and that of his family. (Although the book does not mention it, the changing situation of West Indians from unwanted immigrants to members of society can be seen from the career of his brother Trevor Phillips (b. 1953), which includes the presidency of the National Union of Students, TV researcher and presenter, newspaper columnist, and chair of the Commission for Racial Equality. Trevor Phillips was a Marxist who had a major role in convincing black militants that the times had changed; he became a leading member of New Labour under Tony Blair.)

Empire Windrush: Fifty Years of Writing about Black Britain (1998), edited by Onyekachi Wambu with a preface by E. R. Braithwaite, includes white and Asian voices and brings out the changes in context from early immigrant memories of home, the excitement and hurts of immigrant life in London during the 1950s, the racial tensions of the 1960s, followed by a black–Asian alliance, and such subsequent developments as the collapse of an older nationalism, the formation of a post-imperial outlook, and a new England existing alongside the old. Towards the end of the anthology Mike Phillips tells of travel through the north of England, a part of the country with few non-whites. Decades earlier, a schoolboy new immigrant, he felt threatened outside his house; now he feels only at home in England—Africa and black America are foreign cultures. The provincial white England of the north appears left behind. England's money, culture, and energy are in the large urban areas, mostly in the south, where people of different races and cultures live side by side. There are still racists, but England is not segregated socially like the USA.

The Windrush story gave the British West Indians a usable past, a mythology of arrival, struggle, even the romance of black criminals in Notting Hill during the 1950s and 1960s and their influence on national politics as represented by Christine Keeler (the white girl-friend of a black gangster) who bedded both a cabinet minister and a Russian agent. Like other legitimizing social myths, this one disregards the West Indians who already held university and other professional positions, and that the West Indians are one of the smaller immigrant groups in England. The Windrush legend, however, does reflect the centrality of the West Indians politically and culturally whether in the number of the writers, the popularity of reggae and other Jamaican music, or the way Jamaican English has influenced black and white speech.

The second half of the 1990s was a time of trying to take stock of how immigration had changed England. There were many anthologies including *Writing Black Britain 1948–1998: An Interdisciplinary Anthology* (2000) edited by James Proctor. Using the arrival of the SS *Empire Windrush* as a starting place, the first section goes to the late 1960s which is seen as a period of laissez-faire when neither the British nor the immigrants had a clear picture of each other, discrimination was not organized, and well-meaning whites were patronizing. The second period begins about 1968 with Enoch Powell's 'Rivers of Blood' speech in Birmingham, the Kenyan Asian Act, the 1971 Immigration Act, and the various political and cultural groups formed at this time in response, as well as the police raids on blacks which led to a polarized society of whites and blacks. The third period, starting in the late 1980s, is multi-ethnic and multi-sexual.

A project started by the poet James Berry eventually became *Voices of the Crossing: The Impact of Britain on Writers from Asia, the Caribbean and Africa* (2000), edited by Ferdinand Dennis and Naseem Khan. Funded by the Arts Council, it contained memoirs by writers who had come to England from the 1930s onwards. The essays range from E. A. Markham's memories of how life in England no longer consisted of the large house, cars, and servants his family had known in Montserrat to Desani arriving penniless and living a year with newspapers stuffed in his clothing as he could not afford a coat. Whereas Rukhsana Ahmad remains strongly nostalgic of her past and speaks of some day writing in Urdu, Dom Moraes says English is the only language he knows and England was so familiar from books and talk that when he arrived he felt no cultural conflict or surprise. Hosain laments the inability of the English language to convey the social nuances of the feudal north-Indian Muslim culture in which she was brought up, while Ferdinand Dennis tells of a young West Indian from a broken working-class family whose teachers were not encouraging.

The establishment by the actress Marsha Hunt of the Saga Prize for black fiction, meaning by those from Africa and the African diaspora, came into being with a new generation of black British writers and gave them visibility as the winner was guaranteed publication. The first winners were Diran Adebayo's *Some Kind of Black* (1995), Joanna Traynor's *Sister Josephine* (1996), and Judith Bryan's *Bernard and the Cloth Monkey* (1997). In the theatre there were several initiatives to encourage production of plays by black and Asian dramatists, such as the London Arts Board 'Diverse Acts', started in 1995. Tanika Gupta and Biyi Bandele-Thomas were among those whose plays were performed by theatre groups with such grants. Many of the new playwrights were born in England and had experience writing for television before the theatre.

Further visibility was provided by many new anthologies of creative writing, from the excitement produced by poetry raps, performance poetry, workshops, public funding, and the Arts Council's policy to stimulate arts by minorities. *Fire People: A Collection of Contemporary Black British Poetry* (1998), which Lemn Sissay edited, includes those familiar to the workshop and reading scenes. Besides poets of mixed race, the volume includes the new generation of those of African parentage. *Afrobeat: New Black British Fiction* (1999) edited by Kadija Sesay, backed by an Arts Council grant, draws its contributions from a black cultural scene that includes performance poets, TV presenters, and journalists.

The ethnic basis of black British literature was changing from primarily West Indian as Africans settled and brought up their children in England. Such youth as well as children of mixed couples meant that black writing in England increasingly was by those of recent African origin; they, like many of the Indians, were more middle class than those West Indians who had rebelled against education and career aspirations as part of a system which discriminated against them. Even Brixton had become largely North and West African, rather than Jamaican, and was becoming fashionable to young whites. Kadija George Sesay's *Burning with Flaming Images* (1996) was an anthology of 'poems and short stories by writers of African descent', the majority of whom were of recent African or part-African background.

Many of the younger writers in *IC3: The Penguin Book of New Black Writing in Britain* (2000), edited by Courttia Newland and (once more) Kadija Sesay, are of African origins, and several are consciously mixed-race, a category which was increasingly separate from black in ethnic politics. Several stories and memoirs concern lost black fathers, including Hope Messiah's tale of a daughter's continuing bond to the father who has left her mother for a younger wife. Ray Shell's ironic 'Sister Girl' is about a black transsexual singer. Margaret Busby recalls moving from her middle-class family to Notting Hill to be part of a black scene. Colin Babb contrasts the past significance of cricket with the Americanized sports later followed by black youth. Ben Bousquet tells of organizing a black section of the Labour Party and the election of the first black MP. Many of the concluding pieces concern conflicts of values and identity. There are young people exploring racial mixing at school, and on dates, or learning in Africa that English blacks are English. How does an African family in England react when a daughter decides to marry a white man? In another story, a girl backs out of a traditional arranged marriage when she meets the man. Leone Ross engagingly tells of how the pop singer Prince was important to her in discovering her bisexuality.

During the 1990s the shift of critical interest towards narrative, the reluctance of many university English departments to require the study of poetry, and the emphasis on literature as politics and critical theory, resulted in a diminishing readership for poetry. The publishing of contemporary poetry was taken on by a few, usually subsidized, presses, such as Carcanet, Bloodaxe, and Anvil. As a result small presses became moderate-sized (in contrast to the giant international organizations that now dominated publishing) and published black and other minority poets. This was useful as the Woman's Press and Virago were no longer as active as in the past. The Carcanet or Bloodaxe imprint meant entering the mainstream, becoming an accepted part of the national canon. The development of oral or performance poetry into popular competitive poetry 'slams' was part of the process through which what was once primarily a protest form became normalized. Roger Robinson was one of those who participated in the poetry jams at Brixton Art Gallery from 1994 and was a member of Urban Poets Society. Other performance spaces included Urban Griots and Black Pepper. Canongate's division Payback Press published many oral poets.

The popularity of oral poetry, the money being devoted by various official bodies to arts and literary festivals, the commercialization of black arts along with recognition that they had an audience, opened new careers and entrepreneurial opportunities. As the oral presentation of literature became a feature of British culture so did advisers, agents, consultants, and companies earning money by putting together programmes for literary festivals, arranging tours, and promoting the careers of new writers. Paul Beasly was programme co-ordinator at Apples and Snakes, 1986–92, then director at 57 Productions. Roger Robinson later became programmer for the Apples and Snakes performance poetry agency. The Write Thing (TWT), started in 1990, promoted readings by novelists and arranged tours to the United States. Support for poetry came from the Arts Council directly in subsidies to Carcanet and other publishers, but also indirectly through various regional arts boards and the Poetry Society, which sponsored writers-in-residence, writers' workshops, and reading tours. The British Council was active in sending many young writers to conferences and on tours abroad. Centerprise's Black Literature Development Programme offered regular creative writing workshops and short courses in East London. Many poets studied in an Afrostyle seminar run by Kwame Dawes, a Jamaican who taught literature in the United States. In his workshops Dawes examined traditional poetic forms to see how they could be extended and transformed for use by black poets.

The growth of theoretical approaches to literature and culture soon produced a body of postcolonial theory. Several leading theorists were British. The most important postcolonial literary critic in England was Homi Bhabha (b. 1949), an Indian who later moved to distinguished professorships in the United States. Although too often writing at a high level of abstraction, Bhabha is concerned with minorities, immigrants, the meeting of cultures and peoples, and how they interact and the stories that result—whether in the story of the 'nation' or creative writing. He is one of the few high-profile postcolonial theorists to discuss recent writing in English rather than texts of the colonial period or texts in other languages. From a Parsee Mumbai family he is especially aware of ways minorities may be endangered by nationalists claiming to represent the majority. His autobiographical essay in *Voices of the Crossing* is useful preparatory reading for *The Location of Culture*

(1994) and for *Nation and Narration* (1990), which he edited. The latter consists of essays by others showing how notions of nation change as a result of particular conditions; there is no essential nation based on such characteristics as a language, religion, geography, or race. The nation is a narrative or text constructed in relation to varied pressures which are continually in flux. Most of the essays take a single text and pick at it to reveal its relationships to what otherwise might seem marginal to notions of the nation.

The Location of Culture, a collection of twelve of Bhabha's essays discussing such writers as Fanon, Salman Rushdie, and Derek Walcott, looks at mimicry as a starting place for resistance. Whereas nationalist-influenced theory assumes that there is an essential 'native' culture which needs liberation, Bhabha sees those who have learned the oppressor's culture as the starting place for resistance and liberation. His interest is in subjectivity and change, the hybridization that develops between the colonized and colonizer, or between the migrant's culture and the place of immigration. Instead of choosing between separatism and integration Bhabha speaks of a process of interaction in which character and culture are fluid. *The Location of Culture* includes an essay significantly titled 'How Newness Enters the World'.

In the *Voices of the Crossing* essay Bhabha distinguishes between the international postcolonial elite and the ordinary immigrant. He says that the 'double life of British minorities . . . makes them "vernacular cosmopolitans", translating between cultures, renegotiating traditions . . . Their specific and local histories, often threatened and repressed, are inserted "between the lines" of dominant cultural practices . . . From the perspective of the "in-between", claims to cultural authenticity and sovereignty—supremacy, autonomy, hierarchy—are less significant "values" than an awareness of the hybrid conditions of inter-cultural exchange' (p. 139).

Bhabha speaks of the influence of V. S. Naipaul's early novels, rather than that of any Indian writer, on the formation of his own vision. Bhabha was intrigued by the ability of Naipaul's characters 'to make their way in the world acknowledging its fragmented structure, its split imperatives, its sense of an absence of authority'. Bhahba felt 'the ability of his characters to forebear their despair, to work through their anxieties and alienations towards a life that is radically incomplete yet intricately communitarian, busy with activity, noisy with stories, garrulous with grotesquerie, gossip, humour, aspirations, fantasies—these are signs of a culture of survival that emerges from the other side of the colonial enterprise' (pp. 140–1).

For Bhabha the lesson of Naipaul's characters is the possibilities of personhood, the many possibilities of ordinary life for those on the margins of society. In a reply to the crude simplifications of some postcolonial theory, Bhabha speaks of translation as 'not simply appropriation or adaptation' but cultures revising their own norms and values. Bhabha differs from such older cultural theorists as Raymond Williams who talked about the feelings and values of the British working class and who argued for a political left rooted in such national authenticity. Towards the conclusion of 'The Vernacular Cosmopolitan' Bhabha mentions the way notions of black culture had developed a resonance during the 1980s in response to British politics. Bhabha feels that British society changed and points towards Rushdie's *The Satanic Verses* as an image of how the energy, what Bhabha terms the 'vibrancy and insurgency', of immigrant life was transforming London: 'Suddenly the intimate lives and concerns of London's migrants and minorities emerge as major metropolitan themes and, in this translated terrain, they become agents of a historic transformation' (p. 142).

Bhabha's theories have been influenced by his life, first as part of a minority in India, and then in England as part of an international elite distinct from the other immigrants, a distinction that was sharpened with publication of *The Satanic Verses*. What Bhabha saw as a celebration of the transformation of England by its minorities became an example of the problems that could accompany the 'insurgency' of immigrant life.

Routledge, which had done well as publishers of the post-structuralist theorists, noticed that postcolonialism was a new academic interest and became one of the first major publishers pushing the study of black British literature and culture. It took over the publication of *Wasafiri*, the journal of Caribbean, African, Asian and Associated Literatures in English from ATCAL. Routledge published several readers and companions for the new market including *Black British Culture and Society: A Text Reader* (2000), edited by Kwesi Owusu, and *Companion to Contemporary Black British Culture* (2002), edited by Alison Donnell.

Official recognition of black British literature can be seen from the 1997 'Tracing Papers' conference at the Museum of London, to discuss black British literature and the 2001 'Write Black, Write British' at the Barbican Centre, besides conferences at universities in England and abroad. There had been books of literary criticism about V. S. Naipaul (usually as a West Indian writer), followed by books about Sam Selvon and Salman Rushdie, but the first survey was *Other Britain, Other British: Contemporary Multicultural Fiction* (1995), edited by A. Robert Lee. It joined Anne Walmsley's *The Caribbean Artists' Movement: 1966–1972* (1992) as places to start in understanding the new literature. They were joined by Susheila Nasta's *Home Truths: Fictions of the South Asian Diaspora in Britain* (2002), C. L. Innes's *A History of Black and Asian Writing in Britain 1700–2000* (2002), and several collections of German and American conference papers discussing recent British writing. Innes's excellent book only has a short 'epilogue' on post-Windrush writing, but is useful for understanding how the rapid development of a tradition of black and Asian literature since 1948 contrasts with sporadic earlier writing.

As book-length academic studies of individual authors had for some decades been considered unprofitable, there had been few beyond those concerning Naipaul and Rushdie. The situation began to change when John Thieme convinced Manchester University Press to start Contemporary World Writers which, beyond including Rushdie along with such world-famous writers as Peter Carey, Derek Walcott, and Wole Soyinka, published studies of Ishiguro, Mo, Kureishi, and Caryl Phillips. Peepal Tree Press also announced a series of studies of British Caribbean writing, while the British Council, in renewing its Writers and Their Works introductory booklets, commissioned titles concerning the new black and Asian writers including Cynthia Wong's *Kazuo Ishiguro* (2000).

At the end of the century another feud developed over the nature of black literature which had earlier lost its Asian component. While African children faced problems at school from West Indians who felt that the new immigrants were invading their territory, and as black Britain was becoming darker, a division developed within the black community based on 'shade'. Those with lighter skins were being termed mixed race (a category which became widely used) and accused of acting white. This was an old accusation aimed at light-skinned mulattos, but a strange one as in comparison to Africans few of West Indian origins were black. Indeed there are black and brown Africans. Behind such hostility were class tensions. The West Indian community had been the leader among minorities because for decades its brown professionals and black working class shared the same politics and culture based on Caribbean tastes, nationalist history, and the prejudice undergone by decades of immigrants. But this was changing. A West Indian middle class of university graduates and professionals was leaving behind the alienated unemployed, often unemployable, youths on the estates. Moreover, Africans and those of mixed race appeared to be getting ahead in society through education and finding or creating niches in the middle class. The continuing fashionable 1980s pose of a young black rebel did not help the unemployed nor did some of its characteristics copied from the USA of speaking in black dialect and treating schooling as a white plot. The black middle class could drop into such poses for a weekend, unemployed youth were stuck in them. Such tensions found their way into literature with many short stories and chapters of novels being concerned with the meetings and conflicts within a now stratified black society. In some cases authenticity was no longer a matter of colour, whites who were brought up around and shared working-class black culture became honorary blacks. Just as 'black' had become 'black and Asian' so now 'Asian' was starting to fragment into its various components. Shelly Silas's play *Calcutta Kosher* (2000), performed by Tara Arts during 1998, concerns Indian Jews.

What then was black literature? There were generational differences. Some considered older writers such as Berry and Markham colonial immigrants and not really black British like themselves. Among those who proclaimed their black Britishness the question of which social class was authentically black began to be heard. At the 'Write Black, Write British' conference, September 2001, Steve Pope of Xpress claimed that black Britain read and bought his publications which reflected black life and speech in England. While arguments about cultural or group authenticity are always being debated, they reflected an increasing division within black Britain between the professional and working class, a division accented by such matters as who gets recognition and patronage. Mike Phillips has complained that white reviewers and arts-granting bodies favour those who write about unemployed and criminal blacks.

Tensions, confrontations, even battles, between racial minorities and the police remained news throughout the 1990s. There was the death of Stephen Lawrence by white racists which the police seemed unwilling to investigate or investigated incompetently in such a way as to make conviction of the guilty impossible. Such murder might have been ignored in the past but the Lawrence family had influential contacts which led to the Macpherson report branding the police as racist. There were other cases, such as blacks picked up on vague charges and later found dead in their cells, supposedly as suicides or resulting from some medical problem. The police appeared permeated with hate towards people of colour and unwilling to distinguish between criminals and ordinary blacks and Asians. Such active discrimination could be seen in the framing of an Asian police officer for inciting racial hate, an injustice which the police were unwilling to correct despite being told so by commissions. Riots in the north of England were instigated by racist groups which the police allowed to demonstrate while arresting Asians who protested. Rather than defending public order the police created disorder.

The social background of English literature continued to change. Mimi Khalvati was from Persia, Tony Hanania from the Lebanon. Many writers were mixed race and born in Britain. Jackie Kay was Scottish-Nigerian as was Luke Sutherland; Gabriel Gbadamosi was Irish-Nigerian. Official recognition of the multicultural and multi-racial nature of English literature was further seen in honours awarded to writers. V. S. Naipaul was knighted by the Queen in 1992; in 1994 James Berry was awarded an OBE on his seventieth birthday. John Major remained prime minister until 1997 when Tony Blair and Labour came to power. Although backed by most artists and minorities, this Labour government had little interest in the arts which it viewed as snobbery in contrast to popular entertainments. V. S. Naipaul described it as a government of philistines and to prove him right his being awarded the Nobel Prize for

Literature in 2001 was ignored by the government. Naipaul was a British citizen, with origins in the West Indies and India and with a Muslim East African Pakistani wife. For a government which had made so much public display of supporting multiculturalism, the failure to recognize that Naipaul had won the most important literary award in the world was revealing. The last British author to be so honoured was William Golding in 1983. While part of official England had promoted its multiracial literature through Arts Council Grants and British Council tours abroad, other sections seemed unaware that such writers already had recreated England's literary tradition and how readers imagined England.

The decade began with the apparent collapse of the notion of English literature; it concluded with its restoration as a multiracial literature. By now there were several generations of immigrants who had settled, and brought up and educated children in England. There was racial mixing socially, culturally, and genetically. There were active policies to discourage racial discrimination. The cities and their suburbs had become international, a mixture of peoples, tastes, religions. The literature of the 1950s about finding housing and work, filled with recent memories of the warm tropics, was replaced by wondering what it was like in those lands their parents had left, and visits to ancestral homes, followed by affirmations of black Britishness. Some writers had found refuge in England from the brutalities of ancestral homes. The poet Jack Mapanje (b. 1944), imprisoned for over three years in Malawi because of his writings, came in 1991 after an international campaign for his release. After 1948 most writers of colour were concerned about the problems of immigration. By 1970 many were young black radicals. By 1985 they were affirming the right to be in England and claiming a racial history in England. By 1995 they were writing about middle-class lives, or those who had been left behind in black ghettos, and notating the social history of the recent decades that had produced them. Some writers seemed more interested in private lives than racial and political matters. Recent immigrants seemed to fit in without the anguish and problems of the past.

Increasingly writers from elsewhere were using England as a base either because of its publishing and literary worlds, or because easy communications made an international life possible, or because their own place of origins had become threatening or undesirable. London had become an international city with a large community of resident writers from elsewhere who were either employed in England or used it as a home while being part of the literary scene. Neither immigrants nor birds of passage, such resident migrants had similarities to those at the end of the colonial period in the 1940s and 1950s who were at home in England while retaining homes elsewhere. Instead of being part of the Empire they were products of internationalization.

II. Prose: Remapping England

Black Britain

Black British became the usual term for the new black popular fiction, the urban naturalism that evolved from such models, as well as the serious detective stories written by Mike Phillips, and a generation of new writers, many of whom were of mixed race. If black British could be the basis for separatist assertion, it could also mean racial pluralism. There was an increasing interest in what might be thought the white side of blackness, how white working-class and women's lives were like those of blacks and Asians, what it was like to be white in a mixed marriage. A small but significant number of writers avoided racial or ethnic classification. Besides the increasing prominence of Nigerian, British Nigerian, and British Asian authors, there was now a large community of resident writers from parts of Asia.

Black British pulp fiction started when Xpress published *Yardie* (1992), the first of Victor Headley's trilogy about D, a Jamaican sent to England as a gang courier. Instead of delivering the consignment, he uses the cocaine to become a British gang lord and is soon being pursued. Intended as a film script, a British version of Michael Thelwell's classic *The Harder They Come*, a violent Jamaican movie about a tough young man, *Yardie* concerns becoming self-sufficient in an environment of poverty, drugs, and crime: the main character, a criminal, is treated as a hero, someone to identify with, rather than a villain.

Two journalists who worked for *The Voice* hoped to raise money for the *Yardie* film by getting the script published. Unable to attract a publisher, they printed the novel themselves. It attracted attention in the press, sold 12,000 copies, and was taken on by Pan, a mainstream paperback publisher. Steve Pope and Dotun Adebayo had stumbled on a previously untapped literary market, black Britons who wanted to read books about themselves and the places where they live, written by one of themselves in a language and manner that approximated black urban life—books by those felt to be part of the community. As journalists who wrote for black publications, Pope and Adebayo knew how to reach their community and make it identify with their product. Xpress advertised in black areas of London the way dances or records were publicized with fliers that looked like record covers. The novels often allude to Pope, Adebayo, other Xpress books, or Adebayo's radio programme. Xpress asked its readers to submit manuscripts about their lives; many of the characters in the novels think about turning their lives into stories for Xpress. Such novels gave their readers a feeling of being intimately part of the contemporary black, especially West Indian, scene in Brixton and the estates.

Xpress novels assume that blacks live and have their own society in a racially prejudiced nation in which life can be tough and many youths become criminals. The law of the street is survival. The novels also assume free will, the ability to distinguish between what becomes harmful and what is useful to the individual and to the black community. There are moral choices to be made, and the morals are conservative, although not those of white Conservatives. While the novels of Selvon, Lamming, and Okri were felt to be written for whites, here was something that followed the conventions of popular black West Indian culture, yet was British. Xpress novels used black street talk, had black British characters in situations where they were not often portrayed in fiction. The novels were designed to be pulp fiction with much sex, violence, excitement, humour, and sounding off about such issues as the difficulty of young blacks finding jobs, the brutality of white police, and the unwillingness of black men to settle and bring up families. There was another social reality, often ignored by those advocating multiculturalism, behind such fiction. Large-scale new immigration brought new criminals. British criminals were being challenged and replaced by Chinese Triads (as in Mo's *Sour Sweet*), Jamaican Yardies, and other newcomers.

Yardie was a runaway success; *Excess* (1993) and *Yardie 3* (1994) were Headley's sequels about D in the criminal world and 'front line' (where police and the community clash) of black London. Soon Xpress books were being sold at W. H. Smith and other chains, first print runs of 10,000 were usual, and such trade publishers as Abacus and Fourth Estate began looking for books about black Britain, involving Jamaican immigrants, set in black ghetto communities, written in black street talk, and concerned with crime and the dangerous life of inner-city youths. This reinforced, as Mike Phillips complained in *London Crossings* (2001), an existing stereotype of black England, especially of black urban youth, as trapped victims in a culture of drugs and violence imported from the West Indies, a model itself based on stereotypes of black American inner-city violence, a stereotype earlier exploited by Chester Himes and more recently by Walter Mosley.

Yardie was an immigrant novel, a hybrid, that transferred a Jamaican stereotype to England. England was tough, but not as violent as Jamaica. While England was another territory in which to hustle for a living, it offered hope of a better life than the islands. The close relationship of early Xpress writing to Jamaica can be seen in Tony Sewell's *Jamaica INC.* (1993), which traces a century of Jamaican history from shortly after slavery until recent murderous drug-riddled politics. Because of the large Jamaican presence among British West Indians and because of the associations of the island with crime, many Xpress novels are set in Kingston. Dirk Robertson's *Highland T'ing* (1998) begins in Kingston with a throat slashing followed by setting aflame cigarette-lighter fluid in the victim's ear. Although the narrative soon shifts to London and Scotland, it is the Jamaican connection that matters. Colin Moore's *Obeah*, a thriller told in patois about murder in rural Jamaica, was awarded the 1995 Xpress prize for new fiction. In such tales about Jamaican brutality and crime, a New World vision of Caribbean and black American crime as deriving from slavery and being part of the black man's survival was imported to England.

Besides creating a formula for stories about the lives of blacks in Britain's inner cities, Xpress fiction avoids white characters. The assumption is that blacks want to read about black lives, not about blacks in a white or a mixed society. Xpress also redefined how black British patois was written. This was not the language of Selvon, but something more contemporary, a patois heavily influenced by Jamaican English. Its notation was difficult to understand for those unfamiliar with the sounds.

Cop Killer (1994) tells of how two sons of Jamaican immigrants respond to the murder of their mother by corrupt white police who mistakenly kill her while seeking a drug dealer from whom they are not getting their percentage. Her one son is studying for qualifications and a better life and settles for financial compensation after the police literally get away with murder. He also returns to the West Indies for a period where he learns that he is not a Jamaican and must accept being British. He will have a career, marry, and have a family. The other brother, a taxi driver, trains himself in the arts of revenge, kills several police including those involved in his mother's death, and at the end of the novel is still driving his cab undetected. The story can be said to show, 'There ain't no justice—just me!', a line several times repeated in the story and quoted on the cover. He learns, however, that his mother's death was caused by a black giving false information to the police which made them suspect that his own brother was a drug dealer. While justifying black anger Donald Gordon shows, through the mother and brother, alternatives to violence when faced by white hostility. A common formula in black British fiction is such doubling, the use of a brother, sister, or close friend whose behaviour is the opposite of the protagonist's. Often the double is killed or wounded by the police. As bad as England may appear, Jamaica, we learn, is more corrupt, crime filled, and violent, and the authorities more unjust. The taxi driver reflects that if he had not taken to revenge killings he might have written a love story for Xpress.

Xpress novels are moralistic about the bad effect on the black community of drugs, guns, and male irresponsibility. Rather than joining in gangsta rap, the novels are written against their valuation of the macho killer as urban black hero. The readership of Xpress novels is overwhelmingly black women and the novels show how a culture of drugs and violence destroys the family and leaves children fatherless, perpetuating from generation to generation a community pathology of single-parent families and irresponsible men. Karline Smith's *Moss Side Massive* (1994; rev. 2000), set in Manchester, concerns war between two gangs of young blacks. The narrative inevitably leads to a bloodbath in which the gangs shoot it out to see which survives. Such a conclusion is inherent to the basic notion that life consists of a struggle for territory over which a person or gang rules and needs to expand their domain which leads to a war for survival once 'respect' (fear of one's violence) is lost. The story shows the terrible effect of the macho gangland culture on families. Once part of a gang the men become trapped and no longer have a family life. Towards the end of the novel the leader of the stronger gang realizes that a member of the other gang is his half-brother. His father left his mother and had a family by another woman. Male irresponsibility, caused in part by the economic problems of black men, destroys the family as the basis of community and creates a culture of male bonding in which gang competes with gang.

After *Yardie* the best-known Xpress books were Patrick Augustus's *Baby Father* trilogy, republished as *The Complete Baby Father* (1999), followed by *Baby Father 4*. The series observes four black men through their early manhood, relationships to women, and their fathering of and separation from their children. Written within conventions of TV soap opera, in which the stories reflect on each other, with each scene often ending with the unexpected and outrageous, the novels portray representative successful, desirable black men. The central incidents involve men straying outside relationships, their lies to women and themselves, and what they and others suffer as a result. Now that there are child-support laws men can no longer increase and multiply without paying for it, yet by law are denied access to their children. Many Xpress novels portray black women as more serious about work, finances, and security than black men. Carl Peters's amusing *Diary of a Househusband* (1998) indicates some of the social and gender tensions in contemporary England, especially in the black community, where women may hold better paying, higher powered jobs than their men and where other roles might be reversed.

Many Xpress novels seem shaped by the same editorial hand, Dotun Adebayo (b. 1959), the newspaper and radio columnist and older brother of the novelist Diran Adebayo. There are recurring types of jokes, allusions to Xpress books and Adebayo's columns, ways in which chapters end, and social and ethical comments, which feel familiar and will either seem predictable or make the reader part of the Xpress circle of readers. Dotun Adebayo edited almost ninety titles, of which some thirty have been heavily edited, and some totally rewritten. He probably should be considered the author of many Xpress novels. Dotun Adebayo's only book of his own work is a collection of essays and newspaper columns, *Can I Have My Balls Back?* (2001). The Adebayos had become a significant British literary family. Besides the novelist Diran Adebayo and Dotun there is a third brother, Yinka Adebayo (b. 1957), who has written children's books for Xpress beginning with *Age Ain't Nothing but a Number* (1998).

Besides publishing original books, Xpress republished black classics and had its own Xpress Book Club. The reprints and club selections were usually of American texts such as James Weldon Johnson's *The Autobiography of an Ex-Colored Man* and Charles W. Chesnutt's *The House behind the Cedars*. These are established older classics of African-American literature which could be republished at no cost for royalties. In this Xpress followed the formula of Virago, which made a reputation and money from rediscovering out-of-print female authors.

Xpress's pulp fiction helped give birth to a more serious black popular fiction, an inner-city naturalism, about the young British of West Indian origins who feel trapped on the estates and other black neighbourhoods among drug dealers and gang violence and who see no way to better themselves. While highlighting the situation of a decaying West Indian working class and how society's neglect of the problem results in crime, these are not protest novels addressed to white liberals. Although sold by mainstream publishers, the novels intended for black readers combine social determinism with a moral perspective. Besides helping map part of black Britain, the novels are rich in the language and speech of the community. They are a new urban fiction distinct from previous novels about London.

Courttia Newland's fiction developed beyond the Xpress formulas and influenced others through his ability to convey a sense of inner-city life, his complexly structured action-filled plots, and his notation of black speech. Newland wrote intricate plots with action and suspense, and brought an intensity to Xpress conventions, making them almost Gothic in bloodiness, urban squalor, danger, and the inevitability of disaster. Using pulp fiction formulas he wrote serious novels about black British communities. The characters are Linton Kwesi Johnson's rebels after the revolution failed. They are victims of race and economics, but more directly of their environment, of other blacks, and their own lapses and wrong choices. There are also criminals of an intensity unusual to serious fiction. The problem is how to survive and leave such a hard world. What should a black youth do? As in much black British fiction survival is a main theme, but what a person does to survive can be self-destructive.

Newland's first novel *The Scholar* (1997) is subtitled 'A West Side Story'. The narrator carefully describes Greenside Estate, a mis-conceived, unfinished housing project whose time has passed. Greenside and nearby estates have become holding pens for immi-grants, especially those West Indians who have not made it in England. Crime and drugs flourish, the youth are unemployed except as drug dealers and petty criminals. There is a subculture in which gangs rule, survival requires gang loyalty, and the police are viewed as enemies by thugs and their victims. Most of the youths lack the discipline to progress through education and some parents are supported by their children's dealing in drugs. The youths are in a trap from which escape is unlikely especially for those already wounded or unable to ignore the pains of others. Whenever the characters are faced by uncomfortable decisions, they light up a joint or take drugs. They appear always to be high on drugs and unable to make or stick to decisions. The line between documentary and judgement is fine.

The interrelated stories in *Society Within* (1999) portray a group of people whose vision and contacts is limited to Greenside Estate, and the volume has the tight focus that the unities give classical theatre, with a similar concentration of effect. This is a book about what 'cool Britannia' ignores. No one goes to a university or belongs to the professional classes. Some parents returned to the West Indies; there are single mothers with out-of-work, live-in lovers; the adults smoke dope while warning their children against becoming involved in drugs. There is always the temptation to drift into crime. While people need to survive, violence results from displays of pride and seeing life as a predatory battle (which is implied to be the ideological inheritance of Thatcher's England).

The volume begins and concludes with portraits of Elisha, who has just arrived from another estate, and who is one of the few self-disciplined characters who actively seek work; at the conclusion she has gained a boyfriend who is a drug dealer. How long will she remain different from the others? The penultimate story is ambiguously upbeat; Nathan wants to create a pirate radio station and manages to bring his friends and some dealers together to finance and run it. However, it is a 'pirate' station outside the law and there are allusions to other stations being busted or going broke. Nathan had not even thought of getting advertising. While for those brought up in such an environment the way out begins beyond law, most of the youths are too undisciplined for work; they prefer 'signing on' as unemployed to taking boring jobs: assuming something better will turn up, they become involved with petty crime. As in *The Scholar*, there is an inevitability about events, a feeling that given the social and economic situation, worse crime and killings will happen. Newland has tried to vary the routine with a love story as a way of showing that there is more to such people than crime and drugs, but he is less convincing about romance.

Newland tried to avoid getting stuck in a niche as novelist of black urban ghettos and phonetically rendered black British speech. He has written a black detective story about the murder of a black MP and his daughter. *Snakeskin* (2002) combines Xpress's sex and violence and its almost totally black world with Mike Phillips's black private detective who surveys society while trying to learn about the past of the murdered. *Snakeskin* suggests that the black professionals and the brown mixed race are as immoral and violent as those from the estates.

Each of the novelists who followed Newland's direction in writing about black Britain made a particular location their speciality as if the mapping of the place was itself of importance. Stephen Thompson's first novel *Toy Soldiers* (2000) concerns the rise and fall of a young drug dealer in Hackney, East London, during the 1980s. Alex Wheatle also portrays the political, economic, and social history of his community, noting its particular problems, and recording its speech, turning the chaos of the recent past into an understandable narrative. Whereas Newland's focus is on the estates which are regarded as black ghettos, Wheatle looks at the black working class in Brixton, especially during the early 1980s, a period now as mythic as the earlier Notting Hill has become.

Wheatle's first novel *Brixton Rock* (1999) is set in Brixton during six months of 1980 when an angry young man of mixed Jamaican-English parentage attempts to find his parents and in the process discovers something of his origins and the dangers of love, a theme which recurs in Wheatle's *Seven Sisters* (2002). Brenton Brown is raised in a brutal children's home and at 16 is hardened, amoral, and filled with rage. He meets, falls in love with, and has a child by his elder half-sister, who, in giving him the love and family that he lacked, takes on his pain and her mother's guilt. Wheatle offers a portrait of second-generation black Britain with the young following sound systems and making social distinctions between going to soul rather than reggae clubs. It is the time of 'sus' law under which black youth were stopped, searched, questioned, and often roughed up by the police. As seen from the death of Blair Peach, a white activist killed while campaigning for nuclear disarmament, police brutality can be colour blind. Wheatle tries to be colour blind; if the police are always 'pigs' and 'the beast' who speak and act like racists, there is enough black violence and crime in the novel to make liberals uncomfortable. Regardless of the causes, this is a portrait of a largely lawless community.

Several well-known black British authors have written about being given away by parents unable to face the personal and social pressures at the time. *Brixton Rock* is a *Brighton Rock* for contemporary England, a story about the inner life of a wounded social outcast who is redeemed while becoming a criminal. Unfortunately the development of the story is predictable and feels contrived and its realism is too literary. There are few sentences without clumsy foregrounding of black slang; the piling up of tough-guyisms becomes unintentionally comic.

Wheatle's *East of Acre Lane* (2001), also about black south London during the 1980s, begins with Biscuit being threatened by a feared Brixton crime lord for whom he sells marijuana and commits petty crimes. Biscuit wants to quit but he has no other career. Barely out of school, he is the oldest of three children and he supports his family. His young brother and his sister, who does little beyond demand more clothes to go to dances, have different fathers, while his mother pretends not to know the source of their family income. Eventually the sister leaves home and is forced into prostitution which leads to a battle in which the crime lord is killed by a gun originally purchased to murder a white policeman. As the novel ends, Biscuit and his family are reunited, he has given up dealing and intends to start studying at a university. He also wins over the woman he loves.

In 1981 Thatcher's England was stunned by riots in the black communities. *East of Acre Lane* shows black youth unemployed with no chances for jobs, and continually hounded and often treated brutally by the police. They live in a demoralizing environment of poor housing, broken homes, and a culture which sees its problems as the result of British racism, a view which has become an ideology of resistance proclaimed in the popular music that is continually played at home and dances. Such an attitude is self-fulfilling. The youths refuse to join training schemes, feel that they must have the latest clothing, and deceive themselves that they will escape without making an effort. The final events in the novel are set against the April 1981 Brixton riot and even here there is irony as the disturbances begin with the locals mistakenly thinking that a policeman had wounded a black youth when actually the policeman wants to take him to hospital after he had been hurt by someone else. The novel is filled with black British social history including fashionable shoes, clothing, and records. As in many books about black Britain, an excess of historical facts clogs the flow of the story while the social determinism works against the message that life can be improved with will and education.

The most successful of the black ghetto novels is Rocky Carr's *brixton bwoy* (1998) published by Fourth Estate. This story of a young rural Jamaican transplanted to England and his evolution from school bully through various stages of petty crime to a hardened criminal seems a descendant of *Moll Flanders*. Want to be a pickpocket? Use your first two fingers as pinchers. Best to do it as part of a gang so that if caught you can scare your accuser, even beat up the unarmed British police. Know how to avoid being caught as a 'creeper' stealing from offices? And if you have many women, two already mothers of your children, are regarded as a hero at local dances and nightclubs, and live from day to day, waiting to see what might come up, it could be a good life while it lasts, especially if by the time you are 20 you are unqualified to do anything else and are bored by monotonous, poorly paid jobs.

Carr is both moralist and determinist who shows how lack of discipline affects schooling thus blocking future employment, how the brutality of one generation is passed to the next, how the excitement of living for the moment become addictive and destructive. This is not a novel about racial victims, but about the ways personality and early choices influence economic survival. Pupatee is already a truant from school in rural Jamaica and hardened to punishment from his father and teachers when he is sent to England to live with an older, sadistic brother. Pupatee is a social misfit, awaiting gangs, reform school, and older criminals to teach him the tricks of what will be his only trade. Many of the West Indians he knows, however, have jobs, are planning careers, live in racially mixed neighbourhoods, go to racially mixed schools and social events. People belong to their neighbourhoods; even the West Indian gangs have some Asians and whites. Some police are prejudiced, brutal, and plant evidence; others are sympathetic softies. The police are themselves injured when outnumbered while making arrests. The real problem is Pupatee's lack of discipline as represented by the difficulties he has in learning Standard English, reading and writing. In this novel conventional morality and the ways of social advancement sit side by side with the fascination of criminal life.

Mike Phillips's fiction differs from the black British ghetto novels, set in the estates or Brixton, that became popular during the 1990s. Although his novels include similar scenes and concerns about the problems of black British youth, they are also about university-educated adults, portray the interaction of whites and blacks, include mixed-race children, and are partly set among the professional classes. The novels mediate the problems, tensions, and successes of the West Indian immigrants as they become part of the middle class—tensions which include the increasing distance between the successful and those left behind, especially among the youth. Phillips is concerned that black British writing should not follow African-American or African models. Set in the immigrant and ethnic areas of New York City, with concluding car chases in California and Arizona, *Point of Darkness* (1994) contrasts the sense of community still found in black England with the United States where, despite talk of black brotherhood, it is dog eat dog. Phillips assumes that the West Indian community in England has become British, that a person has many potential identities which appear in varied situations, and that the West Indian experience is central to the development of a multiracial England. His position is political and sociological, not cultural or racial.

In *Smell of the Coast and Other Stories* (1987) he shows that there is no essential 'black', no essential West Indian, no international black community. Several stories take place in the United States, which at first appears a paradise as blacks rise to the top and become millionaires in sports and entertainment, are sought by prestigious colleges, and hold university professorships. The land of opportunities is also a land of violence and social fragmentation in which black youth turn towards drugs and crime. The stories criticize simplistic notions of racial or Third World identity. Phillips is concerned with representation (an interest he shares with many literary theorists in recent decades); how people are represented in fiction or art reflects cultural assumptions and creates prejudices. In *Windrush* he claimed that the presence of an overwhelmingly unemployed, young male West Indian immigrant population had in the 1960s and early 1970s led to crime and confrontations with the police, leaving an image which persisted although the black population of England was mostly now settled, employed, married, bourgeois.

Exploring such topics, Phillips adapted the conventions of crime novels using a cynical, financially insecure detective and his girlfriend. Sam Dean, the 'detective', is a black journalist and his girlfriend a partly black, partly British, Argentine. Sam also has a son—which allows Phillips to comment on the situation of black youth in England. While the novels can be read as allegories of racial and class relationships, there are numerous parallels, echoes, and ironic vibrations in each novel between the stories of different characters so the themes are treated from various angles. In *Blood Rights* (1989) Sam is constantly aware of how black England has changed since mid-century, of which districts have black histories, of black–white relationships, of black British politics, of the differences between West Indians from diverse islands, and of dissimilarities between black West Indians, Nigerians, and black Americans. He wants his son to know black British history and its social and cultural nuances. Now that there are blacks in the professions and in politics, whites ignore how difficult it is for many young black men to rise from poverty and living by crime. A theme of the novels is how males learn from their fathers, and the consequences to the individual and society when there is no father present to pass on the wisdom of experience.

The exploitation of and rejection by the white British of the black part of their past is represented in *Blood Rights* by Roy Akimbola Baker, the unacknowledged son of Greville Baker, a wealthy powerful Tory MP who in his youth had a black mistress. The story shows that white Britain and black Britain need to accept that history has made them a family which will continue to hurt itself until there is mutual recognition and accommodation. The punning title of *The Late Candidate* (1991) alludes to those running for nomination in a parliamentary election in a traditional Labour borough. The two black candidates are killed and the police—following stereotypes—blame black men, although the obvious candidates for the murderer belong to an Irish group challenged by the new minorities. In showing England and the Labour Party changing, the novel warns about resentments that result from social change. Besides the killings being compensations for the murderer's own humiliations, they represent the rage of white working-class losers.

In a Phillips novel what begins as a chase goes in other directions and brings in different stories. The conclusion rounds off the novel, but much of what was initially sought remains unsolved or found to be unconnected. *An Image to Die For* (1995) begins with a murder that has no bearing on the story, and the murder of the white wife of the black man is never solved. There is a psychopathic killer who pretends to be a detective. Life is chaotic without much predictability. The results of actions are often unexpected. As Phillips moved from the detective story towards complicated thrillers which are not resolved by catching the criminal, he also turned towards the international novel about the world's migrants. Besides wanting to distinguish the black British from black Americans, Phillips was interested in the blacks and other minorities, such as Romas (gypsies) and Turks, in Europe who he felt had much in common with the black British. Migration and refuge were international problems. At the conclusion of *The Dancing Face* (1997), Osman, a Nigerian studying in England, destroys a great work of African art and says 'I turned my back on history. After that it was easy' (p. 251). Osmond, the son of a former minor chief, had served in the Nigerian army and seen opponents of the government massacred; he knows it is time to forget dreams of an ideal Africa as home, better to begin again in England.

As can be seen from the *Wasafiri* special issue, 'The Long March: Migrant Writing in Europe' (no. 32; Spring 2000), as the black and Asian British community felt settled it began to explore its relationship to people of colour in Europe. The 'shadow' of Mike Phillips's *A Shadow of Myself* (2000) is a previously unknown brother in Eastern Europe of a well-off black Briton, but also the many other people of colour who are the 'blacks' of Europe. The novel opens in Hamburg with an image of Africans, gypsies, Turks, Uzbeks, a young German, and others drumming, playing musical instruments, hustling, begging, selling lottery tickets, perhaps picking pockets—a small international crowd outside the train station being watched by George Coker, an East German born to a Russian mother and a father from Ghana. George dislikes the sight, resents the Africans who he feels mock his desire for a more inspiring ancestry and as representing what so often happens to the uprooted. His father studied in the Soviet Union and was separated from his mother by Communist Party officials who were racists. The image of the Africans drumming among a crowd of hustlers, beggars, and tourists is one of many pictorial images that visually communicate themes, emotions, psychology, or history. This early image includes migrants from many lands seeking or forced to seek new lives in alien lands. *A Shadow of Myself* is about the hopes and social upheavals that brought people from throughout Eastern Europe and Asia to England. Phillips interweaves an action-filled plot with the remembrance of things past by many people, using six different narrative voices.

Phillips offers a vision in which the West Indian turned black Briton is representative of the ways people and societies change and form new communities, and especially of England, which for all its faults, including racism, is a place of refuge and comparative innocence from the greater violence of most of the world. The novels show how the desire for excitement leads people to migration, inter-racial love, and attempting to solve mysteries. One theme is the unwillingness of the white liberal to accept the black as an individual in contrast to a victim. Life is more complicated than simple racial or national categories. Phillips reverses the each-man-for-himself existential universe of most crime fiction; what begins as a quixotic search through a labyrinth of false clues, dead ends, and wrong solutions shows that people are part of a community—no matter how chaotic society may seem, life depends on others, even if the others are unreliable. People are products of a time and place which gives them their consciousness. Phillips's stories are about moving on, neighbourhoods changing, and his plots and the structure of his novels are themselves designed to create excitement and surprise. It seems likely that some later black detective fiction such as Nicola Williams's *Without Prejudice* (1998), in which race is significant, had Phillips in mind.

Kinds of Black and White

By the 1990s the presence of writers from various backgrounds and cultures as well as those born in England and those of mixed race, was strengthened by an increasing number who, although British by birth, had lived part of their life in other countries. The size of the black and Asian literary community, the patronage given through various literature boards and arts councils, and a general liberaliza-tion concerning matters of race and sex meant that such writers were no longer outsiders. The range of themes and subject matter also increased. There were such tendencies as the imagining of a black British history beyond tales of slavery, a complementary need for people of colour born in England to learn about the places from which their parents came to England, and the setting of stories in areas of the imagination and society beyond the usual territories of black fiction. In some novels the race of the characters was insignificant or not emphasized as if the authors felt they could now be writers without feeling their tale need directly to be about race.

One of the more influential novels of the 1990s was S. I. Martin's

Incomparable World (1996). Steven I. Martin was born in 1961 in Bedford to black parents of Antiguan descent. After Bedford Modern School, he worked as a postman and in a hospital before becoming a journalist. Set in late eighteenth-century London, *Incomparable World* tells of those American blacks who fought on the side of the British during the American War of Independence and of their lives afterwards in London where they became part of an impoverished black underclass which had existed for centuries. Rich in historical detail, social notation, criminal slang, and the ways the poor survived, if they did, the novel emphasizes the grotesque, the filth, the horrors of the period, and the insecurity of life at the time whether from criminals, mobs, or lack of sanitation. The Americans stand together as ex-colonials trying to live by their wits as the British government fails to honour its promise of pensions to these former soldiers. Means of surviving include crime, prostitution, working on slave ships, being a servant to rich whites, ornamental guardsman if young, and for the few who manage to accumulate some wealth, shop owner. Those who travel abroad learn that rather than being African or Brazilian they are now English, bound by a shared language to the whites, that London is home. A recurrent question is how many centuries it will take before the blacks in England are no longer impoverished beggars who turn to crime to survive.

Incomparable World is a product of research in the micro-history of black England to find a usable past for people of colour in their claim to be British rather than recent alien immigrants. Although part of several decades of retrieval, such as Joan Amin-Addo's *Longest Journey: A History of Black Lewisham* (1995), *Incomparable World* shares in the specific interest in the prominent black presence during the eighteenth century. *Incomparable Worlds* influenced Dabydeen's novel *A Harlot's Progress*. Fred D'Aguiar's poetic novel *Feeding the Ghosts* (1997) used economic and legal details of the slave trade during the eighteenth century. Martin's *Britain's Slave Trade* (1999), with an introduction by Trevor Phillips, includes a discussion of the influence of the slave trade on racism, how representations of black people were formed as a consequence of whites defending slavery, the part-white parentage of many British blacks, and the need for England to recall the past and understand its continuing effects if it is to become a multicultural society.

Ferdinand Dennis (b. 1956), a Jamaican who came to England during the 1970s and then taught for a few years in Nigeria, continued an earlier tradition of seeking roots in Africa. Besides *Back to Africa* (1992), he wrote *Duppy Conqueror* (1998), a novel about a West Indian who must visit Africa to lift a curse on his soul. Dennis also helped record recent black British history in *Beyond the Frontlines: Journey into Afro-Britain* (1988) and *The Last Blues Dance* (1996). Whereas the former tells of individuals from previous generations, such as an African sailor from the Second World War, whom Dennis met in England, the novel is about a West Indian immigrant who recalls the excitement of black night life in earlier days, which is contrasted to his unsuccessful club which he gambles away, symbolic of the passing of a generation and an era.

During the 1990s the history and origins of black England had become a recurring theme of its literature. Andrea Levy is a light-skinned, mixed-race West Indian whose autobiographically based fiction is set in North London where she was born. *Fruit of the Lemon* (2000), her third novel, shows the need of black Britons, especially the children of West Indian parentage, to gain knowledge of their history. Faith, whose parents came from Jamaica, grows up in London among white English students and friends, knowing nothing about her family. Having been taught in school about slavery, she imagines her parents as captives on banana boats, although her parents tell her that they paid for their passage, ate at a proper table, and danced every night. Their troubles began when as a married couple they arrived in England soon after the Second World War and found the British and themselves living in conditions far worse than those in Jamaica. Their story is that of the Windrush generation as West Indians made their way from families sharing one room and looking for work to middle-class careers, often in professions they had to learn to survive. Her father, trained as an accountant in Jamaica, owns a large business as a house painter and decorator in London.

Levy recounts social history for those confused about their 'blackness'. Faith, who has a good job, breaks down after experiencing unexpected racial discrimination and witnessing a National Front attack on a black women. She accepts her parents' suggestion that she visit Jamaica for two weeks. There she is told a complicated family history including poor whites, wealthy blacks, black Americans, Cuba, Panama, Africans, blacks passing as whites, browns sending their children to England to become white, near whites going to Africa to become African—a West Indian past far different from the clichés of tropical paradise or slaves on plantations. Her family genealogy becomes longer and longer as former generations and various branches are added. She starts to feel at home in what at first appeared a strange foreign culture and can return to England knowing who she is and from where she comes. As she leaves, Faith is told that her parents sent her to Jamaica as she was making a mess of her life in London. Their version of her life is unlike her own and contributes to the notion of history as an uncertain story told from different perspectives. Indeed she keeps being told different versions of family history.

Joanna Traynor shares in another tendency of black fiction during the 1990s, the use of models developed in popular and pulp fiction. Traynor herself is part Nigerian and her life is the source material for her first novel. *Sister Josephine* (1997), winner of the second Saga Prize, is a house of distorting mirrors as it mixes pulp fiction with Jacobean grotesque. The central character, Josie (Josephine), is half West Indian. Her father is unknown and she does not know her mother who abandoned her. Not chosen as an orphan child, probably because of colour, she is eventually sent to strictly observant Catholic foster-parents with whom she carries on a war, until she is passed to another terrorized family which uses influence to have her accepted as a trainee nurse. Unable any longer to harm others by acting spoiled, she begins making friends, has sex, faces racial prejudice, and describes operations as if they were comic horror films: 'They were birthing them in one room and bottling them in another' (p. 159).

At the intersections the drill went in. Brrrrrrrrrrrrrrrrrr! Blood spurted out of the head in jets. Squirts and squirts of it in all directions. The theatre, surgeon, anesthetist, nurses—drench in blood. The lights dripped with it. The floors awash. The excitement. My little legs jellied. (p. 164)

The hospital represents society; besides the professional hierarchy with its various titles, there is a sexual pecking order with doctors having their choice of nurses. Access to drugs offers a source of corruption which is protected by violence and links the hospital to the outside community. Towards the end Josephine fears for her life as she has witnessed a killing.

While *Sister Josephine* can be contextualized in relation to blacks abandoned by parents and brought up in white foster-homes and the new awareness of 'mixed race', its power is its instability of tone, its theatre of repulsion, its grotesqueries. As we see through Josie's eyes we empathize with her, but she is as nasty as others in the book. Instead of a hospital romance or even comedy, the book keeps veering towards shock comics. It asks why we live, and the only answer seems to be fear of death. Yet it is upbeat in its energy and in-your-face attitudinizing. The language mixes the banal with the unexpected in ways literary language rarely does.

Divine (1998) is poised between serious literature and a popular thriller with a trial providing much of the excitement. It offers a portrait of English youth, especially its university students continually using soft drugs, and the police framing minorities. Both portraits are part of larger implied picture of England as a land governed by class and money; the drug culture with its financial and organizational hierarchy is a reflection of the larger economy. Although those at the bottom through class, poor jobs, lack of money, or bad looks are discriminated against, that is no reason to whine and give up; for those who strive there are opportunities and pleasures. The novel's structure is of interest because of its split time scheme. Framing and interspersed throughout the story are various phases of a trial. The narrative, which if rearranged chronologically would lead up to the trial, concerns Vivian Jackson, a 20-year-old university student who is part-black, facially deformed by a childhood accident, and who has indeed sold soft drugs but not the hard ones she is accused of selling (as she was still working her way up the hierarchy of dealers and was not yet given the chance to sell heroin).

Vivian's face is used symbolically for race, class, sex, and other relationships in which people are judged by appearances. Vivian's father is black working class, a miner living on a pension, her mother white, and her sister a graduate with a First Class degree from Oxford with a good job in Paris. Vivian resents her attractive bright sister as having everything in her favour. Although Vivian complains about racism, she does not divide the world into races.

Those with money, regardless of race, avoid problems. A wealthy British Pakistani friend uses drugs, sleeps with white men, but will have an arranged marriage, divides the world by colour, and feels her culture is superior. The novel's title not only alludes to the sister, who in an unexpected ironic development has a lesbian lover with whom she is going to live in a commune in Vietnam, but also to the irrational chances life offers: at the novel's conclusion Vivian has two men competing and there is a possibility of improving her appearance by new surgical techniques. If she is found not guilty she will move in with the man she wants, a drug dealer.

Traynor's third novel, *Bitch Money* (2000), a thriller, begins with a gang planning a crime in Manchester. Jonathan, a black layabout, is the driver of a van of stolen TV sets. Returning from the robbery he runs into a car, killing the driver, and flees to Spain where he does odd jobs among the British along the Costa del Sol, meets an old girl-friend, and is torn between wanting to live off and loving her. He is tracked down by one of the Manchester criminals, who wants his money. The girlfriend is forced into a porno film where she is drugged, gang-raped, slashed, and becomes crazed. She and Jonathan escape to England where while going through customs she starts tossing piles of money into the air, claiming it is his. Her bag is filled with drugs she has stolen from the pornographers.

Jonathan is part of the yob culture produced in an England where money is all that counts and where many of the working class are unable to climb out of a life of near-poverty, violence, and crime. Unwilling to study or discipline himself to any job, he even makes a mess of his crimes. All he can do is complain, especially at his father who tells him to get and stick to a boring but steady job. Traynor provides a map of the British abroad in Spain where they stick together yet remain divided by class, and avoid the 'natives'. 'Abroad' is the good life of getting drunk or laid; selling property or sex has replaced the romance of the Med. Set during Thatcher's England, the novel shows a violent free enterprise society of winners and losers in which money and love are both 'bitches' and in which there are no values beyond success. Jonathan and his family are the only blacks in the novel except for some illegal 'African' immigrants in Spain.

An extreme example of writing without race can be found in the novels of Mike Gayle (b. 1970), the Birmingham music and advice columnist whose softie lad's fiction includes *My Legendary Girlfriend* (1998), *Mr Commitment* (1999), *Turning Thirty* (2000), and *Dinner for Two* (2002). Written within formulas made popular by Nick Hornby and Helen Fielding, the novels concern the relations between the sexes, especially the problems that arise about dating and marriage for urban British whites in their twenties and thirties. The sexual attraction, the fights, the breaking up, the reconciliations are set within the context of the differing tastes and expectations of men and women, a context sketched in by references to meals, records, TV shows, restaurants, clothing, to make the story seem up to date and trendy.

While Gayle works within a kind of best-selling British fiction without trying to revise it from a black perspective, the way Mike Phillips has with the detective story and thriller, the kind has been reworked for a black readership in some of the Xpress novels, such as the *Baby Father* books. The Xpress novels offer more sex, more sociology, show men more irresponsible and women more combative and angry, and have a less convincingly realistic texture to the narration, but the formula is similar to *Mr Commitment* in which the male feels threatened by being tied down for life to one woman while the woman feels she is wasting her life with someone who will not make a commitment to marriage. A difference between the Gayle novels and the Xpress books is that Gayle offers basically weak 'new' men who are self-conscious and ashamed of their selfishness and who easily cave in when, for example, the woman becomes pregnant, and the women are less demanding of material things, whereas in the Xpress books the men father children without a sense of responsibility towards the mother, and the mother is often financially demanding.

An intensely serious writer with an interest in popular fiction, Leone Ross (b. 1969) appeared in many anthologies during the 1990s including books of pulp and science fiction. Ross, the product of a broken West Indian family, was born in England, spent part of her youth and received her first degree in Jamaica, and lived in the United States, before settling in London. Her writing reflects her varied background including being of mixed race. *All the Blood is Red* (1996), which was nominated for the Orange Prize, tells a complicated tale of three West Indian women in England and their insecurities concerning appearance, men, careers, and colour. Tall, light-skinned Nicola, who when young thought she was ugly, always wanted to sleep with white men and has become a famous actress in a play by a famous white director who wants to marry her. Nicola forgoes the chance of starring in a Hollywood film to care for her new friend Jeanette who was badly harmed by a black serial rapist who, thinking he is ugly, revenges himself on women. During the trial the black press and protest groups accuse a leading police officer of having made a racist comment, while the rapist is judged not guilty after the defence gets one of Jeanette's former lovers to testify falsely that she likes roughing up. Alexandrea, who feels rejected by Nicola's new friendship with Jeanette, loses her job working for an independent television company when she rejects the advances of the black man in charge. The three women are part of a new Britain in which black women go to university, have careers in the media, and are the subject of media attention. Interwoven throughout the novel is another story told in thick patois by an uneducated black Jamaican who recounts her impoverished childhood, then life as a prostitute, and her present condition cleaning toilets in England where she has come in the hope that her two daughters will escape from the kind of life she has led. They are already turning bad. A powerful novel about the ways in which people corruptly use power, the ways in which people think and act in racial categories, and in the ways women are disadvantaged in society, *All the Blood is Red* suffers from passages which sound like teenage gush about insecurities, appearance, and male–female relations. Like several other new writers in the late 1990s, Ross mixes serious with popular, even pulp, fiction. Her verse in Kadija Sesay's anthology *Burning Words, Flaming Images* (1996) sacrifices technical sophistication for amusing sexual realism.

Orange Laughter (1999) descends from Dostoevsky's *Notes from Underground* by way of that African-American classic, Ralph Ellison's *Invisible Man*. Tony Pellar, the narrator, is literally underground, living in the tunnels of New York City's subway system while recalling his youth in Edene, North Carolina and telling of the present. He is desired and haunted by dead Agatha, whom he calls the Soul Snatcher. At first it appears she wants him sexually as he imagines her being angry when he is with other women, but this is because he uses sex and is used erotically in the North to avoid recalling his past. Agatha needs Tony to take over her task as story-teller. The narrator's story is also an allegory of African-American history, including the migration from the rural South to northern cities. Tony's language is colourful, knowing, and allusive, close to rapping, filled with rhymes, that of black popular music. It is also unpunctuated, an ongoing flow, as Ross creates an equivalent to an oral hip-hop style for her narrator.

Agatha, Mikey, and other Southern characters were part of a community whose lives Tony recalls, explaining how the characters are related; they show how the civil rights movement of the 1960s changed the South, often at the cost of bloodshed by those intending to end segregation, and the fears and violence suffered by Southern blacks as a consequence. The unexpected inclusion of the con-ventions of protest fiction within this otherwise original novel is part of the meaning—the need for contemporary urban black culture to retell its past in new ways. Agatha, as we learn in her story, is a hero, a black feminist role model, and white Mikey (now a university pro-fessor) turns out to be related to her in one of those complicated, violent, interracial stories that are often part of Southern family histories. This brilliant novel about America written by a black Englishwoman is an example of ways literature has become inter-nationalized as a result of the continual movement of people back and forth across national boundaries and of how the literature of other countries and races has become assimilated within what was formerly a specifically white British cultural tradition.

Pauline Melville, who appears white, is of white British, black, and Amerindian Guyanese origins and shares in the ways many writers from Guyana cross races and cultures in personal background and in imagination. Although the magical in her writing is offered as an ironic Indian readjustment of the European world view, it is also in the tradition of Wilson Harris. In her writings the unexpected is even more unexpected because her tone is flat, understated, spare, even dispassionate. She is also an amusing, witty writer, whose barbs at first bring a quiet smile, but leave an after-sense of the intensity of her dislikes. The stories in *Shape-Shifter* (1990) begin in Guyana, move on to the West Indies and London, and then return to Guyana. There are the usual diaspora feelings of nostalgia, of not being at home any-where, of always thinking life is elsewhere, as well as celebrations of small triumphs. Melville's characters are not heroes and heroines, indeed are seldom likeable. Nor is Guyana a tropical paradise. In the first story it is ruled by tyrants; in the concluding story a woman in London returns to her childhood home and finds Guyana now a place of poverty, shortages, economic failure, decay, intense racial awareness, and small-minded bitterness. Yet the England of the stories is a place of failed marriages, bad jobs, isolation, loneliness, for the English as well as for the immigrants. 'McGregor's Journey' tells of a working man who feels that 'Mud. Cold. Shit. Wind. Steel. Rain. Tiredness. That's all I've got to look forward to for the rest of my life' (p. 94). In the underground he is attracted to a drunken black woman who asks him to dance and whom he thinks the only person who has treated him decently. His temporary happiness is shattered when a black cleaner warns him to be cautious as many black youths will consider him another white man exploiting black women. That night he is arrested for smashing shop windows while shouting 'I want you to know that I never owned a ficking slave in my life. Never' (p. 98).

Many of the stories are about imagining and the artist's relation-ship to evil. In the most striking story, 'You Left the Door Open', a minor cabaret artist tries to create a new character, a criminal, and decides the act will not work. Soon she is attacked by a male who claims that he gained entry because she left her door open. She fears he will rape and kill her. After a protracted battle she escapes but the people find her story odd as there is no evidence of the events. Later when another woman is harmed and the police ask her to testify that it is the same man as her attacker, she finds that he is identical to the character she made up for her act. Did she foresee reality or did her imagination create a monster?

In the 1930s a cuckolded and recently converted Evelyn Waugh went to South America hoping to heal his heart. As a result he wrote a travel book *Ninety-Two Days* (1934) and part of *A Handful of Dust*, which concludes with a Waugh-surrogate trapped endlessly reading a Dickens novel aloud to his host who is his captor. Waugh's point is that while civilization can be savage, to be civilized in savage lands can be worse. In Melville's *The Ventriloquist's Tale* (1997) a divorced Englishwoman, Rosa, doing research on Waugh's attitude towards the tropics, goes to what was British Guinea in search of those who remember his visit. She has an affair with a grandson of those she seeks, but she is unable to interview his grandmother who was there and has documents from the period. Rosa will never know that Waugh missed a more interesting story than his own. At the heart of Melville's novel is a tale about a freethinking white Jamaican who goes native in British Guinea, takes Amerindian wives, and whose resulting son and daughter fall in love and commit incest. They flee and are caught and separated by a Catholic priest who will be poisoned by the daughter, who emigrates to Canada where she marries. Their story combines Wapisiana Amerindian incest and creation myths, which are alluded to during the novel and which are its religious context in contrast to the rationalism of the father or the Christianity of the Father.

Melville treats of three generations of Amerindian life with respect. It feels real, complete, unsentimentalized, and is not understood by Europeans who come seeking escape, savages to convert and educate, scenes in which to set their own stories, minerals and culture to mine and exploit. *The Ventriloquist's Tale* shows that where Europeans see nothing and feel bored there are much more interesting and passionate stories than their own. It is a complicated novel with all kinds of parallels, ironies, echoes, and allusions, allusions to the novels of Wilson Harris, even to Andrew Marvell's poem 'To His Coy Mistress'.

The title of the novel, like the title of her first book, *Shape-Shifter*, alludes to Melville's ability to enter the world of others, to offer their perspective dispassionately, without justifying, analysing, or explaining. The Ventriloquist is Macunaima, an Amerindian mythic figure, who mimics his prey, and who here is the story-teller mimicking realism to trap the reader. Melville has a talent for storytelling in depth. She has what appears a natural instinct for making metaphors, images, and convoluted plots. She is also a self-conscious writer who has a character offer a Claude Lévi-Straussian structuralist analysis of Amerindian myths that obviously applies to the novel; Rosa also alludes to such current topics of postcolonialism as the intellectual colonization of others.

Beginning with the opening paragraph of 'The President's Exile', the first story in *The Migration of Ghosts* (1998), there is an extraordinary narrative voice; a captivating storyteller, for whom the imagined and real are the same, moves without hesitation through unusual moods, across spaces. Most of the twelve stories move suddenly into unpredictable territories: 'The Migration of Ghosts', a moody tale of an Amerindian wife's rejection of her husband's Europe, suddenly erupts into her confessed humiliation that her people have not built anything so lasting, although until then the story concerned her more justifiable sense of alienation in a strange, cold, foreign culture. 'The Migration of Ghosts' is, like most of Melville's stories, a metaphor for the relationship of the Old to the New World, the past to the present, and such related themes as cultural contact, cultural memories, and the migrant's sense of alienation. The past lives on in the imagination and emotions. Melville appears to find Europe cold and rational in contrast to Guyana, a topic at the heart of the amusing 'The Parrot Descartes'. A South American green parrot is taken to England in the early seventeenth century as a royal wedding present, observes with Shakespeare a terrible production of *The Tempest* (which being a parrot it memorizes while hating), and is carried around chilly Europe, where it is horrified by Descartes expounding the separation of body and soul, the start of the modern era. Back in Guyana it is shocked to hear priests introducing Cartesian ideas. Captured in 1800 by some strolling players who make him part their production of *The Tempest* and clip his wings, the parrot is taken to North America. The allegory is comic yet suggests how South America has been invaded by Europe, parroted its culture, and consequently become in bondage to North America.

Melville's themes are not, however, only the effects of imperialism, they are primarily the difference between the free imagination and reason. The unfixed imagination of the artist can be seen from the titles of her three books to date, *Shape-Shifter*, *The Ventriloquist's Tale*, and *The Migration of Ghosts*. She is the opposite of a dreamer or dreamy. Her language is often straightforward about sex, and her Amerindians are unsentimental and tough, unlike the Europeans, who for all their rationality and cruel sense of business, are romantic and soft about personal matters. These are stories in which death is seldom feared. Central characters kill without emotion or bringing any condemnation from the narrator. We are told that in some Indian mythology people live on after death for a time, then evaporate. These stories celebrate a different kind of imagination, a non-European vision. In Melville's fictions there is an implied parallel between the mysteries and seeming irrationalities of the story, the cruelty and lack of taboos in Guyanese myths, and the imagination of the author.

Nigerians and British Nigerians

During the 1990s Nigerian as well as mixed-race perspectives on London were beginning to replace the West Indian eye. It is significant of the new role of Africans in the literary scene that the most active anthologist and promoter, London-born Kadija George (b. 1962), is of Sierra Leonean descent, while the co-founder of Xpress, Dotun Adebayo, is Nigerian. As conditions in Africa deteriorated and as Africans settled in England, England had its own African literature. Although many continued to write about Africa, others started to write about life in England. Some writers from racially mixed families moved back and forth between cultures and wrote about life in elite British schools or found a place in the London cultural and intellectual scene. Nigerians who planned to use London as a base for careers in journalism stayed on. Soon several Nigerians wrote their own version of earlier British literary works. Gbenda Agbenugba is the pen name for Ola Opesan (b. 1966), the London-born author of *Another Lonely Londoner* (1991) and *Many Rivers to Cross* (1998). The former novel updates Selvon's classic, partly in Nigerian pidgin, by having a British Nigerian portray the Nigerian scene in London. The main character is British-born but after being taken to Nigeria in his youth, he flees to England a decade later. Although sympathetic, he and many of the Nigerians seem unable to tell the truth, stay within the law, or keep a job. He returns to Nigeria having been influenced by Black Power and claiming racial prejudice. Although the main character of *Many Rivers to Cross* is also a young Nigerian in London and part of the novel is set in Africa, Opesan combines such Xpress formulas as showing how black youth culture leads young men into trouble, black men ignoring responsibility for their children, conflict between the youths and the police, and a setting of drugs and violence. England, however, is shown a better place for blacks to live than the lands the immigrants left.

Simi Bedford's (b. 1942) *Yoruba Girl Dancing* (1991) was a sign of the changing times as writing by British Nigerians moved on from themes of cultural assertion and nationalism to the social differentiation of West Africans and to examine life in England for its African immigrants. In its history of a Yoruba family that returned from Brazil to Sierra Leone and then eventually settled in Lagos where it became part of a westernized elite, *Yoruba Girl Dancing* refers to a similar Yoruba past to Bernardine Evaristo's *Lara*, while its semi-autobiographical descriptions of life in a British public school during the 1950s brings to mind such stories of outsiders as the Nigerian Dillibe Onyeama's *Nigger at Eton* (1972). Bedford's tone is light, and perhaps aimed at a young adult readership, as Remi offers an amusing portrait of a wealthy family of eccentrics in which she was brought up in Lagos until the age of 6 when her father sent her to be educated in England to prepare her for a role in a soon to be independent Nigeria. At first everyone she meets assumes she is an uneducated savage whereas Remi is far ahead of British children her age and part of a family which for generations has demanded high achievement. Tired of people expecting stereotypes, Remi invents stories about her savage African family.

Once she has left school and moved to London while awaiting entrance to university, she enjoys the social life of other outsiders from Africa, Asia and Latin America, and becomes the Yoruba girl dancing of the novel's title. More like Meera Syal's upbeat social comedies of young Indians learning the ropes in England than the studies of cultural conflict common to African literature, *Yoruba Girl Dancing* is also about losing identity while undergoing a western education and later regaining a sense of one's self.

Adewale Maja-Pearce was brought up in both Nigeria and England. An intellectual and essayist rather than a creative writer, he has written about the Nigerian novel, a journey through Nigeria, Wole Soyinka, and a volume mixing essays on race and nationality with autobiography. *In My Father's Country: A Nigerian Journey* (1987) discusses problems of Nigeria ranging from corruption and polygamy to its excessive number of languages, and the squalor in what is a wealthy country. *How Many Miles to Babylon?* (1990) began as a British version of the Nigerian journey but became an extended autobiographical essay on race, nationality, and identity. During the late colonial period Maja-Pearce's father went to England in search of a medical degree which would place him among the Nigerian elite. He returned a decade later qualified, with a Scottish wife, and tried to be European although it took Nigerian independence before he was appointed to the hospital position he sought. The marriage eventually failed, as did many mixed marriages of his class in Nigeria, and Adewale at 11 was sent to relatives in England where at school he was called a 'wog' which puzzled him as in Nigeria he was thought 'white'. He saw, however, that the British called others 'Krauts', 'dagoes', and 'dirty Jews'. All classes disparage the ethnicity of others as a way to feel superior. Caryl Phillips is criticized for making too much of being black, a Hull multicultural feminist sees nothing wrong in young Muslim women being forced into arranged marriage, and many people, whether Tory, leftist, or black, are obsessed with racial and cultural stereotypes. *How Many Miles to Babylon?* is, like the writing of Bernardine Evaristo and Ferdinand Dennis, an attempt to mark a position in society as black British without losing the reality, complexity, and history of what both black and British mean.

Maja-Pearce aims to be a truth-teller rather than an apologist. In his two books about Nigerian literature and African politics Wole Soyinka is used as a model unlike those who hide social and political faults by blaming history. *Who's Afraid of Wole Soyinka?* (1991) contrasts the acceptance of tyrannical government, corruption, and cruelty in most of Africa since independence with Soyinka's bravery in defence of democracy, human rights, and freedom of speech. Governments have been little more than a 'legalized thief' as Africans torture and oppress each other for wealth and power. While the West and its wealth contributed towards such corruption, the situation becomes worse with each decade of independence. *A Mask Dancing: Nigerian Novelists of the Eighties* (1992) returns to the intellectual dishonesties that hide behind 'African' thought.

Biyi Bandele-Thomas, also known as Bandele, came to England, like Ben Okri, to be published, found a publisher within two weeks, and stayed. While his fiction is about the corruption rampant in

Nigeria, the stories, characters, and storytelling seem the reason for Bandele's writing. Like others who have followed Soyinka's direction, he blends modernist techniques and a Yoruba tradition with social and political subject matter. *The Man Who Came in from the Back of Beyond* (1991) has an elaborate introductory frame within which the main story is told—supposedly a history of real events about others contained in an incomplete manuscript. At the conclusion of this main story we are returned to the frame story which we now learn was a lie, as was what we were previously told about the history and authenticity of the main story. Bandele's post-modern hall of changing perspectives with its emphasis on the art of art might be regarded a further stage in Nigerian fabulation in which storytelling is mixed with social comment. Bozo, the hero of the main story, describes Nigeria as 'a faceless society of godfathers, nepotism, tribal chauvinism, ethnocentricism, shady deals, cold-blooded cruelty, mutual distrust and greased palms' (pp. 111–12). While Bozo, who turns into a killer, is not a reliable narrator, Bandele's works often have such tirades along with brutal characters and scenes of violence. Violence may be necessary for reform.

The Sympathetic Undertaker and Other Dreams (1991) cleverly mixes satire on a range of Nigerian topics, especially the police, army, and head of state, with tales about the narrator's brother who, we learn, has recently become insane. At the conclusion the narrator is found to be the same person as the brother and we learn that his mother is taking him to a local medicine man to be cured of such abnormalities as writing fiction. The form cleverly allows a variety of tales and portraits, including an amusing depiction of the tyrannical head of the government. *The Sympathetic Undertaker and Other Dreams* shows Nigeria during a time when people lived in fear of the army's arbitrary brutality.

While Bandele claimed that he was not black British nor British Nigerian and his knowledge was of Africa not England, this changed. *The Street* (1999) follows the lives of several Nigerian families in England and might be thought a later version of Selvon's *The Lonely Londoners*, a magic realist portrait of black London in the 1990s. Set in Brixton, often on Brixton High Street, the novel alludes to a now trendy community of coffee houses, an art house cinema, where 'the old mean streets had become the playgrounds and night haunts of

Trustafarians and Afro-Saxon literary, media, and artistic types' (pp. 17–18) while house prices skyrocket. Selvon's picture can be found in a black bookshop and the community is still littered with amusing, weird, and fantastic characters such as Fidel Castro, a bearded and bible-wielding street preacher. *The Street* with its many fantastic tales, including Ossie's dreams while in a coma and other dream tales, is post-modern fabulation, self-reflective fiction. It is also a progress report on England, particularly a now fashionable Brixton where Nigerian and mixed couples have replaced West Indians and the lonely Londoners are likely to be self-destructive middle-class blacks in their twenties pretending to trendy counter-culture roles.

Diran Adebayo is a British Nigerian born in England. Unlike Okri and Bandele his subject matter is not Nigerian, but he shares similar tendencies towards blending realism and sociological observations with fable and allegory, especially the mixture of cultural myths found in a modern Yoruba tradition that includes Amos Tutuola and Wole Soyinka. *Some Kind of Black* (1996), Adebayo's first novel, uses the formula of a recent graduate from Oxford exploring London to examine what it means to be black in contemporary England. Dele's father, who arrived from Nigeria in the 1960s, has two university degrees but is stuck in a low-level administrative position, and hopes his son will bring the family honour and wealth by becoming a lawyer. He keeps reminding Dele that in Africa many people walk barefoot and starve to finance their education. The father regards West Indians as criminals and drug dealers without the same drive to succeed through education as Africans, and the Caribbean youths seem to regard Africans as enemies. Dele, however, is British-African. Whether at Oxford or in London he keeps trying to define himself by difference, usually through his musical tastes, clothes, irony, or other matters of style. Adebayo is interested in the various subcultures of England, especially black England. The novel's survey ranges from the African diplomat's son who flies to Paris and Geneva for weekend parties to the working-class Caribbean women Dele meets in London dance halls whose poor speech and sweaty bodies scare him.

Dele's history of self-deception and mistaking appearances for reality provides a key to his behaviour after his foolish friendship with Concrete, a West Indian drug dealer, causes the story to take a serious turn. When Concrete gets in trouble with the police, Dapo, Dele's sister, goes to Concrete's defence and is herself arrested, kept from her medicine (the police think she is high), and falls into a deep coma likely to result in death. This leads to the father expelling Dele from the family house. The novel becomes a version of Ralph Ellison's *Invisible Man* when competing black and leftist groups want Dele to join and lead protests. Seduced by similar musical tastes, he comes under the influence of a Black Power hustler who uses Dele to relaunch his gang. The gang kills a naïve follower and blames it on white racists, a death which results in much publicity, increased membership, and money. As the novel moves towards what appears a powerful illustration of how pride, racial anger, drugs, and irresponsibility can destroy even the brightest and in the process ruin a family, the story takes an improbable turn as Dele wises up, is reconciled with his father, Dapo recovers, and Dele regains his white working-class girlfriend who is culturally black and musically hip.

Some Kind of Black has concerns beyond the sociology of black youth, the London club scene, black alienation, and black British speech. Notions of blackness are questioned; blacks can be as exploitative of blacks as the worst whites. Each episode of white racism is paralleled by black racism. Dele is a racist in his treatment of white women. The novel shows the importance of family, the need not to fall into racial sentimentality, and that shared musical tastes do not indicate shared values. Dele indeed is better off socially, in his educational qualifications, and likely future, than most working-class whites, some of whom, like his girlfriend, have lived in black communities and know them better than he does. Yet they are sometimes attacked by angry blacks who hate whites.

A strength of the novel is its curious language. Dele's grammar and lexis whether in narration or conversation is understood as sociologically black but, except for some of the slang words, seems a private version of English in keeping with his sense of difference. Its strangeness adds to the feeling that while set in contemporary England the novel borders on allegory and fable.

Tendencies towards the hybridity of literary forms from different cultures are even stronger in *My Once Upon a Time* (2000), a strange, powerful, self-parodying, hard-boiled detective story and allegory with a hip, knowing narrator. Adebayo shifts between literary conventions while once more using allusions to popular music and recent British history. The narrator's language is sharp and inventive. There are many incidents, including a palace of hedonism for the rich, a black ghetto dance party, and a find-a-partner dinner party among middle management, where realism is sacrificed for the symbolic. It is a spiritual quest, while also being a variant on the London black ghetto novel with its main characters coming from the wrong side of river and aspiring to move upward, north, and west. The detective narrator, Boy, seeks a perfect wife for a rich black man. If successful Boy will earn a fortune and retire to the good life of wealth and security. It only takes him two days, halfway through the novel, to waste most of his advance payment and to recognize that he has gone about the search the wrong way; in his desire for quick success he has taken short cuts which fail. Those two days of wealth show that money does not bring happiness.

The more he attempts to distinguish himself from his 'brethren', the more Boy seems similar to what he thinks they are like. He visits Race Man, a mysterious Guru, who tells him that if he completes his mission he can work for him and enjoy the peace of belonging instead of the stresses of being concerned about himself. There is a cricket game of the Rest versus the West, a riot in Babylon during which two women Boy likes are killed, and then at the hospital Boy discovers 'Girl', the first woman he really loves. Instead of informing his client that he has found the woman, Boy tries to run away with her and the novel suddenly shifts to a paradise (filled with Nigerian associations and symbols) where 'Girl' tells Boy that the client had told her of his coming and that she is promised to Him (who turns out to be the angel Eshu). Losing his temper, Boy kills Eshu, thus destroying the future he sought, losing his chances of working for Race Man, and losing 'Girl'.

British Asians, Pakistanis, and Sri Lankans

The British Asian equivalent to black British writing developed slowly as most immigrants can write only about a society they know.

Pakistan-born Nadeem Aslam wrote the award winning *Season of the Rainbirds* (1993), contrasting a poetic vision of his childhood with the violence of local Punjabi politics and the need to work abroad. Although most of his life has been spent in England, he has not published another novel. That he lives in Huddersfield away from the literary and publishing communities of London perhaps contributed to his silence. Many earlier Asian writers in England were birds of passage who returned home or moved to North America and did not feel part of an ethnic community in England, while during the 1970s Asian males were attracted towards West Indian black causes. It was only in the 1980s that a distinctive Asian literary presence was noticeable, and that among women influenced by the feminist movement. Rukhsana Ahmad, originally from Pakistan and a founder of the Asian Women Writers' Workshop, wrote one of those rare novels one wished were longer. The large canvas of *The Hope Chest* (1996) has similarities to an earlier tradition of novels in English from Urdu-speaking areas of India and to fiction in Indian regional languages. Ahmad has an awareness of social nuance, class differences, even differences in dress, as well as being more concerned with psychology, upbringing, and other formative influences on character and action than is now common in literature. The author sees individuals and literature as part of society from a woman's perspective. Even her treatment of the men—distant, unlikeable, ruthless, exploitative of women—shows how their behaviour has been shaped by their culture and social situation.

The title points to the main theme, how traditionally a woman's hopes were supposed to be directed towards marriage and how mothers especially have devoted themselves to, and placed their own hopes in, their daughters' marriages. Ahmad takes the 'whom shall she marry' plot of earlier novels and offers a feminist criticism of its assumptions through following the lives of several women including an English woman. Although most of the novel takes place in Pakistan and touches on extremes of Muslim attitudes towards women, it also looks at Muslim women in England and how western individualism can be as destructive as Asian obsessions with family, tradition, and community. *The Hope Chest* focuses on the complex relationship between mothers and their daughters, a relationship which can be destructive to both.

Although the Pakistan families feel dishonoured if their daughters are unmarried or divorced while in England daughters are expected to become independent and have careers, the stories are not straightforward extremes of bad mothering or of typical East–West cultural behaviour. Rani is self-destructive, purposeless, and only survives because her mother is wealthy and her family influential; her mother makes certain that Rani keeps her property and money in case of a divorce. Ruth, despite moments of decision making, is mentally ill and economically unable to support herself. She is similar to Rani in that whenever she feels rejected or judged she breaks down.

In contrast to these two stories there is the case of Reshma, one of the young daughters of Rani's mother's gardener, who makes up for his poverty and lack of social status by bullying his women. Rather than let Rani interfere with his authority by taking one of his daughters to the hospital, the gardener lets her die and then quits his job as a way to assert his pride. He sells 12-year-old Reshma to an older man who is looking for a young wife to rule and who will care for his children from his previous marriage. The man treats his child bride as something he bought and he rapes her to assert his rights. The one woman in the novel who is unharmed is Rani's sister Shehzadi who insisted on a career and avoided marriage.

Unlike the older generation of immigrants, Meera Syal was born and educated in England. Her focus on the relationship between women, the tensions produced by women neither in nor out of Indian traditions, and the way the women unite, shows a continuation of AWWC themes. Her underlying story, similar to Kureishi's, is modelled on her own journey from a provincial working-class town to the excitement and fame of London as an actress, scriptwriter, and TV star. Her novels and scripts offer a portrait of the creation of a new Asian England with both its own identity and integration in British social and cultural life; in the process new forms of identity have been created by a younger generation often at odds with its parents.

Syal's *Anita and Me* (1997) is a tale of childhood friendships and a portrait of a small society. The narrator is a 9-year-old Indian girl in the 1960s who lives in a dreary ex-mining town near Birmingham among a white, downwardly drifting working class where only the women are still employed. Meena rebels against the polite ways of her educated parents. Not wanting the enclosed world of the Indian immigrants who continually visit each other, she imitates and tries to become the best friend of Anita, a toughened, nihilistic product of a broken British working-class family with its violence, poverty, and resentment. The story continues into Meena's eleventh year by which time she learns more about her own family's history, including the horrors of the Partition, and understands that they have come to England for the future of their children. The warm, binding ways of her family and their friends are contrasted to those of Anita's mother who is racist, promiscuous, and abandons her children.

The organization and movement of *Anita and Me* show the influence of Syal's experience as a scriptwriter in its distinct scenes, each of which builds to a major action. Instead of psychology or social exploration, there is recognition of character and a strong sense of location. Cultural nuances are visualized. The characters are forcefully present stereotypes. Shaved hair means skinhead, violent, racist, hopeless, futureless.

Syal's second novel, *Life Isn't All Ha Ha Hee Hee* (1999), concerns the intertwined lives of three young women, the children of Punjabi immigrants, over several decades as they make the transition from rebellious youths, embarrassed by their elders, to early adulthood in a contemporary London where the certainties of the past are becoming nostalgia. This is a hip book in which the characters self-consciously comment on the many stereotypes about youth, love, parents, relatives, marriage, and cultural conflict that they or others experience. This is another novel in which music styles and labels, even hairdos, mark the year and social behaviour. Syal usually manages surprises, unexpected or ironic twists, although by the conclusion the fun has given way to a version of feminist uplift, uncertainty, and as the title says *Life Isn't All Ha Ha Hee Hee*.

The three women live in a London suburb and are a bridge generation between their immigrant parents and their own children, who are unlikely to need to escape from the confined world of relatives and family friends, or resist the pressures of an arranged marriage, or be told that life consists of having babies, staying at home, obeying men, and living one's karma. The three women have the opportunity to go to university, are exposed to feminism, and can have careers. The novel is about what they do with their lives. *Life*

Isn't All Ha Ha Hee Hee describes friendships between women which are almost destroyed by their relationship to men, but which survive and, along with family, are found to sustain when the passions of sex and love have cooled or become destructive. The novel begins with a wedding and ends with the three women united around the birth of a child. It also ends with one broken marriage, one saved marriage, and the third woman, who has recently broken off her affair with the husband of her friend, imagining reconciliation with her dying father. Syal's experience in writing for television shows in the rapid jumps and change in direction in the story, in how she keeps developing several related stories, in rapidly ending scenes, and in skipping ahead years without the novelist's usual anxiety to explain.

Of the same generation as Syal, Atima Srivastava writes of the conflicts, especially caused by love, in the lives of young professional women of Indian parentage as they make their way in London. While her novels are hip and streetwise in the ways expected of British fiction during the 1990s, mentioning all the trendy places, other, Indian values shape the conclusions as tradition wins out over modern liberal ways. Throughout *Transmission* (1992) Srivastava makes the reader aware of cultural specifics, whether in the celebration of Diwali, or in the gender application of 'yaar'. Angie (Ungelliee) and her brother Rax (Rakesh) try to disconnect themselves from their parents' re-creation of India at home where the radio is tuned into broadcasts from India, the father reads *India Today*, and relatives gather to discuss Indian politics and movies over Indian food. At home she has no privacy and is expected to behave Indian although she has been brought up in England and loves London. She is in her mid-twenties, a university graduate, has a multiracial group of friends, and freelances as an assistant to companies producing films for television. At a working-class pub she meets and falls in love with Lol, a reformed Paki-bashing skinhead who was infected with HIV by his wife, Kathi. When Angie is allowed to direct her first film, about Kathi, by an American wanting films about HIV, entrepreneurship and individualism will conflict with security and community. Unlike her parents who worked hard for financial and emotional security, Angie is so obsessed by romantic love that she destroys the film and her career when Kathi comes down with AIDS and does not want the film shown and Lol returns to Kathi to care for her. The sacrifice of self for the protection offered by family and community are Indian values transmitted to Angie and which find ironic expression in her refusal to make use of Lol and Kathi. This contrasts with the ruthless amoral efficiency of the American who hired Angie. While sharing in the 1990s concern with the self, career, and personal life, the novel seemingly criticizes such priorities. Although Angie has become one of the new multi-cultural yuppies, there are also reminders in the novel that working-class resentment and other sources of racial violence against Indians are not solely in the past.

Looking for Maya (1999) appears to be women's fiction (imitating a marketable popular model), a highly self-referential work of art, and an allegory. A young Indian stays on in England to be free after her family returns to India; a product of undemanding multicultural comprehensive schools (in which more Bengali than British history is taught) and a second-rate university, she drifts through London, enjoying it, drugs, and affairs, feeling superior to the British, until she becomes obsessed with an older Indian womanizer, a writer and uni-versity lecturer, with children by several women. The novel concerns this obsession, the emotions and pains, knowing it is wrong to love him, awareness it can lead to nothing, their conversations, conversa-tions with others about him, his lies, and the eventual break-up. There is little sex and even that is not very successful. She becomes pregnant and has an abortion. Maya is the Hindi word for illusion. The novel is about the need for and creation of illusions, the suffer-ing they cause, and the way such experiences seem necessary for a writer. While about romantic love, the novel is about Indianness. On the surface a British confessional novel about young, hip London, it is also an Indian novel about the illusions of individualism and inde-pendence. That the heroine's family comes from Lucknow carries specific associations found in Indian literature and films set in Luck-now. Lucknow culture has a similar obsessive high romanticism mixed with moral warning.

While many of the younger authors of Indian descent do not write of Indian life in England, there is an obvious difference in the way India is treated by writers who lived there from those brought up in England. Ardashir Vakil's (b. 1962) *Beach Boy* (1997), although modelled upon Rushdie's magic realism, is filled with detailed memories as a young boy from a Parsee family explores the Bombay of Vakil's birth, learns different customs and cuisines, while a family drama occurs around him as his mother moves out, his father takes ill and dies in Chicago, and a ceremony for the father's death is improvised in India. A sensitive portrayal of a young boy's developing awareness, *Beach Boy* at times reads like a guide to India for outsiders. By contrast, Rajeev Balasubramanyam's (b.1974) *In Beautiful Disguises* (2000), which like *Beach Boy* earned a Betty Trask Prize for an unpublished first novel, although set in India feels placeless, without scenery, without a specific local. While the lack of social texture is a clear choice, such fictions tend to be produced by those socially isolated or excluded, as there is reason to think Balasubramanyam felt growing up in his native Lancashire where his parents were university lecturers living in a town with few British of similar interests. *In Beautiful Disguises* is a novel about identity in which the acceptance of life's unfairness is mixed with attraction towards innocence; youthful naïvety is seen as admirable, amusing, foolish. A main theme is conflict between responsibility towards self and family, the liberalizing and what is thought to be the past.

A young girl in southern India rejects an arranged marriage and, fearing her brutal father's wrath, flees to some unnamed big city, leaving behind a caring mother and a hopeless, defeated, older brother. In the big city she works for a rich Kashmiri, who treats her like a member of his family. She turns down a good job working at the zoo (which would have freed her from servanthood and put her on the way to financial independence) to return home, as she hopes to liberate her family from her father by agreeing to marriage. Instead, because of her return the drunken father beats the mother and brother. She marries a man who does not want a dowry, once more returns home to tell her father, who again feels humiliated and drags her to her new husband, whom they find in bed with another man.

The characters are exaggerations, stereotypes treated archly, who act in unexpected, absurd ways like the characters in Bidisha's two novels. The psychology seems tongue in cheek. There are suggestions that this is a parody retelling of Indian myths and legends, with the events and characters identified, but the heroine keeps imagining scenes from American films and TV programmes and it is difficult to keep events distinct from the parodies of the scenes she imagines. In the narrator's mind there is no clear distinction between fantasy and reality. The story seems to be a display of imagining, an author's ability to transform dull reality into something strange and exciting. At the same time it is a delightful warning against imagining life is either like Hollywood films or Indian mythology. No one has a karma to be a character in a movie. The novel, like *Candide* and *Candy*, is purposely thin and at times little more than an Indian parody of Capote's *Breakfast at Tiffany*. It shows, however, the influence of R. K. Narayan in its tendency towards myth, its lack of psychology and depth of character, its weird twists in story, its quiet humour, in a stand-offishness from its main character. There is a moral and mythical scheme behind Nayaran's novels which allows characters to act in amusingly unlikely ways; Balasubramanyam's appears to be aiming for a similar kind of comedy. The heroine in her confusions does indeed illustrate the *Bhagavad Gita*'s 'be thyself', although not in the Hollywoodish way she at first desires.

Balasubramanyam's use of parody as a way of refusing to be limited by Indianness is taken further by Bidisha in *Too Fast to Live* (2000), published by Duckworth, a surprising offshoot of the Xpress novels. It is surprising because London-born Bidisha, like Balasubramanyam, is from a family of university lecturers and knows little of black British life. Rather than reporting on ethnicity, Bidisha wanted fame and money. *Too Fast to Live* was meant as an imitation of the Xpress formula which the author hoped would become a best-seller, be made into a film, and make her fortune. Bidisha is a self-conscious young author who, in imitating and parodying the Xpress formula, intensified such characteristics as violence, inevitability, repeated phrases, and a headlong, unchanging narrative rhythm. To this she added much from her own literary education such as basing the characters and many situations on the King Arthur story. The result is gory popular fiction of much intensity.

A cross between an imitation Jacobean tragedy of blood and horror and streetwise sensational trash, *Too Fast to Live* is set in a modern London of drugs, pushers, violent criminals, sadistic police, ethnic tensions, and rundown public housing; it is a contemporary nightmare of the evil that drives the crime scene and its gangs. Bidisha has little interest in sociology except to set a scene; there is no psychology; people are bad, good, strong, weak, mad, of the dead, of the living. Driven by unchanging traits of character, they are not products of complicated lives offering free choices. They seem to have emerged from a horror film: even when they appear to die of brutal wounds they rise again, feel pain, seek revenge, and inflict damage. There is no love; there is rape, sex with hatred, bargains to be paid. Attraction rapidly becomes hate while the most hated may be the most desired.

Bidisha wants to shock. *Too Fast to Live* begins 'Every night, Alun lies awake in the dark and thinks about how he can get her. He knows he is better, stronger, cleverer than her lover Jon Duke.' Within a few pages Isobel agrees to have sex with Alun if he kills Jon. The killing is done in a painful fashion while Isobel calmly waits in another room. As a result of her night with Alun, Isobel will die horribly while giving birth to Rex whom she wants destroyed. Brought up in an orphanage where he leads a gang, Rex inherits the sins of the past—Alun's Soho bar, a centre of drug dealing, gangland contacts, every imaginable crime. The regulars are the perverts of the criminal world. A few characters come from 'good' backgrounds but are attracted by the gutter. Isobel is a white 'Sloan' girl, well-off, who expects much, but badly misjudges her men. By the conclusion Rex's entire gang is dead.

While the advantages and disadvantages of social class and the fate of social outcasts are themes of the novel, race is not explicitly present. In the novel's expressionistic, nerves-on-end manner, people are described as dark and light, or golden, but that has no fixed relationship to skin colour. Although many of the characters seem to be black or part-black, possibly West Indian immigrants or their children, this is unclear. Bidisha uses many literary conventions, including those of the Gothic novel, and hinting at darkness and light as racial as well as spiritual contrasts is one of them. The novel shares in the fashion for trash and shock noticeable with some artists in the Tate Gallery's Sensation show. It seems an unlikely successor to *Seahorses* (1997), Bidisha's first novel.

Bidisha is the pen name of Bidisha Bandyopadhyay (b. 1978). In her mid-teens she began writing for such popular youth magazines as

NME and *Dazed & Confused* and was asked to turn one of her sketches of hip London into a novel. *Seahorses* (1997), published by Flamingo while she was still studying at Oxford, is about as far from an Xpress novel as possible; it seems more like some hybrid of Henry Green, Saki, Ronald Firbank, and early Evelyn Waugh, with early Samuel Beckett's taste for elliptic dialogue and absurdly disillusioning and deflating descriptions. Its opening sentence is typical: 'The dry indistinguishable stone fronts of the university buildings were vacant under a sun whose myopic eye surveyed London through its watery cataract.' Of its five characters, one is a successful avant-garde music composer around 40 who, bored with fame, retires to a country house in search of a minimalist life of pure efficiency. His former lover, a few years younger, is now an avant-garde film maker and an extremely handsome bisexual serial fornicator who ruthlessly leaves them without bothering to spend a night. As the novel progresses, the composer and film maker share a 15-year-old girl, who also sleeps with her handsome father, and who at the time she is taking examinations becomes aware that she is pregnant. *Seahorses* is an attempt to be cool, callous, knowing, and hyper-sophisticated—a novel, like *In Beautiful Disguises*, clearly written in youth, and mocking of literary formulas. Its only emotions concern the way women without educational qualifications or contacts become trapped in such roles as cleaners, servants, and sexual objects. Life itself never offers what is desired. Men are angry at life, disappointed, and take their rage out on women, often brutally.

Then there is Preethi Nair (b. 1971) who came to England from South India while young and who lived most of her life in London except for studying law and economics at Cardiff, international relations at Warwick, and working in Spain. The tale of how, after *Gypsy Masala: A Story of Dreams* (2000) was rejected by two publishers, Nair quit her job as a management consultant and invented a company, NineFish, and agent, Pru Menon, to print and promote the novel, received considerable publicity. Nair received several advertising and entrepreneurship awards although, or perhaps because, the *Guardian* claimed it sold under 500 copies during the short period Nair said it sold many thousands of copies and went through three printings. Although its central story concerns an Indian woman who marries an Indian immigrant and the way their dreams of romance evaporate in London, it is a charming and ironic book of stories told from varied perspectives of characters who try to follow their dreams. The writing, which includes such ingenuities as the characters dismissing the narrator, is, like the novels of Bidisha and Balasubramanyam, of more interest than the story and themes. Such younger Indians who were born or lived most of their lives in England seem part of the world of publicity and media depicted by Syal and Srivastava, and lack the seriousness of Amit Chaudhuri or the complex sensibilities of Sunetra Gupta.

Just as Rukhsana Ahmad brings an Urdu literary tradition to English, Amit Chaudhuri and Sunetra Gupta make use of Calcutta's Bengali traditions, while Aamer Hussein draws on a wide range of literature from the Muslim world. They are part of the internationalization of England's literature due to globalized labour and education rather than immigration. Although Amit Chaudhuri (b. 1962) lives in England and as a literary critic is visibly part of its intellectual life, England is his working 'base'; he remains an Indian national and has mostly limited himself to writing about the society, history, and culture of Calcutta. He came to England to study at London University (1986) and after his DPhil at Oxford (1993), he held positions as a creative writer at Oxford and Cambridge. His style, careful, precise, with close observation of everyday details, psychology, and manners, is also intended to be within a Bengali literary tradition in contrast to the wide-ranging culturally assertive novels that were part of Indian nationalism. Like many foreign residents who work and live in England, Chaudhuri returns for periods to his country of origins and his novels record recent social changes, especially the decay of Calcutta and its once modern culture. While *Afternoon Raag* (1993) is set in England, it is about the life and emotions of an Indian student at Oxford. Chaudhuri's usual setting is Calcutta. In particular he is aware that Calcutta, which was during the colonial period a city of great intellectual excitement as Indian nationalism developed from contact with western liberalism, has now become a decaying provincial place in contrast to Mumbai and other cosmopolitan Indian cities. Its Marxist movement became a foot-dragging local government more concerned with protecting the past than meeting the challenges of the present and future.

Chaudhuri is Bengali in being both highly realistic as a novelist and yet so concerned with style that the writing can seem affected. *Freedom Song* (1998), his third novel, is a finely wrought, sympathetic, at times ironic, portrait of two closely related families in Calcutta during the 1990s. It is a novel in which little happens slowly, a bit like watching a tree grow; its delicate, even deliquescent, realism, is the opposite of the energetic magic realism and fabulation which for a time dominated Indian writing in the wake of Rushdie's success. It uses a family's quest to find a spouse for an arranged marriage as a way to examine a society and its history. *Freedom Song* concerns Calcutta and Bengali culture since independence. The city of Tagore, the Indian renaissance, and the beginnings of the national movement, Calcutta is portrayed as now a place of the old and arthritic which the young leave. This is a book of illness, retirements, decay, monotones, and lives told in ellipses.

Sunetra Gupta is another stylist from Calcutta whose novels of displacement play with Bengali and western literary conventions. Unlike Chaudhuri she belongs among the fabulists and instead of focusing on Calcutta her novels span the modern world and evoke many cultures and mythologies. Although she has been discussed in relationship to modernism and Virginia Woolf's stream of consciousness, her aims are different. Her long, seemingly never-ending sentences, with their many clauses, and continuing shifts in tense and place and perspective, and her pages-long paragraphs, are those of a citizen of the world concerned with memory, complexity of emotion, and using art to link and order experience through imagination. If myth, literary models, parody, and the improbable disrupt mimesis, it is because Gupta, a scientist, has a surprising interest in the non-scientific, the surreal, the witty and amusing. She is unlike other magic realists in her focus on private lives and feelings, and lack of direct interest in the political. Her novels could be stories evoked by strange paintings and poetic films.

Memories of Rain (1992) tells of a Bengali girl who, already in love with the England of its literature, falls in love with an Englishman, follows him to a disappointingly alien England, and after many years of his unfaithfulness leaves him, returning with their children to a Calcutta which she long ago rejected and which is unlikely to offer her much. The story might appear one of cultural conflict, disillusionment, and adultery to which Gupta contributes a woman's perspective and the woman's claim that she is leaving to free the man as he lacks the strength to make such a decision. Gupta, however, told *Contemporary Authors*: 'Memories of Rain was initially motivated by Brendan Keneally's adaptation of *Medea*, though eventually it evolved into a comment and critique of a culture dominated by the dreams of single poet.'[1] Tagore's work is cited, imitated, and parodied throughout the novel as he often is in Gupta's other novels. Her writing is a reply to Tagore's romanticism and his continuing influence on Bengali nationalism. Gupta's writing has its origins in a specific Indian cultural tradition which has continually absorbed European mythology and its modern high culture while being obsessed with its own past achievements. Although deriving from the high culture of Calcutta, Gupta's story is also universal, as is the rain, symbol of both London and Calcutta. Such writing is evidence of Susheila Nasta's claim that while a diaspora remembers its origins it also criticizes them and keeps changing.

Critique through parody, the continual mixing of the highly literary with the mockingly elementary, can be seen in *The Glassblower's Breath* (1993) in which several men representing parts of a woman's past and memories attempt to catch up with her during a day in London. Once more memories move across three continents in this female surrealist version of James Joyce's *Ulysses*. The woman is being chased by her cousin, the baker Avishek, a candlemaker friend named Jonathan Sparrow, and has an affair with Dan the butcher. Gupta told *Contemporary Authors*: 'The Glassblower's Breath is about one day in the lives of a butcher, a baker, and a candlemaker—and a woman they all love' (p. 172). Like the novel's title, such a statement suggests that all art is a product of technique as an artisan creates a version of some object or tale. Yet this is also a novel of passion in which the woman and the men are driven by desire and its memories; as the men attempt to capture her, the woman seeks her fulfilment. The woman thinks of herself and is addressed in the second person 'you', an alienation of narrator from self.

As the title *Moonlight into Marzipan* (1995) indicates, this is another story in which stereotypes are mocked as it moves into

[1] 'Sunetra Gupta', *Contemporary Authors*, 137 (1992), 172.

stranger, more amusingly decadent, directions, although directions others, such as Nabokov, have taken as modern writers began to make the art and fictionality of fiction part of their subject matter. Here a woman scientist, Esha, in Calcutta, sacrifices her career to assist her husband, Promotesh, a scientist who has made a supposedly great discovery, the turning of gold into grass. This leads to their move to England through the patronage of Sir Percival Partridge where after five years the husband is unable to repeat his discovery. He is unfaithful and, in another parody of great literature, Esha commits suicide by throwing herself under an underground train. While parodying the stories of Faust-Prometheus this is a rewriting of the folk tale in which a miller's daughter spins gold from hay. Once more the novel is filled with echoes of Tagore.

There is always a female perspective, something autobiographical, something Bengali, something unusual, along with worldly high culture in Gupta's fiction. *A Sin of Colour* (1999) is strangely beautiful as it moves back and forth from 1931 to the present between generations, several families, and India, England, and the USA in a complex improbable narrative. Gupta's prose is distinctive, brilliant, extraordinary, eccentric. Highly styled, ironic, the dialogue is elevated, and purposefully unnatural. At times the descriptive language is emotional, passionate, absurdly vague; in other places it is dryly ironic and undermining. Two songs are repeated or alluded to throughout the novel; a romantic Tagore song about a dancer's devotion to Lord Buddha predominates, but is displaced by the Brecht–Weill's mocking 'Mack the Knife'. Told in a radically interiorized manner, in long sentences, many of nine to eleven lines, this multigenerational, international novel is a house of mirrors; its intertwined, fragmented stories reflect, echo, invert, and interplay upon one other, and concern the obsessions, traps, and illusions of desire. The perspective changes with circumstances. Late in the novel the reader learns that the idealized Reba may have had other lovers and may have married for money. The title signifies a sin of unusual passion worth doing.

With Gupta British literature gained a highly cosmopolitan writer. Those who want fictionalized social studies and politics need seek elsewhere, but it is because of the presence of such writers as Amit Chaudhuri, Gupta, and Atima Srivastava that the literature of

England has a much larger range of subjects, styles, and modes than those associated with such terms as postcolonialism or the literature of protest and immigration.

Aamer Hussein and Kamila Shamsie, two Pakistani writers who live in London, are dissimilar in their subject matter and kind of cosmopolitanism. Hussein, more sensitively than Rushdie or even Souief, brings non-western literary traditions and conventions into his writing. *Mirror to the Sun* (1993), his first book of short stories, concerns multiple displacements. Some of the characters are North Indian Muslims badly treated as unwanted outsiders in Pakistan. What is their land, their culture, their language? This can lead to collapse of the self and turning to drugs or becoming insane. The stories, like Naipaul's later writings, mix fiction with autobiography. An essay tells of Hussein's insecurity in coming to London. Such mixtures of form, places, nationality, and the stories of ambivalent and interracial sexuality universalize the theme of life as unfixed. There is an autobiographical subtext with the early stories concerning flight and the later ones about wanderers. Throughout the volume love is suppressed, unconsummated, unhappy. The object of desire is married, the wrong sex, likely to bring shame, unobtainable. Writing, migration, desire are forms of infidelity.

In subsequent books Hussein's concerns remain love, desire, exile, betrayal, death, and writing. Like many expatriates, exiles, or immigrants, his writing moves back and forth in time and is concerned with fading memories. In *This Other Salt* (1999) the title story, a complicated tale shuttling back and forth over decades, concerns a writer's love of an older, married woman, and his relationship to another, bisexual woman. Set in Indonesia, London, and Italy, it asks about the relationship of desire to love, whether it makes sense to love a person or place, and suggests a parallel between desiring a person and desiring a home. Is not all life exile, idealized memories of what is lost? Most of Hussein's characters are exiles, an Egyptian married to an Italian, a homosexual Australian guide in Bali, students from various regions and religions at an Indian boarding school; the desire for friendship, love, family, and home is a temptation leading to disaster. The artist's task is to write about desire in its complexity.

Politics come into the stories as influences on personal actions—

Hussein's family leaving for Pakistan after Partition, returning to India after violence started in Pakistan against refugees from the south, a boy needing to keep his Pakistani passport hidden while attending an Indian school—or by allusions to the ways Pakistani literature has responded metaphorically to local politics. The order of stories withdraws from adulthood to childhood. Most of the stories are autobiographical and others can be read as having an autobiographical significance. Although they vary in kind from an experimental patchwork of poems and documents to a romantic folk tale, they are understated, elliptical, change their settings in time and space, and self-consciously use literary conventions. Hussein is the heir of a tradition of writing that began in Persian, found expression in Hindustani and Urdu, and can still be found in some Pakistani writers in English. There is the romantic sadness, the self-conscious artistry, the inserted tales, the indirection, even the imitation and continuation of older forms and conventions. Many writers from this tradition are quoted, cited, and in one case Hussein himself writes an illustrative example of how a classical Persian verse tale is revised and added to and given other significances by later generations. He is a complex and sophisticated writer, but because he works in more than one literary tradition his art is not likely to be fully appreciated, especially as Muslim literary traditions are not well known. There are, however, problems of his own making. Those long, complex, interiorized sentences can lose their obvious reference. There is a sameness of tone and a lack of forward movement throughout the volume. There is much indirection, fragmentation, and reticence. Hussein is an exquisite miniaturist; a rare example of an author who writes in English while developing alien literary traditions.

Kamila Shamsie (b. 1973) attended university in the United States and lives perhaps half of each year in London where she writes about Pakistan and Pakistanis abroad. She is a third-generation female Pakistani writer, her mother and an older relative being authors. This perhaps accounts for the assurance, polish, knowingness, and cleverness of the writing which is swift and witty. Although more concerned with social detail and distinctions, she is also a storyteller in the mould of Rushdie and Zameenzad. *Salt and Saffron* (2000), her second novel, concerns a Pakistani author who is a product of a sophisticated literary culture and cosmopolitan elite within a feudal society in which pride and awareness of the past are valued more than democracy and the present. There is a complicated family map of seven generations of the House of Dard-E-Dil preceding the novel. The intricacies of who begat whom reveal how Indian and Pakistani family relationships are far more complicated, far reaching, and at times absurd, than those in the West. The House of Dard-E-Dil are proud of their history and regard themselves as superior; as the story develops however—and much of its development seems to be an excuse to tell stories about the family—the past is more amusing, bordering on farce, than reason for pride. Besides the long lineage there are such characters as Hairless Nawab, Najeeb (Yak Man), Binky, Smelly, and Stinky. In this self-conscious, very writerly book, Shamsie parodies the conventions of the multigenerational novel and of historical writing itself. The central character, Aliya, we are always aware, is a storyteller. At the beginning she is telling family stories on an aeroplane while others sit cross-legged in the aisle listening as if this were an oral folk culture.

Salt and Saffron offers an allegory of Indian history. The family divides at Partition into two sides who hate each other and continually quarrel about whose fault it was. There is much parody of *Midnight's Children*; characters are born on or near midnight, there are many near twins, people are not who they at first seem. This is a novel about social divisions and the way they are constructed on a past that no one really knows.

A few writers from Sri Lanka have settled in England since the early 1940s when Tambimuttu was a literary entrepreneur. Ambalavaner Sivanandan (b. 1923) came to England in 1958, was part of the *Race Today* group, and became known for his involvement in British racial politics and sociology. He wrote two books of essays, *A Different Hunger: Writings on Black Resistance* (1982) and *Communities of Resistance: Writings on Black Struggles for Socialism* (1990), and *When Memories Die* (1997), a novel about the class and ethnic conflicts which tore apart Sri Lanka. During the 1990s two excellent Sri Lankan writers appeared on the British literary scene, Romesh Gunesekera and Bandula Chandraratna. Neither writes about England, or when Gunesekera does it is about Sri Lankans. Gunesekera's subject matter is the Sri Lankan civil war, its background and its relationship to exile and the writer making use of memories of the past. Whereas Ishiguro sees the usefulness of people lying about their past, Gunesekera worries that the past is unrecoverable yet hidden behind other stories, providing echoes and distorted images. Salgado, in *The Reef*, tells Triton that people are what has been remembered about them, but in Gunesekera's fiction stories tell of what is in the process of being lost.

Several of the nine short stories in *Monkfish Moon* (1992) tell of the Sri Lankan civil war between the Tamils and Sinhalese and how this affects life at home and abroad. In 'Batik', set in London, a husband is more concerned with the ethnic conflict in Sri Lanka than with his young pregnant wife. 'A House in the Country' and 'Carapace' show Gunesekera's ability to let the political and other influences appear indirectly as background or through atmosphere. While in other stories, such as 'Storm Petrel', discussion of the Sri Lankan civil war erupts directly into the tale, Gunesekera's usual method is to focus on storytelling and character while the reader becomes aware of the public corruption, ethnic hatreds, and psychological hurt that communal violence and distrust cause. A main theme concerns the lack of and search for 'home' whether in Sri Lanka or England. Homes or houses figure prominently in his fiction along with the relationships of memory to exile and narrative, as if a writer were burdened by a past, or by the nation's past, which keeps finding its way into his imagination although he cannot trust the truth of what he imagines and indeed might be happier if he could write without such a burden.

Reef (1994), Gunesekera's first novel, is set in the 1960s but told as memories during the 1990s by Triton, who begins as a simple village boy, enters the service of the upper-class Ranjan Salgado, and is now an exile and businessman in London. It portrays the relationship between Salgado, a self-educated marine biologist who wants to save a reef, his servant and cook Triton, and Salgado's worldly lover Nili. After Salgado and Nili break up, he and Triton flee the political turmoil of a Cuban-inspired revolution to London in 1972 (when Ceylon officially became Sri Lanka thus confirming the Sinhalese Buddhist revolution against the Tamil Hindus). In London Triton continues to move up the ladder from houseboy, household administrator, and cook to snack-bar then restaurant owner.

Salgado, however, returns to Sri Lanka to help Nili, who has been a victim of communal violence. The language of *Reef* is sensuous but quiet. The structure is like a book of linked short stories in which needed facts can only be found in other stories. During the course of the novel the reader becomes aware of how ethnic politics have torn apart a society and wounded individuals.

Details of cooking are mouth-wateringly prominent in Triton's telling. His Christmas turkey might be said to be like Gunesekera's writing, something western but with a tangerine Sri Lankan stuffing. This is Gunesekera's chutnification of history. History itself is a sea like the waves which destroy the coral reef. Another symbol is the jungle: the civil war turns the country into a jungle once more.

The Sandglass (1998) is unlike *Reef* in its many characters and the purposeful complexity of narrative method. As suggested by its title, the novel offers an attempt at recall along with reflections on memory. Gunesekera uses a technique of indirectly seeing the lives of others, especially the main characters, by examining scraps of un-reliable evidence, with a story as much about the viewer as the viewed. The novel concerns several generations of two feuding families, the Vatunases and Ducals, and an unexplained murder. It is also about the corruption of society and ethnic tensions, a history of a country in which things are seldom as they appear and relation-ships have become so complicated that they seem mysterious. The story has the lack of resolution of a multilayered soap opera in which each new episode brings further shocks and more suspense. How can you know history when it, like the nation, keeps splintering as do the chapters in the novel into many stories without becoming one?

Gunesekera has said that he tried to write abstract minimalist fiction like Beckett, but the memory of places in which he lived kept finding its way into his writing. *The Sandglass* spans three continents and moves between Sri Lanka and England, but except for a few background details the scenes could be any- or nowhere. Gunesekera's perspective seems quietly sceptical, uncommitted except to writing. Who would want to return to ravaged Sri Lanka? Even the faceless international modern Americanized hotels in which the novel's narrator stays are Japanese-owned in co-operation with local thugs who understand liquidity, international trade, and public stocks.

The intertwined tale of two opposing families can be read as the history of Sri Lanka for the past century, the mingling of its peoples, the struggle over land continuing into an era when it has become irrelevant, the flight by many people from the newly independent nations to Europe and the United States, the elimination after independence of the Burghers, the way history keeps repeating itself, the falsity of paradises, and the fragility of life. We fix the past into grand stories as we move on from regional tales of the last days of European empires to the massive diasporas, jet-set postcolonialism, and global business of the present. Gunesekera has commemorated a past which will otherwise be forgotten as families disperse, die, or assimilate elsewhere. His books are about how the past will remain in one's memory and yet decay and become increasingly a fiction as life moves on.

England became home in 1967 for Bandula Chandraratna (b. 1945), another Sri Lankan, who a decade later worked in various hospitals in Saudi Arabia for five years before returning to England. His *Mirage* (1998) was printed in Sri Lanka and self-published in England. A second printing followed after it barely missed being short-listed for the Booker Prize. Set in a contemporary unnamed Islamic nation *Mirage* is told in short simple sentences which objectively describe events and places: there is little psychology, depth, interiority, narrative tension, or excitement. Significant conflicts within or between characters are briefly mentioned, yet the story is as determined by society as any naturalistic novel. The first half tells of a modern hospital with its foreign experts, who are looked down upon by the local staff who do little work but who regard aliens as inferior. The patients who await treatment also look down on the foreigners who in turn look down on them. In this world of irritability, back-biting, and betrayal Sayeed avoids controversy, does what he is told, and says little. He has come from a desert village to the city where he works as a porter in the hospital and lives in a small mud hut on the city's outskirts. Prematurely aged and unable to read, he dreams of becoming rich as that would allow him to give money to beggars. We do not know whether Sayeed is saintly or a good-natured simpleton. He has a younger brother to whom he has given his half of the family land and who arranges a marriage for him with a young widow. Sayeed soon has an unhappy wife on his hands who fails to adapt to the terrible conditions in which they live. They seem to have no sexual life. One day she nearly dies of dehydration searching for their straying goats in the desert (the goats have been let out by a woman who hates her) and is rescued by Sayeed's friend who rapes her. They have been followed by a local religious leader who has them killed for adultery while Sayeed tries to plead that they be forgiven. The novel notes the great distance between local elites and peasants, the way foreign experts drive up the cost of living (especially in housing), and the corruption and wastage that results when enclosed societies become part of the global economy. But it is mainly about the horrors committed in the name of Islam by those with religious authority. Medical treatment, the comforts of expatriates, friendship, justice are mirages in such a country.

An Eye for an Eye (2001), Chandraratna's second novel, opens with a foreigner who works in the hospital of an Arab county (now clearly Saudi Arabia), being victimized in an automobile pile-up caused by the driving habits of the rich locals. We also learn about medical traditions (use cauterization for everything) and female circumcision (performed unsanitarily, but worse in Muslim Africa). Such topics are aspects of other themes including the pride of Saudi Arabians and the traditionalism and backwardness of a country undergoing rapid change. The main theme, however, is injustice, the injustice of traditional ways in the modern world.

An Eye for an Eye continues the story of Sayeed. Although the rapist confesses he alone was at fault, Sayeed's wife is also stoned to death. Sayeed suffers shock from which he slowly recovers among his relatives who take him to a traditional healer who places burning coils on his head and lets blood from his veins. Yasser, a childhood friend who is now a fundamentalist leader, preaches revolution in the name of justice. Yasser admits that the country formerly was involved in continual tribal warfare, but now that the present ruling family has imposed itself, the king and his clan rule for their advantage. As a consequence young men of other rich families, such as the Bin Ladens, claim only strict adherence to Islamic law will bring justice. Yasser encourages Sayeed's resentment of the injustice he has suffered; he gives him a knife to revenge himself on the mutawah who accused his wife of adultery. Death must be paid for by death, an eye for an eye. Sayeed returns to the city, but he cannot bring himself to commit murder. This contrasts to Yasser and the fundamentalists who invade the Great Mosque, take hostages, kill people, and barricade themselves in the basement. Just as traditional is probably not the best medicine, so fundamentalist justice might not be best solution in a corrupt, rapidly changing society.

That discussion about significant changes within the Islamic world should be the subject of books by Gurnah, Naipaul, Rushdie, and Chandraratna as well as Soueif is another example of how England's literature had internationalized in the ethnic origins of its writers, in subject matter, and in examining the contemporary world. If English, in the sense of anglophone, writing has become a world literature, it is especially England that has a literature about how a nation and the contemporary world is changing.

Zadie Smith and Hybridity

The publishing sensation of 2000 was Zadie Smith's *White Teeth*. A first novel by a young author, it was said to have received an advance of a quarter of million pounds and soon sold 100,000 copies in hardback and nearly a million copies in paperback. An amusing novel about the new multiracial London that had come about during the past fifty years, it had the larger-than-life, cartoonish characters, large billboard themes, and the caricatured ethnic English and improbable events featured in Salman Rushdie's *Midnight's Children*. Like *Midnight's Children* it could be read as a national allegory, but its story was about contemporary England and its colonial heritage rather than Rushdie's India. Its characters were from a range of minorities, including West Indians, Muslims, Roman Catholics, Jews, and Jehovah's Witnesses; many of the themes had to do with race and colonial history including the role of Indians fighting for England in the Second World War and West Indian immigration after the war.

While parodying stereotypes, Smith's aim was to break down the racial categories and representations of victims and complicities that dominated interpretation of the 'postcolonial'. The novel celebrated a new hybridity, a hybridity that in other ways was the theme of such novelists as Rushdie and such British theorists as Paul Gilroy and Homi Bhabha, and which had been noticed by Stuart Hall. *White*

Teeth was the desired multicultural novel of a new multiracial England, a celebration of London as an international city in which the peoples and cultures of the world were cross-pollinating. It did not show, however, a new multicultural homogeneity which was replacing old England. The new generation knew each other from school and lived together, but *White Teeth* was also a story of conflicts, of new resentments, of new stereotypes, a novel of an England still in turmoil. It was not going to be so easy to get beyond race, class, difference.

Part of the excitement over the book was the author's own ethnicity. She was mixed race, as were many other new 'black' British authors. The author's mother was a Jamaican immigrant whose father was colonial British, while the author's father was a Jew. The novel told of several generations of three families. The Iqbals are Bangladeshi, while the Jones are British and Jamaican. Samad Iqbal and Archie Jones first met in the service during the Second World War. The Chalfens are a Catholic Jewish mixture. The novel is mostly about the children and their relationships to their parents. Samad sends one of his twin sons to Bangladesh to turn him into a pure Muslim; he will return more English than the English, whereas his brother who remained in London progresses from a local thug into an Islamic fanatic. The enlightened scientific Jews produce a radical environmentalist son who along with the Muslim fanatic destroys his father's genetically engineered FutureMouse. The heroine, a part-Jamaican, is pregnant but by whom? Who will be heir of the immigrant experience?

The title of the novel comes from an elderly racist character saying that in Africa the natives could be killed in the dark as their presence was given away by their white teeth. This is part of the cultural heritage of England to which the novel alludes. More than that, it is a novel about generational conflict, class differences among minorities, what drives people to extreme behaviour, and how the world is governed by chance and personalities rather than the abstractions of science, ideologies, and literary criticism. It is also a novel which, while being about a multicultural and multiracial England, insists on being considered part of the same literary landscape as such white British authors as Martin Amis. During the course of the novel, the book burning of *The Satanic Verses* is alluded to but so are Amis and Julian Barnes. Smith is as interested in the history of her white as of her other characters. A postmodernist novel alluding to some of its models as well as combining the novel of imperial history with the new black British novel about life in England, *White Teeth* like other novels of the 1990s about black Britain is set in a specific area of London, Willesden Green, which it helped put on England's new multicultural map.

By the time Smith's *The Autograph Man* (2002) appeared, it was clear that she disliked the way literature and people were being tagged with ethnic labels. She was trying to undermine such categorization while insisting on individual difference in contrast to group identity. The Autograph Man is a British Chinese Jew and his girlfriend a black Jew. Smith's views might be thought similar to the passage from Lenny Bruce which prefaces *The Autograph Man*: 'Dig: I'm Jewish . . . If you live in Butte, Montana, you're going to be goyish even if you're Jewish.' Such signifiers are free floating, and people are products of where they live as well as of history, just as the value of autographs is a product of the market.

Both *White Teeth* and *The Autograph Man* belong with novels of the 1990s which map ethnic and ethnically mixed areas of London and which redefine Britishness to include people of colour, colonial history, and recent immigration as seen by those colonized. Many of the writers were born in England and while their main characters may be from minority groups they are more interested in the lives of the characters than in ethnic assertion or protest. They are, however, interested in the history that created them. Hanif Kureishi's earlier screenplays and his novel *The Buddha of Suburbia* initiated a change in subject matter and themes that can be seen in Ayub Khan-Din's play *East is East*. Such writers at times seemed the last British writers as many of their white contemporaries wanted to be Scots, Welsh, Northerners, European, gay, feminists, anything but British. But then their white contemporaries did not have a past of being told they were not British and should go home.

III. Poetry: Returning to the Page and the Self

As the black poetry scene became less militant and its rhetoric conventionalized, oral poetry became even more popular with competitive poetry slams attracting racially mixed audiences. The slams compensated for a slump in elite culture's interest in poetry. Some poets, such as Jackie Kay and Bernardine Evaristo, had begun in theatre groups and while they became experienced at writing for oral performance their approach was (as was the case with E. A. Markham, another poet who worked with theatre) different from that of the performance poets of the 1980s. They gave attention to narrative, plot, character, and different voices; they thought of their work as primarily for the page. Their lines were longer than those of performance poets, they concerned themselves with form. They were part of a general movement away from the fragmentation of lyric poetry as poets became interested in sequences, story, and the long poem. Even such new oral poets as Lemn Sissay and Patience Agbabi insisted on the textuality of their verse.

The change in the ethnic basis of black poetry to African or part-African origins resulted in less West Indianized black English. Kay and Evaristo were born in Britain of mixed, part-African, parentage. Kay was adopted by a white family in Glasgow. Sissay and Agbabi were born in England to African parents. Agbabi was brought up in a white working-class family, Sissay in orphanages. There was now an excellent poet of Persian origins, Mimi Khalvati, and one of half-Pakistani origins, Moniza Alvi, neither of whom were part of an ethnic community. Both are highly textual poets. Most of the new poets were female. A common concern of the period was the coming to terms with ancestry through imagination. Whether African, Persian, or part-white, the poets had been brought up as British and were curious about the occulted part of their past, an interest similar to exploring recent family British history by novelists and dramatists.

Jackie Kay appeared in many of the lesbian publications of the 1980s such as *A Dangerous Knowing* (1985). Those poems belong to a time when black lesbians were confrontational and when mixed race was still not distinguished from black (and black Scots a real unknown), an attitude reflected in the title of 'So you think I'm a mule?'. The poems assert that difference is divisive: 'We are not all sisters under the same moon' ('Great White Mother'). Kay's verse sharpened while working with such new black and lesbian drama groups as Theatre of Black Woman and Gay Sweatshop. By writing plays she learned about narration, the creation of character, economically filling in background, the differences between voices, how to write lines for the speaking voice, how to leave space within a line for breathing and interpretation, and the use of unobtrusive rhyme. Theatre-influenced poetry makes more use than most oral poetry of narrative, changes in direction, and many voices.

The Adoption Papers (1991) revealed a powerful poet who wrote carefully crafted, intricately rhymed verse as good on the page as in performance. Kay's ears were attuned to Glaswegian speech with its stressed rhythms and phrasal cadences. The poems were public, even theatrical, yet felt intimate; they were formal, being governed by syllabic count and visual shape as well as by voice and stress. Varied in length, the lines were rich in rhymes, especially internal rhymes, alliteration, and patterns of sounds. While Kay's themes remained political, they were the start of a shift from generalizations to the self as subject matter. The first half of *The Adoption Papers* consists of a sequence of semi-autobiographical poems (first broadcast on Radio 3 as experimental drama) covering several decades of relationships between the birth mother, the legal mother, and the daughter. The voice shifts among the characters and various times in the daughter's life. The sequence is full of events, a range of feelings, and society— including a social worker, family relatives, schoolchildren. Kay writes about those who are marginal, who do not fit into stereotypes. That she was adopted and brought up by white Communist working-class parents adds to the social complexity. Changes in place, Scotland, London, are expressed through images that can be visualized or used as stage settings. The theme is how difference creates social identities that divide people.

The second half of the volume explores ways to write about AIDS, love between women, and the effects of Thatcherite economics on society. Poems are about the ironies, shifting boundaries, and contradictions of identity. 'Dressing Up' tells of a battered Scottish working-class wife's discovery that her son is a transvestite. Deftly, economically, through speech, manners, and conflicts, a world is sketched in revealing how women live, class differences in Scotland, gay experiences, and the bravado and prejudices of the young.

The poems in *Other Lovers* (1993) are nuanced, oblique dramas of identity, friendships, memories, desires. Feelings surface in well-crafted epiphanies of revealing phrases, scenes, or remembered remarks within an implied story. The title poem reveals how the end of an affair results in people no longer sharing tastes. Kay's poetry takes on complexities when the subject is someone else or there are several characters, so her own feelings of alienation, of not belonging, have other people through or against which to define themselves. There are three sequences including one taken from her play *Every Bit of It* telling of the life and death of the American blues singer Bessie Smith, about whom Kay would publish a short prose biography, *Bessie Smith* (1997). In the poem many lines have the feeling of the blues; in the prose biography she recalls listening to a Bessie Smith album when young and her desire to be Smith's lover after learning that the singer was bisexual. Kay identifies music and musicians with blacks, lesbians, and the marginalized.

Her best poems have been sequences metaphorically treating difference, especially racial and sexual. *Off Colour* (1998) is linked by themes, personal and historical allusions, and such techniques as recurring words, phrases, and images. The central idea is that birth is the start of death, life being a process of dying. Life is made of bacteria, and consists of viruses bringing sickness and decay. To move is to be infected and dying. This sounds a subject for some melancholic Jacobean Anatomy of Bacteria; the humour is at times sardonic and grim, but it can also be an amusing way to allude to serious matters. To be 'off colour' is to be ill, but if you are part-black in a white society you are 'off colour'. Some poems, such as 'Hottentot Venus', 'Christian Sanderson', and 'Gambia' concern the treatment of blacks in the English past. A concluding long poem, 'Pride', imagines a healthy African world in which Kay will be welcomed and dance as part of a community, a fantasy of Eden.

The opening poem, 'Where It Hurts', draws on Kay's Scottish English to establish an alienated non-English voice: 'It's a great muckle hand inside my guts, clawing. | Or a camshachle crow, beat at my kidneys.' Correspondences are immediately created to

Prometheus and between suffering, language, and writing: 'Well, it moves like that. Like a verb.' There are several short sequences including (England being England) poems on teeth. Someone with good teeth is rejected, treated as an alien, and subjected to violence. The speaker falls in love with her female dentist who finds a cavity and is imagined filling her 'hole'. The poems have a strong speaking voice and use of a wide variety of conventions including a Skeltonic rhythm and such forms as a ballad and a skipping rope rhyme.

Blackness, lesbianism, Scottish origins, and 'passing' are themes in Kay's first novel, a book about the complexities of identity. Newspapers had carried stories about a swing band leader who passed as a male and only after death was discovered by others to be a woman, although she had a wife and child. Kay turned the story into *Trumpet* (1998), a novel about Joss Moody (born Josephine Moore), a half-black Scottish trumpet player and jazz band leader, who lived as a male, married a woman, adopted a child, and was found at death to be female. Joss then becomes the subject of newspaper articles and for a freelance journalist, a hack, trying to research and write a book about how Josephine became Joss. This allows Kay to examine the role of memory and writing in creating supposed identities. Whose memory offers the real Joss? This is a story about why a lesbian left home and what makes her run. There are tender and excited love scenes, but little about Joss's formation as a musician. Kay assumes parallels between being lesbian, black, a jazz musician, and an artist, but it is only the lesbian side of the story that is developed.

Kay often transposes parts of the autobiography told in 'The Adoption Papers' to the stories of others who are Scottish, lesbians, adopted, assertive, talkative, black or part black, highly imaginative, and social outsiders. Like her long poems, which make more use of revelation through different voices at various times than straightforward narrative, the tales that emerge in *Why don't you stop talking* (2002) are from passing revelations by or about someone; the conclusions are clever symbols or ironies rather than a necessary causal ending. Kay's previous books have been held together by linkage of images and the punning on different meanings of a word, the way 'talk' and 'silence' are used throughout these short stories; each tale also foregrounds certain words and phrases, often the words of the short story's title. Many of the characters are argumentative, overbearing, assertive, yet amusingly attractive in their obsessions, opinions, and vanity. 'The oldest woman in Scotland' does not want the second oldest to become the oldest after she dies. In *Why don't you stop talking* recurring concerns are speech, language, and their relationship to life, art, and the imagination. Talking (and thus metaphorically being a writer) is dangerous, but it is life. To speak, remember, assert yourself, is to live even if you are different, whether the difference is sexual, national, racial, being eccentric, or having obsessions.

'Big Milk' concerns an obsession and concludes with death. The speaker is a black Scottish lesbian who was abandoned by her white mother shortly after birth as her Nigerian father had already left for Africa. Jealous of her lover's baby who for two years has been suckling, the narrator thinks of her past and decides her whole life has been determined by lack of love, as represented by mother's milk. She leaves her lover and baby in Manchester and drives north to meet her birth mother for the first time without considering whether the mother wants to see her. When she arrives at her mother's house it seems, as the narrative ends, that the woman died a few days previously as bottles of milk on the doorstep have gone sour.

These are lonely people, the wounded, those who want love, the self-destructive, those who usually miss out. In the title story a woman is so driven to non-stop talk, self-righteously justifying her behaviour, that others avoid her, thus making her situation worse. Unable to stop herself talking and unwilling to accept that she is at fault, she blames her tongue which she wounds with a knife. Kay is good at rapidly sketching a character, a scene and situation, and especially good at writing prose that imitates feelings of obsession, anxiety, and panic. There are many nice touches of fantasy and humorous comparisons, such as the oldest woman in Scotland who continually bakes and had one sexual climax in her life: 'It shook her about like the only shortbread in a tin.' It is the woman's 107th birthday and she still complains 'That family of mine will send me to an early grave.' Like the other stories it can be read aloud for performance and is one of those amusing assertions of self that make up for the character's at times disagreeable opinions.

Bernardine Evaristo is also of part-African origins and also began in theatre rather than the West Indian performance poetry scene, which she dislikes. The influence of theatre can be seen in the use of drama, story, speeches, voices, monologues, and dialogue in her verse, which is concerned with what has been neglected or misinterpreted in the past. In *Island of Abraham* (1994) poems recall what is ignored as not belonging to the ways history is recorded by white Europeans. Even when this non-European past is brought to attention it becomes a tourist view of strange ruins without recapturing the actual nature of what it was like. 'Epitaph' is like Keats's 'On a Grecian Urn' with its awareness of loss:

> Ethiopian, Aztec, Ashanti,
> Mongol, Ottoman, Shang,
> Inca, Moor, Mayan.
> Your years did not stand still
> like upright Corinthian pillars
> but were flowing rivers
> carrying the memories of your deeds.

What at first appears a protest changes into an elegy about all civilizations being subject to decay, death, and ruin. The tone, voice, and movement of the poem, the feeling of balance, the way it appears rhymeless yet uses a variety of subtle near and almost rhymes, its pitch, even the piling up of rich-sounding nouns, the use of time as a river, are influenced by Derek Walcott. The movement of Evaristo's poem and the poise are that Jacobean melancholy and compassion that haunt and conclude Walcott's 'Ruins of a Great House'. Walcott is also a part-white poet, having two white paternal grandfathers, and brought up in white British culture in St Lucia. Much of his poetry concerns the conflicts and contradictions of being mulatto, whether in the predominantly black Caribbean or the racially divided USA. In Walcott's manner Evaristo found a temporary vein through which to express herself, a measured elegiac way of treating topics where there is a distance that can only be bridged through accepting unknowableness. One of her themes is her mixed ancestry and how little she knows of Africa.

In her poems the speaker is an outsider. She flies to the 'Island of Abraham' (Ille St Marie off mainland Madagascar; the title translates Nosy Boraha, Island of Ibrahim or Abraham, from Malagasy), one of several poems in which, like Walcott's 'Homecoming: Anse

La Raye', the poet desires to be one with the natives, only to be regarded as another rich foreign tourist, a coloured white. Walking along the beach feeling one with nature she watches a small fishing boat and imagines herself as a small girl in 1666 watching the first white men, pirates: 'the island would never be the same again, | its virginal membrane broken'. The results of history are 'Recalled now in the green-eyed, | dark skinned boy'. This is in part Evaristo's situation, a product of Europe's encounter with other people, and though she attempts to identify with the others she is a tourist on this small island off the coast of Madagascar. There is a desire for rootedness, community, belonging, continuity, associated with family, females, being black, and contrasted to strangers, male culture, whites. In 'Simple Scribe' Evaristo imagines herself like a scribal writer in the past.

The concluding poems in the volume allude directly to her own and family history, although her father did not abandon the family to return to Africa. The lost part of her heritage is a source of unease and an influence on the final stanza of 'Bed Time Story', a poem which invents an African mother who dies in England after telling her that she is an imprisoned deer and who passes on a message: 'Child, you must be a panther. | Agile! Swift! Stalking your prey!'

Most cultural movements involve the rediscovery and invention of a usable past. Evaristo's narrative poem *Lara* (1997) tells a more complicated story than most proclamations of black identity. Omilara on her mother's side is the product of a poor Irish Catholic family that moved to England in the nineteenth century and tried to raise itself out of illegitimacy and the working class to the security of the middle class, a destination intended for Ellen, Lara's mother, until she meets and marries an African, one of the black immigrants who came to England after the Second World War in search of higher education. Taiwo is from a Lagos Yoruba family earlier taken as slaves to Brazil, from which some returned to Africa after emancipation and formed a small elite enclave during the later nineteenth and early twentieth century. The story of the Irish and the working class has its parallels to black history while the continuing movement of people of African stock back and forth across the Atlantic and to England has taken place over several centuries, resulting in a complex history of class and cultural differences. Whereas Caryl

Phillips finds parallels between the white underdogs and black experience, Evaristo writes as a product of both.

The first half of *Lara* tells of Lara's white family history and her life in England. It is a story about Irish Catholics with few comforts beyond family and church. Evaristo knows this world better than Nigeria and Brazil and it feels solidly present in the poems as does the attraction of Ellen towards Taiwo, Ellen's mother's mixture of racial prejudice and fear of losing class status if her daughter marries a black man, Lara's youth in a large household in a working-class suburb, and her experience of the cultural and political fashions that followed the swinging sixties. The large rambling house on the margins of London is symbolic of a new multicultural England. *Lara* chronicles the changing times, like older novels of changing manners and sensibilities.

Ellen, Lara's mother, experiences discrimination for marrying black, and is rejected by her mother until children are born and there is semi-reconciliation. Lara's childhood is both typical and troubled by being different, so that naïve questions of where she is from can wound. She wants to be like everyone else until, sexually awakened, she also becomes colour conscious and has an affair with a black Etonian. She plunges into the world of black England trying to find a supportive identity and towards the end of the poem travels to Nigeria, Brazil, then back to Nigeria before returning to England. This recapitulates the journey of her black ancestors and is emotionally cleansing, allowing her to face London reborn, knowing who she is, a product of two cultures, each with its own complex history.

While the physical journey back to origins is a commonplace of ethnic, religious, nationalist, and racialist discourse, the notion that the purpose is psychological cleansing, rather than a search for an alternative, more authentic culture, sounds like the Derek Walcott of *Dream on Monkey Mountain*. Lara does not stay in Africa, and does not imagine a Little Tradition of Black England; her actual voyage is the equivalent of the imaginative journey back to Africa that Walcott recommends for those conflicted by being raised white with brown or black skins.

It is possible that Derek Walcott's influence will prove greater on the literature of England than on that of the West Indies; he provides those with a British education with a model of a poet who is concerned both with artistic form and with the complications of self-identification. Evaristo, along with David Dabydeen and Fred D'Aguiar, is one of his literary heirs. The form of *Lara*, over a hundred dramatically self-sufficient, individual poems of no more than a page in length, appears to be based on Walcott's practice in such volumes as *Midsummer* and *The Bounty*. Evaristo's rhythm begins as a variable thirteen-syllable line; the line changes according to context. This is a looser, unmetric version of the hexameter with many substitutions that Walcott used as a way of getting a longer line for narrative and a more prosaic feel to his poetry. Similarly Evaristo, like Walcott, but with less texture and less complexity, uses occasional and unpredictable end-rhymes and various other methods to mark line endings, has some internal rhymes, and likes to rhyme a word in the middle of a line with one at the end. Although her style is more open, less dense, less filled with metaphors, she has learned from Walcott the use of backward and forward movement in time and many voices.

The *Emperor's Babe* (2001) is prefaced by Oscar Wilde's 'The one duty we owe history is to rewrite it' and concludes by acknowledging Peter Fryer's *Staying Power: The History of Black People in Britain* (1984) where Evaristo 'first learnt that Africans lived in Britain during the Roman occupation nearly eighteen hundred years ago'. *The Emperor's Babe* is part of the reimagining of a usable past. That Evaristo wrote her poem while a poet-in-residence at the Theatre Museum shows how Arts Council and Arts Board patronage was supportive of the new multicultural writing. Set in the Roman Empire, the story concerns Zuleika, the daughter of Sudanese immigrants who marry her to a much older, rich, fat, aristocratic Roman. After violently deflowering her, he leaves her in their villa while he is away with a Nordic blonde with whom he has a family. Although she has moved upwards socially and economically, Zuleika feels life is passing her by until she catches the eye of Septimius Severus, the Roman Emperor who has come to England seeking to conquer Scotland. He is a Libyan who has fought his way 'from African boy | to Roman emperor'. He and Zuleika have a passionate affair until he dies leaving her defenceless against her husband who, learning of her infidelity, has her poisoned.

Roman London seems at times like swinging London, at times like a culturally diverse mixture of parts of the Roman and British empires. The story of the wandering of Zuleika's family through the Empire to London and their climb up the social and economic ladders has its parallels to black Britain. It is amusing to read of the 'wild sloping grassland of Mayfair', 'the wheatfields of Hyde Park', and 'the humid jungle | at Bayswater' but the playing-off of contemporary British street slang against tags of Latin can tire—'futuo-off'. Evaristo has a wide range of registers of English including cockney, American, black British, and parodied poshness. ' "Once you're dead, | you never existed, baby, so get to it." ' As part of her husband's plan to educate her from street urchin to a proper matron, Zuleika joins in the fashion of the Roman upper class to write poetry. *The Emperor's Babe* is her memorial; it shows how poetry reimagines history in accordance with present racial and cultural needs. Walcott's *Omeros* and Fred D'Aguiar's *Bloodlines* are similar long narrative poems with similar purposes.

The main performance poets who appeared during the 1990s were of African descent, did not use Jamaican dialect, and needed to distinguish themselves from what was becoming routine. Self-promotion continued as did a new sensationalism similar to the pulp fiction influences on the prose of the period. While the model for Patience Agbabi's (b. 1965) *R.A.W.* (1995) is the tough guy, gangster, rebel outside-the-law act of the rappers, she also writes for the page. Some poems are written to hip hop and other dance rhythms, others have iambic pentameter. She writes those 1980s slogans about race and women but to newer rhythms. Many of the poems in *R.A.W.*, published by Gecko Press, are intended primarily for the page as they are either shaped to offer a visual appearance or have a complex stanzaic form. 'Accidentally Falling' tells of beginning, enjoyment, and end of a love affair over bottles of wine. The poem is in the shape of a wine bottle. Agbabi is an Oxford graduate aware of the traditions of poetry. There is a forcefulness to her poetry, an energy that stands out. She can be loud but she also has a colloquial voice like a person speaking to another. The thoughts are expressed in clear images and poems shift direction unexpectedly. They are intended as expressions of the new. 'Serious Pepper' begins:

> Everyone's born
> no-one's found
> until they find themselves

Cultural conflict is expressed by:

> but they held my nose and force
> fed me on two cultures
> eggs and chips or eba and groundnut stew

The desire to remain an adolescent and avoid problems of racial, social, and sexual identity is conflated with the anorexic's fear of becoming fat and unacceptable:

> D'you know I used to stick my fingers down
> my throat so I didn't have to grow up
> and find myself

Much of the poetry is offered as autobiography. In 'London's Burning' Agbabi incorporates street chants and descriptions of violence into a story of her experiences as a protester against Thatcher's poll tax. *R.A.W.* is meant as an attack, 'Uncooked uncut uncaged unchained uncensored'. 'I'm a poet | it's a four-letter word.'

In *Transformatrix* (2000), published by Payback Press, Agbabi, like Evaristo, treats the past as if it were the present, a counter-cultural present. Using the convention that the poet is at the mercy of a Muse, Agbabi offers a streetwise feminist parody in which she is the submissive lover of a cruel, demanding, erratic dominatrice. The title poem which concludes the volume is Robert Gravesian with a twist: 'A pen poised over a blank page, I wait | for madam's orders, her strict consonants . . . She trusses up | words, lines, as a corset disciplines flesh.' The use of a pattern of perverse imagery with a broad range of significance has similarities to Kay's use of off-colour-ness. Agbabi's choice of a central metaphor reflects her period as a Poetry Society writer-in-residence at a tattoo parlour, an example of how the attempt by those in charge of patronage to reach a broad public was reflected in writing. The emphasis on the material body as symbol is also in keeping with those literary and cultural theorists who regard transformations of the human body as political. Agbabi's public readings from *Transformatrix* were advertised as 'Body Language'.

While 'Transformatrix' is clever and sophisticated, Agbabi usually writes for youth pop culture. 'Prologue' introduces the theme of waiting at the computer for inspiration, but the manner is like a cheerleader at a sporting event: 'Give me a word I any word . . . let each syllable vibrate I like a transistor.' While alluding to the Word and saying poetry is sound, the poem's lack of decorum is purposeful. This could be a pop song or a Jimmy Hendrix or Country Joe and the Fish recording of the sixties: 'Is your consciousness on fire? I Then let me take you higher . . . so let me take you to the fifth dimension.' Two of the five sections into which the book is divided have titles recalling a famous pop song and a famous pop group, 'Devils in Red Dresses' and 'Mothers of Inversion.' In many of the poems she is a creature from outer space, on the road, and on drugs, but actually is referring to the paraphernalia of contemporary youth, urban vandalism, and popular culture: 'I'm wicked witch of the wheel, I swapped my broomstick for a gearstick . . . Mad Maxine on amphetamine' ('The Joyrider').

Transformatrix includes several prose stories which read like Agbabi's verse: 'Well, Jack. Take acid, take that risk. Look back over your life, your long long trip' (p. 22). Or for the improbable hard-boiled realism award: ' "Solo. The shit hit the fanny. He was sex on legs in PVC but wore steel in his conga eel" ' (p. 73). As conscious bad taste became part of the cultural milieu, there was a pop fiction scene to which Catherine Johnson and Leone Ross occasionally contributed. Pulp fiction anthologies such as *Britpulp!* edited by Tony White (1999) are colour-blind and include a sprinkling of streetwise black writers including Xpress novelists Victor Headley and Karline Smith. Agbabi is an artist playing with such new areas of tastelessness as the shock art associated with the Tate's Sensation exhibition of Young British Artists.

The title of Lemn Sissay's *Tender Fingers in a Clenched Fist* (1988) indicates how his verse was part of the same trend as Zephaniah's in modifying the posture of the young black rebel for a mainstream audience. His is more a tense relationship. While radicalism had become a style, something to sell, something that draws from and contributes to popular culture, Sissay's racial hurt and feelings of difference are often expressed, as in 'Trendy Places, Liberal Clones', through such puns as 'For breakfast I A bowl of coonflakes'. Being of

African rather than West Indian origins, and brought up by whites, Sissay does not write in dialect. Rather than Caribbean music, he often performs with jazz musicians. Like the other oral poets he identifies, in 'Trendy Places', with the black working classes: 'I'm proud I'm Black and I love my culture | But I hate drinking wine with a liberal vulture.' 'The Invasion of the Mancunoids' connects British loutism with neo-fascism and racism. Wags said of his second book *Rebel without Applause* (1992) that Sissay is neither a rebel nor without applause; there is a drop in intensity and a vagueness about the cause he proclaims beyond his claim that he remembers it when others no longer do.

Beyond protest themes, his subject matter ranges from the boredom of doing nothing, poems addressed to other black poets, descriptions of Manchester where he lives, mocking the black bourgeoisie, and whatever is topical. While too much of Sissay's verse is rap doggerel and political chants it is also amusing, likeable. Sometimes the lines are barely more than a single word, and often his message is not much more than an assertion of being black, but he has a talent for puns and rhymes. His allusions, metaphors, and images are interesting. In *Rebel* (p. 59) the prose 'Can You Locate Planet Ethnic?' retells many of his preoccupations, including claims that being black he is distinct from other counter-culture and progressive causes. Despite Sissay's claims to rebelhood he is mainstream counter-culture. 'Ethnic' like 'minorities' had become another politically incorrect term, actively discouraged by the Arts Council.

Mimi Khalvati appeared on the literary scene through winning two prizes, one of which led to her first book, *In White Ink* (1991), with its notion that women writing are a continuation of mothers nursing their young. Mother's love and breasts remain recurring themes: 'And her child suckled at the wall, drew | the sweetness from the stone and grew' ('The Woman in the Wall'). 'Family Footnotes', 'Shanklin Chine', 'Sick Boy', and 'Blue Moon' are about a mother and her children. Somewhere behind the volume as seen in such poems as 'Stone of Patience' are bad marriages and unsatisfactory love affairs:

> And a woman faced with a lover grabbing for his shoes
> when women friends would have put themselves in hers

no longer knows what's virtuous. Will anger
shift the boulder, buy her freedom and the earth's.

A feminist ideology infuses this poetry without becoming polemical. There is a seriousness in craft as well as in tone and in what it treats. *In White Ink* begins in a free verse hovering around iambic pentameter and as the volume progresses becomes increasingly formal.

Khalvati is unusual in her Persian origins, which are mentioned in several poems based on readings about Iran rather than actual memories, as she was sent for schooling in England while young. 'The Bowl' is prefaced by a passage from a late nineteenth-century English voyager and uses a Persian bowl the way Keats used pictures on a Grecian urn to imagine a world of fancy. In her case it is a past she either never had or lost and is trying to assemble. Such a poem provided a model for Moniza Alvi, who also wanted to explore in poetry her Pakistani family connections before she had visited Asia and had any real memories to tell.

Khalvati not only has traditional poetic technique at her fingertips but has learned to give form and structure to much of what is thought of as free verse. No doubt because she was an actress the kind of techniques more common to American poetry, such as breath groups, voice, indentations, and lineation, have been thought about and used by her with the same conscious craft as conventional metrics. This is possible because her poems are driven by syntax, a syntax that pushes sentences over lines, stanzas: the syntax drives the thought or argument as it does in Milton, piling simile on top of simile. But there are many other forms. An ironic Haiku which concludes the Persian section of *In White Ink*: 'On the verandah | the wet-nurse thinks of her own | pomegranate tree.' Wallace Stevens compressed?

Each poem seems a new start. She is no epic poet, not a writer of big themes, but each volume has its own characteristics, recurring images and words. *Mirrorwork* (1995) aims for lightness and light, many refractions, like some spacious Persian dome with its many little bits of mirror creating light. 'Light' is one of her recurring words. *Entries on Light* (1997) consists of contemplations on light, each poem written at one sitting, an attempt at seeing whether it is possible to make structured poetry directly from moments of inspiration. While not as hermetic as, say, French verse, it concerns the idea rather than objects.

Moniza Alvi belongs with those writers of mixed parentage outside an ethnic community but aware of cultural differences among relatives. Such writers when young often try to avoid what would make them alien; later they begin to think about identity, origins, and culture. For those brought up in England, the culture of India or Pakistan is imagined or seen through a tourist's eyes. Alvi had not visited India or Pakistan until after the publication of *The Country at My Shoulder* (1993), her first book, in which she imagines an India based on what others have told her. The impulse to write such poetry came from Khalvati's 'The Bowl', which, in its rich imagery, showed how to explore one's background.

The first thirty pages of Alvi's *A Bowl of Warm Air* (1996), consisting of poems about India and Pakistan written after she had visited the subcontinent, suggest an autobiographical narrative. They begin with 'And If' which one assumes will be a lament of confused identities, nostalgia for what has been lost, or acceptance of hybridity, 'If you could choose a country | to belong to—', but its few lines of Indian pastoral are soon undermined by mention of castes, subcastes, and an awareness of a Muslim being as much an Other in India as in England:

> you'd be untouchable—as one
>
> defined by someone else—
> one who cleans the toilets,
> burns the dead.

Her father had to flee India for Pakistan. There were and are no pure cultures, races, or nations; traditions and cultures are made. In her poem 'Hindu Urdu Bol Chaal' we are told

> Urdu borrowed from Sanskrit,
> Arabic and Persian.
>
> I shall be borrowed from England.

The Indian-Pakistan section concludes with 'The Laughing Moon' in which the English language and an uncertain grey England offers security to someone who has been thinking of Pakistan. Such poems have an understated philosophical vision expressed with quiet economy, a fatalism that appears cheerful, youthful, hopeful. Alvi has a an instinctive sense of shape, cadence, sound, harmony, and rhythm.

The sudden unexpected shifts in direction of poems are even stronger in the last third of the volume, poems set in England or perhaps purely in the imagination. They begin with 'Exile', a poem about a new classmate from Sarajevo, and conclude with 'Story of a City', another poem where she is in bed at night dreaming or thinking. Here the city tells her 'I need you. Make of me what you can— I my suburbs of ideas, my flames, my empty spaces.' These poems are lively, lyrical, at times surreally fanciful. They move from an insight or description towards outer space, then return to a spiritually transformed reality. In the title poem she has a vision of a man offering her 'A Bowl of Warm Air' which although empty includes all delights. One of the pleasures of her poetry is a shared love of poetry, famous poems, and the visions, obsessions, and techniques of great poets:

> I'd rather be like the miniaturist who works alone
> Painting on rice paper, silk and camel bone
> Polishing an image with a stone.

On the cover of *Carrying My Wife* (2000), Alvi's third book, is a reproduction of Pablo Picasso's 1932 painting *Girl before a Mirror*: a slightly orientalized Cubist deconstruction of a woman is mirrored in reverse in a way that suggests interiority, passion, and perhaps something more oriental or Islamic. It introduces the poems that follow in which a wife is observed and imagined from various perspectives while multiple facets of her emotions are revealed. The volume collects Alvi's earlier two books along with fifty new poems. Of the new ones, about half belong to the *Carrying My Wife* sequence, a fantasy often tinged with the surreal, in which a husband recalls or perhaps imagines characteristics of or life with a wife who has disappeared. The series started a few weeks before Alvi was married, when she started thinking about the various resonances of the phrase 'my wife'. She then tried to imagine herself as a husband using the phrase. The poems bring out the varied aspects of relationships including jealousy, shared tastes and events, passion, discovery, disillusion, and difference. They are amusing and display

Alvi's developing talent for finding short, attractive, even marvellous metaphors, symbols, and images.

Alvi has always been aware of craft and seemed attracted and perhaps limited to the miniature, but these short poems pack a lot of suggestion into a few lines. In 'Missing':

> Hadn't she been orphaned, adopted,
> rejected, married, divorced
> and finally wedded to the stare
> of the planets, the anxiety
> of constellations.

Behind the masked comedy are complex feelings as when the speaker imagines his wife passionately kissing a composer who we learn is actually dead: 'So what was her affair | with the music | of gardens, distance, and solitude?' ('My Wife and the Composer'). The sequence subtly brings out the multiplicity of an individual and the complexity of a relationship. There are many beautiful enigmatic poems, and the sequence leaves an impression of a lyric poet working towards a more exciting, larger expressive form.

Similar to the painting on the cover, *Carrying My Wife* has two distinctive halves; the wife sequence is followed by poems that appear factual and which directly reveal feelings. These later poems are less striking without the boldness encouraged by the mask of the fantasizing husband, but there is a similar tentativeness as poems conclude with a left-in-air feeling. Many poems concern themes of multiple identity. While they seem a step back from the extravagant grand carnival of the *Carrying My Wife* poems into the introverted space of the earlier books, some, such as 'Queen-of-the Night', 'Once', 'Takeaway', 'Thoughts of a Pakistani Woman in an English Jail', and 'Incident at the Zoo' form mini-sequences implying more than the subject matter.

Alvi's India and Pakistan are starting places for the imagination and what it produces, which is her main interest. Here are poems about imaginings. She is commonsensical about desires, and avoids declaring extreme wants: the imagination, however, roams freely as it plays with other possible lives that have been suggested by stories she has heard, phrases that attract her attention, and especially by phrases or images of other writers. Much of her poetry is 'what if'.

Matters of identity, race, and gender are raised, thought about, and dropped. She is a poet of caution and fancy, of craft and lyricism, on the verge of the surreal lyricism sometimes found in American and Central European poetry. Although her poetry might be seen as parallel to the early novels of Hanif Kureishi and Zadie Smith, there is little interest in race and postcolonial issues. Like Khalvati she is an English poet influenced by contemporary American poetry who writes about her own life, including her awareness that she could have had other lives.

After Dom Moraes and Zulfikar Ghose left England, the Indian poets who remained were seldom noticed. Melanie Silgardo (b. 1956), who already had a good reputation in India for a small body of poetry, moved to England in 1984 and quietly self-published a slim volume, *Skies of Design* (1985), which won the Asian regional Commonwealth Poetry prize. She joined Virago and edited several anthologies including *Virago New Poets* (1993) and *Short Circuits* (1996). The Delhi London Poetry Society produced a magazine, *Delhi-London Poetry Quarterly* for over a decade; its editor was Gopi Warrier and among its publications was his *Lament of JC: Poems* (1999). The Spring 1995 issue of *Wasafiri* included a section of poems by Asians of the diaspora in England: Ketaki Kushari Dyson, Debjani Chatterjee, Prabhu Guptara, Melanie Silgardo, Satyendra Srivastava, Sanjeev Richariya, Maya Chowdhry, and Shanta Acharya. Dyson, a bilingual writer, published with the Writers' Workshop of Calcutta. Chowdhry, a member of the Asian Women Writers' Workshop, was better known as a dramatist. Prabhu Guptara compiled the extremely useful *Black British Literature: An Annotated Bibliography* (1986) and took employment in Switzerland. Shanta Acharya's *Not This, Not That* (1994) and *Numbering Our Days' Illusions* (1995) includes attractive short poems about spirituality, mysticism, and the disappointments of reality.

Debjani Chatterjee (b. 1952) attracted some admirers with *I Was That Woman* (1989) and *Albino Gecko* (1998). She edited *The Redbeck Anthology of British South Asian Poetry* (2000), the first anthology of its kind. The anthology gave a national voice to the many writers' workshops for women and ethnic groups which she directed and was a runner-up for the 2001 Raymond Williams

Community Publishing Prize intended for publications which reflect the voices of 'particular communities'. Chatterjee's concern in *I Was That Woman*, published by Hippopotamus Press, is less with the complexities of origins found in the poetry of Kay, Evaristo, Khalvati, and Alvi than, in poems such as 'I was that woman' and 'To the English Language', with the clichés of victimization. Too often her verse is a badly written editorial. In 'Primary Purpose' she claims, 'All know you are an Asian woman. | No matter what your genera- tion, | You will always be an immigrant.' Even the old, disproved, cliché about dreaming in one's mother tongue is resurrected by Chatterjee who apparently does not know the Bengali of her dreams. In 'To the English Language' she argues 'What has proficiency to do with it? | I know I dream it endlessly.' If Chatterjee says too much, Sudeep Sen (b. 1964) is her opposite. A poet of more technical facility than content, beginning with *Lunar Visitations* (1994), he produced a large body of work, with the occasional good poem. Kwame Dawes's *Sudeep Sen: A Bio-Bibliographical Sourcebook* (1996) is admiring. As with many of the Indian poets in England Sen's volumes are mostly self-published.

It was unfortunate that there was no major poet in England of Indian descent to offer a model or to challenge. Vikram Seth (b. 1952) might have been that person but after coming to England to study at Oxford he moved on to the USA and eventually returned to India. He became one of those writers always on the move. Although he is often in England, the subject matter of his writing is inter- national as are the influences on it. The poetry ranges from the Chinese-influenced poems in *From Heaven Lake: Travels through Sinking and Tibet* (1983) to *The Golden Gate* (1986), a verse novel about California written in fourteen-line stanzas modelled on those of Puskin's *Eugene Onegin*. Similarly his fiction ranges from *A Suitable Boy* (1993), an old-fashioned who-should-she-marry study of manners, morals, and their relationship to economics and religion, set in India, to *An Equal Music* (1999), a musically organized novel about an English string quartet. With an inter- national literary market place and the ease of international travel, such a writer no longer needed to live in London to be successful. Seth spent seven years travelling from country to country to give readings from *A Suitable Boy*, as it was translated into many languages. Such international promotion is part of a modern literary life and shows the relationship of the global market place to cultural hybridity.

IV. Drama: Histories

The best-known black feminist dramatist was London-born Winsome Pinnock whose *Leave Taking* (Liverpool Playhouse Studio, 1988) concerns the conflicts among three generations of West Indian women and the costs of survival and independence, pains that have crossed the Atlantic with black British women. Like many works about West Indian families, it explains lack of love as a consequence of the costs of survival. Whereas previous plays were usually about mothers leaving the West Indies for the future of their sons, in this play Enid's mother was abandoned by her husband and worked hard in Jamaica to bring up her daughters, which required concentration on work and prevented giving love. When Enid, wanting to better herself, leaves for England, her mother appears not to care. In England Enid repeats the pattern; she becomes a single parent and is driven by the desire to improve herself and her daughters; she works at menial jobs to earn money for her children's future and resents letters from Jamaica begging for money to care for members of the family. Her children let her down. They refuse to be English, want to know about Jamaica, and rebel against the life Enid planned for them. The older one—seeing herself as condemned to dead-end jobs—parties all night, skips work, sleeps around, becomes pregnant, and leaves home although she has nowhere to stay and will depend on public assistance. The younger one, whose school grades equip her for university, suddenly leaves an examination and wants to travel to, and perhaps remain in, Jamaica.

Pinnock's plays contrast repression of instinct by the mothers who survive with the more instinctual but self-destructive lives of the young. Throughout the play there is a contrast between the level-headed woman Enid makes herself and her emotions. She believes in obeah, has suppressed her lively youth, and feels guilty for not sending more money to her mother. Society gives black women no way to satisfy both the instinctual and the desire for security and respect.

West Indian men are irresponsible and only black women understand the problems of black women. Although lively, *Leave Taking* feels illustrative.

Many of Pinnock's themes recur in *A Rock in Water* (1989), which began as a commission by the Royal Court Young People's Theatre to write about Claudia Jones. Jones, the daughter of Trinidad immigrants to the USA, was active in the Communist Party and deported to England after Trinidad refused her. During the 1950s she worked for the *West Indian Gazette* and helped found the Notting Hill Carnival. First we see Claudia's mother waiting on street corners for work as a cleaner of white houses; the mother idealizes white people and their lives. The mother and father worship America in contrast to the poverty of peasant Trinidad, but the mother holds two jobs and dies working at a factory. Claudia by contrast is educated and bitter at class and racial injustice. The play follows her life from her youth through her years in England until her death of a heart attack during Christmas 1964. Claudia is a black female giant among pygmy male leftists. The play celebrates sisterhood and motherhood; its male characters are selfish and weak, and marriage is a trap. While recovering black female British history and showing contexts in which black militancy developed, Pinnock's heroine can be priggishly self-righteous and unsympathetic. Although a historical pageant, *A Rock in Water* asks whether social activism might displace love into do-gooding and be related to pride. The dialogue has a similar rapid snip-snappiness to Rudet's.

Pinnock offers a Brechtian epic vision of a life with its contradictions. Although this should allow an objective view of the people and situations, the results, as in *Talking in Tongues* (Royal Court Theatre Upstairs, 1991), can reduce life to political illustrations. Where Mustapha Matura appeared easily to find situations and occupations which have political significances without reducing the dramatic action, Pinnock can be reductive. *Talking in Tongues* attempts to get around its illustrativeness through complications and ambiguities, but the characters seem like ideas about behaviour. The play starts with a prologue of West Indian women secretly chanting their pains, a symbol of black sisterhood showing the common anguish of black women in England, especially in relationship to black men and white women. At a New Year's party black women complain about the infidelity and lack of commitment of black men. They are angry at black men preferring white women and hate white women who they claim act superior and use friendship with black women to approach their men. When a desirable black male friend of one of the women has sex with a conniving white woman while the black women improbably are hiding under a load of coats, it is difficult not to feel that the author uses her characters as puppets in a political argument. Two of the women then go to Jamaica seeking their roots, only to use the local black men as sex objects just as white female tourists are said to do. The Jamaicans speak of the black women as broken, meaning that living in white England has ruined them, although it might be thought that the Jamaicans in the play are so dependent on tourist money and whims that they are not reliable judges.

Pinnock's *Mules* (1996), commissioned by Clean Break Theatre Company, first produced at the Royal Court, is another play in which lovelessness, abandonment, and the difficulties of survival for black women pass from one generation to the next. The mules are Jamaican women used as international carriers of drugs. They hope for better lives but they are caught and gaoled. The central figure is Birdie who, abandoned by her mother at 14, has had to make her way on her own and uses women, pretending to be their special friend, as ruthlessly as any man.

The continued relationship between black British society and Jamaica is shown in London-born Roy Williams's (b. 1968?) *The No Boys Cricket Club* (Theatre Royal, Stratford East, 1996; pub. 1999) and *Starstruck* (Tricycle Theatre, 1998; pub. 1999). In the former, two single parents in London, maltreated by their British-born children and mocked by the young black British, recall their youth in Jamaica when they formed a girl's cricket team to challenge the men. The women keep dreaming of returning 'home' although the girls they knew are now sad, unsuccessful older women. The play takes a feminist perspective in showing how men have formed and abused the emotions of the main character, first as a daughter, then as a mother. It ends with her rebelling and demanding that her son stop drug dealing or else move out. Whether things have really changed remains to be seen.

Williams's *Starstruck* complicates the Errol John *Moon for a*

Rainbow Shawl story of a West Indian man wanting to escape to London but being held back by responsibilities to a pregnant woman. Here the mother was made pregnant in England but returned to Jamaica when the man would not marry her. A year later his brother learns of what happened and returns to Jamaica to marry the woman and pretend the child is his own. When the boy grows up, he appears to have no future in Jamaica and is a petty thief until he gets a part in a movie and has an opportunity to leave for London. He, however, has made a 16-year-old girl pregnant. His mother, herself longing for England, asks him to leave the girl—she is trapping him. The husband, however, reveals the mother's past, and makes the son take responsibility for the child. As the play ends, the son has become a happy taxi driver in Kingston and the probable future head of a fleet of drivers. Both of Williams's plays suggest that England changes West Indians, making them selfish, less caring, and while possibly offering better material and career prospects, will result in demoralization and dehumanization. Both plays, although written by a man, show concern with the plight of the female head of a West Indian family. In these plays West Indian men treat their women brutally, coldly, and without concern beyond what they can provide sexually, financially, or as cooks.

Bradford-born Trishe Cooke (b. 1962) fills in the history of those, like her mother, who came to England from Dominica and places their story within the context of how women awaken to sexual desire, become infatuated with predatory men, and are trapped early in life with children. Cooke's *Back Street Mammy* was performed at the Lyric Studio, Hammersmith, 1989, and published in *First Run 2* (1990), selected by Kate Harwood for Nick Hern Books. It combines two basic situations. One is the story of West Indians who came to England in the hope of a better life for themselves and their children only to find disappointment, especially as their children continue a pattern of early pregnancies, quarrelsome or one-parent families, and failure to obtain the educational qualifications that might lead to better employment. Once more there is a tyrannical father, a tired, hardworking mother who has sacrificed her dreams by depending on a man, and rebellious children.

While the West Indian immigrant family provides a setting, Cooke also presents another tale, the universal story of a young woman whose developing sexuality, physical desire, and the illusions of romance and love result in becoming a parent while young. The style of the play with its shifts back and forth in time, use of a chorus, and intense short speeches combines feminist concerns and an earlier expressionism as the young woman, who is 16 and still in school, identifies her unborn child with God who she claims is speaking to her. The situation is intensified by Dynette having been brought up as a Roman Catholic. If the seemingly rational answer to an unwanted pregnancy is abortion, the play's title alludes to a woman's fear that she may never again become pregnant and will become a 'Back Street Mammy' with a career but no child. Instead the play opens with a 30-year-old woman apparently satisfied with her job, her husband, and her child by him, in contrast to a one-night stand when she was 16 that resulted in the child she aborted; it reveals the confusions, drama, and family history in the past when she might have made a wrong choice.

Cooke's *Running Dream* (1993) was first produced at Theatre Royal, Stratford East in 1993 and published the same year in Kadija George's *Six Plays by Black and Asian Women Writers*. It tells of three generations of related women whose lives had taken different paths as a result of whether they were born in England or Dominica and what had caused this split in family history. As in *Back Street Mammy* women are seen as desiring education, employment, and independence, but being undermined by their sexual urges, romantic attachments, and listening to promises of men, with the result that too often early in life they become pregnant and then single mothers without the qualifications for good jobs.

In contrast to dramatists who use the West Indies as an ideal of home, and the plays which continue a battle between the sexes, there is London-born Maria Oshodi's *Blood, Sweat and Tears* produced at the Harmony Theatre, Battersea Arts Centre (1988), and published the next year in *Black Plays 2*; it concerns sickle-cell anaemia, a condition common to perhaps 10 per cent of blacks. Paul Boakye's *Boy with Beer*, produced by This Is Now Theatre Company at Man in the Moon Theatre (1992), published in *Black Plays 3*, is about two gay black men, dominance within sexual relationships, how class complicates race and sexuality, the dangers of AIDS, and the tensions between Africans and West Indians.

Just as poetry and prose by those of African origins became noticeable during the 1990s, there was a parallel emergence of African and Asian dramatists. Several Nigerian dramatists who used London as a base would settle. Biyi Bandele-Thomas draws from the range of the world's theatre, especially modern drama, while working in a tradition established by Wole Soyinka. Bandele's plots are mostly set in a Nigeria of military rule, widescale corruption, obsessed evangelical Christians, and the unpalatable future offered university students. *Marching for Fausa* (1993) retells the history of Nigeria (here called Songhai) from before independence until the corrupt and brutal military regimes of the 1980s and 1990s. The opening scene shows a female journalist being tortured to supply the names of supposed traitors to the regime and admit that the names on a list of students are guilty. Scenes of her being questioned alternate with her memories of the past, especially of teenagers shocked by their schoolmate Fausa being forced into marriage at the age of 16 to a Minister of Culture who already has ten wives and who announces on Woman's Day that purdah is the best place for women.

Two Horsemen (Gate Theatre, London, 1994) begins like an imitation *Waiting for Godot* in which nothing happens in repeated ways and in which the lack of action is kept alive by sudden shifts in mood, the playing of silly games, the taking of puns as literal facts, and reversals of what occurred previously, with a character later in the play repeating the same words the other said earlier. Behind the play is a nihilistic feeling of a world without purpose.

Resurrections in the Season of the Longest Drought (Cochrane Theatre, London, 1994) is another study in Nigerian corruption, a corruption which extends through every level of society from the president through the judges and into families. The corruption is not just financial and ethical it is also moral and spiritual. The drought of the title is spiritual but the trickster god is active. Judge Bassey tricks BB into giving him an immense bribe to save BB and then sentences him to death. The dead BB becomes in folk mythology a hero of the popular imagination. The mixture of myth, ritual, and satire on corrupt society and the politicians, along with the free borrowing among the mythologies of many cultures, is part of the tradition which Soyinka established for Nigerians.

Death Catches the Hunter (Battersea Arts Centre, 1995) was published together with the very short *Me and the Boys* (Finborough Theatre, London). *Death Catches the Hunter* is a short three-act play, with a prologue and epilogue, mostly told in monologues by a prophet, his female disciple, and her sceptical husband. The prophet, one of the charismatic Christian preachers common in Nigeria, is a con man who lies about his past, and the play ends with his death, possibly the result of his foolishly believing in his own powers, or because he has become bored with his deception. Underlying the action are a Yoruba saying that Death will catch the hunter and a myth about the trickster god. *Me and the Boys*, set in a Nigerian gaol cell, is little more than a monologue in which one prisoner tells his cell mate about his days as a student. The narrative ends when the previously silent cell mate says that he was the drug dealer that ruined the lives of the students.

The prime influence on the development of an Asian British theatre was Tara Arts where Jatinder Verma (b. 1954), who came to England from Kenya in 1968, formed a theatre company in 1976. Other companies were started by his actors and writers. Most theatre companies, including Asian Co-operative Theatre, at first recreated versions of traditional Indian culture and its mythology as if their job were preservation rather than the portrayal of South Asian lives in England. Over the decades Tara Arts evolved towards a broader approach including western theatre classics, plays from India, and plays about Asians in England. Many of the British Asian theatre companies were offshoots of the various minority groups sponsored by the GLC. Kali Theatre Company was co-founded by Rita Wolf and Rukhsana Ahmad, the latter a member of the Asian Women Writers' Collective and of Tara Arts where Jatinder Verma had invited her to write plays. Kali's first production was Ahmad's *Song of a Sanctuary* (1990) showing the pressures on Asian communities which led to the murder of a woman in a refuge. The first professional company to concentrate on the 'second generation' of British Asians was the short-lived HAC Theatre (Hounslow Arts Co-op) in the mid-1980s. Parv Bancil (b. 1967) originally wrote for them and then for other new companies until coming to wider notice with his powerful *Crazyhorse* (co-produced by Tara Arts and Paines Plough, 1997), a wild portrait of the fall of an Indian father and son into the British working class, mutual hatred, petty crime, murder, and fantasy. Bancil, born in Tanzania but brought to England when 2 years old, is concerned with Indian life in contemporary England. His *Made in England* (Red Room Theatre/Battersea Arts Centre, 1998), included in *Black and Asian Plays* (2000), tells of how the rebellion and protest of punk music was lost as pop music was ethnicized and British Indian pop stars created.

The Tamasha Theatre Company was founded in 1989 by Kristine Landon-Smith and Sudha Bhuchar to adapt Indian literature and to reflect contemporary British-Asian life. Its first production was an adaptation of *Untouchable*, a novel by Mulk Raj Anand. Among its productions were *Women of the Dust* (Bristol Old Vic, 1992; pub. 1999) and *A Yearning* (Birmingham Rep, 1995; pub. 1999) by Ruth Carter, who is not of Indian origins. The former play was commissioned by Oxfam for their fifteenth anniversary and tells the stories of an all-female workforce at a Delhi construction site; the latter is an adaptation of Federico García Lorca's *Yerma* to the Birmingham Punjabi community. Tamasha adapted Meira Chand's first Indian novel *House of the Sun* for the stage; its production at Theatre Royal Stratford East was voted Critics Choice and broadcast during 1996 on Radio 4.

A major breakthrough for Asian theatre was Ayub Khan-Din's *East is East*. It began as a writers' workshop in 1996 held by Tamasha Theatre Company in collaboration with the Royal Court. It was produced first by Tamasha at the Birmingham Rep and attracted audiences with many Asians in attendance when it transferred to the West End. It was soon made into a film (1999). It is another instance of writers during the later 1990s making art from family history. Set during the 1970s in the neighbourhood of Ordsall, Salford, where Khan-Din was brought up, it is autobiographical and attempts to recall the past before it is lost. It tells of a time when mixed-race marriages in England were unusual. It shows the bravery of both the father, who had left Pakistan where he was already was married and a father, and the English mother, and how close their relationship was despite conflicts in bringing up the children, the terrible brutality of the father, and the courage of the mother in sticking up for her children.

It was the first play to look at a mixed working-class marriage through the eyes of the children and not see it simply as a story of racial prejudice or cultural conflict. Another strength is its attempt to understand what turned the father, who earlier seemed to accept cultural mixing, into an angry destructive brute who demanded absolute obedience from his children including wanting to arrange their marriages; when the children rebelled they were banished from or fled the house, for which he would blame and beat his wife. The remaining children would obey him for fear of how he would treat her. The father wanted to be head of his extended family and live in Bradford where his relatives settled and before whom he felt a failure, a failure he hoped to overcome by proving himself a traditional father who would return his children to the community he left. The father's rages derive from his idealization of the land and culture he left, his conflicts in loyalty between his family in England and his family in Pakistan, his unwillingness to accept that his British-born mixed-race children cannot live the fantasy life he desires, and his failure to accept that his rigidity and violence bring hatred rather than respect to himself and what he believes. That Pakistan is losing the war in what became Bangladesh contributes to his anger. Complex in its psychology, highly effective on stage, *East is East* epitomizes how the immigrant loses touch with the land left behind, fossilizes it in memories which do not take into account change, and purifies it of its realities, while being unable to see that children cannot remake an adult's past.

Ayub Khan-Din's second play, *Last Dance at Dum Dum* (Royal Court, 1999) also treats of mixed-race minorities, in this case the dwindling Anglo-Indian community of India. The Anglo-Indians were the children of a British father and an Indian mother, Christian, English-speaking, and before Indian independence were socially above the 'natives' but were regarded as 'black' by much of English society in India. Like many of the lighter skinned West Indians, they often tried to pass for 'white' or were willing to trade their comforts for marriage to an Englishman and a lower standard of living in England. Those who did not flee to England after Indian independence form an ageing, declining group increasingly at the mercy of Hindu nationalists. *Last Dance at Dum Dum* looks sympathetically at the self-destructive behaviour of such a small group in Calcutta during 1981 in a house which has effectively become the property of a rabble-rousing politician living next to them. While they continue to celebrate former British victories over the Indians, they hate the British for their prejudice and for leaving them stranded and helpless. The Anglo-Indians and their imitation of an older western culture, however, have no future. In this play, as in *East is East*, Khan-Din has tried to present individuals in their complexities, with their hurts and their often unattractive reactions to disappointing circumstances. The people are absurd, but their moments of tenderness and care, as well as their situation, make them sympathetic. Such a play gains its power from its awareness of what motivates people.

At the start of the new millennium there was a strong interest in India and its cultures as seen by several musical shows based on Bollywood movies. There was also now a large Indian business and professional community, a potential audience for theatre that would interest them. The career of Tanika Gupta (b. 1963) reflects ways in which an interest in Indian culture had become part of middle-class culture. Like many of the younger Indian dramatists, she began writing for radio and television before having a play produced on stage. After being a finalist in the 1991 BBC Young Playwrights' Festival, she began writing for Radio 4 Drama, television, and the screen, before the Royal National Theatre workshopped her *Voices on the Wind* (1995). Many of her scripts have been adapted from Indian texts. *Skelton* (Soho Theatre Company, 1997), based on a Tagore short story, tells of a young Indian medical student who falls in love with but resists the seductions of the skeleton of a once beautiful woman who murdered her two husbands rather than lose her good looks by becoming a mother and housewife. As in many Indian tales, a traditional moral is easily perceived.

Although Tanika Gupta's career was furthered by those seeking ethnic authors, she tried to move beyound such labels. Her *The Waiting Room* (2000) is set in England and blurs theological distinctions between Hindu and Christian notions of what happens after death. It includes such customs as the cremation, and is set during a Hindu three-day period in which the soul after death must review and settle its previous life before it begins its next cycle of life or becomes One with the One. The play ranges in mood from the tragic to the comedy of the son and dead mother continuing their arguments. It offers a mixture of social practices. While making use of Indian beliefs and spiritual values, *The Waiting Room* shows British Indians irritated by the ways of the parents; the daughter is a lesbian working in Paris, and the father has accepted his wife's child by his best friend in the hope that this would lead her to love him. That such plays were now produced at the Royal National Theatre and the success of Mehmet Ergen's Arcola Theatre in Dalston based on the Turkish community shows how much the London theatre scene had changed from the 1950s when West Indians were struggling to have a black theatre company.

Conclusion

I began by saying that the internationalization of English literature was part of a larger change. The great events after the Second World War included the Cold War and the decolonization of the former European empires. The latter gave birth to the new English literatures, Commonwealth literature, and, more broadly, postcolonial studies. The model of decolonization set in motion a wave of micronationalisms and liberation movements, such as Black Power and feminism, within nations, which was encouraged by the counterculture of the 1960s and supported by deconstructivist versions of Marxist analysis and their offshoots. The various strands of cultural assertion, liberation, and social criticism remained twined in postcolonial studies long after decolonization had been overtaken by a larger historical movement of which it was a part, the globalization of the world's economy, communications, transportation, education, and the internationalization of modern technology. The accompanying rise in the standard of living, wealth, and health was led by an American liberal ideology of free trade in contrast to imperial and other protectionist systems. During this time English became the world's language while the culture of the anglophone world became dominant in what V. S. Naipaul termed 'Our Universal Civilization'. The internationalization of English literature is part of a liberalism which reappears in varied and unexpected shapes, whether in notions of decolonization or free trade. It aims at a universalism. If the imaginative construction of a nation includes race and ethnicity, the change of 'British' from white to multiracial is part of a modernization brought about by free-market economics and culture.

During the half-century the nature of immigration and the England the newcomers faced changed. England after the Second World War was a place of scarcity, in which West Indians with rural skills were likely to be out of place as well as experience racial discrimination. England at the end of century was a place of abundance, offered the best opportunities for immigrants in Europe, and had an active policy against racial discrimination. People of colour were part of its population, many were British-born, many were highly skilled, educated, and part of the new international economy. There were mixed-race Britons, the recent African immigrants were highly motivated, and the Indians and many Pakistanis were middle-class professionals and entrepreneurs.

Such entrepreneurship can be seen in publishing. Writers came and still come to London seeking publishers. While British publishers from Michael Joseph, André Deutsch, and Faber in the 1950s and 1960s to Bloomsbury, Chatto, and Fourth Estate in the 1990s were welcoming to the new writers, there was always a need for other places of publication and the number of publishing houses created over the decades is impressive. They range from New Beacon, Bogle L'Ouverture, Peepal Tree, Allison & Busby, Hansib, and Xpress to the many small black poetry and feminist presses. There is the phenomenon of writers going outside trade channels and forming their own companies to self-publish their books, as Buchi Emecheta did especially for her children's books, as Timothy Mo did after a dispute over advances with Chatto, and as Chandraratna and Preethi Nair have done when faced by rejections.

History always consists of change and the clash of old and new, especially as the old partly adopts while trying to challenge the new. It is one of those paradoxes that the ideologies leading to national independence and decolonization often, as became obvious in Africa and the Islamic world, turned reactionary as they insisted on some unique past and essential culture long after that was useful in challenging imperialism. Postcolonial studies in inheriting a dialectic of opposites, the dominant and oppressed, took over this older paradigm. Although proclaiming hybrdity, postcolonial studies often continued what had become the language of decolonization, nationalism, and oppression into what was actually a period of great social liberation and emancipation.

The internationalization of the literature of English is mostly a change in subject matter and themes. Seeming changes in form, such as the attempt to create an oral poetry supposedly rooted in African traditions, are superficial; the poems were still published and the forms of black and white poetry were not significantly different from each other. Often only the kinds of dialect differ. The imitation of Indian storytelling within novels was attractive, but the novels remained novels not oral tales or massive epics. Those who argue that modernization imposes western modes on other peoples are basically correct. Multiracialism and multiculturalism in the new literature of England are primarily in subject matter and attitudes to which, at times, other cultural markers, such as dialect, are added.

The background to the internationalization of English literature 1948–2000 is that of mass migration as a result of rising expectations, a globalized economy, and the internationalization of the market place, whether for workers or writers. The literature often tells of the process by which people came to England, recall former homes, were at first ill at ease, wanted to be accepted as equals, and eventually felt enough at home to write of individual lives rather than as part of racial and immigrant communities. The meeting of cultures can be seen in such mixtures as novels of Indian spiritual journeys, performance poetry in a British Jamaican dialect, and Sunetra Gupta's cosmopolitan fictions, as well as the forms created by Rushdie, Okri, and Naipaul. A significant further stage of newness was how, from the mid-1980s on, those of mixed race sometimes wrote of the white side of their family as well as the black, while many black writers were noting similarities between the lives of outsiders regardless of race. A new national narrative was in the process of being written.

There are other stories, such as about those who feel they never took root in England and who remain nostalgic for lands they left; those who fled the results of decolonization; those who tell about the clash of the modern and the old as well as about diasporas; and those who have international lives. As each writer has a different history, each writes from a different position with his or her own concerns. Still, England's new international literature has been either about immigration and its consequences or about abroad, especially European imperialism, the decolonization which followed, and the problems of nation-building, being self-supporting, integrating communities, and becoming part of the modern world. Both immigration and the process of nation building are aspects of modernization, require the revisioning of history, and are the narratives by which people make sense of and justify their lives.

The Second World War, the Cold War, and the conflict between Islam and the West were about freedom. Liberation may often have seemed a slogan and was usually understood as colonial, national, or racial freedom, but social and cultural liberalism was accompanied by integration into the secular modern world and its market. The major writers, such as V. S. Naipaul, Rushdie, and Kureishi, have directly examined the resulting changes and problems. As can be seen from the writings of G. V. Desani, Kamala Markandaya, or Timothy Mo, such themes as cultural conflict, tradition versus modernization, East meets West, and communality versus individualism are aspects of the varied effects of liberalization. Even many of the movements that use nationalist-like slogans, such as gay liberation and feminism, are international and appeal to liberal values; they are unlikely to find sympathy from traditionalists, closed societies, or tyrannies. Personal liberation requires individual rights. Seen this way, writing about immigration, racial prejudice, and being part of a nation and writing about the failures of modernity and consequences of decolonization are concerned with different aspects of radical liberalism's effect on people and societies.

For some readers this will seem too neat an ending. The story I tell of England's multiracial literature needs to be superseded by later stories of the troubles of new refugees from other parts of the world at the start of the new century. Such refugees and their children will eventually produce their own literature which will be the subject of later literary histories. As societies change, their histories need to be revised.

Author Bibliographies

An asterisk beside an edition cited designates the edition from which a text has been cited in the body of the book.

ABBENSETTS, MICHAEL (b. 1938)

The son of Neville John (a physician) and Elaine Abbensetts, he was born in Georgetown, British Guiana. Educated at Queens College (Guyana), 1952–6; Stanstead College (Quebec, Canada), 1956–8; and Sir George Williams University (Montreal), 1960–1, he saw a Canadian production of John Osborne's *Look Back in Anger* and decided his future was as a dramatist. After moving to England he worked as a security guard, then became part of the staff at the Sir John Soane Museum, 1968–71. He took his first script to the agent Peggy Ramsay who told him to write a play about a black man in contemporary England. He began the next day to write *Sweet Talk* (Royal Court, 1973), which won the George Devine award, and was published by Heinemann in 1988. He became a British citizen in 1974. During the next decade there were numerous radio and television plays. *Empire Road* (1978–9) was said to be the first TV series to treat immigrant life without the simplification of happy or racial protest black characters. It was published as a novel in 1979 (Panther). He followed it with *Samba* (Tricycle Theatre, 1980; pub. Eyre Methuen, 1980). *Living Together* contains two plays: 'Royston's Day' and 'The Street Party' (Heinemann, 1988). Michelle Stoby interviews Abbensetts in *Wasafiri*, 35 (Spring 2002), 3–8.

ADEBAYO, DIRAN (b. 1968)

He was born in north London where his family lived at Manor House, Wood Green. His mother, Phebean Olufunke Adebayo (née Agbe), came to England from Nigeria in 1964 on a civil servant scholarship. His father, Solomon Layi Adebayo, who came to England the next year, was a scientist who earned a PhD in chemistry in England. He influenced the children, insisting that they read books and write weekly reports. Diran was a major scholar at Malvern College, Worchestershire, 1981–6, then studied law at Oxford, 1986–9, before returning to London as a news-paper and television reporter, then becoming a full-time writer. His experiences at Oxford were contrasted with those of London in his first novel, *Some Kind of Black* (Virago, 1996), which was awarded the 1996 Saga Prize, a Betty Trask Award, the Authors' Club Best First Novel Award, and the Writers Guild Award for Great Britain's New Writer of the Year in 1996. This was followed by *My Once Upon A Time* (Abacus, 2000).

AGARD, JOHN (b. 1949)

In Guyana, Agard contributed to local publications while still at St Stanislaus College. He published the hippy-influenced *Shoot Me with Flowers* (Candlewick, 1973) before moving to England in 1977 where he soon became a prolific author of such books for children as *Letters for Lettie* (Bodley Head, 1979) and *Dig Away, Two-Hole Tim* (Bodley Head, 1981). He won the Cuban Casa de las Americas Poetry Prize in 1982 with *Man to Pan* (Ciudad de la Haban, 1982), followed by *Limbo Dancer in Dark Glasses* (Islington Community Press, 1983), *Mangoes and Bullets* (Pluto, 1985), and *Lovelines for a Goat-Born Lady* (Serpent's Tail, 1990), the latter alluding to the Guyanese poet Grace Nichols with whom he lives in Brighton. Agard became an established figure on the British poetry scene as writer-in-residence at London's South Bank Centre (1993) and the BBC's first poet-in-residence (1998). The later volumes include *From the Devil's Pulpit* (Bloodaxe, 1997) and *Weblines* (Bloodaxe, 2000), which along with new poems reprints *Limbo Dancer in Dark Glasses* and *Man to Pan*. An actor, Agard also writes plays.

AHMAD, RUKHSANA (b. 1948)

She was born in Karachi, Pakistan. After taking an MA (Hons.) in English literature from the University of Karachi (1970), she was appointed Lecturer in English. Two years later she received another first class MA (1972), this time in linguistics and language teaching, before marrying and moving to England early in 1973. She has an MA (1974) in modern litera-ture from the University of Reading. Later she studied for an MA (1999) in screenwriting from the London College of Printing. Her husband Nobil Ahmad is a dentist and they have three children.

A journalist and actress, her stage-writing career began when invited to write for Tara Arts. In 1988 she and Rita Wolf started the Kali Theatre Company; its first production was her play *Song for a Sanctuary*, published in Kadija George (ed.), *Six Plays by Black and Asian Women*. (Aurora Metro, 1993), 159–86. Her stories are in *Right of Way* (Women's Press, 1988), *The Inner Courtyard* (Virago, 1990), and *The Man Who Loved Presents* (Women's Press, 1991). She translated and edited *We Sinful Women: Contemporary Urdu Feminist Poetry* (Women's Press, 1991); *The Hope Chest*, a novel, was published in 1996 by Virago.

ALI, TARIQ (b. 1943)

He was born in pre-Partition Lahore. His parents were active Communists, his father the editor of the *Pakistani Times*. After graduating from Punjab University (BA (Hons.), 1963) he left Pakistan, a political exile active on the Left. At Oxford University he was president of the Union. Now a Trotskyite, he edited two radical political magazines, *Black Dwarf* and *Red Mole*, and was on the editorial board of *New Left Review*. He was a prolific writer, his works including *The Coming British Revolution* (Cape, 1972), *1968 & After: Inside the Revolution* (Blond & Briggs, 1978), and, with Phil Evans, *Trotsky for Beginners* (Pantheon, 1980). He co-wrote several plays, notably, with Howard Brenton, the short *Iranian Nights* (Nick Hern, 1989) written in support of Rushdie at the time of the *fatwa*. Ali collaborated with Brenton on *Moscow Gold* (Nick Hern, 1990), a theatrical epic concerning the Gorbachev years in the Soviet Union.

During the 1990s he turned his attention to fiction with two novels about Marxism, and three novels tracing the history of Islam in its relations to the West: *Shadows of the Pomegranate Tree* (Verso, 1992), *The Book of Saladin* (Verso, 1998), and **The Stone Woman* (Verso, 2000). He is interviewed in Chelva Kanaganayakam (ed.), *Configurations of Exile* (1995), 1–11.

ALVI, MONIZA (b. 1954)

Born in Lahore, to an English mother and Pakistani father, Dulcie and Zia Alvi, Moniza came to England as an infant with her parents and grew up in Hertfordshire. She studied English at the University of York (1973–6), did a postgraduate certificate in education at Whitelands College, London (1977) and an MA in education at the University of London Institute of Education (1985). She taught in comprehensive schools in London and was head of English at Aylwin Girls' School (1989–97). She married Robert Coe (1996); their daughter was born the next year. Her first two books of poetry, *The Country at My Shoulder* (1993) and **A Bowl of*

Warm Air (1996) were published in the Oxford Poetry series; when the series ended she moved to Bloodaxe Books for *Carrying My Wife* (2000), which included the first two books and new poems, and for *Souls* (2002).

BANDELE-THOMAS, BIYI (b. 1967)

Born in Kanfanchan, he left home when he was 14 and travelled across Nigeria. While studying dramatic arts at Obafemi Awolowo University, Ile-Ife, he won an international student playwriting contest (1988). He came to England on a British Council grant (1990) with the manuscript of his first publishable play, *Marching for Fausa* (Amber Lane Press, 1993), which was performed at the Royal Court Theatre where he became an associate writer on an Arts Council bursary (1992). He won the London New Play Festival Award (1994) with *Two Horsemen* (Amber Lane, 1994), was writer-in-residence with the Talawa Theatre Company (1994–5), which performed his *Resurrections in the Season of the Longest Drought* (Amber Lane Press, 1994), and a resident dramatist with the Royal National Theatre Studio (1996). *Death Catches the Hunter* was published with *Me and the Boys* (Amber Lane, 1995). His prose fiction includes *The Sympathetic Undertaker and Other Dreams* (Bellew, 1991; Heinemann, 1993); *The Man Who Came in from the Back of Beyond* (Bellew, 1991; *Heinemann, 1992); and *The Street* (Picador, 1999). He regards himself a Yoruba-Hausa Nigerian international writer who lives in London.

BERRY, JAMES (b. 1925)

Berry was born in Fair Prospect, Jamaica. After a brief period of working in the USA he moved to England in 1948, where he became a telegraphist in a London post office, 1951–77. Publication of *Bluefoot Traveller: An Anthology of Westindian Poets in Britain* (*Limestone, 1976; expanded edn., Harrap, 1981) led to appointment as writer-in-residence at Vauxhall Manor School, London (1977). *Fractured Circles* (New Beacon, 1979) established him as one of the leaders in the use of black dialect in verse. *Cut-Way Feelins, Loving, Lucy's Letters* (Strange Lime Fruit Stone, 1981) was revised and enlarged as *Lucy's Letters and Loving* (New Beacon, 1982). He edited the influential *News for Babylon: The Chatto Book of Westindian-British Poetry* (Chatto and Windus, 1984), which was followed by his own poems in *Chain of Days* (OUP, 1985), *When I Dance* (Hamish Hamilton, 1988), and *Hot Earth Cold Earth* (Bloodaxe, 1995). His many books for children began with *A Thief in the Village and*

Other Stories of Jamaica (Hamish Hamilton, 1987), the stories in *The Girls and Yanga Marshall* (Longman, 1987), and *Anancy-Spiderman* (Walker, 1988). He was awarded the OBE (1990). He is discussed by Stewart Brown, 'James Berry: Celebration Songs', *Kunapipi*, 20/1 (1998), 45–56; and in such reference books as *Contemporary Poets* (7th edn., 2001), 79–81, and *Contemporary Authors*, 135 (1992), 36–8.

BRAITHWAITE, E[DWARD] R[ICARDO] (b. 1920)

Braithwaite was born and educated in Georgetown, British Guiana. After studying science at City College in New York (1940) he served in the RAF as a fighter pilot (1941–5), followed by an MA in physics from Gonville and Caius College, Cambridge (1949). Unable to find suitable employment in England he turned to teaching (1950–7), an experience recounted in *To Sir, With Love* (Bodley Head, 1959), which made him famous. *Paid Servant* (Bodley Head, 1962) recounts disillusionments as a social worker concerned with minorities (1958–60). He became a human rights' officer in Paris for the World Veterans' Foundation (1960–3), an education consultant for UNESCO (1963–6), and Guyana's permanent ambassador to the UN (1968–9). *A Kind of Homecoming* (Prentice Hall, 1962) tells of travels in Africa, while *Honorary White* (Bodley Head, 1975) concerns being a diplomat in South Africa. *Reluctant Neighbors* (McGraw-Hill, 1972) concerns racial prejudice in the USA where he became a professor of English and an American citizen.

DABYDEEN, DAVID (b. 1956)

He was born on Plantation Zeeland, Berbice, Guyana, to Krishna Prasad and Vera Dabydeen. His father, a Presbyterian, was of Madrassi stock with some mixture of African; his mother an Indian Hindu. After the family broke up he was sent to England to join his father whose new wife forced him to leave. From the time he was 15 until he was 18 he was in the care of the Wandsworth Council. This period is described in 'From Care to Cambridge', *Planet* (1988), 39–43. He attended Ernest Bevin Comprehensive School in Tooting Bec, South London, 1969–74. A BA (Hons.) in English literature from Cambridge University (1978) was followed by a doctorate in English literature from London University (1982), and a junior research fellowship, Wolfson College, Oxford University (1983–7). Appointed in 1984 a lecturer at the University of Warwick, he moved up the academic ladder to professor. He joined the Executive Board of UNESCO in 1993 as ambassador-at-large for Guyana.

Dabydeen edited *The Black Presence in English Literature* (1983; rev. Manchester UP, 1985); and *A Handbook for Teaching Caribbean Literature* (Heinemann, 1988); with Nana Wilson-Tagoe, *A Reader's Guide to West Indian and Black British Literature* (Hansib, 1988); and with Paul Edwards, *Black Writers in Britain 1760–1890* (Edinburgh UP, 1991). His *Hogarth's Blacks: Images of Blacks in Eighteenth Century English Art* (Dangeroo, 1985; Manchester UP 1987) was followed by *Hogarth, Walpole and Commercial Britain* (Hansib, 1987).

His creative writing begins with *Slave Song* (Dangaroo Press, 1984), which won the Commonwealth Poetry Prize, and **Coolie Odyssey* (Dangaroo Press and Hansib, 1988). Concern with black representation in art is found in the title poem of *Turner: New and Selected Poems* (Cape, 1994). The novels *The Intended* (Secker and Warburg, 1991), *Disappearance* (Secker and Warburg, 1993), and *The Counting House* (Cape, 1996) imagine aspects of the Indian diaspora. *A Harlot's Progress* (Cape, 1999) concerns black life in eighteenth-century London. *The Art of David Dabydeen* (1997) is edited by Kevin Grant.

D'AGUIAR, FRED (b. 1960)

Born in 1960 to Malcolm Frederick D'Aguiar, a London Transport bus driver, and Kathleen Agatha Messiah, a bus conductor, immigrants living in London, Fred and his older brother were in 1962 sent to Guyana to be brought up by his paternal grandparents—the Mama Dot at Airy Hall of his first two books of poetry, **Mama Dot* (Chatto & Windus, 1985) and **Airy Hall* (Chatto & Windus, 1989). He returned to England in 1972 and lived with his divorced mother who had remarried a Pakistani and converted herself and her children to Islam, a situation used in the semi-autobiographical novel *Dear Future* (Chatto and Windus, 1996). After studying at Carlton Boys Secondary School, D'Aguiar was a psychiatric nurse in Camberwell and Croydon. He earned his BA from the University of Kent, Canterbury (1982–5). He edited *The New British Poetry 1968–1988* (Paladin, 1988) with Gillian Allnutt, Ken Edwards, and Eric Mottram. After various positions as writer-in-residence, he moved to the United States in 1992 where he became a professor of creative writing. The poems in **British Subjects* (Bloodaxe, 1993) reflect on the contradictions of being black British. This was followed by *The Longest Memory* (Chatto and Windus, 1994), a novel which received the Whitbread First Novel award and the David Higham Prize. **An English Sampler* (Chatto & Windus, 2001) contains new and selected poems. He is married and has children by his present wife along with two children from a previous marriage. Robert Stewart has written about him in *DLB* 157 (1996), 67–78; Harald Leusmann interviews him in *Wasafiri*, 28 (Autumn 1998), 17–21.

DESANI, G[OVINDAS] V[ISHNOODAS] (1909–2000)

Born in Nairobi, Kenya, Desani came to England in 1926 after a fight with his father, and lived between London and India until the Second World War when he lectured in England on Indian topics. His novel *All about Mr Hatterr: A Gesture* (Aldor, 1948) was published in a revised edition by Bodley Head, 1970. The King Penguin 1972 edition was again revised with an extra chapter. Hatterr's absurd search for the truth was followed by *Hali* (Saturn Press, 1950; rev. edn., Calcutta Writers' Workshop, 1967), an allegorical drama about Good and Evil. From the early 1950s Desani travelled for two decades through India and Burma in search of spiritual enlightenment. His short stories during this period are in *Hali & Collected Stories* (McPherson, 1990). In 1968 he began teaching philosophy at the University of Texas, Austin. He took American citizenship in 1979 and had an ashram in Texas until his death. Molly Ramanujan's *G. V. Desani: Writer and Worldview* (1984) can be supplemented by Susheila Nasta's *Home Truths* (2002) and C. L. Innes's *Black and Asian Writing in Britain* (2002). Peter Russell and Khushwant Singh edited *A Note on G. V. Desani's 'All about H. Hatterr' and 'Kali'* (1952), which uses Desani's annotations.

DHONDY, FARRUKH (b. 1944)

His father, a Parsee, was an army engineer. Born in Poona, India, Farrukh studied at Bishop's School, then at Wadia College. After a BSc in engineering, at the University of Bombay, 1964, he took a BA in English, at Pembroke College, Cambridge, 1967. He lectured at the Leicester College of Higher Education, 1968–9 while studying for an MA in literature at Leicester University. Teaching at the Henry Thornton Comprehensive School, he began to observe the students and conditions which he would use in his books about the East End. From 1974 to 1980 he was head of English at Archbishop Michael Ramsay's School, Lambeth. In politics he moved from a British version of the Black Panthers to the *Race Today* collective. He, Barbara Beese, and Leila Hassan wrote for Race Today Publications *The Black Explosion in British Schools* (1982). *East End at Your Feet* (Macmillan 1976), which won an Other Award from the

Children's Rights Workshop, and *Siege of Babylon* (1977) were among the first trade books written for this new educational market.

In 1979 he joined the Black Theatre Co-operative. His TV plays for BBC between 1982 and 1996 include the serials 'Come to Mecca' (1982), 'No Problem' (with Mustapha Matura, 1982–4), and 'King of the Ghetto' (1985). *Romance, Romance* received a Samuel Beckett Award for the best first television show (1983). As commissioning editor of multicultural programming for Channel 4 TV, 1984–97, he commissioned *Salaam Bombay, Mississippi Masala*, and *Bandit Queen* (scripted by Mala Sen from whom he is divorced). His only novel for adults is *Bombay Duck* (Picador/Cape, 1990). C. L. R. James for a time stayed with him, the basis of Dhondy's *C. L. R. James: Cricket, the Caribbean, and World Revolution* (Weidenfeld & Nicolson, 2001). Jane Carducci, 'Farrukh Dhondy', in Emmanuel Nelson's *Writers of the Indian Diaspora* (1993), provides biographical and bibliographical information.

EMECHETA, [FLORENCE ONYE] BUCHI (b. 1944)

Emecheta was born in Yaba, Lagos, Nigeria to Igbo Christian parents. Orphaned young, she lived with relatives who opposed her desire for education. She was forced into marriage when she was 16 to Sylvester Onwordi to whom she had been promised since she was 11. The next year she bore the first of five children. She worked as a librarian, 1960–4, first in Nigeria, then in England, 1965–69, to support her husband and family while he studied. Their marriage broke up in 1969 after he burnt the manuscript of her first book. These years are the basis for *In The Ditch* (Barrie and Jenkins, 1972), which also tells of how she studied at the University of London for a BS (Hons.) degree in sociology (1972), supported her children, and became a writer. Her two early autobiographical novels were combined as *Adah's Story* (Allison and Busby, 1983). Her early novels about Nigeria, including *The Bride Price* (Allison and Busby, 1976) and *The Slave Girl* (Allison and Busby, 1977), protest against the treatment of women in her clan. The ironic *The Joys of Motherhood* (Allison and Busby, 1979) draws upon the experiences of her mother. A disillusioning year at the University of Calabar, Nigeria (1980–1), resulted in the novel *Double Yoke*, published by her own company (Ogwugwu Afo, 1982). She returned to autobiography in *Head above Water* (Fontana, 1986). Her later novels, including **The New Tribe* (Heinemann, 2000), examine mistaken idealization of Africa by blacks in Europe. She has written books for children including *Titch the Cat* (Allison and Busby, 1979) and *Naira Power* (Macmillan, 1982).

Critical discussion includes Katherine Fishburn's *Reading Buchi Emecheta: Cross-Cultural Conversations* (1995); and Marie Umeh (ed.), *Emerging Perspectives on Buchi Emecheta* (1996); and Omar Sougou's *Writing across Cultures: Gender Politics and Difference in the Fiction of Buchi Emecheta* (2002).

EVARISTO, BERNARDINE (b. 1959)

Born in London to a Nigerian father who was a welder and a white English schoolteacher mother of Irish and German origins, Evaristo is the fourth of eight children. She spent four years in a Roman Catholic convent school before attending Eltham Hill Grammar School (1970–7). She trained to be an actress at the Rose Bruford College of Speech and Drama (1979–82). Her first professional play, 'Moving Through', was performed at the Royal Court in 1982, the year she co-founded the Theatre of Black Women (1982–8). She co-edited *Black Women Talk Poetry* (Black Womantalk, 1987). During 1988–90 she lived in Spain and Turkey, and travelled to Kuwait. She became an arts manager and was a co-director (1995–9) for Spread the Word Literature Development Agency. **Island of Abraham* (Peepal Tree, 1994) is based on a journey to Madagascar; *Lara* (Angela Royal, 1997) tells of someone like herself, product of a mixed marriage, who wants to know her family's past. **The Emperor's Babe* (Hamish Hamilton, 2001) imagines a black British woman who became the mistress of a black Roman emperor. Alastair Niven interviews Evaristo in *Wasafiri*, 34 (Autumn 2001), 15–20.

GHOSE, ZULFIKAR (b. 1935)

Born into a Muslim family in Sialkot, Punjab, India (it became Pakistan in 1947), he moved with his family to Bombay in 1942. Coming to England in 1952, he studied at Sloane School, and graduated from Keele University (1959). After working as a newspaper reporter, he was a schoolteacher in Ealing (1964–9). These were extremely creative years. His first book of poetry, **The Loss of India* (Routledge, 1964), was followed by the autobiography *Confessions of a Native Alien* (Routledge, 1965); his first novel, *The Contradictions* (Macmillan, 1966); his second volume of poetry, *Jets from Orange* (Macmillan, 1967); and his best novel, *The Murder of Aziz Khan* (Macmillan, 1967). In 1969 he became a professor of English at the University of Texas-Austin. He married a Brazilian and wrote a number of magical realist novels concerned with South America. His books of literary theory include *Hamlet, Prufrock and Language* (Macmillan,

1978), *The Fiction of Reality* (Macmillan, 1984), and *The Art of Creating Fiction* (Macmillan, 1991). Part of *Review of Contemporary Fiction* 9/2 (1989) is devoted to essays on Ghose who is the subject of Chelva Kanaganayakam, *Structures of Negation: The Writings of Zulfikar Ghose* (1993).

GUNESEKERA, ROMESH (b. 1954)

Born in Colombo, Sri Lanka (then Ceylon), the second of three children, Romesh was bilingual in Sinhalese and English. For a time the family lived in the United States. His father, Douglas Gunesekera, was attached to the Asian Development Bank and they moved to the Philippines when Romesh was 14. He came to London in 1972 for his A levels and studied at Liverpool University, where he took a BA (Combined Hons.) in English and philosophy (1976) and was awarded the Rathbone Prize in philosophy. He held a variety of jobs ranging from bookselling to research and journalism. After being attached to the Institute of Development Studies at the University of Sussex, in 1984 he became assistant regional director, East Asia, for the British Council.

The short stories of *Monkfish Moon* (Granta, 1992) were shortlisted for Commonwealth Writers and David Higham awards, and were followed by a novel, *Reef* (Granta, 1994), which was shortlisted for the Booker Prize, the *Guardian*'s Fiction Prize, and was the *Economist*'s Book of the Month. In 1996 he became a full-time writer. *The Sandglass* (Granta, 1998), his second novel, was *Marie Claire*'s Book of the Month. He changed publisher with *Heavens's Edge* (Bloomsbury, 2002), his third novel, which is set in England and an unnamed tropical island. There are entries in such reference books as *Contemporary Novelists*, 7 (2000) and a survey of reviews in *Contemporary Literary Criticism*, 91 (1995). Nasta's *Home Truths* (2002) discusses his use of memory. A British citizen, he returns to Sri Lanka yearly, is married, lives in North London, and has two daughters. His parents and sister also live in England.

GUPTA, SUNETRA (b. 1965)

A Bengali, Gupta was born in Calcutta to secular Hindus. Her father, Dhruba, was a university reader in art and film criticism, her mother, Minati Sengupta, a schoolteacher. Her youth was mostly spent in Africa. After she received her BA in biology cum laude (1987) from Princeton University, she moved to England where she was a principal investigator at Imperial College (1988–92) while working towards her

PhD in theoretical epidemiology (1992). She became a fellow in mathematical biology at the Department of Zoology, Oxford University, was appointed junior research fellow at Merton College (1993), became senior research fellow in Oxford University's Department of Zoology (1995), and reader in epidemiology of infectious diseases (1999). She is married to Adrian Vivian Sinton Hill, medical doctor and professor of human genetics, Oxford University. They have two daughters. In 1999 she became a British citizen.

Although each of her novels is different, *Memories of Rain* (Grove Weidenfield, 1992), *The Glassblower's Breath* (Orion, 1993), *Moonlight into Marzipan* (Phoenix House, 1995), and *A Sin of Colour* (Phoenix House, 1999) move restlessly between India, England, and Princeton. Her fiction is discussed by Tabish Khair in *Contemporary Novelists*, 7 (2000), who considers her an heir of literary modernism without its cultural critique, and in Susheila Nasta's *Home Truths* (2002). Gupta's comments on 'Why I Write' are in the 'Post-Colonial Women's Writing' volume of *Kunapipi*, 16 (1994), 289.

GURNAH, ABDULRAZAK (b. 1948)

Born in Zanzibar, now part of Tanzania, Gurnah came to England in 1968 and worked as a hospital orderly in Canterbury 1970–3, then qualified for a Certificate of Education (1975) and a BEd (1976) from the University of London before teaching at Astor Secondary School at Dover, Kent, 1976–8. His fiction often shows his personal experiences such as, in *Memory of Departure* (Cape, 1987), the frustrations of the young in Tanzania, or in *Pilgrim's Way* (Cape, 1988), set in Canterbury, the prejudices faced by an impoverished foreign student. During 1980–2 he taught at Bayero University, Kano, Nigeria, while working towards his doctorate (1982) from the University of Kent. After being manager of an access project in Hackney, London, 1983–5, he joined the University of Kent in 1985 as a lecturer in English literature and was made a senior lecturer in 1995. He edited the two volumes of *Essays on African Writing: A Re-evaluation* (Heinemann, 1993, 1995). He is married and has British citizenship.

*Paradise (Hamish Hamilton, 1994), shortlisted for the Booker Prize and the Whitbread Prize, offers a portrait of East Africa before the First World War. *Admiring Silence* (Hamish Hamilton, 1996) tells of a Zanzibarian who, having taken refuge in London, visits Zanzibar two decades later. *By the Sea* (Bloomsbury, 2001) concerns refugees from Zanzibar in England. Gurnah's 'Imagining the Postcolonial Writer' is in Susheila

Nasta's *Reading the 'New Literatures' in a Postcolonial Era* (Brewer, 2000), 73–86. A. Robert Lee, 'Long Day's Journey: The Novels of Abdulrazak Gurnah', in Lee (ed.), *Other Britain, Other British: Contemporary Multicultural Fiction* (1995) offers a survey; Eckhard Breitinger's entry on Gurnah, in *Contemporary Novelists*, 7 (2001), 415–16, discusses *Paradise* and *Admiring Silence*.

HARRIS, [THEODORE] WILSON (b. 1921)

Born in New Amsterdam, Guyana, Harris was educated at Queens College, Georgetown. His work as surveyor for the government gave him the knowledge of the Guyanese interior and time for the readings into German philosophy which went into such early novels as *Palace of the Peacock* (1960), *The Far Journey of Oudin* (1961), *The Whole Armour* (1962), and *The Secret Ladder* (1963), republished as *The Guyana Quartet* (1985), all published by Faber. His first marriage was to Cecily Carew, 1945. He came to England in 1959 when he married Margaret Whitaker. His privately published poetry began with (as Kona Waruk) *Fetish* (1951); *Eternity to Season* (1954, rev. edn., New Beacon, 1979).

Harris's theoretical and critical writings include *Tradition, the Writer and Society: Critical Essays* (New Beacon, 1967, 1973); *Explorations: A Selection of Talks and Articles* (Dangeroo, 1981) ed. Hena Maes-Jelinek; *Womb of Space: The Cross-Cultural Imagination* (Greenwood Press, 1986); *The Radical Imagination* (University of Liege, 1992), ed. Alan Riach and Mark Williams; and *Selected Essays of Wilson Harris* (Routledge, 1999), ed. and introd. Andrew Bundy.

Commentary begins with C. L. R. James's pamphlet *Wilson Harris: A Philosophical Approach* (1965). The main commentator on Harris's fiction is Hena Maes-Jelinek whose publications include *The Naked Design: A Reading of Palace of the Peacock* (1976) and *Wilson Harris* (1982), brought up to date by essays in Maes-Jelinek (ed.), *Wilson Harris: The Uncompromising Imagination* (1991) and Maes-Jelinek and Bénédicte Ledent (eds.), *Theatre of the Arts: Wilson Harris and the Caribbean* (2002), each of which includes bibliography.

HEATH, ROY A[UBREY] K[EVIN] (b. 1926)

Heath, whose parents were teachers, was born in Georgetown, British Guiana, which is also the location of his fiction. He attended Central High School in Georgetown and was a treasury clerk (1942–50) before moving to London (1951) where he received a BA in French at the University of

London (1952–6). After various clerical jobs he became a primary school-teacher (1959–68), then a teacher of French and German. He was called to the Bar, Lincolns Inn (1964). He married Aemilia Oberli and they have three children. His novels are socially detailed and show the many cultures that exist in Guyana. They include *A Man Come Home* (Longman, 1974), *The Murderer* (Allison and Busby, 1978), *Kwaku; or, The Man Who Could Not Keep His Mouth Shut* (Allison and Busby, 1982), and *The Shadow Bride* (Collins, 1988). His autobiography, *Shadows Round the Moon: Caribbean Memoirs* (Collins, 1990), concludes with his leaving for England. He is discussed by Ian Munro in *DLB* 117 (1992), 198–203; by Chelva Kanaganayakam, *Caribana*, 5 (1996), 141–50; and by Lloyd Brown in *Contemporary Novelists*, 7 (2001).

HOSAIN, ATTIA (1913–1998)

Hosain was born in Lucknow, India, into an orthodox Muslim landed family and educated at La Martinière School, Isabella Thoburn College, and the University of Lucknow (1933). The first woman in her family to have a liberal western education as well as studying Urdu, Persian, and Arabic, she became an Indian nationalist and a member of Progressive Writers' Group. After the Partition of India, she and her husband and their two children moved to Britain in 1947. She also had a home in Bombay, but refused to live in Pakistan. She co-ordinated the women's programme on the BBC Eastern Service for many years. She published *Phoenix Fled, and Other Stories* (Chatto and Windus, 1953), introd. Anita Desai (Virago, 1988). Her novel *Sunlight on a Broken Column* (Chatto and Windus, 1961), introd. Anita Desai (Penguin and Virago, 1989), is auto-biographical. She is discussed in Susheila Nasta's *Home Truths: Fictions of the South Asian Diaspora in Britain* (2002).

HUSSEIN, AAMER (b. 1955)

Hussein was born in Karachi, Pakistan; both parents were from feudal, landed Muslim families, his father a businessman. He was educated in Karachi and in Ooty, India, as well as, from 1970, in London, before studying Persian, Urdu, and Indian history at the School of Asian and Oriental Studies, University of London, where he has taught Urdu since 1991. His edition of Han Suyin's *Tigers and Butterflies: Selected Writings on Politics, Culture, and Society* (Earthscan, 1990) was followed by the novel *Mirror to the Sun* (Mantra, 1993), an edition of *Hoops of Fire: Fifty Years of Fiction by Pakistani Women* (International Specialised Book

Service, 1997), and two volumes of his short stories, *This Other Salt* (Saqi, 1999) and *Turquoise* (Saqi, 2002). He is discussed in Susheila Nasta's *Home Truths: Fictions of the South Asian Diaspora in Britain* (2002).

ISHIGURO, KAZUO (b. 1954)

He was born in Nagasaki, Japan. His family moved to England in 1960 when his father, an oceanographer, was employed in developing the North Sea oil fields. Kazuo was educated at Stoughton Primary School, 1960–6, then Woking County Grammar School for Boys, Surrey, 1966–73. He travelled to the United States and Canada before studying at the University of Kent, Canterbury, 1974–5 and 76–8 for the BA (Hons.) in English and philosophy. During 1976 he was a community worker in the Renfrew Social Works Department, Scotland. He then worked as a residential social worker, West London Cyrenians, and wrote four short stories, before studying for an MA in creative writing with Malcolm Bradbury and Angela Carter at the University of East Anglia, 1979–80.

After three of his short stories were published in *Introduction 7: Stories by New Writers* (1981), Faber became his publisher. The Royal Society of Literature awarded his first novel *A Pale View of Hills* (1982) the Winifred Holtby Prize (1983). His second novel, *An Artist of the Floating World* (1986), was the Whitbread Book of the Year and was shortlisted for the Booker Prize. The same year Ishiguro married Lorna Anne MacDougal. They would have a daughter Naomi (1992). *The Remains of the Day* (1989) was awarded the Booker Prize. When the film was released in 1993 it was nominated for eight Oscars. *The Unconsoled* (1995) won the Cheltenham Prize, was shortlisted for the Booker Prize, and Ishiguro was awarded an OBE. *When We Were Orphans* (2000) tells of a detective's life in London during the 1930s and his attempt to learn what happened to his parents in Shanghai years earlier.

While Brian Shaffer's *Understanding Kazuo Ishiguro* (1998) and Cynthia Wong's *Kazuo Ishiguro* (2000) are concerned with Ishiguro's unreliable narrators and readers' response, Barry Lewis's *Kazuo Ishiguro* (2000) offers a synthesis of various critical approaches held together by Freudian notions of displacement.

JOHN, ERROL (1924–1988)

Errol John was born in Port of Spain, Trinidad where he was a journalist and commercial artist while participating in the Whitehall Players as writer, actor, and director. After moving to London, 1950, he became a professional actor. He was in a production of *Othello*, won the London *Observer* Prize for drama in 1957 with his script *Moon on a Rainbow Shawl* (Faber, 1958), and received a Guggenheim Fellowship in 1958. From 1956 to 1966 he performed in films and television plays. His writings include *Force Majeure, The Dispossessed, Hasta Luego: Three Screenplays* (Faber, 1967). He had a wife and two children.

JOHNSON, AMRYL (1948–2001)

Born in Tunapuna, Trinidad, she moved to England in 1959 where she was educated at Clark's Grammar School in London and at the University of Kent, where she received a BA in English. She lived in Coventry and was popular as a performance poet especially on the female circuit. She taught arts and creative writing. Her poetry collections include *Gorgons* (Cofa Press, 1992) and *Tread Carefully in Paradise* (Cofa Press, 1991), which republishes *Long Road to Nowhere* (Virago, 1985) and *Shackles* (Sable, 1983). *Sequins for a Ragged Hem* (Virago, 1988) is a travel book concerning a six months' trip to the Caribbean. Denise de Caires Narian provides an obituary in *Wasafiri*, 33 (Spring, 2001), 64–5.

JOHNSON, LINTON KWESI (b. 1952)

Johnson was born in Chapeltown, Jamaica, and brought up and educated by his grandmother in the parish of Clarendon. He moved to England in 1963 to join his mother in Brixton. While still at Tulse Hill Comprehensive School he was introduced to black literature by John La Rose and joined the British Black Panther Youth League (1970). He studied for a BA in sociology at Goldsmiths College (1973). The next year he became a founding member of the Race Today Collective (1974), its Arts editor, and published a pamphlet of poems and a play, *Voices of the Living and the Dead* (Toward Racial Justice, 1974). His main publications were *Dread, Beat, and Blood* (Bogle L'Ouverture, 1975), *Inglan is a Bitch* (Race Today, 1980), *Tings an' Times: Selected Poems* (Bloodaxe and LKJ Music, 1991), along with such recordings as *Poet and the Roots* (Virgin, 1977), *Dread, Beat, and Blood* (Virgin, 1978), *Bass Culture* (Mango/ Island, 1980), and *The Best of LKJ* (Epic, 1980). He started his own record company, LKJ Music and Records (1981), and has produced a ten-part radio series about Jamaican music, 'From Mento to Lovers Rock', which was broadcast by the BBC in 1982. He stopped touring regularly after 1985. *Mi Revalueshanary Fren: Selected Poems* (Penguin, 2002) covers three decades. He is interviewed by Burt Caesar, *Critical Quarterly*, 38/4

(Winter, 1996), 64–77, and by Allister Henry, *Sable*, 1 (Spring, 2001), 7–18; discussed by the poet Fred D'Aguiar in *DLB* 117 (1992), 123–30 and in Kwame Neville Dawes, *Natural Mysticism: Towards a Reggae Aesthetic* (1998). He has three children.

KAY, JACKIE [JACQUELINE MARGARET] (b. 1961)

Kay was born in Edinburgh, her father a Nigerian (who returned to Africa before she was born), her birth mother a 19-year-old white woman from the Scottish highlands. She was brought up in Glasgow by white adoptive parents, the basis of poems in *The Adoption Papers* (Bloodaxe, 1991), and some short stories in * *Why don't you stop talking* (Picador, 2002). After studying English at the University of Stirling (MA, 1983), she moved to London where she soon published in * *A Dangerous Knowing: Four Black Women Poets* (Sheba Feminist, 1985) and *Stepping Out: Short Stories on Friendships between Women* (Pandora Press, 1986). *Chiaroscuro* (1986) was published in *Lesbian Plays* (1987), while *Twice Over* (Methuen, 1988) was included in *Gay Sweatshop: Four Plays and a Company* (Methuen, 1989). The poems in * *Off Colour* (Bloodaxe, 1998) pun on relationships between skin colour and illness. Her retelling Bessie Smith's life in a sequence of poems in *Other Lovers* (Bloodaxe, 1993) was followed by a biography of the blues singer, *Bessie Smith* (Absolute, 1997). *Trumpet* (Picador, 1998) won the *Guardian*'s 1998 fiction award. She is included in *Penguin Modern Poets 8* (1996) along with Merle Collins and Grace Nichols. She has one son and has written for children *Two's Company* (Puffin, 1992) and *The Frog Who Dreamed She Was an Opera Singer* (Bloomsbury, 1998). Kay discusses her early work and reasons for writing in 'Let It Be Told' in the 'Post-Colonial Women's Writing' volume of *Kunapipi*, 16/1 (1994), 530–9; and is interviewed by Maya Jagi and Richard Dyer in *Wasafiri*, 29 (Spring 1999), 53–61.

KHALVATI, MIMI (b. 1944)

Born in Tehran, she was sent to a boarding school on the Isle of Wight at the age of 6. After her father and mother separated, the mother was unable to pay for Mimi's return to Iran on holidays, except for a trip when she was 14. At 16 she took a secretarial course and the next year studied French in Switzerland. She returned to Tehran where she worked as a secretary and married an Iranian; they divorced after a few years. She returned to work as a secretary to save money to attend the Drama Centre, London (1967–9). She acted for a year and married an English actor

(1970–85) with whom she had two children. They travelled for several years including to Tehran where she directed the Theatre Workshop (1971–4) and relearnt Persian. They returned to London where she wrote two children's books and co-founded the Theatre in Exile. During 1986 at an Arvon writing course she mistakenly found herself in a poetry section and started writing poetry. She also met E. A. Markham with whom she had an off-and-on relationship, including marriage, 1997–9. After co-winning a Peterloo Poets award in 1990 she started concentrating on poetry: *In White Ink* (1991); *Mirrorwork* (1995); *Entries on Light* (1997); and *Selected Poems* (2000), all published by Carcanet. Her unusual relationship to Iran and Iranian culture informs many poems. She studied Persian at SOAS (1992–3), and co-founded the Poetry School (1997). Her work is discussed by John Killick in *Poetry Review* (Summer 1995), 10–13; she is interviewed by Vicki Bertram in *PN Review*, 130 (1999), 58–63.

KHAN-DIN, AYUB (b. 1962)

He was born in Salford. The father, who was already married and had two children in Pakistan, came to England during the 1930s, worked as a bus conductor, and married an Englishwoman with whom he had ten children. Ayub attended Salford Tech and then drama school. After graduation he found himself limited to 'black' roles and as a result objects to non-integrated casting. For over a decade and a half he appeared in soap operas, dramas, and occasionally, films, most notably in the Kureishi–Freers *My Beautiful Laundrette* and *Sammy and Rosie Get Laid*. His autobiographical play was *East is East* (1st pub. Nick Hern Books, 1996 (Instant Playscript); rev. Nick Hern Books, 1997) followed by *Last Dance at Dum Dum* (Nick Hern Books, 1999). *East is East* was given awards in 1997 from the Writers' Guild for the Best New West End Play and the Best New Writer as well as a John Whiting Award. Khan-Din rewrote it as a screenplay, which won the 1999 Best Original Screenplay Academy Award. The screen version has been published with an autobiographical essay as an introduction.

KUREISHI, HANIF (b. 1954)

Kureishi was born at Bromley, Kent, to a Pakistani father, who was a clerk and political journalist, and to an English mother. After attending Bromley Technical High School, 1965–70, he studied for his A levels at Ravenswood College of Art, 1971–3. Expelled from Lancaster University at the end of his first year, he received his BA in philosophy from King's College, University of London (1977).

When he was 18 he sent a short play to the Royal Court Theatre which led to him being invited to spend time at rehearsals and, eventually, working at the Court Theatre. He began as a dramatist with *Soaking the Heat* (1976), *The King and Me* (1980), and *Outskirts* (1981), which received the George Devine Award (1981) and led to him being appointed writer-in-residence at the Royal Court. Influenced by Brecht, he directed *Mother Courage* (1984). Material from the early plays found their way into the film scripts for Stephen Freers, *My Beautiful Laundrette* (1984) and *Sammy and Rosie Get Laid* (1987). The former was judged the Best Screenplay by both the National Society of Film Critics (1986) and the New York Film Critics Circle (1986), and nominated for an Oscar. He wrote and himself directed *London Kills Me* (1991). He also wrote the film script for *My Son the Fanatic* (UK release 1998) based on his short story in *Love in a Blue Time* (1997).

His novel, **The Buddha of Suburbia* (1990), was based on his desire to leave the suburbs for the excitement of London. It received the Whitbread Award for a First Novel. His leaving his long-time companion and mother of his children is the background of *Intimacy* (1998), while many of the stories in his later fiction concern the difficulties of living with another person for long.

Kureishi's usual publisher is Faber which has also issued *Plays*, volume 1 (1999). *My Beautiful Laundrette* (1986); *Sammy and Rosie Get Laid* (1988); and *London Kills Me* (1991) are republished in *London Kills Me: Three Screen Plays and Four Essays* (Penguin, 1992). His major essays are in *Dreaming and Scheming: Reflections on Writing and Politics* (2002). The best introduction to the plays, films, fiction, and contexts is Bart Moore-Gilbert's *Hanif Kureishi* (2001), which includes a selected bibliography.

LA ROSE, JOHN (b. 1927)

Born in Trinidad, La Rose had by the 1950s become a formidable cultural and political activist who acted as general secretary of the West Indian Independence Party in Trinidad and was an executive member of the Federated Workers' Trade Union. In 1961, he moved to Britain and during 1966 founded, with his wife Sarah White, New Beacon books. Its first publication was his book of poetry, **Foundations* (1966) and it also published his *Eyelets of Truth within Me* (1992). He co-authored *Attila's Kaiso: A Short History of Trinidad Calypso* (with Raymond Quevedo

1983), and *Kaiso Calypso Music* (with David Rudder, 1990) (both published by New Beacon). He edited *New Beacon Review*, a half-yearly journal, and was one of the founders of the International Book Fair of Radical Black and Third World Books. He is discussed in *Foundations of a Movement: A Tribute to John La Rose on the Occasion of the 10th International Book Fair of Radical and Third World Books* (John La Rose Tribute Committee, 1991); Anne Walmsley, *The Caribbean Artists Movement: 1966–1972* (1992).

LEVY, ANDREA (b. 1956)

She is one of four children born in London to parents who emigrated from Jamaica. Her father, Winston, arrived on the SS *Empire Windrush* with his brother who had earlier served in the RAF. Winston was descended several generations back from a North African Jew who had married a woman of mixed origins including Indian. The mother, Beryl, a school-teacher, was descended from slaves. The family lived in a council flat in Highbury, North London. Each of her three novels (published by Head-line Review) is semi-autobiographical. *Every Light in the House Burning* (1994) is largely about her parents and their life in London. *Never Far from Nowhere* (1996) concerns two sisters who live in a council estate. One wants to know about the family past and return to Jamaica. The other passes for white. *Fruit of the Lemon* (2000) reflects a visit to Jamaica during which time Levy, like her main character, met relatives and looked up family history. See Maya Jaggi, 'Redefining Englishness', *Waterstone's Magazine*, 6 (1996), 62–9.

MAHJOUB, JAMAL (b. 1960)

Mahjoub was born in London to a Sudanese father and an English mother. His father was the student officer at the Sudan House in Rutland Gate. In 1961 the father was transferred to Liverpool where Jamal attended Booker Avenue Comprehensive in Allerton. Every summer the family returned to the Sudan for three months. In 1968, they moved to Khartoum, where Jamal lived for the next ten years and attended Comboni College in Khartoum, an Italian Catholic school. In 1978, he left on a scholarship for Atlantic College in South Wales. He studied next, 1981–4, at the University of Sheffield where he received a BSc in geology. Afterwards he lived in London, holding odd jobs. In 1988 he moved to Denmark where he married, and had two children. Jobs included selling futons. He learned Danish on top of his English and Arabic and became a librarian in the Department of Ethnography at the University of Aarhus for which he translated academic books into English. His first and second novels, *Navigation of a Rainmaker* (Heinemann, 1989) and *Wings of Dust* (Heinemann, 1994), reflect the difficulty of those educated abroad returning to Sudan. The siege of Khartoum in the nineteenth century is the setting of *In the Hour of Signs* (Heinemann, 1996). 'The Cartographer's Angel' won the 1993 Heinemann/*Guardian* Short Story Prize. In 1997 he divorced and moved to Barcelona, Spain. *The Carrier* (Phoenix House, 1998) concerns a seventeenth-century slave who, sent to Holland to obtain one of the first telescopes, becomes stranded in Europe. Mahjoub writes about Sudan in 'Dreams, Ghosts, Nightmares', the *Guardian* (15 May 1998, C section, p. 4). He is discussed in Gareth Griffiths, *African Literature* (2000), 309–13.

Maja-Pearce, Adewale (b. 1953)

Born in London, but raised in Ikoyi, Lagos, Maja-Pearce led a privileged life with his Nigerian physician father and Scottish mother. When he was 10, his parents' marriage broke up and he was sent to live with his grandparents in Streatham. He went back to Nigeria for boarding school, then, at age 16, moved to London with his mother. He has an MA from the SOAS, University of London, and resides in Sussex.

Maja-Pearce's first book was *Loyalties and Other Stories* (Longman, 1986) followed by his Nigerian travels *In My Father's Country* (Heinemann, 1987). His essay in the form of a short novel called *How Many Miles to Babylon?* (Heinemann, 1990) discusses the difficulties associated with his mixed heritage. In *Who's Afraid of Wole Soyinka?* (Heinemann, 1991) he explores issues relating to Africa which are taken up again in *A Mask Dancing: Nigerian Novelists of the Eighties* (Hans Zell, 1992). He edited *Christopher Okigbo: Collected Poems* (Heinemann, 1986) and *The Heinemann Book of African Poetry in English* (1990). He has been the editor of the Heinemann African Writers series and Africa editor for the *Index on Censorship*.

Markandaya, Kamala (b. 1924)

Kamala Purnaiya Taylor was born in Bangalore, India. After attending Madras University, and working as a journalist, she moved to London in 1948 and married an Englishman with whom she has a daughter. Under the name Kamala Markandaya she had a run of transatlantic successes beginning with *Nectar in a Sieve* (Putnam, 1954). Relations between the

British and Indians became a recurring theme beginning with *Some Inner Fury* (Putnam, 1955). Other novels are *A Silence of Desire* (Putnam, 1960), **Possession* (Putnam, 1963), *A Handful of Rice* (Hamish Hamilton, 1966), *The Coffer Dams* (Hamish Hamilton, 1969), **The Nowhere Man* (Allen Lane, 1973), *Two Virgins* (Chatto and Windus, 1973), *The Golden Honeycomb* (Chatto and Windus, 1977), *Pleasure City* (Chatto and Windus, 1982; as *Shalimar*, Harper, 1983). After publishers became less interested in her work, she stopped writing and devoted herself to Indian cultural affairs in London. Her work is examined in Uma Parameswaran, *Kamala Markandaya* (2000). Fawzia Afzal-Khan offers a postcolonial approach in *Cultural Imperialism and the Indo-English Novel* (1993).

MARKHAM, EDWARD A[RCHIBALD] (b. 1939)

Markham was born in Montserrat. His father was a prominent Methodist pastor in Canada. In 1956 Archie's mother moved from Montserrat to England. Archie attended Kilburn Polytechnic in London (1960–2), St David's University College, University of Wales, Lampeter (1962–5), where he earned his BA in English and philosophy, University of East Anglia in Norwich (1966–7), and the University of London (1967). He lectured at Kilburn Polytechnic (1968–70) and at the Abraham Moss Centre, Manchester (1976–8). He was director of the Caribbean Theatre Workshop (1970–1), a creative writing fellow at Hull College of Higher Education at Yorkshire (1979–80), and assistant editor for *Ambit* magazine (1980–6). His time in Papua New Guinea (1983–5) is recalled in *A Papua New Guinea Sojourn: More Pleasures of Exile* (Carcanet, 1998). Returning to England, he became editor of *Artrage* (1985–7). In 1991 he became senior lecturer, and later professor of creative writing at Sheffield Hallam University.

*Human Rites: Selected Poems 1970–1982 (Anvil Press, 1984) was followed by **Living in Disguise* (Anvil Press, 1986), and **Towards the End of a Century* (Anvil Press, 1989). His time as a writer-in-residence at the University of Ulster is reflected in **Letter from Ulster and the Hugo Poems* (Littlewood Arc, 1993). *Marking Time* (Peepal Tree, 1999) is a campus novel. He has also written plays and published collections of short stories. He edited the influential **Hinterland: Afro-Caribbean and Black British Poetry* (Bloodaxe, 1989) and the *Penguin Book of Caribbean Short Stories* (1996). *New & Selected Poems* (Anvil, 2001) and *New & Selected Short Stories* (Peeple Tree, 2001) might be places to start. Freda Volans and Tracey O'Rourke (eds.), *A Festschrift for E. A. Markham* (1999) contains interpretive essays and bibliography.

MATURA, MUSTAPHA (b. 1939)

He was born as Noel Matura in Port of Spain, Trinidad, where he was educated at Belmont Boys Roman Catholic Intermediate School, 1944–53. His parents were Anglicans of Asian Indian origins. Between 1954 and 1961 he held numerous temporary jobs. He came to England in 1961, worked as a hotel porter in Italy during 1961–2 when he became acquainted with African-American theatre while assisting a production of Langston Hughes's *Shakespeare in Harlem*. Returning to England he was a factory assistant, 1962–70. During the 1960s he began calling himself Mustapha. *As Time Goes By* was produced at the Traverse Theatre Club, Edinburgh, 1971, then taken to London. The same year Matura received an Arts Council bursary, and in 1972 the John Whiting award for the most promising new writer. During 1978 he co-founded with Charlie Hanson the Black Theatre Co-operative in London. He has co-written for the television series *Black Silk* and *No Problem* (the latter with Farrukh Dhondy, 1983–5). *The Coup* (1990), about an attempted Black Power revolution against the government of Trinidad in 1970, was commissioned by the National Theatre, a first for a black British author. Trinidad awarded him its Scarlet Ibis, 1991.

'*As Time Goes By*' & '*Black Pieces*' (Calder and Boyars, 1972) was followed by *Play Mas* (Marion Boyars, 1976), and volumes including *Nice, Rum an' Coca Cola*, and *Welcome Home Jacko* (Eyre Methuen, 1980), and *Play Mas, Independence*, and *Meetings* (Methuen, 1982). See Judy Stone, *Studies in West Indian Literature: Theatre* (1994) and Malcolm Page, 'Matura, Mustapha', *Contemporary Dramatists* (1999), 443–4.

MELVILLE, PAULINE (b. 1948)

Melville was born in Guyana to a British mother and a Guyanese father of Amerindian, Scots, and black origins. During her childhood she went back and forth between London and Guyana, attending school in both. She spends several months each year in Guyana where she has family on the coast as well as among the Amerindians. A trained psychologist, sometimes poet, scriptwriter, and former stand-up comedian, she was 19 when she had her first parts in films and began appearing in such TV series as 'Girls on Top' and 'The Young Ones' during the early 1980s. She acted in *Mona Lisa*, *Shadowlands*, and other films. The short stories in **Shape-Shifter* (Women's Press, 1990) won a *Guardian* award and Commonwealth prize for the best first book. *The Ventriloquist's Tale* (Bloomsbury,

1997), set in Guyana, won the Whitbread First Novel Award; the stories in *The Migration of Ghosts* (Bloomsbury 1998) range through Guyana and Europe. Her writing is witty and quietly malicious, especially when showing European incomprehension of the Indians of Guyana.

MENEN, [SALVATOR] AUBREY [CLARENCE] (1912–89)

Menen (an Anglicization) was born in London to Kalipurayath Narayana Menon, an Indian expatriate businessman, and Alice Violet Everett, an Irish Roman Catholic. He attended the University of London (1930–2) and became a drama critic for the *Bookman* (1934), afterwards holding various positions and occupations including director of the Experimental Theatre, London (1935–6), affiliate for the Personalities Press Service, London (1937–9), head of the English drama department of the All-India Radio (1940–1), and script editor of information films for the Government of India (1943–5). *The Prevalence of Witches* (Chatto & Windus, 1947), his first novel, was based on his time in the civil service in India. He became head of the motion picture department at J. Walter Thompson Co. (Eastern) Ltd., an advertising agency, until 1948 when he moved to Italy as a freelance writer. He wrote several travel books including *Rome for Ourselves* (McGraw Hill, 1960), *London* (Time Life Books, 1976), and *Venice* (Time Life Books, 1976). Menen died in Trivandrum, India.

Penguin India republished many of his books. *Aubrey Menen*, by Mohammed Elias (1985) offers an overview, while Susheila Nasta's *Home Truths* and C. L. Innes's *Black and Asian Writing* (both 2002) provide a British postcolonial perspective.

MO, TIMOTHY (b. 1950)

Mo was born in Hong Kong to an English working-class mother and a Chinese lawyer father who divorced when he was 18 months old. He was educated at the Chinese language Convent of the Precious Blood and then at the Quarry Bay International School. At 10 he came to England where after prep school in Finchley he continued his education at Mill Hill School, London, and St John's College, Oxford, where he studied history (1969–72). Between 1975 and 1976 he was a part-time journalist for the *Times Educational Supplement*, an editor at *New Statesman*, a trainer in a gym, and a part-time reporter for *Boxing News*, the latter until 1990. He was formerly a bantamweight boxer.

The Monkey King (Deutsch, 1978) won the Geoffrey Faber Memorial

Prize. His second novel, *Sour Sweet* (Deutsch, 1982), won the Hawthornden Prize and was nominated for the Whitbread Prize and the Booker Prize. His later works include *An Insular Possession* (Chatto and Windus, 1986) and *Redundancy of Courage* (Chatto and Windus, 1991), both of which were nominated for the Booker Prize. After a dispute with Chatto over advances, Mo published his next two novels, *Brownout on Breadfruit Boulevard* (1995) and *Renegade, or Halo²* (1999), through his own Paddleless Press. Elaine Yee Ho's *Timothy Mo* (2000) is the basic introduction.

NAIPAUL, SHIVA[DHAR SRINIVASA] (1945–1985)

The younger brother of V. S. Naipaul, he was born at his uncle's home in a suburb of Port of Spain, Trinidad. After their father died Shiva lived with his mother and five sisters, which probably contributed to his portrayals of women. After attending Queen's Royal College, and then St Mary's College, he won an Island Scholarship to study abroad. At University College, Oxford (1964–8) he took a degree in Chinese. He met Jenny Stuart at Oxford; they married in 1967 and had one son. While at Oxford he started his novel, *Fireflies* (1970), which was published by André Deutsch who remained his publisher throughout the 1970s. *North of South: An African Journey* (1978) reflects Naipaul's six-month trek through Kenya, Tanzania, and Zambia. *Black and White* (1980), the first of his books published by Hamish Hamilton (published in the USA as *Journey to Nowhere: A New World Tragedy*), chronicles the mass suicide by an American cult in Guyana. He returned to writing novels with *A Hot Country* (1983; published in the USA as *Love and Death in a Hot Country*). It uses Guyana for another portrait of a Hindu family's degeneration in the tropics. *Beyond the Dragon's Mouth: Stories and Pieces* (1984) includes memories of Trinidad and life in Earl's Court along with articles about India and Islamic fundamentalism in Morocco. *An Unfinished Journey* (Hamish Hamilton, 1986), published posthumously, includes an essay on his relationship to his older brother, and the start of a book about Australia. See Harold Barratt, 'Shiva Naipaul', *DLB* 157 (1996), 218–26.

NAIPAUL, [SIR] V[IDIADHAR] S[URAJPRASAD] (b. 1932)

V. S. Naipaul, born in Chaguanas, Trinidad, is the second of seven children. After attending Tranquility Boys School (1939–42), and Queen's Royal College (1943–9) in Port of Spain, Vidia won a scholarship to study for his BA (Hons.) in English from University College, Oxford (1950–3). His university years are recounted in *Letters between a Father and Son: Family Letters*, ed. Gillon Aitken (Little Brown, 1999). Moving to London he became an editor of BBC radio's *Caribbean Voices* series (1954–6) and married Patricia Ann Hale in 1955.

Memories of colonial Trinidad were the basis of *The Mystic Masseur* (1957), *The Suffrage of Elvira* (1958), and *Miguel Street* (1959). The life and death of his father Seepersad, a journalist with literary aspirations, is the basis of *A House for Mr Biswas* (1961). Travel in the Caribbean during 1960 resulted in *The Middle Passage: Impression of Five Societies* (1962). *Mr Stone and the Knights Companion* (1963), a novel about England, was written while touring India for *An Area of Darkness: An Experience of India* (1964), the first of three books about India. His experiences during 1965–6 when he was a writer-in-residence at the University of Makerere, Uganda, and travelled in East and Central Africa, provided details for several of his later novels including the central story of *In a Free State* (1971), which won the Booker Prize. Until the late 1980s his publisher was André Deutsch with Penguin paperback editions.

His settling in Wiltshire during 1970 was the theme of his autobiographical novel * *The Enigma of Arrival* (Viking, 1987). Travels to Iran after the overthrow of the Shah, and then to Pakistan, Malaysia, and Indonesia during 1979, resulted in *Among the Believers: An Islamic Journey* (1981). During 1990 he was knighted in England for his services to literature and received the Trinity Cross from Trinidad; three years later he was awarded the first David Cohen Prize (1993) for British authors. *A Way in the World: A Sequence* (1994) mixed fiction, autobiography, and history to examine Caribbean lives and myths. After his wife Patrick Ann Hale died (1996), Naipaul married Nadira Khannum Alvi, a journalist of Pakistani origins raised in East Africa. His revisiting Iran, Pakistan, Malaysia, and Indonesia during 1995 resulted in *Beyond Belief: Islamic Excursions among the Converted People* (1998). Publication of the novel *Half a Life* (Picador, 2001) was followed a month later by the award of the 2001 Nobel Prize in Literature. *The Writer and the World* (Picador, 2002) republishes many essays including 'Our Universal Civilization'.

Kelvin Jarvis's *V. S. Naipaul: A Selective Bibliography with Annotations* (1989) is continued in Jarvis's 'V. S. Naipaul: A Bibliographical Update, 1987–1994', *Ariel*, 26 (Oct. 1995), 71–85; Feroza Jussawalla's selection of *Conversations with V. S. Naipaul* (1997) and Robert Hamner (ed.), *Critical Perspectives on V. S. Naipaul* (1977) remain useful. Bruce King's *V. S. Naipaul* (2003) discusses the life, writings, and criticism.

NAMJOSHI, SUNITI (b. 1941)

Born in Bombay, she worked for the Indian Administrative Service (IAS), 1964–9, during which time the Calcutta Writers' Workshop published her *Poems* (1969). After taking an MA in public administration at the University of Missouri, she resigned from the IAS and earned a PhD (1972) on Ezra Pound's *Cantos* from McGill University in Montreal while publishing with the Calcutta Writers' Workshop *Cyclone in Pakistan* and *More Poems* (both 1971). While teaching at Scarborough College, University of Toronto, she spent the 1978–9 academic year in England where she participated in the feminist and lesbian movements of the time. She moved to England in 1987 where she lived with Gillian Hanscombe in Devon. Namjoshi's *The Conversations of Cow* (1985), *The Blue Donkey Fables* (1988), and *The Mothers of Maya Diip* (1989), consisting of amusing lesbian fables, were published by Women's Press. *Because of India: Selected Poems and Fables* (1989) was published by Onlywoman Press. Her work is discussed by Diane McGifford in Emmanuel Nelson's *Writers of the Indian Diaspora* (1993), 291–7. She is interviewed in Chelva Kanaganayakam (ed.), *Configurations of Exile* (1995), 45–58.

NEWLAND, COURTTIA (b. 1973)

A third-generation British West Indian of Jamaican-Barbadian origins, born in Hammersmith and raised in White City, Newland began writing in his early teens at school where a teacher introduced him to black African and American writing. At 15 he left school and tried unsuccessfully to be a rapper. After four years of unemployment, when he was 21 he began a novel about the black urban ghettos of West London. *The Scholar* (Abacus, 1997) was followed by *Society Within* (Abacus, 1999), another novel about Greenside Estate. Now active as a touring poet and course tutor, Newland co-edited with Kadija Sesay *IC3: The Penguin Book of New Black Writing in Britain* (2000). He expanded his interests to the theatre, starting with a monologue (1997) for the Post Office theatre company. Their adaptation of Euripides' *Trojan Women* was followed by Newland's *The Far Side* (2000) at the Tricycle Theatre. He wrote a black detective novel, *Snakeskin* (Abacus, 2002), and was Harrow's first writer-in-residence (2002).

NICHOLS, GRACE (b. 1950)

Born in Guyana, she was the fifth of seven children and attended the Highland elementary school where her father was headmaster and her mother was piano teacher. She attended St Stephen's Scots School after her family moved to Georgetown, then the Progressive and Preparatory Institute, and the University of Guyana, where she received a degree in communications. She was a teacher (1967–70), newspaper reporter (1972–3), assistant for Government Information Services (1973–6), and freelance journalist until 1977 when she moved to England. Her first book was for children, *Trust You, Wriggly* (Hodder and Stoughton, 1980). She continues to write and edit books for children including *Come on into My Tropical Garden* (A & C Black, 1988). She lives in East Sussex with John Agard, and two daughters. Nichols and Agard co-edited *No Hickory No Dickory No Dock: A Collection of Caribbean Nursery Rhymes* (Puffin, 1992).

Her first published collection of poetry, *I is a long memoried woman* (Caribbean Cultural International, 1983) won the Commonwealth Poetry Prize. *The Fat Black Woman's Poems* (Virago, 1984) offers amusing contrarian attitudes. Her novel *Whole of a Morning Sky* (Virago, 1986) appears autobiographical. *Lazy Thoughts of a Lazy Woman, and Other Poems* (Virago, 1989), containing new and selected poems, was followed years later by the sequence of lyrics in *Sunris* (Virago, 1996). She is discussed by various authors in Gina Wisker (ed.), *Black Women's Writing* (1993); by Brenda Berrian in *DLB* 157 (1996), 235–40; by Gudrun Webhofer in *Identity in the Poetry of Grace Nichols and Lorna Goodison* (1996); and interviewed by Maggie Butcher, *Wasafiri*, 8 (Spring 1988), 17–19.

OKRI, BEN (b. 1959)

Okri was born in Minna, northern Nigeria, of an Igbo mother and Urhobo father, who brought him to England in 1961 when the father studied law. They lived in Peckham, then returned to Nigeria in 1968 during the civil war. Okri was educated at Children's Home School, Sapele; Christ High School, Ibadan; and Urhobo College, Warri (1973). He started publishing in Nigerian newspapers and by the time he was 17 he had completed *Flowers and Shadows* (Longman, 1980) and other manuscripts before moving to England in 1978. He studied comparative literature at the University of Essex (1980) until his Nigerian scholarship ended. His second novel was *The Landscapes Within* (Longman, 1981). Two books of short stories followed: *Incidents at the Shrine* (Heinemann, 1986) and *Stars of the New Curfew* (Secker and Warburg, 1988). He won the Booker Prize with *The Famished Road* (Cape, 1991) and was visiting fellow commoner in creative arts, Trinity College, Cambridge (1991–3). He continued the story of *The Famished Road* in *Songs of Enchantment* (Cape, 1993) and *Infinite Riches* (Phoenix House, 1998). **Astonishing the Gods* (Phoenix House, 1995) is an allegory.

His essays can be found in *A Way of Being Free* (Phoenix House, 1997). He is interviewed in Jane Wilkinson's *Talking with African Writers* (1992); the relation of his style to Nigerian politics is the subject of Ato Quayson's 'Esoteric Network as Nervous System: Reading the Fantastic in Ben Okri's Writing', Gurnah's *Essays on African Writing*, 2 (1995), 144–58; while the significance of his use of Yoruba literary conventions is discussed in Quayson's *Strategic Transformations in Nigerian Writing* (1997).

PHILLIPS, CARYL (b. 1958)

Born in St Kitts, Phillips was brought to Leeds when he was 4 months old, the oldest of what were to be four brothers. He is of mixed race: African, Madeira Portuguese, Indian. His parents divorced when he was 8. After his mother took ill, he was fostered with white families and then lived with his father. He attended schools in Leeds and Birmingham until 1976 when he entered Queens College, Cambridge (BA (Hons.), 1979). At Queens racial identity became a major concern and he had a nervous collapse. He travelled to the United States and decided to become a writer. He was founding chairman (1978) and artistic director (1979) of the *Observer* Festival of Theatre, Oxford. He was a stage hand at the 1979 Edinburgh Festival, then lived on the dole while writing a play, *Strange Fruit* (Amber Lane Press, 1981). After he moved to London his plays *Where There is Darkness* (Amber Lane, 1982) and *The Shelter* (Amber Lane, 1984) were staged at Lyric Hammersmith. His first novel *The Final Passage* (Faber, 1985) was about his parents and the Windrush generation. When he was 22 he visited St Kitts, and bought a house, a visit which influenced his novel *A State of Independence* (Faber, 1986). A trip across Europe during 1984 provided the theme for *The European Tribe* (Faber, 1987). *Higher Ground: A Novel in Three Parts* (Viking, 1989) was followed by *Cambridge* (Bloomsbury, 1991); *Crossing the River* (Bloomsbury, 1993); and *The Nature of Blood* (Faber, 1997). Starting in 1990 he taught at Amherst College; then became Henry R. Luce Professor of Migration and Social Order at Barnard College, Columbia University (1998). *Extravagant Strangers: A Literature of Belonging* (Faber, 1997) is Phillips's anthology of foreign writers who lived in England. **A New World Order* (Secker & Warburg, 2001) consists of selected essays.

Reinhard Sander's entry on Phillips in *DLB* 157 (1996), 307–22, and

Bénédicte Ledent's *Caryl Phillips* (2002) might be supplemented by Maya Jaggi's 'Rites of Passage' profile in the Saturday review section of the *Guardian* (5 Nov. 2001), 6–7.

PHILLIPS, MIKE (b. 1943)

He was born in Kitty Village, Georgetown, British Guiana. His parents, George and Marjorie (Jones), were of African descent with some Indian and European ancestors. He emigrated to England in 1956 where he was educated at Highbury School, received his BA (1967) from the University of London, his MA (1974) in politics from the University of Essex, and a Postgraduate Certificate in Education from Goldsmiths College. He worked as an unskilled labourer, founded a youth hostel in London, and worked as a community activist in Birmingham and Manchester, cities which feature in his fiction: *Blood Rights* (Michael Joseph, 1989); *The Late Candidate* (Michael Joseph, 1991), awarded a Silver Dagger by the Crime Writers Association; and *The Dancing Face* (HarperCollins, 1997). *Point of Darkness* (Michael Joseph, 1994) takes place in the USA where Phillips's parents and relatives settled. Travel in Eastern Europe forms part of the background of his international thriller *A Shadow of Myself* (HarperCollins, 2000). *An Image to Die For* (HarperCollins, 1995) reflects his experience as a freelance journalist and broadcaster, and TV producer. He was education officer (BBC 1977–9); senior lecturer in communications at the University of Westminster (1983–93); and is on the Board of Trustees of the National Heritage Memorial Fund (2002). He lives with Jenny Owen, an academic and writer.

Concern with the history of black life in England found expression in *Notting Hill in the Sixties* (Lawrence and Wishart, 1997); *Windrush: The Irresistible Rise of Multi-Racial Britain* (HarperCollins, 1998), which he co-wrote with his brother Trevor Phillips; and *London Crossings* (Continuum, 2001). He is discussed in A. Robert Lee's *Other Britain, Other British* (1995), 84–6 and Sauerberg's *Intercultural Voices* (2001), 166–72.

PINNOCK, WINSOME (b. 1961)

Born to Jamaican parents in Islington, she often writes plays about Jamaican women immigrating to England. At Goldsmiths College she received a BA (Hons.), 1982, in English and drama. Pinnock was playwright-in-residence at the Tricycle Theatre, London for the 1989–90 season, and starting in 1991 at the Royal Court. Her first play, *Wind of*

Change, was produced at the Half Moon, London, and taken on tour 1987. *Leave Taking* (1988) is in *First Run: New Plays by New Writers*, selected by Kate Harwood (Nick Hern Books, 1989). *A Hero's Welcome* is in Kadija George (ed.), *Six Plays by Black and Asian Women Writers* (Aurora Metro Press, 1993). *A Rock in Water* (1989) was first developed in workshop improvisations for the Royal Court Theatre Upstairs before being scripted. It is available in Brewster's *Black Plays 2* (Methuen, 1989). *Talking in Tongues* (1991) is in Brewster's *Black Plays 3* (1995). *Mules* was published by Faber (1996). See Lizbeth Goodman, 'Winsome Pinnock', *Contemporary Dramatists* (6th edn., 1999), 558–9.

RANDHAWA, RAVINDER (b. 1952)

An Indian of Sikh parentage, Randhawa was born in the village Dhanowali in the district of Jalandhar. She came to England when she was 7. Her father came to England to work in a factory, only knowing Punjabi. Her family moved from Gravesend to Leamington Spa where in junior school she was for a time the only Indian girl. She took a degree in English in 1973 from the London Polytechnic (now the University of East London), followed by postgraduate work in sociology. Between 1975 and 1984 she was employed as a teacher, then in the civil service, and most importantly by an Asian women's workers' community group to develop centres for women needing refuge and resources. After attending Black Ink sessions in Brixton, she became the initiating member of the Asian Women Writers' Collective in 1984. Her story 'India' was published in Rosemary Stones (ed.), *More to Life Than Mr. Right: Stories for Young Feminists* (Piccadilly, 1985). She married in 1986 and has two children. Many of her experiences are the basis for events in her novel *A Wicked Old Woman* (Women's Press, 1987). She has four stories in the Asian Women Writers' Workshop, *Right of Way* (Women's Press, 1988). Her second novel, *Hari-Jan* (Mantra, 1992), is about mother–daughter tensions and teenage romance in multicultural England. *The Coral Strand* (House of Stratus, 2001) concerns moral debts. Randhawa is introduced in Emmanuel Nelson's *Writers of the Indian Diaspora* (1993); she is discussed in Susheila Nasta's *Home Truths* (2002) as among the new writers who enjoy being 'unhoused' rather than seeking stability.

RILEY, JOAN (b. 1958)

She was born in St Mary, Jamaica. After coming to England, she studied at the University of Sussex (BA, 1979) and London University (1984). *The*

Unbelonging (1985), *Writing in the Twilight* (1987), *Romance* (1988), and *A Kindness to the Children* (1992) are published by the Women's Press. She received the 1992 *Voice* award as the literary figure of the decade. She discusses 'Writing Reality in a Hostile Environment' in the 'Post-colonial Women's Writing' issue of *Kunapipi*, 16/1 (1994), 547–52.

RUSHDIE, [AHMED] SALMAN (b. 1947)

Born in Bombay, the eldest child in a wealthy, liberal Muslim family, Salman attended Cathedral School, Bombay, before leaving for England and Rugby School, 1961–5. During 1962 his family moved to England and became citizens; in 1965 they moved to Pakistan. After taking his BA (Hons.) in history at King's College, Cambridge, 1965–8, Rushdie visited Pakistan where he was a television actor, then returned to London where he worked as an actor and in advertising from 1969 to 1980. During 1970 he met Clarissa Luard whom he married in 1976 and divorced 1987; their child Zafar was born in 1979.

Grimus, his first novel (Gollancz, 1975), was followed by travel to India for research on *Midnight's Children* (Cape, 1981), which won the Booker Prize. It was in 1993 named the 'Booker of Bookers' as the best novel in the twenty-five years of the prize. During 1986 he went to Nicaragua where he consorted with the Sandinistas and wrote *The Jaguar Smile: A Nicaraguan Journey* (Pan, 1987). He married the American writer Marianne Wiggins in 1987; she divorced him in 1993. *The Satanic Verses* (Viking, 1988) won that year's Whitbread Prize, but was followed by Muslim demonstrations in Bradford against the novel. In February 1989 Ayatollah Khomeini issued his *fatwa*, as a consequence of which Rushdie and Wiggins were forced into hiding for several years. Rushdie published several defences of his position as a writer including the essay 'Is Nothing Sacred?' (1990), the children's tale *Haroun and the Sea of Stories* (Granta, 1990), and an essay in *Imaginary Homelands: Essays and Criticism 1981–1991* (Granta, 1991).

He met Elizabeth West the year he published the short stories in *East, West* (Cape, 1994) and married her in 1997, the year of the birth of their child Milan. They co-edited *The Vintage Book of Indian Writing, 1947–1997* (Vintage, 1997). In 1998 the Iranian government announced it would no longer support the *fatwa*. By the time of *The Ground beneath Her Feet* (Cape, 1999) Rushdie had moved to New York where he was often accompanied by an Indian beauty queen. *Step across This Line* (Cape, 2002) collects his non-fiction 1992–2002.

Criticism includes Catherine Cundy, *Salman Rushdie* (1996). Interviews are collected in *Conversations with Salman Rushdie*, ed. Michael Reder (2000). There is Joel Kuortti, *The Salman Rushdie Bibliography: A Bibliography of Salman Rushdie's Work and Rushdie Criticism* (1997). The politics of the *fatwa* are discussed in Lisa Appignanesi and Sara Maitland (eds.), *The Rushdie File* (1989); and Daniel Pipes, *The Rushdie Affair: The Novel, The Ayatollah, and the West* (1990).

SELVON, S[AMUEL] D[ICKSON] (1923–1994)

Born in Trinidad to a mother of Scottish descent and an Indian father, Selvon attended Naparima College, 1935–9; was a wireless operator in the Trinidad Royal Naval Volunteer Reserve, 1940–5; and a journalist for the *Trinidad Guardian*, 1946–50. He married a Guyanese, Draupadi Persaud, in 1947. In England he worked as a clerk in the Indian High Commission, London, 1950–3. After the success of his first novel *A Brighter Sun* (Wingate, 1952), and being awarded a Guggenheim fellowship for 1954, Selvon became a full-time writer. The idea for *The Lonely Londoners* (Wingate, 1956) first came to him while in New York on his Guggenheim. His London novels, *The Housing Lark* (MacGibbon and Kee, 1965), *Moses Ascending* (Davis Poynter, 1975), and *Moses Migrating* (Longman, 1983; *Three Continents with Special Preface, 1993), reflect stages in the immigrant experience. His second marriage was to Althea Nesta Daroux, 1963, with whom he had two sons and a daughter. After visiting his wife's relatives in Calgary, Alberta, Selvon moved in 1975 and a few years later became a Canadian citizen. He died in Trinidad during a visit.

Foreday Morning: Selected Prose 1946–1986 (Longman, 1989), ed. Kenneth Ramchand and Susheila Nasta, includes bibliography. Two volumes of plays, *Eldorado West One* (1988) and *Highway in the Sun and Other Plays* (1991) were published by Peepal Tree Press. Book-length criticism begins with *Critical Perspectives on Sam Selvon*, ed. Nasta (1989), and an issue of *Kunapipi* (17/1, 1995), published as *Tiger's Triumph: Celebrating Sam Selvon*, ed. Nasta and Anna Rutherford. Roydon Salick's *The Novels of Samuel Selvon: A Critical Study* (2001) offers close readings and surveys criticism. There is a useful discussion in Nasta's *Home Truths* (2002).

SISSAY, LEMN (b. 1967)

Born in Manchester as a result of an affair between an Ethiopian Airlines pilot and an Ethiopian woman who came to England to study at a religious college (and married a vice-minister of finance under Haile Sellasie), Sissay was first brought up by white Baptists in a village in Lancashire, where he was the only black child, and then in various children's homes. From his late teens onwards he was obsessed with learning about his parents and his family history, a story told in the BBC documentary 'Internal Flight' (1995). A performance poet, his first published poems appeared in *Tender Fingers in a Clenched Fist* (Bogle L'Ouverture, 1988), followed by *Rebel without Applause* (Bloodaxe, 1992). He edited *The Fire People: A Collection of Contemporary Black British Poets* (Payback, 1998). He lives in Manchester and has acted in and written stage and TV plays.

SMITH, ZADIE [SADIE] (b. 1976)

Born in London to a Jamaican model and psychotherapist and an older English father (they divorced in 1990) who worked in direct mail and was a photographer, she has two brothers. She grew up in Kilburn and Willesden Green, in north-west London, where her first novel is set. She attended a local comprehensive school, then studied English (Double First, 1997) at Kings College, Cambridge, where she started *White Teeth* (Hamish Hamilton, 2000) while she was still 21. It won the *Guardian* First Book Award and a Commonwealth literature prize, sold over a million copies, and was dramatized on Channel 4 TV (2003). She wrote an introduction to a republication of Lewis Carroll, *Through the Looking Glass* (Bloomsbury, 2001). Her second novel *The Autograph Man* (Hamish Hamilton, 2002) is about being famous. Claire Squire's *Zadie Smith's White Teeth* (2002) is a useful 'Reader's Guide'.

SOUIEF, AHDAF (b. 1950)

Souief's mother, Fatma Moussa, is a well-known translator of English into Arabic. Born in Cairo, Souief learned to read English in England before she learned to read Arabic. After studying English at Cairo University (BA, 1971) and English and American literature at the American University, Cairo (MA, 1973) she taught in Cairo while earning a doctorate in literary stylistics at the University of Lancaster (1978). The stories in *Aisha* (Cape, 1983) and the novel *In the Eye of the Sun* (Bloomsbury, 1992) are autobiographically based. The latter book produced a scandal in the Arab world as the heroine, a married Egyptian woman studying for a doctorate in England, has an affair with an Englishman. The book was assumed to have some relationship to Souief's first marriage and divorce (1972–8). She taught at King Saud University, Riyadh (1987–9) before returning to London where she is an executive officer at the Al-Furqan Centre for

Islamic Studies. Soueif has been active on behalf of the Palestinians and translated from Arabic the autobiography of the Palestinian poet Mourid Barghouti, *I Saw Ramallah* (2002). She lives in Wimbledon and was married to the poet Ian Hamilton from 1981 until his death in 2001. Their two sons were born in 1984 and 1989.

SRIVASTAVAS, ATIMA (b. 1961)

Born in Bombay into a family of several generations of Hindi poets, she came to London with her parents in 1970. She attended Moat Mount Comprehensive School, 1972–80, afterwards doing a degree in English (1983) at the University of Essex. After 1984 she worked as a freelance film editor and television director, which forms the context of her first novel *Transmission* (Serpent's Tail, 1992), as well as since 1989 a writer of screenplays, short stories, novels, and 'Cross Currents' (2001), an opera libretto. A British citizen, she considers herself a Hindu Indian Londoner, a complex identity reflected in her second novel *Looking for Maya* (Quartet Books, 1999). She is interviewed by Mala Pandurang, *Wasafiri*, 33 (Spring 2001), 3–5.

SYAL, MEERA (b. 1963)

Syal was born in Essington near Wolverhampton, a working-class town near Birmingham which forms the backdrop of her novel, *Anita and Me* (Flamingo and HarperCollins, 1997), which like her second novel, *Life Isn't All Ha Ha Hee Hee* (Doubleday, 1999), treats of what happens to childhood friends. During her final year at the University of Manchester, where she was awarded a Double First in English and drama, (1984), she co-wrote and acted in a one-woman play, *One of Us*, about a young Indian woman from Birmingham wanting to become an actress. It won a National Student Drama Award, a Yorkshire Television Award for 'outstanding personal achievement', and at the 1983 Edinburgh Festival she received the Scottish Critics' award for Most Promising Performer. She acted in stage plays at the Royal Court and Theatre Royal Stratford East (1989), and a National Theatre production of *Peer Gynt* (1989) as well as in the film *Sammy and Rosie Get Laid*. An active feminist, her films include the TV script for her *Sister Wife* (1992) and the screenplay of *Bhaji on the Beach* (1993). She is perhaps best known for the BBC TV series *Goodness Gracious Me* (1997–2001) with its comedy of Asian British life. She wrote the book for Andrew Lloyd Webber's musical *Bombay Dreams* (2001). See Syal's 'Finding My Voice' in M. Sulter (ed.), *Passion: Discourses on*

Blackwomen's Creativity (Urban Fox Press, 1990), 57–61; and Susheila Nasta's *Home Truths* (2002).

TRAYNOR, JOANNA (b. 1960)

Born in Merton, Surrey, to a Nigerian father (later a politician) and English mother (whom Joanna did not meet until the 1980s), she was brought up in foster care by a cleaner and postman in Devon. This experience was the subject of her first novel *Sister Josephine* (1997). It won the 1998 Saga Prize and Bloomsbury became her publisher. After attending Ursuline Convent School, Chester, and Loreto Convent School, Altrincham, she studied psychology at Plymouth Polytechnical (1980–3), then moved to London where she held various jobs ranging from shop assistant to computer trainer. *Divine* (1998) was based on people she knew, although she gave the main character a facial scar so that it would be a novel of alienation, the main theme of her books, rather than race. *Bitch Money* (2000) by contrast was fiction, and allowed her to write from a male perspective about such themes as instant riches and crude exploitation, symbols of England during the 1980s under Thatcher. Because of her skills in writing three novels she was hired as a TV producer.

WHEATLE, ALEX (b. 1963)

Born in South London of Jamaican parents, he spent his childhood in care homes and foster-families, a background reflected in his novel *Seven Sisters* (Fourth Estate, 2002). Brought up in Brixton, he worked as a carpenter and trained as an engineer. From the age of 16 to his early twenties he was called 'Crucial Rocker' and ran a sound system. While he was in prison for two weeks for 'Taking and Driving Away' a Rasta man influenced him to read; this changed his life. During the early 1990s he became a performance poet on the Brixton poetry circuit. He evolved into the novelist of *Brixton Rock* (Black Amber, 1999) and *East of Acre Lane* (Fourth Estate, 2001) by writing about the lives of his friends and himself, especially the black working class of Brixton during the 1980s. He is married with three children and lives in Brixton.

ZAMEENZAD, ADAM (b. ?)

Zameenzad makes a mystery about himself and published biographical details are often mixed with misinformation. His unlikely name is derived from Urdu for Man, Son of Earth. Although his parents were Muslims, the father a Punjabi, Zameenzad lived the first six years of his life in Nairobi, Kenya, and later in other parts of East Africa including Uganda where his parents were then teachers. His parents moved to Pakistan when the father inherited land in Sindh. Zameenzad started school in Lahore when he was 11 where he lived with his mother and entered Government College when 14. He studied for an MA in English and American literature at Karachi University and afterwards taught in a Christian college. Zameenzad came to England from Canada during 1974 to teach English. His father's money enabled him to travel widely, which is reflected in his five novels. *The Thirteenth House* (1987) won the David Higham award for a first manuscript before it was taken on by Fourth Estate which also published *Love Bones and Water* (1989). He was at various times a Buddhist, a Protestant evangelical, a Quaker, and attended Catholic masses, but now has no religion. He is married, and has children.

ZEPHANIAH, BENJAMIN OBADIAH IQBAL (b. 1958)

Born in Handsworth, Birmingham to Oswald, a Post Office manager, and Valerie (Eubanks) Springer, a nurse who migrated to England in 1954, Benjamin was the oldest of his mother's nine children. As she kept moving to avoid his father, there were continual changes of school and he was sent to Jamaica for some years. A dyslexic who did not learn to read and write until his twenties, he was often in trouble at school, and was expelled from Ward End Hall Secondary and from Canterbury Cross. He became a burglar, was sent to an approved school at 15, then borstal, and afterwards was imprisoned for two years. After a lung illness he became a Rastafarian. He lived in Handsworth as a DJ during the 1970s and became a poet performing to music. In 1980 he moved to London where *Pen Rhythm* was published by Page One Books, a co-operative he helped found in the same year. *The Dread Affair: Collected Poems* (1985) was published by Arena. He married Amina Iqbal Zephaniah in 1990; they later divorced. Now a popular poet he was a favourite of the *Guardian* and the BBC. He became one of the poets published by Bloodaxe: *City Psalms* (1992), *Propa Propaganda* (1996), and *Too Black, Too Strong* (2001). He was nominated for the Oxford professorship of poetry (1993) and awarded an honorary doctorate by the University of North London (1998). Mostly a performer who also writes plays, his books for children include *Talking Turkeys* (Viking, 1994), *Face* (Bloomsbury, 1999), and *Refugee Boy* (Bloomsbury, 2001).

Suggestions for Further Reading

General bibliographies of creative writing are Prabhu Guptara's *Black British Literature: An Annotated Bibliography* (1986) and Susan Croft's 'Bibliography: Black and Asian Playwrights in Print' in *Black and Asian Plays* (2000). *Black and Asian Plays in Performance* (2003) by Susan Croft is essential. For children's literature see Rosemary Stones (ed.), *A Multicultural Guide to Children's Books 0–16+*, bibliography compiled by Judith Elkin (1999), which also contains useful short essays.

For biographies, bibliographies, and short essays on individual authors consult present and past editions (as the contents change) of such reference works as *Contemporary Poets*, *Contemporary Dramatists*, *Contemporary Novelists*, and *Contemporary Authors*. There are full essays and bibliographies on some authors in such relevant volumes of *The Dictionary of Literary Biography* as *Twentieth-Century Caribbean and Black African Writers*, ed. Bernth Lindfors and Reinhard Sander, vols. 117 (1992), 125 (1992), and 157 (1996), and *British Novelists since 1960*, vol. 194 (1998), ed. Merrit Mosley. Another starting place is Emmanuel S. Nelson (ed.), *Writers of the Indian Diaspora: A Bio-Bibliographical Critical Sourcebook*. Websites include Contemporary Authors Online (1999), reproduced in Biography Resource Center (http://wwwgalenet.com/serviet/BioRC).

General studies include David Dabydeen and Nana Wilson-Tagore (eds.), *Reader's Guide to West Indian and Black British Literature* (1989), which has introductory essays by various hands, while Lars Ole Sauerberg's *Intercultural Voices in Contemporary British Literature: The Implosion of Empire* (2001) discusses authors within the larger context of how the literature of England changed during second half of the twentieth century. Graham Huggan's *The Postcolonial Exotic: Marketing the Margins* (2001) finds postcolonial literatures and criticism complicit in selling post-imperialist nostalgia to the West. It includes discussion of Naipaul, Rushdie, Kureishi, and the Booker Prize. There is a useful short 'epilogue' to C. L. Innes's *A History of Black and Asian Writing in Britain 1700–2000* (2002) and a privately circulated 100-page 'report' concerning *South Asian Women Writing in Britain* (1994) by Ranjan Sidhanta Ash. Randall Stevenson's *The Last of England* (2004), Vol. 12 in the Oxford English Literary History, which covers 1960–2000, should be consulted for other perspectives on contexts and many authors I discuss.

For literary criticism of novelists, Susheila Nasta's *Home Truths: Fictions of the South Asian Diaspora in Britain* (2002) discusses Sam Selvon, V. S. Naipaul, Salman Rushdie, Hanif Kureishi, Ravinder Randhawa, Romesh Gunesekera, Sunetra Gupta, and Aamer Hussein among others. A. Robert Lee (ed.), *Other Britain, Other British: Contemporary Multicultural Fiction* (1995), includes essays on Selvon, Ishiguro, Gurnah, Naipaul, Rushdie, Lamming, Kureishi, Dabydeen, and Mike Phillips. Steven Connor's *The English Novel in History 1950–1995* (1996) has interesting readings of works by Mo, Rushdie, Kureishi, and Ishiguro in relation to nation and outsiderliness. Sukhdev Sandhu's excellent *London Calling: How Black and Asian Writers Imagined a City* (2003) shows how Selvon, Rushdie, and others wrote about the joys and excitement of London. Mark Stein's *Black British Literature: Novels of Transformation* (2004) looks more theoretically at the formation of such writers as Kureishi, Dabydeen, Levy, and Evaristo.

A good short introduction to black poetry is Fred D'Aguiar, 'Have you been here long? Black Poetry in Britain', in Robert Hampton and Peter Barry (eds.), *New British Poetries: The Scope of the Possible* (1993), 51–70. Dennis Walder's *Post-Colonial Literatures in English* (1998) has a section on black British poetry. Oral poetry is discussed in Christian Habekost, *Verbal Riddim: The Politics and Aesthetics of African-Caribbean Dub Poetry* (1993); *Critical Quarterly*, 38/4 (Winter 1996), an issue edited by Jean Binta Breeze; and Asher Hoyles and Martin Hoyles (eds.), *Moving Voices: Black Performance Poetry* (2002).

Research on drama begins in the Theatre Museum's Alby James Collection and other holdings about black theatre. Judy S. J. Stone, *Studies in West Indian Literature: Theatre* (1994) includes material on Errol John, Edgar White, Mustapha Matura, Caryl Phillips, and bibliography. Mary Karen Dahl, 'Postcolonial British Theatre: Black Voices at the Centre' in J. Ellen Gainor (ed.), *Imperialism and Theatre* (1995), 38–55, supplies an introduction to the contexts of black British theatre and interprets plays by Hanif Kureishi, Jackie Kay, and Maria Oshodi.

Ferdinand Dennis and Naseem Khan (eds.), *Voices of the Crossing: The Impact of Britain on Writers from Asia, the Caribbean and Africa* (2000), has original memoirs by Rukhsana Ahmad, Mulk Raj Anand, Berry, Bhabha, Dabydeen, Dennis, Desani, Farrukh Dhondy, Emecheta, Figueroa, B. A. Gilroy, Hosain, Markham, and Moraes. Onyekachi Wambu (ed.), *Empire Windrush: Fifty Years of Writing about Black Britain* (1998), preface by E. R. Braithwaite, is a collection of writings ranging from theory and reporting to creative. Courttia Newland and Kadija Sesay (eds.), *IC3: The Penguin Book of New Black Writing in*

Britain (2000), and James Proctor (ed.), *Writing Black Britain 1948–1998: An Interdisciplinary Anthology* (2000), offer surveys of creative and other writing for the half-century. Other interesting anthologies of prose are Rukhsana Ahmad and Rahila Gupta (eds.), *Flaming Spirit: Stories from the Asian Women Writers' Collective* (1994), and *Afrobeat: New British Fiction* (1999), ed. Patsy Antoine, which includes Judith Bryan, Newland, Traynor.

The selective *Hinterland: Caribbean Poetry from the West Indies & Britain* (1989), ed. E. A. Markham, includes Berry, Markham, L. K. Johnson, Nichols, D'Aguiar, and good introductions. *The New British Poetry* (1988), ed. Gillian Allnutt, Fred D'Aguiar, Ken Edwards, and Eric Mottam, devotes a section to black poetry. Lemn Sissay (ed.), *Fire People: A Collection of Contemporary Black British Poetry* (1998), reflects the black poetry scene of the late 1990s. Debjani Chatterjee's *The Redbeck Anthology of British South Asian Poetry* (2000) is an unselective anthology of South Asian poets living in England.

For drama anthologies see the three volumes of *Black Plays* edited by Yvonne Brewster for Methuen. *Black Plays 1* (1987) includes plays by Michael Ellis, Alfred Fagon, Tunde Ikoli, and Jacqueline Rudet; *Black Plays 2* (1989) has plays by Maria Oshodi, Winsome Pinnock, and Benjamin Zephaniah; while *Black Plays 3* (1993) includes Fred D'Aguiar, Paul Boakye, Bonnie Greer, and Winsome Pinnock. Aurora Metro Press's two anthologies are Kadija George (ed.), *Six Plays by Black and Asian Women Writers* (1993), which includes Rukshana Ahmad, Maya Chowdhry, Trish Cooke, Winsome Pinnock, Ayshed Raif, Meera Syal, Zindika Macheol; and *Black and Asian Plays* (2000), introd. Afia Nkrumah with a bibliography by Susan Croft, which includes Parv Bancil, Wayne Buchanan, Michael McMillan, Manjula Rabmanabham, and Shelley Silas.

Special issues of literary journals are *Literary Review* 34/1 (Fall 1990) devoted to black British writing; *Wasafiri*, especially no. 21 (Spring 1995) 'India, Asia, and the Diaspora'; no. 29 (Spring 1999) 'Taking the Cake, Black Writing in Britain'; and no. 36 (Summer 2002) 'Writing in Britain: Shifting Geographies'; *Kunapipi*, especially Dabydeen (ed.), 'The Windrush Commemorative Issue: West Indians in Britain 1948–1998', vol. 20/1 (1998); and 21/2 (1999) 'Post-Colonial London'; while Lauri Ramey (ed.), *Sea Change*, a special issue of *BMa: The Sonia Sanchez Literary Review*, 6/2 (Spring 2001) contains conference essays on black British writing and bibliographical notes.

For theory see Paul Gilroy, *The Black Atlantic: Modernity and Double Consciousness* (1993); Paul Gilroy, *Small Acts: Some Thoughts on the*

Politics of Black Cultures (1993); Homi Bhabha, *The Location of Culture* (1994); Kobena Mercer, *Welcome to the Jungle: New Positions in Black Cultural Studies* (1994); and Houston A. Baker, Jr., Manthia Diawara, and Ruth H. Lindeborg (eds.), *Black British Cultural Studies: A Reader* (1996). Vijay Mishra, 'The Diasporic Imagery: Theorizing the Indian Diaspora', *Textual Practice*, 10/3 (1996), 421–7, is excellent. For post-colonialism see Robert Young, *Postcolonialism: A Very Short Introduction* (2003) and the essays by Helen Tiffin, Gareth Griffiths, and especially Stephen Slemon in Bruce King (ed.), *New National and Post-Colonial Literatures* (1996).

For British ethnic minorities there is *The Arts of Ethnic Minorities: A Reading Guide* (1983). Works on black history include Chris Mullard's autobiographical *Black Britain* (1973) and Peter Fryer's influential *Staying Power: The History of Black People in Britain* (1984). A short work with contexts is S. I. Martin's *Britain's Slave Trade* (1999), introd. Trevor Phillips. More specialized studies include Joan Amin-Addo, *Longest Journey: A History of Black Lewisham* (1995); Hakim Adi, *West Africans in Britain, 1900–1960* (1998); and Susan Okokon, *Black Londoners, 1880–1990* (1998). Rozina Visram's *Ayahs, Lascars and Princes: The Story of Indians in Britain 1700–1947* (1986) should be consulted along with Visram's later *Asians in Britain: 400 Years of History* (2002). The journalist Tony Sewell has written *Keep On Moving: The Windfall Legacy. The Black Experience in Britain from 1948* (1998).

Books on politics include Trevor Carter, *Shattering Illusions: West Indians in British Politics* (1986), and A. Sivanandan, *From Resistance to Rebellion: Asian and AfroCaribbean Struggles in Britain* (1986). Michael Keith's *Race, Riots and Policing: Lore and Disorder in a Multi-racist Society* (1993) provides detailed analysis of the riots of the 1980s. David Mason's *Race and Ethnicity in Modern Britain* (1995) is a general introduction with useful bibliography. Ian R. G. Spencer, *British Immigration Policy since 1939: The Making of Multiracial Britain* (1997) is good on details concerning ethnic communities and the contrasts between what governments said and intended.

In the area of culture see Naseem Khan's *The Arts Britain Ignores: The Arts of Ethnic Minorities in Britain* (1976). Kwesi Owusu and Jacob Ross, *Behind the Masquerade: The Story of Notting Hill Carnival* (1988) is a popular introduction with information about Carnival in Trinidad, the social history of Notting Hill, and many photographs. Paul Gilroy's *Small Acts: Thoughts on the Politics of Black Culture* (1993) is stimulating as are Gilroy's many essays on culture in various collections including Catherine Ugwu (ed.), *Let's Get It On: The Politics of Black Performance* (1995).

Various aspects of Bhangra music are discussed in the essays in Sanjay Sharma, John Hutnyk, and Ashwani Sharma (eds.), *Dis-Orienting Rhythms: The Politics of the New Asian Dance Music* (1996). *Black British Culture and Society: A Text Reader* (2000), ed. Kwesi Owusu, has good material although the introductions are jargonish. Alison Donnell (ed.), *Companion to Contemporary Black British Culture* (2002), includes introductory essays on theory and useful information in many areas such as fashion and design, films and cinema, popular music, organizations, broadcasting, and the visual arts. There are also short entries on literary authors.

For cinema see Therese Daniels and Jane Gerson (eds.), *The Colour Black: Black Images in British Television* (1989); Manthia Diawara, 'Power and Territory: The Emergence of Black Film Collectives', in Lester Friedman (ed.), *Fires Were Started: British Cinema and Thatcherism* (1993), 147–60; Lola Young, *Fear of the Dark: Race, Gender and Sexuality in the Cinema* (1996).

Useful social documents and books of sociology are Henri Tajfel and John Dawson (eds.), *Disappointed Guests: Essays by African, Asian, and West Indian Students* (1965); and John Brown, *The Un-Melting Pot: An English Town and its Immigrants* (1970), a detailed study of British minorities and their differences. *The Empire Strikes Back: Race and Racism in 70s Britain* (1982) consists of densely written influential essays concerning the relationship of the economy to nationalism and the state which examine such issues as policing, education, and feminism, to argue for a racial approach distinct from Marxian theory. Winston James and Clive Harris (eds.), *Inside Babylon: The Caribbean Diaspora in Britain* (1993), examines critically the history of West Indian immigration in terms of racialization and exploitation especially towards black women. Michael Keith's *Race, Riots and Policing: Lore and Disorder in a Multi-Racist Society* (1993) knocks down the usual explanations given for causes of the 1980s riots. Yasmin Alibhai-Brown, *Mixed Feelings: The Complex Lives of Mixed-Race Britons* (2001) is a partly autobiographical discussion of 'mixed-race identities' by someone who feels that the problems outweigh advantages.

Women are discussed in Beverly Bryan, Stella Dadzie, and Suzanna Scafe (eds.), *The Heart of the Race: Black Womens' Lives in Britain* (1985). Valerie Mason-John and Anna Khambatta (eds.), *Making Black Waves* (1993), is about black British lesbians; as is Valerie Mason-John (ed.), *Talking Black: Lesbians of African and Asian Descent Speak Out* (1995).

Language is discussed in Edward Kamau Brathwaite, *History of the*

Voice: The Development of Nation Language in Anglophone Caribbean Poetry (1984); David Sutchiffe, *Black British Language* (1986); David Sutchiffe and Ansel Wong (eds.), *The Language of Black Experience* (1986); Roger Hewitt, *White Talk Black Talk* (1986); and Mark Sebra, *London Jamaican* (1993).

Books on political and artistic movements are *Foundations of a Movement* (1991) and Anne Walmsley's *The Caribbean Artists Movement 1966–1972* (1992). Brian Alleyne, *Radicals against Race: Black Activism and Cultural Politics* (2002) provides a history of John La Rose, Sarah White, and New Beacon Press. For painting and other arts see Maud Sulter, *As a Black Woman* (1985); Rasheed Areen, *The Other Story: Afro-Asian Artists in Post-War Britain* (1989); Mora J. Beauchamp-Byrd and M. Franklin Sirmans (eds.), *Transforming the Crown: African, Asian & Caribbean Artists in Britain 1966–1996* (1997); and issues of *Third Text*.

Gareth Griffiths's *African Literature: East and West* (2000) discusses Okri, Gurnah, and others. For Indian literature see Arvind Krishna Mehrotra (ed.), *An Illustrated History of Indian Literature in English* (2002); Bruce King, *Three Indian Poets: Nissim Ezekiel, A K Ramanujan, Dom Moraes* (1991); and Bruce King, *Modern Indian Poetry in English* (rev. 2001). For West Indian Literature see Bruce King (ed.), *West Indian Literature*, 2nd edn. (1995), and Louis James's *Caribbean Literature in English* (1999), which offers a concise historical introduction to areas, themes, and authors along with a short chapter about Britain. The paradoxes of nationalism and modernization are discussed in Bruce King's *New National Literatures: Cultural Nationalism in a Changing World* (1980).

Index

Page-references in **bold type** represent major discussions of the subject. Grouped entries are given for the following: anthologies; awards and prizes; drama companies and theatres; and publishers.

Lightning Source UK Ltd.
Milton Keynes UK
UKOW02f1245260815